D0949892

End of the Line

End of the Line

THE RISE AND COMING FALL OF THE GLOBAL CORPORATION

Barry C. Lynn

DOUBLEDAY

New York London Toronto Sydney Auckland

FOR ANYA

PUBLISHED BY DOUBLEDAY
a division of Random House, Inc.

DOUBLEDAY and the portrayal of an anchor with a dolphin are
registered trademarks of Random House, Inc.

Cataloging-in-Publication Data is on file with the Library of Congress.

ISBN 0-385-51024-1

Book design by Tina Thompson

PRINTED IN THE UNITED STATES OF AMERICA

September 2005

First Edition

1 3 5 7 9 10 8 6 4 2

CONTENTS

End of the Line

SHOCK WAVES

We live in a world where a sixty-second earthquake in Taiwan can nearly shatter the American economy. We live in a world where an epidemic in China can threaten America's ability to build cars and airplanes. We live in a world where the shuttering of a single factory in England can deprive Americans of half the nation's supply of flu vaccine.

Consider the earthquake that slammed through Taiwan on September 21, 1999. Few Americans paid much notice that day, when the news flashed onto their computer screens or was broadcast from their car radios. The reports were dramatic enough. The quake had registered 7.6 on the Richter scale, buildings had toppled and others were on fire, electricity was out, and so too most transport. By the time the Taiwanese had cleared the rubble, the death toll would hit 2,400. Yet with the obvious exception of anyone who had family or friends on the island, most Americans showed little concern that Monday afternoon, the second-to-last day of summer. Judging by the nightly newscasts that week, Americans were much more interested in North Carolina, where Hurricane Floyd had dropped twenty-eight inches of rain, or the introduction of Ford's new supersized SUV, the Excursion, with its forty-four-gallon gas tank.

One man who did notice the quake was Willem Roelandts, CEO of the semiconductor design firm Xilinx. Awakened by a call from his home office in San Jose, Roelandts sat up in a hotel room in Tokyo staring at his television set, watching live feed of the disaster. For a few hours, Roelandts thought he was witnessing the first act in the collapse of the world economy.

Xilinx's business is to design and manage the production of highly specialized semiconductor chips for manufacturers around the world. This gives Roelandts a view into one of the nexuses of today's global economy. He knows which companies use his firm's chips, how they use those chips, where those chips are manufactured, and what are the alternatives should anything happen to the firms that actually build the chips to Xilinx's specifications. And herein lay the problem that day in September. Almost all such manufacturing was done by only two firms in Taiwan, which had located most of their capacity in a single industrial park. Roelandts therefore knew that any severe disruption of commerce in Taiwan had the potential to cause economic damage on a scale far greater than most conceivable terror attacks. And he knew the semiconductor business is not the only industry where work has been hyperconcentrated on the island. "There is not an electronic product in the world," he says, "that does not contain a Taiwanese component." For that matter, such specialization and concentration is increasingly found in every production system in the world, from automobiles to medical devices, from petrochemicals to aerospace.

The shock wave from the Taiwan quake hit the American economy within days. Although the quake's epicenter was far from Taiwan's main industrial center in Hsinchu, and although key plants reported only slight damage, the weeklong break in the island's electrical and transportation systems meant production could not take place and that what little inventory existed could not be shipped. The first Americans to feel the effect of the quake were therefore workers at factories that depended on components made in Taiwan; within days, thousands of manufacturing employees were sent home from assembly lines from California to Texas. The next Americans to feel the quake were investors. As Wall Street began to make sense of the disaster, traders quickly off-loaded stocks of some of the biggest American electronics firms, with Dell, Hewlett-Packard, and Apple among those that fell furthest. Last of all, Americans felt the quake as consumers. By Christmas, shoppers faced shortages of everything from laptop computers to Furby dolls to Barbie Cash Registers, all of which had been hit hard by parts shortages. The overall figures were dramatic. The one-week shutdown in Taiwan cut world output of electronics by 7 percent below predictions, just in the month of October, and disruptions continued well into the new year.

Even so, Americans were able to count themselves lucky. The problems they actually experienced were quite small compared to what might have happened had the quake been stronger, had it been centered closer to Hsinchu or the capital Taipei, had it more severely damaged power plants and transport facilities. The warning, however, was clear. Our corporations have built a global production system that is so complex, and geared so tightly and leveraged so finely, that a breakdown anywhere increasingly means a breakdown everywhere, much in the way that a small perturbation in the electricity grid in Ohio tripped the great North American blackout of August 2003. Nor was the Taiwan quake our only warning. There was also the fire in a small Dutch-owned semiconductor plant in New Mexico, which cost a Swedish cell-phone maker a half-billion dollars in lost sales. There was also the spread of SARS through China and industrial East Asia in 2003. There was also, as we will see, the effects of the September 11 attacks and the subsequent four-day closure of U.S. airspace. The list goes on and on.

Our corporations have built the most efficient system of production the world has ever seen, perfectly calibrated to a world in which nothing bad ever happens. But that is not the world we live in. Not only is human civilization riven routinely by earthquakes and hurricanes, but so too is it shattered by wars and acts of terror and simple human error. Which means it is only a matter of time until we experience our next industrial crash, perhaps one much worse than any we have yet known.

Most Americans would not live in a house where architects every day removed a few bricks from a load-bearing wall, or a few beams from the ceiling, to test the real-life absolute minimal limits of the structure. Few would book passage on a ship where the owners had cut out watertight bulkheads to save on weight, and hence on fuel, to charge a few dollars less per ticket. America has repeatedly spent treasure and blood to ensure that no one other nation controls more than a small share of the total world supply of oil. Yet somehow, this highly reasonable instinct rarely kicks in anymore when it comes to trade in industrial goods and business services. Instead, in the name of efficiency, we accept life in a house whose frame is so finely wrought that as we lie in our beds we feel every breeze, the rubbing of every branch on every gutter. It is a house that every day is more likely to collapse, and when it does it may fall far faster and harder than we can imagine.

For Alexander Hamilton, the suffering he had seen in Valley Forge still rankled as he drew up America's first plan to promote manufacturing. Keeping the American army in shoes and blankets and guns was an all-but-impossible task throughout the war, but that winter in Pennsylvania was especially rough. Cold, disease, and outright hunger killed nearly a quarter of the American soldiers, while British troops slept snugly in the towns, fully outfitted with English-made uniforms and English-made boots and English-made powder. As George Washington's top aide, Hamilton lived through it all. So it is not surprising that fourteen years later, as America's first Treasury secretary, he prefaced his "Report on Manufactures" with words about the liberty won in that war. Manufacturing is not merely a matter of putting coats on citizens' backs or plates on their tables; nor is it only a matter of creating wealth for the owners of factories. Manufacturing, he wrote, was key to America's "independence and security." To be free, Americans must have the power to make what they need when they need it.

And so, with a little help from their government, Americans became very good at making guns and textiles, as well as sewing machines and steel and locomotives and many other things. Even before the Civil War, American manufacturers had become renowned around the world for their creativity, the quality of their work, the rationality of their systems. By the beginning of the twentieth century, Americans had built more factories than any other nation, and these factories tended to be bigger and more productive. Americans succeeded not only in keeping themselves free but in developing the power to project their will far beyond their nation's borders. Americans not only succeeded in making themselves rich, but their technologies and techniques improved the lives of peoples around the globe.

The crowning achievement of American industry came after the Second World War destroyed much of Europe and Asia. Americans used their manufacturing might to restart many of the world's economies, seeding the rubble with machinery and technology and dollars. American leaders then did something entirely new in the nation's history—they encouraged corporations to entwine America's economy with those of other industrial nations, both victor and vanquished. The immediate goal was simple—to make the West's system of production more efficient to better serve the common struggle against the Soviet Union. Their other goal was more sublime. American leaders sought through such interlinking of industry to make future conflict with our new allies much more difficult, by all but preventing these nations from rebuilding an independent capacity to make war.

In a sense, the postwar economic system set into motion by Harry Truman was a radical inversion of Hamilton's doctrine. Rather than seek security through industrial *independence from* other nations, America would now seek security through industrial *interdependence with* other nations, especially Europe and Japan. At a more basic level, however, the postwar system did grow directly from Hamilton's vision. American presidents from Truman to Ronald Reagan remained unwavering in their conviction that government must play a role in structuring industry to promote security as well as prosperity. Even as many preached "free trade," all these administrations proved through their actions their fundamental belief that markets and machines are tools to be directed toward certain ends by rational people, that the arts of production must be cared for and husbanded, that the interests of the nation trump the interests of the investor. When the Soviet Union collapsed in 1991, much of the credit went to the great industrial system that stretched from Western Europe through North America to Japan. This vast, highly rational complex had, many believed, bankrupted the Communist regime. It was the bicentennial year of Hamilton's Report, and this victory seemed proof of his wisdom.

Which is why Americans should find it absolutely shocking today, a mere decade and a half later, to find themselves dependent on an industrial system that is rapidly whittling away at both their national security and their economic security. Fifteen years of turbocharged "globalization" of industry, unchecked by any American state strategy or vision, has left the American people relying on a global industrial "commons" that is largely out of their control and that is riven by fundamental structural flaws. Corporations, answering these days only to investors, have forged a marvelously efficient industrial network that extends far beyond the boundaries of 1989, into dozens of countries, from Budapest west across two oceans to Bangalore. But in the absence of any thinking about the link between industry and national security, in the absence of any real efforts to prevent or understand the nature of today's industrial consolidation, these corporations have built a system so hyperspecialized and so lean that a relatively small glitch in production on the far side of the world has the potential to devastate large swaths of the American economy. A spat between peoples twelve time zones away? A natural disaster in a nation whose name we cannot spell? Today, as we will see in this book, the effects of such events are often transmitted on a just-in-time basis right to the heart of our own society, as if by a global vena cava.

This book is about the rise of our new global industrial system, and the many grave and growing dangers this system poses to America's citizens and to the world. It is a story of how the laissez-faire free market and free-trade policies that were supposed to ensure us lasting prosperity are in practice every year leaving us far less safe and far less free. It is a story of how our recent governments—intoxicated by a potent mix of greed, hubris, ideology, and just plain naïveté—shifted the hard political work of managing the American and the world economies from their own desks onto a mindless "marketplace" that was somehow supposed to do the job automatically. It is a story of the abandonment of a strategy that for 200 years has ensured the health and well-being and independence of the American nation.

There is no reason we must live in such a world. There is nothing ineluctable or necessary about today's global industrial system; no person or corporation has the power to determine that we must depend on such a precarious structure. There are far safer and more intelligent ways to run our lives, and we should take them. And we can do so even while keeping in mind the rational wisdom inherent in free-trade theory, even as we keep in our hearts the great hope of "globalization," which is to extend prosperity and peace to ever more people around the globe.

The term "outsourcing" has inspired a lot of outrage in recent years, and a lot of outrageous statements. The outrage comes mainly from

Americans who have watched their employers hire workers in other countries to do their jobs. The outrageous statements have been made mainly by economists, who claim that any shifting of American jobs offshore is absolutely and incontrovertibly good for the American economy and hence for America as a whole, at least when the system is viewed from a sufficient distance and with sufficient dispassion. This is a stance so extreme that it was finally renounced by one of the high priests of today's economic profession, Paul Samuelson.

For anyone listening to this debate, the prime lesson from outsourcing would seem clear enough. It is that Americans must now compete for their jobs to a degree we never had to before, with people in Guangdong, in Karnataka, in Kuala Lumpur. And if we look honestly at outsourcing, we will see that it does indeed tend naturally, to some degree intentionally, to set workers into more intense competition with one another, not only across borders but often right here at home within the borders of the United States.

This is not really something new. Outsourcing is new relative only to the tendency of most manufacturers in the twentieth century to "vertically integrate" the activities that went into the making of their products. Economists are absolutely correct when they point out that outsourcing is as old as manufacturing itself. It is really nothing more than hiring another company to manufacture a component for you, or to perform some service. It has long been used to boost efficiency, as companies replace small and perhaps inefficient in-house operations with high-quality purchased inputs. And outsourcing has long served as a strategy to reduce the power of workers, especially those in unions, as Bennett Harrison made clear a decade ago in his book *Lean and Mean*.

But today's outsourcing has created something that is very new, something entirely outside of all our previous experience as a nation. Traditionally, companies that outsourced work tended to hire suppliers located nearby, usually within a few miles of their main factory. But the global communications and transportation revolution has in the past few years enabled companies to hire suppliers located not simply on the far side of town or the far side of America but on the far side of the earth. And inspired by "just-in-time" production strategies, these companies have often linked these scattered operations together far more efficiently than was true even when they were all within the walls of the vertically integrated factory of yore. In other words, even as they were designing a system that set American workers more and more into competition against one another and with workers overseas, America's corporations were simultaneously tying the American nation to many other nations whom we do not know well nor much trust.

This new and intimate interdependence with other nations was forged not in the name of love. It was almost literally manufactured in the name of efficiency. Today's border-busting interdependence was stitched together not by trade ministers toiling fitfully in the hotel ballrooms of Geneva and Rio and Bangkok, nor was it stitched together by a tweedy cabal at the State Department working with the Brylcreemed internationalists of Bonn and Tokyo. Rather, it is the product of a handful of visionary industrialists who first figured out how to explode their factories and spread the constituent parts around the globe. This hyperinterdependence of nations is not a product these industrialists intended to produce; many do not even understand what it is they have produced. Yet the visceral connections they have forged with other nations have changed our lives profoundly.

For this reason, I focus the book largely on the actions of people like the computer maker Michael Dell, John Chambers of Cisco Systems, Jack Welch and Gary Wendt of General Electric, Paul Galvin of Motorola, Fred Smith of FedEx, Jurgen Schrempp of DaimlerChrysler, Jose Ignacio Lopez de Arriortua of General Motors, and Sam Walton of Wal-Mart. It was these businessmen and these companies who responded first or most effectively to the new competitive pressures, and the new market opportunities, and new political liberties of the past two decades. Specifically, these companies figured out how to prosper in a world remade by the "invasion" of Japanese manufacturers, the collapse of the Soviet Union, the opening by developing nations of their markets, the introduction of new information technologies and new transport systems, the emergence of new thinking about the purpose of the corporation, and the American government's decision to all but abandon its antitrust powers and regulatory powers and decades-old support for labor.

We carry in our minds certain iconic images of manufacturing. The most powerful, perhaps, is of Ford's immense River Rouge complex of the 1920s, where oceangoing ships unloaded ore and coal at one end to be spun into complete Model A automobiles that were rolled onto rail cars at the other. The General Motors of the 1950s, meanwhile, has served as a sort of archetype of the "Corporation," providing us with a picture of a private-sector entity able to shape demand to meet production, able to shape society though collective contracts, able to shape itself to serve the interests of the state, and able to reshape the state to serve its own corporate needs. Then there is the IBM of the 1960s, which serves as a model of the technology-centered business, wherein ink-stained geeks wander across leafy campuses imagining the high-tech gizmos of the future. These core images have not changed much in recent years. In the 1980s, our iconic factory often flew the Japanese flag. In the 1990s, it kept its American flag while relocating to China. But a factory was still a factory, a corporation still a corporation.

One point of this book is to show how the factory we thought we knew, and the corporation we thought we knew, no longer exist. The vertically integrated corporations of the twentieth century have for the most part been taken apart and blended together to the point where it is increasingly hard to tell one from the next. In place of a collection of distinct individual companies, we increasingly see a global production "network." In essence, the Fords and IBMs and Xeroxes of America have mixed their constituent pieces together with each other, and with pieces of companies like Nissan and Sanyo and Phillips and Siemens and Samsung and TSMC. The result is a system of production controlled by no one of these companies nor any one country. On the contrary, it is a system into which all participating nations increasingly mix their technology, and their capital, and their labor, and from which all receive products.

Viewed in the abstract, as for instance by an economics professor at the University of Chicago, the result is truly a wonder of efficiency. Viewed by the average investor, the global production network seems the very quintessence of the rational use of capital. Viewed from the checkout line at Wal-Mart, through the eyes of the consumer, the global production network appears to be a veritable conveyor of wealth.

Unfortunately, judged from any other conceivable facet of the American citizen, the new global production system appears to be nothing short of a disaster. The taking apart of the "modern" twentieth-century corporation has precipitated a slow-motion collapse in America's pension and health care insurance systems. It has put an end to the traditional role of the corporation in forging communities of workers. It has dramatically shifted power over wages and work environment away from the average employee and toward the investor. It has undercut the ability of elected representatives to regulate business activities, be it to promote safety, or a cleaner environment, or more fairness in society. It has eroded the power of entrepreneurs to maintain the value of their investments or to bring new ideas to market. It has eroded the freedom of workers to shift from one job to another. It has eroded the freedom of the United States to act in ways contrary to the wishes of a growing list of foreign nations on which we depend. It has undermined much of the stability of the system itself, in terms both of investing in future economic growth and even of simply sustaining present levels of activity.

Of all these points, the last one is perhaps the most counterintuitive. Why, after all, would the corporation, if it truly is more powerful and more free than before, accept a vastly greater degree of risk? Yet the answer to this question is actually quite simple, if we look in more detail at how the nature of the corporation has changed. As we will see, power over the production system has shifted away from companies that view themselves primarily as manufacturers and producers into the hands of companies designed mainly to trade in the production of others, and which have never had any reason to identify, track, and limit risk in the production system. The most clear example of this is the rise of Wal-Mart, a firm able to exert immense power over almost any company whose products it sells. But this shift also explains the secret of the success of "manufacturers" like Dell Computer and Cisco Systems, which to a large extent simply package up components manufactured by other companies. This new focus on selling the work of others also increasingly describes the operations even of traditional heavy manufacturers like General Motors and Boeing, which in recent years have off-loaded many of their plants, machinery, and work onto suppliers, from whom they buy what they used to make.

Through most of the last century, the safe functioning of any assembly line was the natural responsibility of the managers at the vertically integrated corporation that owned the line. If your revenue depended on the efficient and steady use of the machines and workers who made up a manufacturing complex, it was only rational to devote a lot of effort to ensuring that there were no breaks in production.

And indeed, one of the prime attractions of outsourcing lies right there, in the fact that hiring other companies to handle the hard work of manufacturing also entails the ability to shift responsibility for managing risk to these companies. Unfortunately, most of these suppliers, which are under near-constant pressure to cut their costs, have responded quite naturally by outsourcing much of their own work to other companies farther down the chain. And so on. The result, when outsourcing has spread widely and deeply enough through any industrial system, is that many responsibilities are not so much shifted from one company to another as from one company to no company.

Another way to understand what has happened is to look not at the process of outsourcing but at the network of production that results naturally from any systemwide outsourcing. In a sense, any such network can be viewed as common property that belongs to all the companies that rely on it. Yet as is true of all common properties, such a production network obviously belongs to none of the corporations that use it. In a networked system of production, no one, quite naturally, is ultimately responsible for ensuring that the system is safe. Nobody looks for risk in the system, nobody analyzes risk in the system, nobody seeks to lessen risk in the system, nobody accepts any liability for risk in the system. If anything, the nature of competition results in a race among users to exploit the common system most effectively.

In today's global production network, nobody walks the line. No one even understands where it leads.

In the early 1960s, MIT meteorology professor Edward Lorenz discovered that extremely slight alterations in data would, given enough time, hugely disrupt his computerized weather models. It soon occurred to Lorenz that what he was observing might be of use in understanding what actually takes place in real-life weather systems. It was, Lorenz wrote later, as if a butterfly flapping its wings in Brazil could set in motion a chain of reactions that led ultimately to the touchdown of a tornado in Texas. Thus was born the term "Butterfly Effect," and thus was laid one of the foundation stones for the "science" of chaos, which is the effort to create concepts and models by which to make some sense of extremely complex and dynamic systems.

Scientists were not the only people influenced by Lorenz and his followers. Their set of concepts, sometimes called "deterministic chaos," has also shaped how many thinkers perceive social systems such as the global economy. Indeed, in recent years a surprisingly large number of writers have depicted the global economy as an immensely complex, almost chaotic, mechanism that operates mainly according to its own rules, largely unresponsive to the will of the individual, the community, or the nation. In many cases, the writers saw the workings of this mechanism as mainly a good thing. Former Labor secretary Robert Reich viewed economic globalization as an unstoppable natural force, but he hoped that the ineluctable crushing of the state would leave more space for the individual. For *New York Times* columnist Thomas Friedman, it was the globalization of cultures that was the unstoppable power at work, but he felt confident that the overall result would be to forge a more global community of interest. A similar line of thinking lies at the heart of the teachings of free-market fundamentalists, like the economist Milton Friedman, who envision the global marketplace as an almost sentient being able to direct humans toward actions much more wise than they could have ciphered out using their own limited and inherently corrupt faculties, or even the institutions of government. In other cases, however, this vision of a great, unknowably complex mechanism at work has led to much bleaker conclusions. A good example is journalist William Greider, who in a 1997 critique of globalization relied on an image of an immense machine blindly destroying the works of man.

It is not clear why so many writers believe—or want to believe—that the global economic system is so far out of human control. In some cases, it is probably due to the influence of Karl Marx's theories of economic determinism, in which he held that capitalism was leading inexorably to Communism. In others, it probably grows from what is sometimes called technological determinism, the now common belief that modern technologies shape human beings and direct their actions at least as much as humans shape technologies. In other cases, it is probably no more than a product of intellectual laziness, the invocation of an all-powerful deus ex machina to explain away what the writer finds too complex to communicate or analyze. The overall effect, however, is of profound importance. It is to declare unequivocally that the global economy itself is out of our control. It is to abandon humanity's millennia-old struggle to nurture and grow our faith in our own free will, and to nurture and grow the institutions through which we exercise it.

This book is very much not of that group. Deterministic imagery serves only in the writing of tragedy. A deterministic economics serves only to ensure that someone other than us shapes our lives. Nothing of what you read on these pages is meant to seem inevitable. None of the potential futures has yet been decided.

Indeed, if we tease out Lorenz more carefully, we see that the mechanistic imagery of these many writers on global economics is a clear perversion of his intent. By declaring that even in chaos there is predictability, Lorenz sought to extend humanity's ability to understand complex natural systems, which is of course to exert a form of control over the world. As applied to human systems, determinism is also a perversion of our common experience. Even if we take weather in its pre-Lorenzian state, and perceive it as a purely chaotic system, the simple inability to predict an event does not mean we must therefore be entirely at its mercy. We learned long ago how to shelter ourselves from the cold, how to build our homes above the floods, how to steer our ships around storms. If anything, our goal with our global production network is just this—to structure this human system so as to make it able to survive almost any conceivable act of God or man.

Which leaves us with the issue of blame.

At times there may seem to be a tension in this book. I rely heavily on the actions of businesspeople to illustrate some of the basic flaws in our global system, and I am clearly disgusted with the greed and selfishness and shortsightedness of some individuals. But I also admire businesspeople as a group. This is not a contradiction. Businesspeople, as I hope I make clear, are merely tools of society, who can be used wisely or not. Every business operates entirely within a set of contexts created by the action—and failure to act—of government. Ultimately, all businesses do only what we the people direct them to do, or what we fail to direct them not to do. Therefore, if the marvelous energy and imagination and initiative of America's business community have placed us in danger, it is not the fault of the businessmen and businesswomen themselves. It is because we as a society have been too lazy or too shortsighted or too blinded by ideology to use these assets well.

Hence I concentrate in the first third of the book on how and why American governments set certain general rules by which to direct business activity, especially in terms of trade across borders. I describe three main periods. The first and longest, which began with Hamilton and Washington, lasted to 1945. It aimed generally at a rational national self-dependence, though by no means an absolute autarky. The second stage began at the end of the war and lasted to the collapse of the Soviet Union in 1991. This was a time when the government acted with great deliberation to enable both American and foreign corporations to entwine the European and Japanese industrial systems into a loose, liberal, American-centric system. The third stage began in 1993, when Bill Clinton defied the will of his own party to adopt the most laissez-faire international economic policy in the nation's history.

Fingering the Clinton Administration may surprise some. Ronald Reagan certainly preached laissez-faire economics, yet his trade policy was in fact highly interventionist, shaped always foremost by concerns for national security. George Bush Sr. truly believed in laissez-faire policy, more so than any president since Calvin Coolidge. But given Democratic control of both the House and Senate during his time in office, he lacked the power to change much in practice. The younger Bush, although quarried of the same philosophical vein as his father, has faced almost no major battles on trade. This is because all the hard work was done over the previous eight years.

Bill Clinton during his first term in office devoted more energy to fighting battles over trade than to any other issue, including his plan to reform America's health care system. Many of us will remember the grand showdown over the North American Free Trade Agreement in 1993. It was by far the loudest and most public discussion of trade policy in America in the twentieth century. But this book will show how that was only the first in a series of battles to overturn the previous policy, and that the true intent of that agreement was much more complicated than may first seem. The book will show how Clinton acted contrary to the mandate of the voters in 1992, contrary to the majority of the Democrats in the House and the Senate, and contrary to the thinking of many of his top advisors. It will show how he relied on a classic bait and switch, as he took his victory in getting the semiprotectionist NAFTA agreement passed and parlayed it into approval for the truly laissez-faire system expressed into the World Trade Organization.

All in all, Clinton's abandonment of 200 years of American strategic thinking can be viewed as one of the great snookers in American history, a far more subtle and effective sleight of hand than that used to prepare the invasion of Iraq a decade later. And as we will see, it was a set of actions that in its entirety will likely prove far more damaging over the long run.

In the Pentagon, America's military strategists are debating what the new system of global production means for the security of our nation. On one side, a group of young thinkers declares that globalization has changed everything, that the global production network has in essence stitched the individual industrial nations of the world into a single system within which war has become all but impossible. In their view, conflict will take place only on the "periphery" of this "core" system; conflict within the system is simply too illogical for any state in the system to allow. The other side, by contrast, holds that globalization has changed little if anything, and that the world is still composed of a collection of discrete nations, each of which acts mainly in its own interest. According to this group, the only intelligent course of action is to do what we have always done, which is count their missiles, planes, and ships and make sure we have more.

The point where these two schools of thought come most clearly into conflict is over how to treat China. The integrationist school at the Pentagon now declares that the act of extending the West's production system into China during the 1990s, for all intents, pacified that nation. Their basic argument is that by filling China's homes with washing machines and microwave ovens, and by tying this new good life to the willingness of the Chinese to continue to serve *our* needs and not to upset the global system on which *all nations* depend, America has all but literally domesticated that great nation. The realist school at the Pentagon, by contrast, declares this pacific vision to be the most dangerous sort of bunkum.

Differences in the two nations' political systems and geopolitical goals remain so profound that it would be foolhardy for the United States not to remain very much on guard. And indeed, the United States routinely engages in shows of military force in the region, not least the stationing of aircraft carriers off the China coast in the summer of 2004.

The absurdity, and extreme dangerousness, of today's global industrial system is nowhere more plain than here. The United States shares the selfsame production system with another nation, yet also feels obliged on occasion to cow that nation through gunboat diplomacy.

The debate in the Pentagon does not reflect some lack of imagination among America's military planners; they're doing their best with what they've got. Rather, it reflects the failure of the U.S. government as a whole, since the collapse of the Soviet Union, to think through the tough questions. Does sharing the same industrial system with China ultimately make peace more likely? Or war? Will intimate industrial interdependence ultimately force China to compromise its political ideals? Or America? Does the United States have the freedom to welcome political change in China? Or will the specter of economic disruption at home lead us to join in the suppression of democracy there and elsewhere? In every case, the answer is that we do not know.

What we can say for certain is that we now depend on work done in Suchow in a more immediate way than we depended two decades ago on work done in San Jose. And we can say for certain that any conflict between these two nations, if it does occur, will be vastly more devastating economically than we could have imagined only a few years ago. And we can say for certain that, nations being nations, mutual dependence on the same system of production does not guarantee peace. Finally, we can say for certain that the U.S.-China relationship is far from being the only potential source of disaster. America depends intimately on capacity located in many unstable regions, on the Korean Peninsula, in the Indian Subcontinent, in the Middle East, on the periphery of Europe.

I named the book *End of the Line* for many reasons. The title refers, of course, to the end of the traditional River Rouge–style, vertically integrated assembly line. It also serves to emphasize how we in America have come now to depend on chains of activity that stretch to points far beyond the reach of our government and our law. The title refers also to the end of the traditional borders that existed for so long between our nation and the other peoples of the world. And it refers to the end of the borders that for most of the last century existed between companies.

I also hope to show how we have reached the end of the line for "free trade" as a central organizing concept for our global economy. The ideal of free trade is, fundamentally, a story of becoming. Its aim is to create economies of ever-greater scale, economies that are more efficient, more interlinked, more global. Yet these days, when it comes to production, the fact is we already live in a global system. In many industrial sectors (not all, yet), the scale of organization today is as big as it can ever get. Further expansion of the world market for many goods is therefore no longer a direct function of trade policy. Bringing more Chinese and Indian peasants into the system, or increasing the buying power of consumers in America or Europe, requires different policies. Free trade, in other words, as an organizing concept is of less and less use. In many senses, its job is done. The global system is a fact. It is a fait accompli.

The current debate—free trade or no free trade—entirely misses the point. Free trade has been of immense value over the years in enabling people to imagine and justify a more rational organization of human activity. As a concept, it will surely continue to be of use as we work to make other areas of our lives more rational and efficient. But going forward we must admit that when it comes to manufacturing, when it comes to certain services, increasingly when it comes to agriculture, our primary need is no longer to promote more global-scale efficiency. These systems have already been made more efficient than is safe. The challenge now is to ensure their stability and their ability to keep growing.

This means that the main concepts by which we should manage our global economy in the future will be closely related to those we used to manage our national economies of the past. This means, to some degree, viewing the world the way we viewed America's oligopolistic economy in the 1950s, or in the 1930s, or in the 1890s. This means that the most important economic tools going forward will look a lot like the tools developed and honed a century ago. These are tools that aim to perpetuate intelligent competition, to promote innovation, to limit the abuse of market power, to ensure a reasonable and intelligent distribution of profit, and to ensure that the system itself is safe and sustainable.

Not paradoxically, the judicious use of such once purely "domestic" policies is the only way to complete the crafting of a truly global economy that is built to last, no matter what happens. Hence it is the only way today to protect the legacy of Hamilton and Washington and Lincoln and both Roosevelts and Reagan. And hence, it is perhaps the only way to demonstrate once again to the world the truly peaceful nature of the American vision.

CHAPTER ONE

THE OLD WEST

Running from Japan

He had been called an "ax murderer," a "hitman," the "grand inquisitor." But the first public appearance in America by the man tapped to save General Motors, Jose Ignacio Lopez de Arriortua, revealed an executive who knew exactly what his audience wanted to hear, and who seemed a little goofy besides. "We are in a war," Lopez declared to an audience of GM executives and reporters in Saginaw, Michigan. The fight was "to save the auto industry and our lives," to keep "our sons and daughters" from becoming "second-class citizens" in the global economy. "We must act. We must win. We cannot afford to lose."[1]

It was August 1992, and America's carmakers had for years longed for a savior in their battle against the Japanese. Lopez seemed the perfect man for the role. A native of Spain's gnarly northern Basque region, the fifty-one-year-old Lopez was dark, wiry, electric, and he came to the job with a reputation as a visionary who could turn vicious. In a twelve-year career with GM in Europe, he had earned such nicknames as "Lopez the Terrible," "Hurricane Lopez," and "The Spaniard Who Makes the Germans Tremble." And he had delivered, slashing the cost of the parts that went into General Motors' European cars. Best of all, he bragged that he had improved on Japan's vaunted and seemingly invulnerable manufacturing model, adding "scientific method" to Japanese "intuition." Yet Lopez also exuded a quirky charm. In Saginaw, he told reporters that his role model was Mother Teresa, whom he called a "great service provider." He explained that he and his staff had moved their watches from their left wrists to their right and that they planned to keep them there until GM reported "record profits." The point, he said, was to feel "something like pain."[2]

Financial pain was exactly what General Motors had been feeling for years. In 1991, the company had lost some $7 billion in North America, and the erosion of GM's share of its home market was accelerating. The crisis had become so bad that GM had taken to acting out of character. The world's largest corporation, the company had long been famous—and increasingly infamous—for the extreme deliberation with which top management made decisions. Yet in April, GM's board had staged an unprecedented coup, abruptly dumping CEO Robert Stempel after less than two years on the job. In his place the board named Jack Smith, the head of GM's European operations. And Smith came loaded with Lopez, who had been one of his key lieutenants in GM's European headquarters in Zurich.[3]

Lopez took little time in making a name for himself in his newly created job as GM's purchasing czar, mainly by forcing suppliers to cut their prices drastically if they wanted to keep GM's business. Though he was virtually unknown in America when tapped for the job in April, by August *BusinessWeek* was able to write that "not since Ralph Nader has one man so shaken Detroit." Autoworkers and suppliers quickly came to regard Lopez as more akin to the Grim Reaper, and the UAW quickly responded to Lopez's all-out assault on suppliers with a nine-day strike in Lordstown, Ohio, which ultimately forced the shutting of seven big plants. The owners and managers of the supply firms seemed no happier, though they dared not criticize Lopez openly. Yet for many Americans, after years of bad news about the failings of the country's manufacturers, Lopez seemed a welcome, even bracing, change. And he certainly made great copy.

However much he bragged of the rationality of his methods, Lopez also injected a rather pre-Enlightenment ethic into the climate-controlled corridors of General Motors. His procurement team, he said, was made up not of midmanagers but "warriors." On-target bids by suppliers were welcomed not with congratulatory memos but loud shouts and pounding on tables. Lopez reminisced of his peasant upbringing, and claimed inspiration from his "namesake" St. Ignatius de Loyola, the founder of the Jesuits and a fellow Vizcayan. He arrived at work at 6:30 A.M., stayed fifteen hours, worked weekends. To journalists, he lamented how much he missed his wife and three daughters, how he had lost weight since taking the job in Detroit. *USA Today* published a copy of his "Warrior Diet," reporting that "its popularity is growing at General Motors." The diet was designed to provide "maximum energy" for long days. "You may eat meat, seafood, cheese—whatever you like," Lopez told the reporter. "But don't combine them with vegetables or salad."[4]

The Lopez regime seemed the perfect prescription for America in the early 1990s. In the popular imagination, American manufacturers had grown lazy and fat, and now an ascetic visionary had arrived to preach austerity. And he did it in a language Americans understood. Lopez seemed able to translate the secrets of Japanese-style manufacturing into America's rougher culture. Japanese companies may boast about how they provide "lifetime employment" to their employees, who are treated as members of "teams," who wear spotless uniforms, who gather in the morning for calisthenics. Lopez instead prescribed a good old-fashioned American-style cracking of the whip. And sometimes his methods came to seem like a Detroit-style gang rumble. As the sales manager for one supplier put it, Lopez "hits you over the head with a two-by-four and starts you bleeding." But it was all for your own good. Once Lopez had captured your attention, the sales manager said, he then "helps you heal." And Lopez also seemed to understand that the American appetite for flagellation is limited. So he tossed out bonbons of praise for the American worker, along with chunks of raw meat, assailing the Japanese as well as anyone. "Japanese competition is unfair," he said. "We mustn't be naïve [and] give advantages to someone without receiving anything" in return.[5]

Lopez's success ultimately would have to be measured not in the American press but on the factory floor and on GM's bottom line. By almost all accounts, he did exactly what he was hired to do. Within a year, General Motors had cut some $4 billion in costs, and upon Smith's retirement in 2003, Lopez was still receiving much of the credit for GM's strong performance in the intervening ten years. Yet Lopez's real importance was due to much more than a simple cost-cutting campaign. Rather, it was the shift in attention from the assembly line to the "chain" of supplies that fed onto the factory floor. For much of the 1980s, American executives who fretted about competitiveness focused much of their attention on the efficiency of their great assembly plants. Debates centered on the arrangement of machines, the number of robots to put on the line, the integration of computer controls, the ability of managers to tap into the knowledge of their workers.[6]

Now Lopez put on the table an even more formidable issue—how to improve the workings of the suppliers. The scope of the task was immense: Up to 90 percent of the value of any product is created before the final assembly process, and the manufacturing of parts and components is often scattered among hundreds of small plants. And so, too, the inertia. For more than a half century, the basic model for supplier relationships in the automotive industry—as in all mass manufacturing—had remained largely unchanged. Big manufacturers expected suppliers to locate near the final assembly plants. They expected them to provide good products; if not, the company might shift work to another supplier or take over the activity itself. And they expected suppliers to follow orders, or at least to follow the blueprints drawn up by the engineers in the central design office. The ultimate goal was an uninterrupted flow of components of reasonable quality to the final assembly line. Now Lopez and a few fellow pioneers in other companies set out not only to remake this system from the ground up, but to dig up the foundations as well.

By no means was Lopez the first executive to target the supplier base, but he was one of the loudest and most successful. And his work was important not least because of the target of his efforts. General Motors for decades had served as one of the main standards against which the wages of the nation were set, against which productivity was measured, against which the relative political power of other corporations was weighed. Although the firm had begun to reconsider how work was distributed between in-house operations and suppliers in the 1980s, the initial efforts were limited in scope and strongly opposed by unions. Now Lopez had greatly accelerated GM's outsourcing, had carried the effort into parts of the firm that had long been off-limits, and most dramatically was now ramming the process down into and through the supplier base itself, dictating to an ever-greater degree how companies external to GM would do their business and where.

At GM's European operations, Lopez had forced purchasers at Opel to cut off local German suppliers in favor of companies as far away as Spain and Turkey. Now in America he did the same, sending his buyers to seek out new suppliers in Canada, Mexico, even back in Europe.[7] Then, to take full advantage of this escape from geography, Lopez pushed his buyers to "rationalize" their purchases, which meant buying as much as possible from one supplier, even if far away, in order to enjoy the efficiencies of bigger production runs. Finally, Lopez sought to overturn the rules on who in the supply chain did what. The top-down, command-and-control relationship between GM and its suppliers led, he believed, to stasis and waste. Lopez now not only demanded that GM's suppliers deliver more for less, but he also urged them to take more responsibility for engineering their products and for managing lengths of the assembly line. Lopez not only wanted GM's suppliers to be leaner, he wanted them to be smarter and more self-directing as well.

Lopez was not a shy man, and he very much wanted everyone to understand what was happening. What was taking place, he declared repeatedly, was nothing less than a "third industrial revolution."[8] First came the introduction of machines to make textiles early in the nineteenth century. Then came the rise of mass manufacturing early in the twentieth century. Now, in 1992, Lopez presented himself as a leader of a movement that was chopping the assembly line into new pieces, giving many of these away to suppliers, then scattering the suppliers around the world.

It was a radical change. And because it took place at a time when politicians were reconsidering the role of the state in managing the global economy, and at a time when new information technologies were exploding onto the marketplace, the overturning of the old industrial order that Lopez was helping to set into motion would have ramifications far greater than anyone at the time imagined, and would spin off in directions no one expected. Its effect went far beyond the American production system and America's competition with Japan. In America, the outsourcing revolution would speed up radically a process that was remaking a society that had structured itself to a large degree around the modern industrial corporation. Around the world, it would speed the abandonment of many of the political strategies that for decades had served to keep the world peaceful and prosperous.

In our popular memory, the 1980s often look pretty good. After defeat in Vietnam and humiliation in the Iranian hostage crisis, President Ronald Reagan urged Americans to feel proud again. He stared down the Soviets and oversaw a long economic boom. After the wild times of the 1970s, America seemed to have regained its balance. OPEC had been cracked, inflation sapped, Studio 54 closed, the Bee Gees relegated to the cutout bin of history. America was back, sober, strong, purposeful. The feeling reached a sort of apotheosis in July 1986, when *Time* magazine published a cover of a beaming Reagan surrounded by exploding fireworks. The article was titled "Yankee Doodle Magic."[9]

On the streets of much of America, though, the 1980s were also a time of great economic pain and fear, even a sense of national drift and decay. In the first few years of the Reagan Administration, a series of huge layoffs shook the Northeast and Midwest. Steel and textile plants were shuttered, automobile and truck manufacturers laid off workers by the tens of thousands. The media began to refer to America's "Rust Belt." Bruce Springsteen sang gloomy odes to a lost industrial-town paradise. In the past, change had always seemed a prelude to progress and growing national power. Now many Americans felt they would have to lower their expectations, to compromise, both at home and around the world. A famous ad for Reagan's 1984 reelection campaign declared it was "Morning in America."[10] Perhaps so, but in much of the country the factory whistle no longer sounded the start of work.

For many Americans, Japan symbolized all these various pains. It was Japanese competition that meant unemployment here at home and the loss of industrial arts. It was Japan that meant a weaker America and the loss of our cherished isolation. A low point of sorts was hit right at the end of the decade, when a unit of the Japanese conglomerate Mitsubishi forked over $846 million cash for 51 percent of Rockefeller Center. Pearl Harbor II it wasn't, but the October 1989 deal delivered a shock to the American psyche. The country's long, lazy national economic decline seemed complete. A far-off Asian nation, one that had been smashed by American military and industrial might only four decades before, had seized hold of one of the premier landmarks in America's greatest city.

And it did so only four years after driving the most famous occupant of that building—the once all-mighty electronics pioneer RCA—into a desperate merger with General Electric.

The response to the sell-off of Rockefeller Center revealed much about American thinking at the time. First came gallows humor. On NBC's *Late Night with David Letterman,* as the opening credits rolled and the camera swooped up the sleek facade of the GE building, the announcer welcomed viewers to "New York, a subsidiary of Mitsubishi." On the street nearby, a woman sold T-shirts advertising "Wokafellar Center." In the Associated Press building, which is part of the Rockefeller Center complex, one enterprising reporter, perhaps by way of welcoming the new landlord, assured readers that "the Rockettes were not kicked out of Radio City by Godzilla." But a deep underlying tension and anger also became clear. New York's local Fox newscast broadcast grainy black-and-white film of Japanese carrier planes—a onetime product of the Mitsubishi consortium—on their bombing runs over Honolulu. Senator Joseph Lieberman of Connecticut lamented that New York's famed celebration of Christmas would take place on "Japanese property." The general mood was summed up by a professor of American history at Columbia University, sixty-five blocks uptown: "If the Japanese had won [World War II] and raised their Rising Sun flag, what more triumphant place to raise it than over the Rockefeller Center?"[11]

The temptation to blame Japanese competition for economic pain in America was not new. All the way back in the 1930s, cheap imports from Japan gave rise to the concept of "social dumping," which can be defined as when solid domestic jobs are undermined by the sale of foreign goods made using cheap and unprotected labor. In 1971, when the United States ran its first merchandise trade deficit of the twentieth century, President Richard Nixon pinned the blame on Japan. As a balance-of-payments crisis forced the United States to abandon the gold standard, Nixon even evoked the specter of Pearl Harbor and used the Trading with the Enemy Act to restrict imports of Japanese textiles. But anti-Japanese sentiment never grew deep roots in America, nor was it allowed to undermine the nation's basic policy in favor of ever-deeper trade. If nothing else, Americans are sophisticated consumers, and for years they welcomed Japan's cheaper and sometimes better-quality products: toys in the 1950s, transistor radios in the 1960s, compact cars and televisions in the 1970s.

By the mid-1980s, the tone began to change. As vast freighters spilled immense loads of Toyota Celicas and Sony televisions onto American docks, many came to believe a sort of reverse invasion was under way. In 1985, Theodore White, one of the American journalists with the most experience covering Asia, wrote in the *New York Times Magazine* of "The Danger from Japan." Forty years after the end of the war, he wrote, the Japanese "are on the move again in one of history's most brilliant commercial offensives, as they go about dismantling American industry." Even the staid magazine *Foreign Affairs* got into the fray. Echoing the anti-Semitic writings common in Europe in the decades before the war, the magazine published an article under a headline that referred to America's "Japan Problem."[12]

It would be wrong to ignore the strong sense of friendship that many Americans and Japanese still felt for each other, or to ignore the recurrent bouts of self-doubt that racked Americans. Through the rest of the decade, Americans' attitudes seemed to skitter back and forth almost by the day. First we blamed ourselves; our poor economic performance was our fault and we should work harder, study longer, make better-quality products. Next we blamed unfair Japanese protectionism. How could Japanese manufacturers capture a quarter of the American car market and sell us 90 percent of our motorcycles, yet no one American product could capture even 10 percent of any market in Japan? First we were eager to work arm in arm with Japan in the common struggle to protect the "Free World" against the Soviets. Thousands of college grads flew off to learn Japanese and teach English, and Japanese tourists and their cameras were welcomed in Times Square and on Waikiki Beach. Next, the factory workers of Japan were held up as a bigger threat than the ranks of soldiers goose-stepping through Red Square, and a congressman bemoaned an invasion by "little yellow people."[13]

By the fall of 1989, many Americans were settling into a sense of betrayal. One of the best-selling books that year was *The Rise and Fall of the Great Powers,* by Yale history professor Paul Kennedy. On the book's cover was a drawing of Uncle Sam, stepping down from a pedestal to make way for a Japanese man in a business suit. Many Americans felt the picture would have been more accurate if it had shown Uncle Sam being pushed. More and more now agreed with Chrysler's feisty and verbose

CEO, Lee Iacocca. "I'm no Communist, folks," Iacocca declared, "but it's not Russia that's laying waste to my business and to most of the rest of business in this country. It's Japan, our friend. While we stack the missiles up in the front yard, all aimed at our enemy, our friend is taking over the backyard."[14] Sometimes it felt as if Japan was pushing into the living room, propping its feet on the coffee table, asking America to go fetch a beer from the fridge. During forty-five years of Cold War, Americans had armed, fought, and bled to protect the world's industrialized democracies. In the case of Vietnam, U.S. soldiers had died at least in part to protect a piece of Japan's old empire; the last "domino" in line was, after all, Japan. A country that had been offered refuge within our walls was now taking over, parasite-like, the world we had made. Worst of all, the Japanese weren't even willing to say "thank you." On the contrary, a 1989 book by right-wing politician and novelist Shintaro Ishihara and Akio Morita, the CEO of Sony, urged Japanese to just "say no" to America's entreaties to act as a more responsible member of polite commercial society.

In the days after the Rockefeller Center deal was announced, the passions were not to be calmed. Americans fretted that they would have to work for Japanese companies, learn to speak and read Japanese, that American women would be turned into geishas and bargirls. London's *Economist* magazine, ever sober, scolded. Both sides, the magazine wrote, were acting like "bad sports." But it was to no avail. Malcolm Forbes, in a column for the magazine his father had founded, declared that enough was enough. "The fallout from this sale," he wrote, choosing his words with care, "is just beginning."[15]

Yet to many, such tough talk seemed little more than a way to sell magazines. America's saber was rusted hopelessly into its sheath. Not only was it not in our character to punish a nation for selling us products that were cheaper and better than ours, but we did not even have the ability to do so. We had caught Britain's disease, and like that once great imperial nation our only wise choice, it seemed, was to rock on our porch remembering better days.

Yet more was at stake than the relative political power of nations. For many Americans, the deterioration of the nation's manufacturing position was even more fundamentally disturbing. To understand the full magnitude of the psychological blow dealt by the headlong retreat of a company like General Motors and the outright collapse of a company like RCA, it is necessary to look back at how Americans, almost from the first days of the nation, have viewed manufacturing as central to their purpose in the world. Manufacturing had long seemed to be America's special art, a product of the nation's industriousness and innovative spark and work ethic and democratic spirit. America, the historian Henry Adams had written, was a nation that recognized the dynamo as a "moral force."[16] Building things bigger and better and cheaper had long ago become one of our most basic missions.

Was it not Americans who had invented the steamboat and the lightbulb and the farm tractor and the telephone and the airplane and the instant camera and plastic tape and the pop-up toaster and the Pop-Tart? Hadn't it been American enterprises that long set the standards for manufacturing quality, quantity, innovation, organization, finance, sales, and market intuition, that had turned our democratic energies toward the feeding and clothing and transporting of the People itself? Not merely was America the forge of the future, America was the forge of future human freedoms. In the same way that American democracy served to help release humanity from the toils of political tyrannies, American industry did the same for the corporeal body, releasing the individual from the toils of labor—the hoeing of earth, the scrubbing of clothes, the shoveling of coal. Socialists promised salvation though seizure of the means of production. Americans promised salvation by running those machines and using that capital better and smarter and more creatively than anyone ever imagined.

If there was a single image that best captured the populist power we perceived in our industry, it was the powered assembly line at the Ford factory in the Highland Park suburb of Detroit. The Ford company didn't invent the assembly line, but it did apply the idea on a scale and with a success that grabbed the imagination of the world. The big jump took place in August of 1913, when the engineers began to experiment with the final assembly of the Model T. Until that time, automobile chassis had been set atop wooden sawhorses, where a team of highly skilled assemblers would attach axles, wheels, transmissions, engines, and gas tanks, before bolting on the body. The new idea—first inspired by slaughterhouse "disassembly" lines in which hog carcasses were sequentially butchered—was now to separate each of these activities in space as well as in time.[17]

Ford's first big experiment gleams like a cameo of American capitalism itself. The setting was an empty patch of factory floor. At one end, engineers set up a windlass, from which they stretched a rope 250 feet to a bare chassis. Along the path of the rope, the engineers used chalk to mark off "stations," where they piled components. The windlass pulled the chassis along the floor, as six assemblers walked alongside attaching components. Though the rope soon broke, the engineers knew they had discovered something big. Whereas it took more than twelve hours to build a car using "static" assembly, the line method cut work time by more than half. Over the next few months, the engineers continued their experiments, shortening then lengthening the line, reordering the sequence of work, replacing the rope with a thicker rope and then a chain. By the following April, Ford was ready to launch three chain-driven assembly lines, with specialized workers standing at intervals rather than walking alongside the moving chassis. Total work time had been cut to ninety-three minutes. This phenomenal gain in productivity was the main factor that enabled Ford to slash the price of a Model T from $850 in 1908 to as low as $260.

Yet mass manufacturing was a power that was not so much discovered as perfected. Ford's great achievement came at the end of a line of innovation that stretched back at least to the magnificent Benjamin Franklin, who studied ocean currents, perfected the woodstove, and drew electricity itself down from the heavens. It was no one less than Thomas Jefferson who introduced America to the concept of interchangeable parts—a concept that lies at the heart of mass manufacturing—in a letter from Paris in 1785, written when he was the nation's first secretary of state. By the time Tocqueville careened through America in the 1830s, he reported seeing almost everywhere an "all pervading and restless activity," which he identified as a natural product of democracy itself.[18] By 1851, the products of this restless activity would, when displayed at the Crystal Palace exhibition in London, astonish the British, who soon dispatched a commission to study American industrial techniques. In 1876, the fruits of this restless activity, on view at the Centennial Exposition in Philadelphia, would shame the

Germans; no less an expert in the potential political power of industrial production than Adolph Hitler would later credit that event with inspiring German manufacturers to set their nation on a course toward the domination of Europe.[19] By the 1890s, America's shipyards were turning out steel battleships not only for the U.S. Navy but for the Japanese and Russians as well. In the early twentieth century, the perfection of the assembly line process brought a rush of industrial pilgrims to America, as many of the nation's manufacturers openly and gladly shared their techniques and even technologies with would-be foreign competitors. Ford's River Rouge complex especially became a sort of Mecca for manufacturers, who came for inspiration and for very practical advice.

In the twentieth century, the assembly line would remake American life. For the 70 years after Ford, mass manufacturing set the pace of the day and the week and the year. Americans no longer rose with the chickens, but set off to work and to eat and to sleep on highly regulated, almost mechanized, schedules. No longer did Americans rest in winter from the rigors of harvest; factories increasingly operated year-round. Ever-expanding industrial complexes lured workers from the farms to the cities, and lured African Americans from rural poverty in the south to the urban north. Mass manufacturing gave birth to massive workforces, which in time won the right to create the great industrial unions, in the process redistributing power within American society. Mass manufacturing led to mass advertising, mass credit, mass obsolescence, mass retirement.

Mass manufacturing meant mass prosperity. Mass-production techniques radically cut the relative cost of everything from lamps to chairs to refrigerators to furnaces to telephones to processed food. By the mid-1920s, with the maturation of the used-car market, many working-class Americans could afford to own a car. And mass-production jobs paid well. The rise of the industrial union, combined with the low rate of immigration during and after World War I, meant that more and more factory owners had to follow Ford's lead in paying more to attract good, steady workers.

Mass manufacturing meant mass scientific progress. Modern integrated manufacturing corporations came to provide the principal pathway along which advances in science and engineering were delivered to the average citizen. In the modern corporation, the assembly line was ever more closely integrated with the research laboratory itself. For two generations, American children grew up expecting that an American corporation would soon put them into a flying car or an interplanetary rocket. For a sort of proof we can turn to the 1960s television show *Star Trek,* where the interplanetary starship was named *Enterprise.*

Mass manufacturing also meant mass security. It was America's industrial might, more than old-fashioned valor, that brought victory in war. Although in some industries American technologies proved superior, in many it was much more a matter of brute industrial capacity. In the Second World War, German engineers designed better tanks and airplanes and rockets and submarines and artillery than did their American counterparts, at least early on. But America could manufacture so many ships and so many bombers and so many tanks that in time the Germans were simply overwhelmed. Americans could even afford to give industrial goods away to their allies. The Soviet Army, in its great push west in 1944 and 1945, often rode in Studebaker trucks.

Of all America's industrial arts, we felt a special pride toward two. Americans from the first had excelled at putting electricity into use and in putting people into motion. And the 1950s and 1960s had stood out as a golden age for both endeavors. It was during these years that Americans brought to the world color television and the computer, and that American carmakers turned out more and faster cars than we had imagined possible. Not only were we harnessing electricity into truly magical products, but we had transformed our very selves into so many loose electrons hurtling across our vast empty land.

And now the Japanese were beating us at these most American of arts. But they were doing so not by taking the arts to new levels but by being more practical, more efficient. Toyota and Sony weren't pushing the limits of technology so much as simply pushing the limits of process. And so it sometimes seemed as if America's new weakness was a weakness that affected all mankind.

The day after the 1992 presidential election found the Japanese government fretting. Bill Clinton had trounced George H. W. Bush, not least by promising to get tough with the Japanese on trade. American voters had made very clear that this is what they wanted; add the 19 percent of the vote won by protectionist Ross Perot to the 43 percent won by Clinton and the result is a very resounding mandate for economic change. In Japan, the question now seemed to be how swiftly reaction would come and how severe it would be. It was a time, one Japanese reporter wrote, of sleepless nights in Tokyo, as officials lay awake pondering "the specter of a bullying America."[20]

It is surprising the Japanese weren't more fearful—or at least the Japanese automotive industry. Lopez stood as proof that the American carmakers were ready to respond in dramatic fashion. And now it looked like the U.S. government would finally back them up. If anything, the rhetoric among the politicians was more hard-line than what was coming out of the ranks of the CEOs. In America, the specter of Japan Inc. had overshadowed the presidential campaign all year. And throughout, the auto industry had been among the main points of contention.

The election campaign season had started with one of the most humiliating moments in the history of American foreign policy. In January, a vigorous-seeming President Bush had flown to Tokyo to wrangle more market for American-made automobiles. Instead, during a state dinner in his honor, he had keeled over and vomited on Japanese prime minister Kiichi Miyazawa, who then gently cradled the president's head in his lap. In the months afterward, conservative television-commentator-turned-candidate Pat Buchanan would show surprising strength in Republican primaries, not least by touting a stoutly nationalistic America First economic plan. Over the summer, the torch would be picked up by the protectionist Perot, who in November would post the highest showing by any third-party candidate since Theodore Roosevelt ran as a Bull Moose in 1912. In such an atmosphere, it was not surprising that Clinton talked tough on trade, which he did often and with gusto. In the last debate before the election, he vowed to impose a "hardheaded realistic policy" that emphasized "fair trade," a phrase that in recent years had been a favorite of Democrats who wanted to slap big tariffs on Japan.[21] So strident was Clinton that Bush thought he saw an opening, and he blasted Clinton as an outright protectionist who sought to exploit the "darkest impulses of this uncertain age, fear of the future, fear of the unknown, fear of foreigners."[22]

Once in the White House, Clinton discovered that the global economic environment was much more complex than it seemed on the campaign trail. The world had changed radically over the previous three years, and the United States now looked much stronger than it had in decades. The Soviet Union had collapsed, the Gulf War had demonstrated remarkable new American technologies, and many American manufacturers seemed to be doing everything right—American semiconductor makers had outflanked the Japanese with new technologies, America's lead in software looked more secure than ever, even the automobile manufacturers were successfully implementing Japanese-style production in places like Mexico and Germany. Japan, by contrast, now looked weaker than it had in a decade. The Bank of Japan had recently popped the country's massive stock market and real estate bubbles, and now the country's economy was shrinking and its export juggernaut sinking. This new world was already increasingly reflected in radically and rapidly evolving debates within the policymaking community. And so it was that Clinton came to office with two road maps, which led in very different directions.

Clinton's first potential course of action was to live up to his pledge to be "hardheaded" and to demand "fair trade." By this time, after more than a decade of debate, a certain consensus about how to treat the Japanese was taking shape. That the Japanese were unfairly protecting their own market—and thereby distorting the entire world system by engaging in what Peter Drucker termed "adversarial trade"—was now widely accepted. Just as widespread by this time was the rejection of one of the more popular responses set forth by anti-Japanese hard-liners, which was to radically reform the American economy to make it look and act more like Japan's.[23] After all, was the nation where Teddy Roosevelt had busted the trusts now supposed to embrace permanent bureaucratic planning and the *zaibatsu* model of conglomeration?

Instead, support had grown in recent years for a more old-fashioned approach, one that wouldn't require any drastic changes at home. Much of this thinking was collected in a book edited by economist Paul Krugman. Amid a thick spray of caveats, Krugman acknowledged that most of the international-trade models built by economists no longer fully explained what was happening in the world, and that tangible national interests might "provide a potential rationale for a turn by the United States toward a more activist trade policy," including perhaps even higher tariffs.[24]

Clinton's second potential course of action with respect to Japan was to do nothing. This proposal was much more radical. Not only did it reject the protectionist approach but it rejected the status quo as well, calling for a de facto abandonment of the long, drawn-out, painful negotiations with Japan in favor of simply letting them engage in whatever mercantilist activities they might wish. Although this may seem to have been the natural answer for an American nation that had for so long preached the value of free trade, as we will see in Chapter Three, the United States had only rarely in its history allowed the international marketplace to operate freely. Now, however, more and more people were declaring that this was just the cure for all that was ailing us. Not only was the Japanese invasion not bad for us, it was quite good for us, bringing us better products for less money, providing good jobs right here at home.

The one key actor in bringing this philosophy into the Clinton White House was a man named Robert Reich, a forty-six-year-old lawyer who had worked in the Carter Administration before recasting himself as a professor of political economy at Harvard's Kennedy School of Government. Reich was one of the oldest Friends of Bill, having met the future president on the boat to England when both were Rhodes scholars. And he had seemingly impeccable progressive credentials; his books included such titles as *The Resurgent Liberal* and *Minding America's Business,* one of the first efforts to imagine a new industrial policy for the United States.

Not long before the election, however, Reich had published a new book, named *The Work of Nations,* in which he sought to make sense of the real workings of the post–Cold War global economy, not least the import of the rise to power of Japanese manufacturers like Toyota. The title of this book was a play on Adam Smith's *The Wealth of Nations,* and without any doubt, *The Work of Nations* was a worthy—albeit not always fact-based—effort to account for some of the great changes that had taken place in the global political economy. For the average American, Reich wrote, the big economic issue was a good job close to home. It was therefore much more in the interest of this American citizen to convince Toyota to manufacture cars in Kentucky than to fret about whether Ford had the right to manufacture cars in Nagoya. The role of government, Reich concluded, should therefore be to invest more in infrastructure and in education, and to pay for this by taxing the upper classes, not to reward inefficient American entrepreneurs by protecting them. In a globalized economy, Reich wrote, the fixation of so many Democrats on making "American" corporations more competitive vis-à-vis the Japanese, and the fixation on forcing Japan to accept more American investment, although somewhat "charming," was also "naively vestigial." The globalization of industrial activity had all but erased the borders of the nation-state, Reich concluded, and this meant that almost all of our economic assumptions had to be rethought.[25]

All in all, Reich's book amounted to perhaps the most tight embrace of laissez-faire trade policy ever to emerge from the mind of a self-described left-wing Democrat. And although Reich later insisted that the heart of the work was a "radical" call for taking money from the wealthy and spending it on educating poor and middle-class Americans,[26] its most immediate political effect was to confound and confuse many of the traditional critics of laissez-faire economics. This indeed may have been one reason why the book so clearly appealed to Clinton.[27] Not only did brandishing the book mean Clinton could claim the mantle of post–Cold War visionary, but following its recipes closely meant he could avoid any really tough fights with either the U.S. business community or any foreign government.

To understand just what Reich packaged up in *The Work of Nations,* it helps to take a closer look at the work of Kenichi Ohmae, a McKinsey & Co. consultant and one of the writers who apparently most influenced Reich in the early 1990s. A onetime nuclear physicist, the American-educated Ohmae had carved out a lucrative niche as a man able to explain the Japanese business environment to Americans. By the mid-1980s, however, like many other consultants Ohmae felt ready to weave what he had learned helping businesses into a full-blown theory to explain the global political economy that was taking shape. The result was a book named *Triad Power,* in which Ohmae described the emergence of three largely autonomous but highly interlinked economic blocs, in Asia, North America, and Europe. Ohmae soon followed this with a book he titled *The Borderless World,* published in 1990 right after the fall of the Berlin Wall. This was a much more radical volume, heavily influenced by the writing of Milton Friedman. In it Ohmae declared that the nation-state was dead or should be dead, and that even if it wasn't dead it was certainly every day more decrepit and irrelevant. At another moment in time, Ohmae's assault on not only the efficiency but the morality of the nation-state would have been dismissed as little more than a sort of pornography for businessmen who like to stay up late fantasizing about a world without regulation. But in the heady days after the collapse of the Soviet Bloc, Ohmae's rather saturnalian vision of commerce quickly made its way to the upper reaches of the American policy community.[28] In the case of Reich's book, published in early 1991, the debt to both *The Borderless World* and *Triad Power* is clear. If anything, Reich went Ohmae one better, by conflating the consultant's two works, using Ohmae's vision of a naturally emerging system of three semi-autonomous economic blocs to reassure American readers who might fear the security implications of a truly "borderless world."

It is not clear whether Reich fully understood the significance of the argument he made in *The Work of Nations*. Like many in the early 1990s, he may have been rendered giddy and uncritical by the sudden and unexpected collapse of the Soviet Union. Another possibility is that Reich saw his book as no more than a creative way to grab Clinton's attention, and to land himself a high-level job wherein he could pull the levers of power in order to do good work. It is also possible that Reich simply believed that the best way to drum up more support for old-fashioned social programs was to get the minds of Democrats off their fixation on trade. The only thing that is clear is that even after Reich had been amply warned about the potential significance of his argument—by baffled fellow progressives, by grateful laissez-faire economists, by observant journalists (*Fortune* called Reich's book a "fascinating flip-flop"[29])—he never developed any supplemental set of arguments by which to explain his intentions.

In his first months in power, Clinton took care not to reveal which of these two paths—"fair trade" or laissez-faire—he planned to take. Early appointments seemed to tilt strongly toward a more liberal approach. These included the naming of conservative Senator Lloyd Bentsen of Texas as Treasury secretary and the tapping of Goldman Sachs co-chairman Robert Ruben for an obscure but very powerful position as the White

House's main coordinator of economic policy. But then Clinton counterbalanced by naming Laura D'Andrea Tyson, a Berkeley economics professor often associated with the more aggressive pro-tariff trade "activists," as head of the Council of Economic Advisors.

And so, as would prove so often the case with Clinton, the new president managed to assure both sides that they would be the ones in control of policy. While many conservatives felt reassured that the general makeup of Clinton's team meant a free-trade tilt, others felt equally certain that nothing less than "industrial policy [was] on the way."[30]

"Nature Boy vs. Texas Chihuahua" is how one newspaper described it.[31] And the 1993 debate over the North American Free Trade Agreement between Vice President Al Gore and Ross Perot did at moments seem more like a professional wrestling match than, as the *New York Times* observed, a reprise of "Webster and Clay."[32] But the debate was important nonetheless. Refereed by Larry King, the showdown marked the culmination of the most intense public discussion of trade policy in America since the Smoot-Hawley Tariff in the depth of the Great Depression.

Whether any of the viewers who watched Gore slowly pick apart Perot's rather simple argument that night learned anything of value about the shape of the world economy or the aims of NAFTA is not clear. In focusing entirely on whether the agreement created more jobs here or more jobs there, the debate ended up being couched in terms more fit to discuss the tariffs of the 1920s or, for that matter, the 1830s than an agreement of the complexity and scope of NAFTA.[33]

And even under the best of circumstances it was not easy to understand the true intent of the trade agreement. For one thing, NAFTA lies far outside the tradition of American trade policy in the decades after the Second World War. Also, NAFTA is much more about investment than trade, and most of its nearly 2,000 pages were devoted to the rewriting of rules that somehow restricted cross-border investment by businesses, especially into Mexico.[34] Then there is the fact that the U.S. government's aims with NAFTA were much more fundamentally political in nature than the governments of the era usually admitted, and the agreement was designed in no small part to head off a political collapse in our next-door neighbor.[35] Last, and most important, NAFTA was really more about America's relationship with Japan—and with Europe—than it was about Mexico and Canada.

This last point may seem most surprising. But it is important to remember that when President Bush first proposed the agreement in 1990, the European Union was in the middle of transforming its economic "community" into a political "union." Many Americans assumed this "New Europe" would form itself into a strong and highly protectionist regional trade "bloc" tilted against the interests of American companies, and there was widespread sentiment that Japan would try to do the same thing in Asia. So when Bush proposed not merely a North American agreement but a "free-trade area" extending from Canada through Argentina, the idea was widely perceived as a strategic counterstroke to moves already taken by Brussels and Tokyo. So although NAFTA was very much about opening up the economies of North America to one another, viewed within a global context the agreement was clearly a protectionist device. To qualify a product for low- or no-tariff treatment under NAFTA, a minimum of 60 percent of the work on that product had to be done in the United States, Mexico, and/or Canada. In essence, NAFTA was a sort of negatively defined tariff wall, which clearly could be raised higher if necessary.

For Bill Clinton—who during his campaign had vowed swift action against the Japanese but who once in office saw so many reasons to hold his fire—NAFTA could certainly seem the most perfect of instruments. Here was a device designed to respond to whatever next move the Europeans and Japanese might make, yet which did not commit the United States to any irrevocably protectionist path. If Brussels and Tokyo chose to turn their economies even more inward, so could we. If they opted for a more global approach, NAFTA could be blended into whatever global trading system might emerge. And in the meanwhile, NAFTA would manage a radical liberalization within North America itself. Viewed in this way, it is really not surprising that Clinton in his first year dispatched his entire economic team—and spent much of his political capital—not in cracking the Japanese nut but in getting this new plan through Congress.

Therefore, to understand NAFTA's real influence on the course and evolution of the world economy in the 1990s we must steer way clear of Ross Perot's fears of a "giant sucking sound."[36] On the contrary, it is much more useful to focus instead on how the policymakers of the era argued the pros and cons of dividing the global economy into three great blocs, as opposed to pushing toward a more perfect single global economic system. This was no minor debate. The main point of contention was whether economic blocs like NAFTA and the European Union would lead the industrial nations of the world toward a more harmonious relationship or toward more conflict.

A good primer for arguments in support of organizing the economy around three big blocs is Ohmae's book *Triad Power.* In this, Ohmae delivers two main messages—that the move toward three blocs would be politically innocuous, and that it was already happening. Indeed, Ohmae presented what was at bottom a deeply political argument in the form of a neutral presentation of recommendations to help businesses thrive in the emerging global economy. His points are worth noting, as they very much captured how many leading businesses of the time actually were organizing their operations. Ohmae urged big companies to set up full-scale operations in all three regions rather than try to export from one home base. Not only should a company replicate its entire production operation three times, but it should also give each separate unit sufficient leeway to adapt its products and thinking to the local tastes and local social structures.

Organizing operations according to a three-bloc structure was no more than smart business, Ohmae wrote. Compared to companies that tried to serve all markets out of a single home production base, triad-structured manufacturers would be more global in outlook, more local in their knowledge of markets, and better insulated from swings in the value of currencies. Such a structure was also smart politics.[37] Organizing production into distinct economic blocs would allow officials to more easily groom regional economies to the democratically expressed desires of local workers and consumers. And the extensive cross-investment by global corporations would ensure that extremely powerful forces based in each of the three regions would work hard to keep any one of the governments from drifting into true autarky.[38]

The breakdown of the world economy into three blocs could, however, also be made to seem downright scary. Not only did Japan remain plenty feisty, but now it seemed Americans also had to worry about reunified

Germany. The collapse of the Communist regimes of Eastern Europe meant that the captains of West German industry could now marshal millions of new Germans to their machines, as well as dip liberally into the great discarded empire just to the east. Scarier yet was to imagine an aggressive Germany in alliance with France and Italy and the United Kingdom. Europe, after a long chrysalidal sleep, seemed to be awakening young and refreshed, and unified. That something was seriously awry was confirmed within months of the fall of the Wall. German chancellor Helmut Kohl, in a speech, declared that the 1990s "will be the decade of the Europeans, and not of the Japanese."[39] No mention was made of America. The assumption, it seemed, was that America was no longer a serious contender.

Those opposed to breaking the world into distinct economic blocs based their reasoning on two main points. The first was that such a division would be politically unfair, as it would mean acquiescing to Japanese and European plans to block off even more of the world economy from the reach of American businesses. The second and even more important objection was that over the long term the three blocs would likely fall into dangerous and ever more heated competition with one another. This argument was well captured by MIT economist Lester Thurow in his book *Head to Head: The Economic Battle Among Japan, Europe, and America.* Not that Thurow felt there was really any alternative. The end of the Cold War, he wrote, had made the breakup of the Western economy "irresistible," so there was nothing America could really do except gird for the battles ahead.[40]

In the end, NAFTA's influence on the global economy of the 1990s would be profound, though in ways no one expected. First, its overall effect on the distribution of work in North America proved to be remarkably innocuous, especially compared to the effect that China would begin to exert later in the decade. Although in certain sectors NAFTA did result in a shift of American capital and jobs south to Mexico, much of the "sucking sound" created by NAFTA was heard not so much in Ohio and Michigan as in Nagoya and Bavaria. In its first years in force, the agreement helped to convince dozens of Japanese, German, British, and French companies to invest tens of billions of dollars directly in operations not only in Mexico but also in the United States and Canada, to make sure they would receive "national" treatment inside the walls of the fortress. Nor were foreign firms the only ones affected; a number of

American manufacturers also credited NAFTA with convincing them to shift some of their growing investments in Southeast Asia and China back to North America, at least to Mexico.

Much more lasting was NAFTA's effect on the attitudes of business. Much has been written about how America's big manufacturers—not least the Big Three automakers—worked to shape the agreement to their interests. But at least as important is how NAFTA shaped how these manufacturers viewed the world. NAFTA served to educate a whole new generation of America's corporate managers that the U.S. government did not plan to help them sell abroad so much as move abroad (for reasons we will review more closely in the next two chapters). And in pushing these firms abroad, NAFTA taught many that cross-border operations give them more power vis-à-vis the individual worker and lower-level supplier. Neither of these lessons was new to NAFTA; the agreement, as we will see, lay very much in the tradition of other pro-investment initiatives pursued by the U.S. government over the years, such as in Western Europe and Taiwan in the 1950s and 1960s. But the debate over NAFTA attracted so much attention that it helped to teach these lessons to many firms much lower down the supply chain than those that had gone abroad in the previous waves of government-induced offshore investment. Not least among these students were the many auto supply manufacturers that had come under pressure from Lopez and other like-minded executives.

Yet NAFTA's most important legacy may be in the realm of national security and strategy. The agreement did prove moderately successful at stabilizing Mexico both politically and economically, at least in the short term. More important, it helped to counter any ambitions Europe and Japan might have had about forging yet more isolationist and mercantilist trading blocs. But as we will see, NAFTA did so not by circling the wagons around greater North America. Rather, it did so by coaching America's manufacturers in how and why they should invest big-time in the one great part of the world that lay outside of any of the economic blocs, which was, of course, China.

Corporate breakups tend to be fast, and Jose Ignacio Lopez de Arriortua was gone from General Motors less than a week after the first rumor of infidelity was reported in the *New York Times*. Actually, he made his final decision to leave so abruptly that GM CEO Jack Smith learned of the fact at a press conference called to celebrate Lopez's decision, made a day earlier, to stay. As Smith faced reporters alone, Lopez and his family were already on a flight across the Atlantic, where he had taken a top job at Volkswagen.[41]

Lopez's departure less than a year after his so loudly heralded arrival was one of the great C-Suite dramas of the decade. But for our purposes what is important is why he left and how this illustrates the changing dynamics and structures of cross-border business. Lopez, we learned in the flurry of coverage that followed his departure, had a dream. Unlike many of his colleagues at GM, Lopez understood that his efforts to reform the giant company's supply base had the potential to overturn much of the power structure within the firm's entire assembly system. After all, Lopez was calling on the suppliers not merely to cut their prices but to assume much more of the responsibility for the overall manufacturing process. This, he believed, would allow a complete redesign of the final assembly system, as suppliers now would be called on to deliver a few very large clusters of components, or subassemblies, to the lead manufacturer, where a greatly stripped-down contingent of workers would quickly bolt the pieces together. Lopez wanted to be the first to do this in the automotive industry. He called his plan Plateau 6, and later he would redub it Plant X.

As we will see in Chapter Seven, Lopez late in the decade would try to take advantage of this new distribution of work to grab power for himself. Yet in the early 1990s, he apparently seemed content to try out his idea within the confines of General Motors. Even before being tapped for the job in Detroit, when he was still toiling at Opel division headquarters in Zurich, Lopez repeatedly made clear to GM honchos that he wanted a chance to try out his experimental production system. The main catch— and this was Lopez's dream—was that he wanted GM to locate the new complex near his hometown of Amorebieta, in northern Spain. Which means we are left to regard Lopez as either one of the most accomplished hypocrites of modern business, or a type of tragic hero blind to the inconsistencies of his own teachings. Because even as he instructed American and European executives in how to denationalize their thinking about production, and gave them the strategies to cut themselves loose from the communities in which they had so long been rooted, Lopez himself remained fixated on his own hometown to an almost desperate degree—and with disastrous consequences for his career.

Once in Detroit, Lopez repeatedly proposed his idea directly to the GM board. But, in part because of a glut of capacity and in part because board members saw little reason to build a new plant in a mountainous area on the periphery of Europe, GM rejected the idea each time. And so, although it was never clear how much Lopez's Plant X dream played in his subsequent decision to leave GM, what is known is that soon after starting work in Detroit, Lopez began to flirt with Ferdinand Piech, the chairman of Volkswagen, another automaker in serious trouble. And it was later reported that one of the main topics they discussed during this courtship was Plant X.

After Lopez left, GM unleashed one of the most personal vendettas ever by a large corporation against a single individual, and to this day the man who once stood as the great hope of American industry still cannot enter the United States without risking jail. GM also sued Volkswagen, basing their case on a charge that Lopez had spirited away corporate secrets. After four years in court, the American carmaker won $100 million in damages, an agreement by Volkswagen to buy $1 billion in supplies from GM, and a promise that VW would sever all ties with Lopez forever. In the end, Lopez did get to build his experimental production system for VW, but he had to do so not in northwest Spain but in northeast Brazil. And he had to leave VW almost as soon as the plant opened.

Yet in 1993, as Lopez took off and as Clinton settled into office, Americans could look around with some confidence that the world was at last getting fixed, and that the actions being taken were highly prudent, practical, and rational. The world's biggest corporation at last seemed truly intent on wringing out waste and improving quality. And the nation's new young president was taking careful steps to counter any of many potential threats to American prosperity, not least that from Japan, by pushing a trading bloc that somehow managed the brilliant feat of blending together the Monroe Doctrine with Ricardian economics.

Yet when stirred together over the coming years, both the corporate strategy and the government strategy would whip into something entirely different. Lopez had truly helped to revolutionize how Americans manufacture. In breaking up old supplier relationships, by declaring that General Motors would go even to Mexico and Turkey for key components, by outsourcing more and more of the activities and skills of manufacturing, Lopez helped free the minds of American executives to envision operations that would be global not only in scale but in organization, and he thereby helped to deracinate the manufacturer from the nation.

Clinton, meanwhile, had truly helped to revolutionize how Americans viewed their economy. As he stood with his freshly signed NAFTA deal in hand in December, he seemed still to be prudently holding back on deciding between implementing the more hard-line approach against Japan or opting for Reich's laissez-faire policy, leaving the decision up to the Japanese and Europeans. And yet by this time Clinton had clearly made a decision of sorts. By the end of 1993, the NAFTA debate had made it amply clear that despite the strong demand for action expressed by voters in the election of 1992, Clinton intended to raise no real barriers to anyone's plan to go anywhere. NAFTA, even though focused on Mexico, also served to give the deracinated manufacturer a sort of license to go global. And so was set into motion a process that within a remarkably short period of time would yield a single global economic system and overturn everything we thought we knew about not only manufacturing but global economics, the global monetary system, and global politics.

CHAPTER TWO

CHINA AND THE GLOBAL MOMENT
Clinton's Counterstroke

The boom is for real!" It was May 1993, and Motorola executive Lai Chi-sun announced that his company was selling 10,000 pagers per week in China, the full output of its new factory in Tianjin. "We no longer talk of the 'potential' Chinese market," Lai said. That market, he felt sure, had "arrived."[1] And it was about time, too. The two decades since Richard Nixon had crossed the Pacific to shake hands with Mao Tse-tung had not been kind to American investors. Many companies had sallied into the Communist economy with great hopes, and most had retreated, often in a rout. The majority had simply held back, commissioning studies, hiring consultants, deploying executives on grand tours of China, closely watching for signals from American and Chinese officials, but keeping their capital dry.

Now Motorola, one of the high-tech stars of the moment, was proclaiming China was at last on track. This was not Nike announcing it could sell sneakers in Shanghai or McDonald's claiming it could vend burgers in Beijing. From its origins building automobile radios in the 1920s, Motorola had grown into one of the powers of America's high-tech industry. Its products ranged from satellites to telecom switching equipment, and it was a leader in the intensely competitive business of designing and building semiconductors. Nor was Motorola renowned only for its research and engineering prowess. The company was also admired worldwide for its manufacturing skills, and its Six Sigma quality-control program had been adopted by firms even in Japan. In effect, Motorola was making two simultaneous dramatic declarations about China—that the country was a place to manufacture not only toys and T-shirts but also moderately advanced electronics, and that China was also a place to sell high-tech consumer goods.

Motorola's sales in China were still small relative to the company's business in other countries, but what was important here was that the volume was swelling much faster than anyone had expected. Motorola managers had originally planned to export half the plant's production, but now Lai found himself assuring anxious investors that the company had plenty of additional capacity in the pipeline to serve the China market itself, including an advanced semiconductor plant. In all, Motorola had by this time already committed to invest upward of $160 million in China, and talk within the company was of much, much more. Indeed, the company had already designated its China operation as one of its three big strategic plays for the coming decade. Another was a much-ballyhooed alliance with IBM and Apple to design and manufacture the PowerPC chip. The third was the audacious and highly complex Iridium global satellite phone system, which was to provide voice service anywhere on earth.

Motorola's longtime CEO, Robert Galvin, had been fascinated with China for years. Son of company founder Paul Galvin, Robert had started as a stock boy in 1940 and worked his way up through various positions before taking over as CEO after his father's death in 1959. Over the next twenty-seven years, Galvin grew the company from 6,000 to 100,000 employees and from $250 million in annual sales to more than $8 billion. Galvin also added his name to America's long list of freethinking corporate titans with a slim ode to commerce titled *America's Founding Secret: What the Scottish Enlightenment Taught Our Founding Fathers.* Even though Motorola was a publicly owned company, like many "founding family" CEOs, Galvin often operated more from instinct than careful study. The China gamble, he said, was one of his most visceral decisions.

Galvin first traveled to China in the fall of 1986, a few months after having stepped down as CEO while retaining the title of chairman. His team—which included his son Chris, whom he was grooming to take his place—toured the country for three weeks, meeting with officials in Beijing and at various provincial governments. What Galvin saw was a nation of huge challenges, but also of vast opportunity and little competition. And, as son Chris later recollected, it was at this point that the elder Galvin decided to invest big in China, and to do so whether the rest of upper management at Motorola liked the idea or not. "I'm gonna write the memo and commit a hundred million to China," along with smaller operations in India and Brazil, Galvin reportedly told his son. If he didn't take the initiative, Galvin lamented, no one else would. His handpicked executive team, which included future Kodak CEO George Fisher, was simply "too timid."[2]

The China venture capped Motorola's move out into the world. Compared to most of America's big electronics firms, the company had long been a homebody, refusing to move any production overseas until the 1970s. In the mid-1980s, Motorola began to aggressively target sales into a few tough markets, including Japan. But the China venture was to be something special. As one internal company publication put it, the country would serve as Motorola's "second home."[3] And so the company's vast investment in Tianjin also represented a break of sorts with America. Galvin had long been one of the most stalwart of American manufacturers. For years he had tried to get the Reagan Administration or the Democrat-controlled Congress of the 1980s to adjust trade policy or tax policy to make it easier to compete with the Japanese while still manufacturing in the United States. Although he was a longtime Republican, Galvin had warned, pleaded, threatened, blustered, and in the end bucked strong opposition from the Reagan Administration to support a hard-hitting trade bill sponsored by Congressman Richard Gephardt. Galvin palled around with archprotectionist Lee Iacocca, and took out full-page advertisements warning that unfair Japanese competition was putting Motorola at risk. Without government help, Galvin said, Motorola would have to move half of its jobs abroad, and much of its research-and-development work as well. "It's no contest," he told a reporter in 1987. "We're in business to make a buck," and as priced at the time, "American labor can't compete."[4]

Not only did the Reagan and subsequent Bush administrations simply ignore Galvin's pleas, when the U.S. government did offer the company some help, it was of a very different sort than Galvin had expected. Over in China, at the time when Motorola executives were weighing the attractiveness of different sites for their big investment, the U.S. government was paying consultants to coach officials in various Chinese provinces in the finer arts of luring American investors. The effort was centered around what was called the Trade Development Program, run out of the U.S. Embassy in Beijing. Through the TDP, U.S. taxpayer money was used to hire top experts, train local Chinese officials, and prepare and translate documents. Of all the many cities that took part in the program, one of the most eager pupils was Tianjin. And the city's efforts would pay off many times over. In the three years after Lai's comments, Motorola would invest more than $1 billion more in Tianjin, as well as in a headquarters in Beijing, and by the end of the 1990s the total would top $3.4 billion. Motorola's China operations by then would directly employ 12,000 Chinese, oversee nineteen research-and-development centers, and report sales of $5.7 billion. Most spectacular of the investments was the $720 million integrated-circuit wafer foundry in Tianjin. Once completed, the Tianjin facility would be comparable only to Motorola's operations in its home base of Schaumburg, Illinois.[5]

So in the end, not only did the U.S. government not provide Motorola the protection Galvin sought, it went out of its way to show Motorola the door, and that door led straight to China. Which means that as much as the Galvin family may want to present their big venture as the result of rational discussions by executives in full control of the destiny of a large corporation operating in an environment of free trade, much of the decision was actually made—both passively and actively—in Washington.

Yet as will soon become clear, Motorola's investment would also prove to be—in terms of both business and government strategy—much more the end of an era than a beginning. Thanks in no small part to outsourcing, fewer and fewer corporations would in subsqent years feel obliged to make that sort of commitment of time and money and people ever again. And less and less would governments be able to force corporations toward any particular action. In one way, however, the Motorola announcement did herald the future. And this was to sound the arrival of China, and thereby the opening of the great "global" boom of the 1990s, in which China would emerge as the industrial center of the world.

Only four years before, the idea that a company of Motorola's stature would open an advanced semiconductor plant in Mainland China was unimaginable. This was because in early June 1989 Communist Party hard-liners in Beijing had decided to quash China's long-simmering democracy movement, which over the previous few weeks had bubbled up into a mass demonstration in Tiananmen Square. The bloodiest battles, which took place on the roads leading to central Beijing, were not witnessed by foreign journalists. Yet there was no shortage of satellite-transmitted images of demonstrators who had been shot, bayoneted, or run over by tanks. In all, at least 700 Chinese protesters were killed, and the real number may have been four times higher.[6]

For Western businesses, the crackdown seemed to end any hope that this great market would really open up anytime soon. For years, Washington and Beijing had carefully managed a political and commercial rapprochement, and the hope on the American side was that the interchange of goods and knowledge would over time slowly liberalize Chinese society and undermine the Communist regime. And so it had seemed for a time to be doing. But in sending the troops against the unarmed students and workers, China's leadership had made it starkly clear that they meant to keep control. The message to business seemed unequivocal. In the future, commerce with China would have to serve the desires and needs of Beijing, and as what Beijing wanted was the polar opposite of what Washington wanted, few if any Western businesses were surprised when the Bush Administration and Congress ratcheted trade sanctions back up early in November. The massacre and the political upheaval were widely regarded as proof that China still suffered from debilitating political instability and economic immaturity. What for many businesses had been a go-slow strategy now became a no-go strategy.

Yet hardly had boards of directors signed off on this plan when the world was shaken by another tectonic shift. On the morning of November 10, 1989, the East German government opened the gates of the Berlin Wall. Within hours, more than 100,000 East Germans rushed through Checkpoint Charley and other crossings into West Berlin and West Germany. For twenty-eight years the Wall had stood. Germany had been severed for forty-four. Now the German people had shoved aside the barriers that separated them, and the immediate result was a spontaneous mass celebration, as Germans quaffed beer, launched fireworks, and danced atop the graffiti-covered concrete.

The collapse of the Wall was one of the great political shocks of the twentieth century. The twelve-foot-high strip of concrete had become a defining feature of the modern world, and it seemed very much a fixture of that world. Every U.S. president since John F. Kennedy had called on the East Germans and their Soviet sponsors to, in the words of Ronald Reagan, "tear down the Wall." Yet few people really expected this to happen; fewer yet dreamed it would ever happen so suddenly. For all the relief that had greeted Soviet president Mikhail Gorbachev's policy of *glasnost,* for all the political experimentation already under way in the nations of Eastern Europe, for all the hundreds of thousands of marchers demanding freedom on the streets of Prague and Budapest—always lurking had been the fear that hard-liners in Moscow would seize power and herd the reformers onto trains bound for Siberia, or worse. In the months running up to the final collapse of authority in the Eastern Bloc nations, the image that loomed in everyone's mind was of the brutal crackdown in China.

For the purposes of our story, the stand-down at Checkpoint Charley did two things. First, it marked the official opening to Western investment of many markets that for a half century had been locked away, first in the trade empire of Nazi Germany and then in the Warsaw Bloc. Not only was it now clear there would be no reaction in East Germany, it became clear there would be no Soviet-sanctioned reaction anywhere in the rest of Eastern Europe, and if anything the collapse of the Soviet government itself now seemed possible. Second, the fall of the Wall recast entirely how the crackdown in China could be interpreted. Rather than the beginning of the next stage in the evolution of an all-controlling Maoist state, the Tiananmen massacre now looked a lot more like a last spasm of a dying tyranny.

For many Americans, the collapse of Soviet Communism was disorienting. For two generations, the Soviet threat had defined America's sense of place and purpose in the world, and countering that threat had been the guiding principle of the nation's foreign and defense policies. Leninism for nearly seventy-five years had been one of the main forces shaping the global political environment. Marxism for 150 years had provided the most compelling counterpoint to the liberal democratic vision born in

America in the eighteenth century. Their sudden disappearance created a crisis almost existential in nature. America, and the West as a whole, was suddenly free to be itself. It was unclear, though, what that self would be, and how that self would manage commerce with the world's last great authoritarian socialist government, in Beijing. The only thing clear was what business planned for the markets deemed to be open.

On November 15, 1989, General Electric announced plans to pay $150 million for 50 percent plus one share of the Hungarian lightbulb manufacturer Tungsram. Less than a week had passed since East Germans had breached the Berlin Wall. And now, with startling swiftness, one of America's biggest corporations had grabbed a choice piece of what so recently had been the Soviet Bloc economy. Other American companies soon followed, not only into Hungary but into Poland and Czechoslovakia and East Germany, even Bulgaria and Romania. Among the biggest early investments were Coca-Cola's buy-up of bottlers in East Germany and Hungary and Poland and Schwinn's takeover of Hungarian bike maker Csepel. Overnight America's business and financial communities began to buzz with terms that had rarely been heard in recent decades, as countries that for forty years had been hidden away behind the Iron Curtain scrambled to off-load state-owned ventures in manufacturing, services, and utilities. Privatization, concession, acquisition, joint venture, and merger became the order of the day, twenty-four hours per day. Failure was common. Many if not most early foreign ventures into Eastern Europe came to grief. Marriott turned a profit on a new hotel in Warsaw but lost money in Moscow, Budapest, and Sofia. General Motors abandoned a transmission plant in Czechoslovakia, as the country split into two. But new firms kept rushing in.

Within months, the frenzy spread from Eastern Europe to other parts of the world, and Latin America especially became a hot destination. Inspired by the "Chicago School" reforms imposed on Chile by dictator Augusto Pinochet, a half-dozen nations from Mexico to Brazil to Argentina had already begun to disassemble statist economic policies and open themselves to foreign investment. Now the collapse of Eastern European socialism served only to speed the process, and what had been a careful timber-by-timber dismantling gave way to a liberal use of dynamite charges in all-in-one reform packages known as economic "shocks."

Soon the frenzy spread further still, to Indonesia and Malaysia and Vietnam, even to distant outliers like Turkey and South Africa.

Investors often arrived in hordes, from America, from Europe, from Japan, grabbing up local manufacturers, setting up new plants, taking controlling stakes in newly privatized local water companies and power companies and telephone networks and airlines and ports. The mantra was to get in early, roll up as much of a sector as could be got, then move on. Every so often, the process would turn sour. In Venezuela, mobs enraged by the cutoff of subsidies for bread and gasoline sacked and burned much of Caracas, and the army shot hundreds dead before the rioters returned home. In South Korea, strikes by fearful industrial workers brought the country to a halt. But the setbacks were only temporary. Investors took the last flight out and the first back in.

Before the 1992 election, Bill Clinton had made clear that he would do little to impede American investment in most of the world, but that was only if you measured the world geographically. No one, as we have seen, was quite sure what he planned for Japan. Even more of a mystery was what he planned for China. But his strategy for Eastern Europe and Latin America and Southeast Asia was simple—go fast and go big. Once in office, the new Administration moved quickly to drive this message home, appointing a team of energetic and confident policy makers who seemed almost desperate to help American corporations push out further and farther into the world. Profits, the Clintonians declared, lay not in convincing the conservative executives of Tokyo and Berlin to buy American products, but rather in moving fast to outflank these old-fashioned, government-addled economies by rushing instead into eager and hungry nations like India and Indonesia and Brazil.

It was a heady time for business, a frenzied time, those early days of expanding into the newly opened world. Yet always there lingered a feeling of incompleteness, a nagging sense that the initial stage of globalization had left the world not yet perfectly round. And this was because China since Tiananmen had been kept in a sort of limbo, caught between the back-to-business attitude that had been personified by the Bush Administration and the starve-'em-out convictions of many hard-core trade realists in Congress who sought to hold back investors until Beijing had made much deeper political reforms.

The first round of globalization was certainly nice enough. But Poland was still a penny-ante game, and Argentina was, well, Argentina. China was where the big bucks lay.

China had always been where the big bucks seemed to lie. From well before America's independence, China had beckoned Americans toward the setting sun, and the force of China's allure on American history is far greater than it might at first appear.

It is not possible to really understand how and why America managed its relationship with China in the late twentieth century unless we review what China meant to Americans in the past, unless we understand the strength and durability of the China fever.

And so consider for a moment a man named Thomas Hart Benton. Little remembered today, in the years before the Civil War Benton was one of the giants of the U.S. Senate, representing Missouri at a time when that body was filled by the likes of Daniel Webster, Henry Clay, and John Calhoun. Benton was not held as quite the equal of these other men in rational debate, though many contemporaries gave him the edge when it came to outright bombast (which, given the standards of the era, is saying a lot). Today, Benton is recalled mainly as Andrew Jackson's strongest ally in the Senate—despite having fought a famous duel with Jackson in his youth—and as one of the South's more powerful opponents of the coastal plantation gentry.

For our purposes, Benton's importance lies in the fact that he was one of America's most ardent expansionists, a man whose avid desire to trade with China serves to illustrate just how profoundly the dream of commerce with that nation shaped America's sense of place in the world. Of all the westward-gazing politicians of that era, Benton boasted perhaps the gaudiest vision, his goal being to transform his adopted city of St. Louis into the "Venice of the New World," the jumping-off point for caravan routes across the western deserts and mountains to San Francisco and thence to Asia.[7] Benton also serves as a convenient connection between the first generation of American expansionists who saw China as the farthest object of what would come to be known as the nation's "Manifest Destiny," and those later actors who would stake very real claims to China's market, mind, and soul. Benton's link to the past was forged during a visit the senator paid to the dying Thomas Jefferson at Monticello in 1824, which in the words of historian Henry Nash Smith "was the occasion of a laying on of hands, a ceremony in which Benton received the mantle of the first prophet of American expansionism."[8] The link to the future came in the form of a widely admired and popular biography of Benton written decades later by none other than Theodore Roosevelt, who in 1898, as acting Secretary of the Navy, would help engineer the capture of the Philippines to use as a base for operations along China's coast.

America's direct commercial relationship with China began within a year of the end of the Revolutionary War, when in 1784 the merchant ship *Empress of China* became the first to sail from the newly independent United States to Canton. China at this time was a source of tea, yarns, cinnamon, porcelains, silks, and textiles, which could be got in exchange for seal pelts, ginseng, Spanish silver dollars, and Turkish opium. This trade could be very lucrative, as Robert Morris, the Revolutionary-era financier, discovered when his stake in the *Empress of China* voyage returned him 30 percent. Over the years, dozens of American families would make their fortunes on the China trade, including the Forbeses and Delanos of New York and the Browns of Providence and the Perkinses of Boston.

So diligent were American traders in expanding the China trade that by early in the nineteenth century their commerce up the Pearl River surpassed that of all European nations except Britain, and the Americans had managed this feat without war or any major display of power. From the beginning, Americans sought to trade with China very much on the cheap, without any of the expense of formal empire. Not that the Americans were shy about taking advantage of the wars of others. They solidified their originally tenuous place in Canton while the Europeans were tied up fighting with or against Napoleon. Later, after the British victory in the first Opium War in 1840, the United States immediately wrangled its own Treaty of Wanghia, which in some ways was even more liberal in its benefits than the deal the British won for themselves with arms.

By the twentieth century, the driving force of America's trade with

China would flip, as the New England trading families would cede primacy of place to the newly formed National Association of Manufacturers, a group whose main purpose was to promote the export of goods made in American factories. No longer was China viewed primarily as a source of exotica, but rather as a market for America's growing surpluses of agricultural products and manufactured goods. With European nations increasingly protecting their markets, many viewed China as the best place to off-load this production, surfeits of which were blamed for a series of deep depressions in the 1890s. In a policy statement that could have been written by the Commerce Department of Bill Clinton, the Grover Cleveland Administration held that "the future of America's trade expansion lay not with Europe but with the undeveloped areas" of the world with which the American economy was now more "complementary."[9]

Over the years, many of America's more aggressive and even imperial acts in the Pacific were shaped by what one historian has called the nation's one "overriding ambition" in the region, which was "the penetration and ultimate domination of the fabled China market."[10] America's war against Mexico in the late 1840s was fought in no small part to acquire the port of San Francisco, not least for the China trade.[11] A few years later, when Commodore Perry's Black Ships sailed into Tokyo Bay, the goal was not so much to open Japan to trade as to force Japan to protect American sailors shipwrecked on the long voyage to China, and to provide coal to the steamers that were beginning to replace clipper ships on the China routes. The most dramatic of America's experiments in formal empire—in the Philippines—was driven mainly by the desire to secure a military base from which to police European aggressions in China.[12]

And so the taking of that archipelago served as a sort of formal entry by America into European power politics. In the 1890s, Russia, Germany, France, and Austria were all threatening to cut off pieces of coastal China. The process was already well under way; in recent years, the French had seized Indochina, the Japanese Taiwan, the Russians Manchuria, the British northern Burma. And so it was now that the McKinley Administration adopted the famous Open Door Policy, which held that all China's markets should be open to all traders, rather than carved into an African-style mosaic. The policy did not so much reflect a deep American conviction in the rightness of protecting China's political integrity, as a belief that America's interests were best served by ensuring that America's highly capable manufacturers had access to as much of the China market as possible. It was in and around China in these years that America would develop a sense of confidence in dealing with Europeans, and the overall strategies, that helped to set the stage for the much greater revolution in the nation's policy that would take place in 1917.

The modern U.S.-China relationship would not begin until 1971 when Henry Kissinger, during an official dinner in Pakistan, feigned a stomachache and slipped away from his entourage to fly secretly to Beijing to meet with Chinese leaders. That trip marked the end of more than two decades in which there had been almost no official contact between the two nations, but rather often violent animosity. The United States and China's Communist government had after all been on opposite sides in China's civil war, in Korea's civil war, and in the ongoing face-off between Beijing and Taipei across the Taiwan Straits. For President Richard Nixon and Kissinger, his national security advisor, there were many compelling reasons to reach out to Beijing. Common sense called for some form of direct communication with a nuclear-armed state that still fervently preached world revolution and that was at times subject to outbreaks of terror and famine. A second reason, of very immediate interest to Nixon as he prepared to campaign for a second term, was to enlist China's aid in fashioning a respectable retreat from Vietnam. And, of course, there was the mutual fear of the Soviet Union, from whose orbit Mao had broken in 1960.

Kissinger used the term "realpolitik" to describe America's outreach to China, intentionally evoking the highly "realist" diplomacy of such Central Europeans as Austria's Prince Metternich and Germany's Otto Von Bismarck. Kissinger's goal in doing so was to emphasize that his policy toward China, however ideologically unsavory an alliance with a radical Communist regime might seem, was an intelligently framed act of greatpower balancing, in the highly refined style of nineteenth-century Central Europe. And in so doing, Kissinger also set a pattern that would prevail for the next two decades. China itself was not to be seen as the goal; China was simply a "card" to play in the extremely high-stakes game America was playing with the Soviet Union. Yet this justification was always at least half based on myth. However calculating Kissinger may have wanted the policy to seem, it was also clearly shaped by America's age-old fascination with the great nation across the sea.

"Who lost China?" was one of the defining slogans of one of the nastiest periods in postwar American politics, a time when Joe McCarthy and Richard Nixon sought to use the Communist victory over the Nationalists in 1949 to cripple the Democratic Administration of Harry Truman. Of course, in order to "lose" China, the United States first had to have China. And as one historian has written, "no such notion [has] ever arisen in American public life about any other nation."[13] It was this sense of proprietorship—in many different guises—that shaped America's conception of China for more than a century, and that guided much American policy well into the 1990s.

By the time Motorola executives decided to settle into Tianjin, they faced no shortage of case studies detailing what worked and what didn't for other companies that had invested in China. The result was two strategic decisions. First, Motorola insisted on full control over the business, rejecting any idea of the "joint venture" approach that China's provincial governments usually required. Second, Motorola came to China fully expecting to build the electronics equivalent of Ford's River Rouge complex à la 1926, as well as a modern version of a West Virginia coal company town circa 1890, complete with streets, power plant, and church.

And so Motorola in its first decade of operation would construct a vast complex of manufacturing operations, and invest extensively in developing a base of local suppliers, and build two branches of Motorola University to train engineers, and establish an institute to instruct Chinese officials in the intricacies of Western intellectual-property-rights regimes. And so Motorola also built hundreds of houses and apartments, and parks and playgrounds, and thirty elementary schools for which it hired and trained the teachers. Motorola even paid for a panda support station near the city of Chengdu, in Szechwan province, complete with a program to propagate the rare animals through artificial insemination.

The extent of this investment may seem extreme. But it helps to illustrate just how daunting most early investors found doing business in

China to be. In recent years, we have come to view China as a vast industrial paradise. Yet right through the 1980s, investing directly in the country was still a very speculative affair, and there was no shortage of stories that seemed to prove that in China it was a lot easier to lose a fortune than to make one.

Many of the first investors into China in the 1970s had expected to find a sort of tabla rasa, ideal for the massive, vertically integrated industrialization then in vogue in places like the Venezuela llanos or the Malaysian jungle. From afar China seemed, if anything, more industrially advanced than most other developing nations; after all, the country had exploded a nuclear bomb and was able to assemble Soviet-designed fighter jets. Yet what the first investors found was not only no tabletop on which to build, but no legs to the table, and no floor beneath it. The first companies entered a country that in many ways was still physically in the nineteenth century and, in terms of its understanding of commerce and capitalism, was in a world very much unto itself.

China never had much heavy industry. In the late nineteenth century, the Western powers that dominated China's coastal regions consciously strove to avoid the cost and effort required for formal colonial control. Foreign governments rarely concerned themselves with the construction of railroads, postal systems, or other basic infrastructure. To make matters worse, most of these governments actively opposed efforts to develop China industrially. This policy was formulated first by the British, on behalf of the Manchester textile mills, but it was later adopted by the American government.[14] The only real early effort to industrialize China was made by Sun Yat-sen after the founding of the Chinese Republic.[15] But Chinese industry for the most part remained highly inefficient and corrupt, and these were the good old days. Beginning in the 1930s, it entered a long period of decline, decay, and destruction.[16] The one break in the pattern came with the infusion of Soviet industrial technologies and techniques in the 1950s, but much of that energy was lost in anarchic revolutionary spasms such as the Great Leap Forward, with its backyard pig iron furnaces, and the Cultural Revolution.

The first real glimmer of what was to come in the 1990s was the set of radical economic reforms Deng Xiaoping imposed beginning in 1978. Deng's program, which he had slyly labeled his "Open Door Policy," integrated many lessons learned from a series of spectacular failures in the late 1970s.[17] Coca-Cola was one of the first companies to accept Deng's bait, and it was soon joined by R. J. Reynolds and Nike, among others. But the real poster child of this second generation of investors, at least from the U.S. point of view, was American Motors, which planned to build Jeep Cherokees for the Chinese market.

The Beijing Jeep project was to illustrate how American manufacturers and Chinese labor could thrive together. Instead, it came to be viewed as proof of just how immense a distance still yawned between the two cultures. Journalist James Mann's history of the project details how the American Motors executives were overwhelmed from the moment the project went into operation in 1985 with challenges both mundane and fundamental. To keep the plant running, they had to import everything from sandpaper to batteries to tires. To do business with local politicians and suppliers, they had to learn the intricate customs of Chinese business relationships. To keep their employees on the job, they had to make do without such "Western" incentives as bonuses and promotions. To obtain supplies and services, they had to learn the dynamics of "Five Year" economic plans, even while accustoming themselves to sudden radical shifts in the most basic of economic policies. To keep their expatriate executives only moderately comfortable, Jeep had to spend huge sums on barely functioning Western-style hotels. Most daunting of all was a chronic lack of hard currency. Both China and American Motors were cash poor.[18]

So even before the Tiananmen massacre, the flagship of the second fleet of investors was widely seen as having foundered. And Jeep—which by this time was owned by Chrysler—was not alone. Nike, a company that since 1964 had focused almost entirely on selling Asian-manufactured shoes in the United States, found itself unable to make a profit off its four factories in China, despite the fact that local wages were a fraction of those at its operations in Taiwan and Korea. After years of effort, Nike never got the cost of production down even to that of the company's factory in Maine.[19] Chronic problems included spotty supplies of high-quality rubber and an oversupply of surly workers. Early on, Nike vice president David Chang was still hopeful that the company would learn the "whole different set of rules" needed "to play the game." After five years of trying, though, Nike finally admitted it just couldn't do it.[20]

Not that all the work of these pioneers was entirely for naught. Even though many of their businesses proved unsustainable, their efforts left behind many important achievements, such as new commercial laws and banking practices, experienced expatriate and Chinese managers, even new building techniques and construction standards. The individual venture often died, but the commercial counterrevolution would live on and grow.

In 1994, an article in *Fortune* claimed to reveal one of Silicon Valley's best-kept secrets—which was that much of the most advanced manufacturing work being sold by America's high-tech manufacturers was in fact being performed in Taiwan by Taiwanese firms. Suppliers on the island, the magazine reported, provided a "vital edge" for almost every American "brand name" in electronics, not least such market leaders as Hewlett-Packard, Apple, Cisco, and Dell.[21] So much work was being done in Taiwan that the island nation had emerged seemingly overnight as one of the great electronics powers in the world, third behind only the United States and Japan, with annual sales of hardware topping $10 billion.

The story of this "Taiwanese connection" is vital to an understanding of the evolution of the U.S.-China commercial relationship in the 1990s. And it also illuminates how modern cross-border outsourcing strategies can reshape both economic and political relationships far faster and far more profoundly than most traditional forms of trade. The alliance also helped to teach American firms two key lessons: how to create a modern global cross-border networked economy (which we will see in more detail in Chapter Four), and how to manufacture in China without risking nearly as many resources as did American Motors and Motorola, or going through any of the hassle of direct investment in that nation. Indeed, at the same time that Motorola was in the midst of its immense build-out in Tianjin, many of its American competitors were gaining the same benefits without ever stepping onto Chinese soil, without tying up a single dollar of capital, and with design work and fresh capital thrown into the deal, all in exchange for a relatively small fee paid to middleman companies based in Taiwan.

The rise of Taiwan as an electronics powerhouse was a very different event from the rise of Japan that culminated in the 1980s. This was not the story of Sony relentlessly eating away at RCA's control of television, or of NEC and Hitachi dumping their way to control of the global market for DRAM memory chips. Rather, it is an example of Taiwanese firms learning how to thrive by allying with but not challenging the leadership of big U.S. electronics manufacturers. Taiwanese firms, the *Fortune* reporter wrote, know their "place in the world value chain"; and this place was midway between "low-end, labor intensive economies like the People's Republic of China and the high-tech domains of the U.S. and Japan." A good example was a firm named Mitac. Early in the 1990s, Mitac tried to sell PCs in the U.S. market under its own brand, in competition with the American giants to which it had long supplied components. After the venture failed miserably, the chastened company, on the verge of collapse, was able to resurrect its earlier business model of building components for IBM, Apple, and others, and it has done well ever since. Such examples are not limited to electronics. One Taiwanese company, named Pou Chen, grew to enormous size simply by making shoes designed and sold by Nike.

The success of the U.S.-Taiwan alliance represented a payoff of sorts for the U.S. government's sustained efforts over the years to build up the island's economy. The process began in the mid-1950s, not long after the American-supported Nationalist Army retreated to Taiwan after being routed by Mao's troops.[22] The State Department soon launched a number of programs and policies designed, most immediately, to wean Taiwan from an expensive aid program.[23] But Washington also had a strategic goal in mind, which was to transform Taiwan into a "showcase of noncommunist development" just off the coast of Communist China.[24] So extensive was the U.S. government effort to build up Taiwan's economy that it should be viewed as a sort of mini–Marshall Plan. Not only did Washington direct significant military and economic aid to the island, U.S. officials also helped Taiwan rewrite its laws regulating business, structured trade agreements to promote imports from the island, funded efforts to lure American companies to invest in Taiwan, arranged for the transfer to Taiwanese electronics firms of radar, avionics, and other advanced technologies, and paid to educate thousands of Taiwanese engineers and scientists at American universities.[25] The effort was a huge success—for

Taiwan, for American manufacturers, and for U.S. policy. In the five years after 1964, the island's exports to the United States quadrupled. By this time, at least twenty-three American companies—including Texas Instruments and General Instrument—had opened manufacturing plants on the island,[26] and many more were on the way.

Taiwan was not the only target of such efforts by the U.S. government and the closely interrelated attentions of American corporations. Much the same thing happened, on a smaller scale, in Singapore, Malaysia, Thailand, the Philippines, and Indonesia, in all of which American firms formed informal alliances with ethnic Chinese business communities. The only real exception to this pattern was South Korea. Americans did forge many key industrial alliances in that nation, often to counter Japanese competitors, but these businesses tended to be dominated by Korean-owned conglomerates.[27] For a number of reasons—not least the fact that Taiwan combined a relatively large-scale economy with generally small-scale firms—that island became a much more popular location.

Beginning in the 1980s, Taiwan's success was also due to a special competitive advantage, which was a close and highly unusual alliance with firms located in Mainland China. Contractors in South Korea and Malaysia also offered good work done cheap. The Taiwanese companies offered the added bonus that they had figured out how to farm much of the work out to a disciplined and increasingly skillful labor force that worked for a fraction of the pay required anywhere else in the region.

Take, for instance, Mitac. When the firm restored its fortunes by re-casting itself as a loyal subcontractor to IBM and Apple, it also increasingly chose to locate this manufacturing work on the Mainland. Take also Pou Chen. After Nike's headlong retreat from manufacturing directly in China in the early 1980s, the company would soon return, but now in partnership with Pou Chen and other Taiwanese manufacturers. It was Pou Chen's work as a sort of foreman rounding up Mainland Chinese labor for Nike that helped to transform it into, by some measures, the world's single biggest manufacturer of shoes.

On the surface, Taiwan seems the nation least likely to serve as a link between American corporations and the workers, manufacturers, and governments of Mainland China. Taiwan and China have been in a state of near war since 1949, and the government in Beijing considers Taiwan to be a province in rebellion. Internationally, Taiwan for the past thirty years has lived as a sort of a non-nation, relegated to a political netherworld ever since President Carter unceremoniously lifted diplomatic recognition of the Taipei government. Not only are there no official relations with the Mainland, but during most of this time there was no direct transportation of cargo or people, no direct communications, and harsh official restrictions on direct investment and trade. Yet beginning in the late 1970s, both Taipei and Beijing quietly fostered highly symbiotic commerce across the Strait, with most early ventures clustering first in Fukian province and later in and around Shanghai.[28]

During the 1990s, the only real downside to tapping into China indirectly through relationships with Taiwanese firms was that the American corporation received no quid pro quo guaranteed right to sell its product in China itself. Motorola was able to sell its pagers in China because it had been granted the right to do so as part of its investment deal. Then again, contracting for manufacturing work in China via Taiwan did not by any means require a company to give up hope of getting its branded products onto the China market. On the contrary, China's marketplace was so complex and segmented, and so subject to the whims of authorities in different cities and provinces, that foreign companies with only minimal direct investment were still often able to carve out commanding shares of key markets.

And so by the middle of the decade, the triangular industrial relationship forged by American, Taiwanese, and Chinese firms—and winked at by the governments of all three countries—would evolve into the real secret behind not only the competitiveness of top U.S. electronics firms but the political interrelationship of these three states. The economic integration of the United States, Taiwan, and increasingly China—in a process largely unregulated by the governments or by traditional vertically integrated manufacturers—was for the well-being of the average American a far more important political event than the formation of NAFTA. Indeed, the tristate relationship would soon emerge as the true center of today's global economy.

In October 1997, President Clinton made one of the most important foreign policy speeches of his two terms in office. During the 1992 campaign, Clinton had presented himself as a hawk on China, and he harshly condemned the Bush Administration for continuing to "coddle" the Communists despite Beijing's "crackdown on democratic reform, its brutal subjugation of Tibet, its irresponsible export of nuclear and missile technology . . . and its abusive trade practices."[29] That summer, Clinton invited Chinese dissidents to address the Democratic Convention in New York. Once in power, however, Clinton began to drift away from the real China hard-liners in Congress. And now, on the eve of the first state visit by a Chinese leader in twelve years, Clinton was desperately seeking to hammer together a new framework for the bilateral relationship.

The ultimate issue was how far to go in trading with Beijing. The collapse of the Soviet Union had destroyed any excuse whatsoever for maintaining the "special" political relationship Kissinger had developed in the early 1990s. It was now impossible to hide the fact that the United States and China shared only two true mutual interests—to avoid conflict with each other, and to exchange cheap labor for investment. So the question for many Americans now became whether this trade was helping or hurting the Communist regime. After the Tiananmen massacre, and what was widely viewed as a weak-kneed response by the Bush Administration, many in Congress insisted on a direct role in managing the relationship. Their main threat became to revoke China's status as a Most Favored Nation for trade, which would force the administration to collect the prevailing basic tariff on imports from China.[30]

Clinton's 1997 speech, which he delivered to a small group of Asia experts in Washington, was masterful. He touched on all issues of the bilateral relationship, delicately acknowledging areas of conflict. China's response to instability, he noted, was to stifle "political dissent to a degree and in ways that we believe are fundamentally wrong." But Clinton also insisted it would be a mistake for the United States to judge China by our morality and our political beliefs, and that it would be an even bigger mistake to try to coerce the nation in a particular political direction. Nor, he quickly added, was any aggressive use of trade "sanctions" necessary. The very forces of history, and of progress itself, were now sweeping China toward liberal democracy. Global television and the Internet, he said, were exposing China's citizens to the "people, ideas, and the world beyond China's borders." The best course of action was simply to continue to do exactly what we were already doing, which was to criticize lightly and to trade like mad. It was, Clinton concluded, a "pragmatic policy of engagement."[31]

If there was a single biggest problem with Clinton's speech, it was that it was delivered four years after his administration had actually established its policy on the issue. For all intents, the decision to keep hands off of trade with China had been made during Clinton's first year in office. Even before Clinton had launched the campaign to win passage of NAFTA, many of America's biggest corporations began to rush back into China. The mere fact that the new administration raised no objections was then read as proof that, no matter his campaign rhetoric, Clinton would not interfere later. And so the rush quickly became a stampede. Beginning in 1993, Clinton's first year in office, cumulative investment in China would soar by a phenomenal fifty times to $500 billion over the next decade, and this does not count the reinvestment of profits earned in China by foreign-owned companies like Motorola. Nor does it count the massive amount of business managed in China for American companies by Taiwanese partners. So by the time Clinton, early in his second term, claimed in his big speech to be sketching out a very nuanced policy on trade with China, his own decisions four years earlier had already radically altered the relationship, and direct commerce between the two nations had as a result built up an extremely powerful momentum all its own.

Clinton's speech is nevertheless still of value in understanding how trade and politics are often thought to connect. Yet since the gist of the speech was apparently lifted almost straight from a report published by the Trilateral Commission, it is probably more useful to look not at Clinton's words but at that text. The Commission is a private organization dedicated to bringing together political, business, and academic leaders from North America, Europe, and Japan, and it had long been one of the more influential voices in favor of policies that promote economic and industrial interdependence among nations. The Commission's 1994 report on China was a clear effort to apply to that nation the industry-centric integration strategy developed during the Cold War to help manage the Western alliance. Noting that "China's rise coincides with the globalization of manufacturing processes," the report then went on to declare that this presented Western nations with an opportunity "of weaving China into an interdependent world at a relatively early stage in its rise, thereby increasing its stake in a stable world order." Political change would then surely follow, the authors wrote. "Deng Xiaoping and his reformers, while certainly not intentionally, are establishing the basis for a more open polity: they are creating a strong middle class . . . that will demand the opportunity to influence public policy." In other words, the Trilateral Commission was concluding that the Chinese Communist government was run by a bunch of suckers.[32]

The profound contradictions of China trade policy that were evident in Clinton's 1997 speech were not new to his administration, nor to the Trilateral Commission in 1994. They had been very much present in American policy toward China since the mid-1980s. The Reagan Administration had presented trade as a force somehow able simultaneously to reinforce China in its struggle against the Soviet Union,[33] and to lead the nation toward political freedom.[34] But the difference was that through the 1980s, such a contradiction could still largely be ignored; trade with China remained highly circumscribed and small in scope, and any concerns about fortifying China were easily trumped by the seemingly much greater and more immediate threat posed by the Soviet Union. In the 1990s, however, the Trilateral Commission and the Clinton Administration, rather than reexamine and update the Reagan Administration's policy toward China, simply attempted to transmute these fundamental contradictions into high strategy or, perhaps more accurately, into hybrid strategy.

The idea that liberal trade was a force able to subvert state power was not new to the debate over China. Until the 1980s, American governments had generally believed that it was unwise to trade with unfriendly nations, and so hard-core trade restrictions became a staple of the West's relationship with the Soviet Union, the Warsaw Bloc nations, China, and lesser powers such as Cuba and Libya. In the 1980s, however, many progressives began to demand that trade sanctions also be applied to right-wing authoritarian nations, most especially Apartheid-era South Africa and Pinochet-era Chile. But the Reagan Administration did not much like this idea. For one thing, American corporations were heavily invested in both of these nations, and there were also many close political ties, especially with the regime in Chile. And so U.S. officials began to develop the argument that liberal trade was a power able to subvert authoritarian governments—in other words, that liberal trade was a force able to liberalize politics. Reagan-era officials backed up this contention with high philosophy of a sort; Milton Friedman was quoted to the effect that economic freedom was the "necessary condition" for political freedom, as opposed to the century-old belief that the exact opposite was true.[35] And the officials backed up their new contention with evidence from the field—the authoritarian regimes in Taiwan and Korea were said to be moving toward more democracy precisely because of their robust liberal trade with the West. There was no evidence whatsoever of any direct link between liberal trade and the liberalizing political systems in these nations, but there was also no clear evidence to the contrary.

Nevertheless, however much the argument may or may not have applied to Chile and South Africa, China was obviously another matter altogether. Politically and economically, China had far more in common with the Soviet Union than with small and highly dependent nations at the far corners of the earth. Further, China was far bigger than any other nation that had been integrated into what was once called the "first world" economy, and it was also far poorer than any other nation within this system. Although circumscribed trade with China was defensible while the Soviet Union remained intact, there seemed to be no reason whatsoever to continue such a policy once Soviets had disappeared, let alone expand it radically by lifting all restrictions whatsoever. Yet that is exactly what the Trilateral Commission recommended and what the Clinton Administration did.

Although both tried hard to imply that an extensive private-sector-managed integration of China into the Western economy represented a sober continuity with the strategies pursued in the West from the late 1940s through 1989, the fact was this policy represented a radical reversal. During the Cold War, as we will see in the next chapter, America promoted extensive trade and cross-border investment as a sort of cement to cohere an alliance of democratic nations against a common enemy. And Washington did so very much conscious of the fact that the creation of such deep interdependencies would in time make it almost impossible for any member of the alliance to set out on its own. The obverse face of this Western policy was that it also prevented any of the benefits of trade from flowing to nations viewed to be strategic threats. And, if anything, the withholding of trade from the Soviet Union almost certainly contributed greatly to the collapse of that system. Now, however, no sooner was this victory won than the strategy was abandoned.

Various arguments can be made to explain why Clinton chose to discard a strategy that had proven so effective over the previous fifty years and that had roots tracing back two centuries. One possibility is that his Administration was simply panicked into a pro-China, pro-trade stance by the specter of a new no-holds-barred competition with the Japanese and Europeans. And indeed, after the massacre in Tiananmen, governments in Tokyo and Bonn did soon let their companies begin to push back into China, while American firms generally held back, not least to await the results of the 1992 election. The Japanese proved especially aggressive, increasing their exports to China by 40 percent in 1991.[36] So Clinton's decision to pursue highly liberal trade with China could be said to reflect the fear that, in a new tripolar world, America was about to lose a commercial advantage in China that had been built up with great effort over the course of two decades, and which now looked much more important than ever.

An alternative interpretation is to view the opening to China not as a decision by the Clinton Administration but more as a sort of policy coup by American corporations, a takeover of U.S. trade strategy by firms intent on keeping their hard-won beachheads in that nation. In support of this thesis is the fact that many American businesses began to turn their attentions back to China even before Clinton was elected. Within a year of the massacre, DuPont and Polaroid were expanding existing operations, and Procter & Gamble and Avon had embarked on new ventures. Within another year, the *New York Times* would note that foreign investors ranging from Digital Equipment to Electrolux to McDonald's were again "pouring into China." Given this reality, Clinton's 1997 speech can be viewed more as a rather pitiful attempt to drape the flag over a monstrous political fait accompli delivered to his desk by an expedition of commercial filibusters.

Unfortunately, both interpretations beg the question of why Clinton, if he really believed that liberal trade with China was not in America's interest, or if he simply did not know yet one way or the other, did not carry his campaign into the public realm (after all, much of the investment by Japanese and European firms was simply a response to the failure by the Bush Administration to raise any objections). Both interpretations also ignore the fact that however much investment flows into China recovered in 1992, they only really shot up in 1993, right after Clinton took office. And both interpretations ignore the fact that many if not most American corporations would have been happier to have trade with China regulated in such a way that they could have moved more slowly and carefully into that market; and in Taiwan many had already found an alternative entryway that seemed superior both politically and economically to direct investment.

In point of fact, there is almost no evidence that in his first four years in office Clinton ever actually tried to exert any strategic control over the flow of investment into China by companies based in the United States or any other industrialized nation.[37] Rather, Clinton instead devoted most of his energies to undermining the position of his erstwhile allies in Congress who continued to insist on linking any further expansion of trade to further political liberalization in Beijing. When it came to China policy, Clinton's overriding goal in both of his two terms was not to use trade carefully and prudently and patiently to help influence the process of political reform in China, but to get the U.S. Congress to "normalize" the trade relationship once and for all—in other words, to get the U.S. government out of the business entirely.

There is a third potential explanation for why Clinton abandoned a national strategy that had such a long history and such deep bipartisan support, and this is that he had come under the influence of thinkers guided less by practical experience than by ideology. We saw this in the last chapter, in the writings of Clinton's economic guru Robert Reich, whose take on trade and cross-border investment wended back through Kenichi Ohmae to the libertarian musings of Milton Friedman. And we can also see this by reviewing the history of an idea, set forth by a man named Francis Fukuyama, which early in the 1990s came to be read as a sort of proof that America could at last relax its long anti-Communist vigil.

Until 1989, Fukuyama was a largely unknown planner working in the State Department, but that summer he published an article in the policy magazine *The National Interest* in which he sought to make some sense of the seeming collapse of Communist ideology, as evidenced by the ever more open policies of Soviet president Mikhail Gorbachev. Fukuyama's piece played brilliantly off the mood of the moment with two of its central ideas. The first, somewhat self-evident yet immensely gratifying, was that "Western ideals" had "triumphed" in the great competition with Communism. The second, found right in the title, "The End of History," provided just the right prod to provoke whole evenings' worth of debate. The German philosopher Georg Wilhelm Friedrich Hegel, Fukuyama reminded an audience that with few exceptions had never read Hegel's work, defined history essentially as the product of friction between ideologies. Now, since we were down to one ideology, there could be no more friction, hence no history. "What we may be witnessing is not just the end of the Cold War, or the passing of a particular period of postwar history," he wrote, "but the end of history as such: that is, the end point of mankind's ideological evolution and the universalization of Western liberal democracy as the final form of human government."[38]

Any close reading of Fukuyama's article, and his subsequent book by the same name, reveals his underlying playfulness. "The End of History" was much more an intellectual exercise than an effort by Fukuyama to develop ideas that might be of use in his day job. Fukuyama went out of his way to emphasize that his thesis had little practical value in the real world. He noted, for instance, that Hegel himself had already once declared history "to be at an end," and that was nearly two centuries previously, after Napoleon's 1806 victory in the Battle of Jena "actualized the principles" of the French Revolution. That "actualization" had not, of course, prevented the restoration of monarchy in France or the rise of Socialism. Fukuyama also emphasized that this latest victory for liberal democracy would probably soon spawn a fresh antithesis of some sort, which would begin the whole process anew. "The end of history will be a very sad time," he lamented, and it would be dominated by a "prospect of centuries of boredom." Such boredom, he concluded, might well "serve to get history started once again."

However playful Fukuyama's intent, "The End of History" soon became one of the cornerstones of a set of very serious arguments put forth by those who favored a much more liberal management of the American and world economies. At first, this group held up Fukuyama's work in support of their efforts to head off the then-common belief that the U.S. government should intervene more in the economy to improve the "competitiveness" of American firms. The clear lesson of the collapse of Soviet power, they said, was that Margaret Thatcher and Ronald Reagan had been right, and those who urged Americans to imitate the interventionist policies of Japan and Europe were desperately wrong. The more radical liberals soon began to take these arguments much further. The collapse of the Soviet Union they increasingly held up not merely as a vindication of Thatcherite liberalism but as proof of the wisdom of the libertarian ideals of Milton Friedman. It was time, they declared, to put an end once and for all to the state's efforts to direct the actions of individual businesses, and indeed of individual human beings. Every person on earth should be free to meet, greet, trade, make markets, sign contracts, and direct private economic power wherever, whenever, however, and with and at whomever they pleased.

All of this, Fukuyama said later, came as a surprise. And there is certainly an absurdity to the image of radical proponents of laissez-faire economics embracing any Hegelian argument. Although Hegel had read Adam Smith and admired his work, he believed Smith had failed to factor the element of power into his discussions of how the marketplace interacted with society. Once power is factored in, Hegel wrote, laissez-faire does not result in Smith's "general plenty" but rather an accumulation of wealth and power by a tiny elite and the corresponding impoverishment of the great many.[39] The energies and revolutionary power of capitalism fascinated Hegel, much as it would Marx a generation later. But its effects on society horrified him. Hegel's analysis of how capitalism worked in and on society would be largely adopted by Marx, though the student strayed far when the time came to imagine a solution. Where Marx would later call for the abolition of property, Hegel had imagined, vaguely, some sort of state effort to ensure that citizens were able both to keep their families fed and clothed, and to enjoy honorable work.

So in a way, "The End of History" did help set history back into motion again. Even as Fukuyama celebrated the collapse of a system of thought devoted to bringing about radical material equality, and which squashed the human spirit to do so, he had warned that liberal democracy could in the future be subverted by very powerful people seeking absolute and unrestrained freedom in which to exercise their personal power. And so it now proved. The liberal democratic state, which for so long had been attacked for doing too little, was now attacked for doing too much, indeed for existing at all. The fundamental challenge was no longer "what more can you do?" but rather "why are you still here?"

And so it was here, it seems, that Clinton found his answer about how to manage China's rise.

Not only could the market be put in charge of directing the economies of the traditionally liberal democracies of the West, which was what Reich taught in *The Work of Nations,* but this market could also be put in charge of managing the entire task of reforming the economy even of a nation as gargantuan and complex and backward and potentially dangerous as China. All the tough dirty work of politics, of diplomacy, of keeping the business community in line? In a moment, it was made to vanish.

So at the dawn of the global economy, at the moment when the rational next step for a liberal democracy would have been to ask how to use our political powers—as efficiently and unobtrusively as possible—to manage the world that was becoming, we were informed that the world didn't need any managing at all. Not at home, nor globally. Not in our relations with our friends, nor in our relations with our potential enemies. If only we would take our hands off the rusty old levers of the "immoral" state, the market would take care of us all.

Yet let's not debate the wisdom of that decision right now. For the moment, let us savor the memory of that wonderful feeling in the spring of 1993 when we were told that China's market had "arrived." The world, it seemed, was once again our oyster (not Japan's). And China was our pearl, industrialized river delta and all.

CHAPTER THREE

OUR WORLD

America's System in Transition

Long before Jose Ignacio Lopez de Arriortua came to General Motors, and long before the Galvins settled Motorola into Tianjin, Jack Welch took over General Electric. Between when Welch assumed the role of CEO in 1981 and when he retired in 2001, no one in business did more to shape the global production system. Nor did anyone do so more consistently ahead of the pack. And so to really understand the full panoply of forces that shaped the global economy of the 1990s, it helps to go back a few years, to GE's December 1985 buyout of the Radio Corporation of America.

The deal was Jack Welch's first big offensive move since he had taken control of the giant conglomerate. In his first four years atop GE, Welch had slashed the company payroll, surrendered markets to better-positioned rivals, and reoriented entire industrial units. Manic, visionary, ruthless, Welch seemed to much of America to be a force of pure destruction. He was Neutron Jack, a man who like the neutron bomb could kill people—in his first two years, he fired 72,000 GE employees—while leaving the buildings intact. Now, though, Welch at last appeared ready to grow his company, and he did so in spectacular style, plunking down $6.3 billion for RCA after a secret thirty-six-day courtship. It was a deal filled with significance. RCA was one of the great industrial pioneers of the twentieth century, the firm that had introduced color television to the world. And the takeover itself was the biggest manufacturing acquisition in history. The deal even had a back story, marking a reunion of sorts between parent and child—the Wilson Administration had coerced GE into creating RCA in the first place (to make radio equipment for the Navy), and the Hoover Administration had later used its antitrust power to make RCA independent.[1] Now, more than six decades later, that child was being reabsorbed, in a deal that would be sealed in high fashion, as the famous RCA logo atop Rockefeller Center was replaced by the letters GE.

Welch took great pains to reassure the public that he had gotten all the layoffs out of his system, and that his intentions now were only of the purest and most patriotic sort. The takeover of RCA, he declared, would "help America's competitiveness in world markets."[2] Yet this was the era of the leveraged buyout, and the journalists who covered GE immediately took a highly jaundiced view of the deal. So well regarded was Welch as a businessman that no one ever doubted the wisdom of the move, but plenty of observers were willing to question his stated motives. RCA's share price was low and the company had almost no debt, so reporters accustomed to comparing the purchase price of a company with its breakup value were quick to declare the buyout a big winner. RCA seemed well worth Welch's investment if only to get hold of NBC— widely viewed as RCA's "crown jewel"[3]—and RCA's highly profitable and naturally protected defense technologies unit.

But the day after the deal was announced, Welch, in a round of interviews, criticized the reporters who had characterized the takeover as a mercenary act. The articles in that morning's papers "didn't capture the story," he insisted, and he berated one skeptical questioner for having "missed the point."[4] And what exactly was the point Welch wanted them to emphasize? It was that GE and RCA in tandem would be, in the words of one journalist, a sort of "new breed [of] colossus powerful enough to beat" all foreign rivals, especially the Japanese. Welch clearly wanted the world to view him as a changed man. He was Neutron Jack no more. He had no plans for major sell-offs of RCA units, he said. It was way too "premature" to discuss layoffs.[5] Reporters should focus instead on how the deal "just has to be good for America."[6]

No one doubted that RCA was very much in need of saving. Over the previous two decades, a once lightning-fast company that for half a century had pioneered electronic technologies had instead set new standards for management incompetence. Rather than develop new innovative uses for the vacuum tube and transistor, RCA managers had instead devoted their fat profits to buying up firms that dealt in greeting cards and frozen foods and carpeting.[7] Yet many still believed that RCA remained an important font of new technologies; after all, its inventions included radar and lasers and infrared sniper scopes. RCA had even invented the television-guided missile during the Second World War.[8] The headline that Welch wanted lay somewhere in these details: that his hardheaded management style was just what was needed to keep this iconic trove of American technologies intact.

It wouldn't be until 1987 that Welch finally got the coverage he sought. The turning point came when GE announced that rather than hire the Japanese firm Matsushita to manufacture GE-branded sets, the company would now build them at a former RCA plant in Indiana. One result was a long and glowing feature in *Fortune*.[9] Welch, the reporter wrote, had given his television production team at least two more years to prove they could produce sets as inexpensively as the Japanese. It was an inspiring tale of American spunk and tenacity, complete with driven executives scrambling to "keep Welch's finger off the destruct button" even as they laid audacious plans for a "revolution" in television technology.

Yet by this time Welch no longer needed any red, white, and blue clippings. RCA was long since fully under his control, so he had nothing to fear anymore from Democrats in Congress, some of whom had initially joined the journalists in questioning Welch's real game.[10] And in fact, by the time the *Fortune* article was published, Welch had already secretly pulled the plug on RCA's television division. In a short tête-à-tête in June with Alain Gomez, chairman of the French state-owned electronics conglomerate Thomson SA, Welch agreed to swap GE's entire consumer electronics unit for Thomson's medical equipment subsidiary CGR and $800 million in cash. It was, Welch said later, a deal simply too "nifty" to pass up. Both companies walked away smiling. Thomson had transformed itself into one of the top three electronics firms in the world—adding GE's 25 percent share of the U.S. TV market to its already substantial holdings—and GE had grabbed second place in the global medical equipment field. Welch offered no apologies. "We acted in good faith and gave the consumer electronics people a chance," he said.[11] But in the end the decision came down to a simple fact, which was that "I like the medical business strategy more."[12] And why not? Welch had exchanged a low-margin, high-competition business for a high-tech and high-profit enterprise that brought GE an all-important beachhead well inside Europe's medical regulatory wall.

Wall Street, on hearing the news, once again exalted the man who had become its supreme hero. Once more Welch was Jumping Jack Flash, an executive ready to leap at a moment's notice on any deal that looked good.[13] Once again, Welch had proved himself the world's preeminent value maker, dumping a rattling commodity business on a French state enterprise whose boss had been appointed by Socialist president François Mitterand. And he had proven the cynics right; he never had viewed RCA as anything more than a bundle of assets to be sold off at the right time. Only now did reporters add up what Welch had done over the previous eighteen months. Consumer Electronics, it turned out, was actually the sixth RCA unit that Welch had off-loaded.[14] He had already managed to rid himself of 51,000 of the 87,000 RCA employees whose jobs he had angrily implied he would protect, and now he was off-loading another 31,000. Given such a record, Welch was perhaps not inaccurate when he said the latest sale would prove "good" for the American workers affected.[15] The French could hardly act with any more severity.

Elsewhere, the reaction ranged from stunned silence to outright anger. One Japanese competitor characterized the deal as a sad retreat, due to a "lack of self-confidence" by GE in its own ability to compete in the manufacture of televisions.[16] London's *Financial Times*, meanwhile, reported a "hollow feeling" in America's manufacturing "revival."[17] To many Americans, the lesson seemed simple enough. The long retreat and ultimate collapse of RCA under the often brutal assault by Japanese competitors, and the subsequent cold butchery of the company by Welch, seemed to make it clear that the United States had simply decided that the principle of free-market competition trumped any perceived need to intervene in the workings of the market, even when it cost American jobs, even when it threatened one of America's most established technology leaders.

Yet a more careful appraisal of U.S. government policies of the 1980s reveals a very different picture. The Reagan Administration, despite its laissez-faire rhetoric and laissez-faire policy at home, was in many ways a highly protectionist government—indeed, more consistently so than any other postwar American administration. Since taking office, Reagan had imposed tariffs on steel imports and on select Japanese electronics, set de facto quotas on Japanese auto imports, restricted trade in textiles, radically increased enforcement of anti-dumping laws, and launched the Sematech consortium to support American semiconductor manufacturers. He had even stuck a 50 percent surcharge on big motorcycles, to allow Harley-Davidson time to reengineer its operations.

More to the point on RCA, U.S. governments for the previous three decades had intervened time and again in the global consumer electronics market. Usually, however, the goal was not to protect American companies but, on the contrary, to force them to spread their knowledge and their market share around the world. If we step far enough back, the overall picture that emerges is of an American state that, rather than being in the clutches of free-trade idealists, intentionally engineered the sharing out of RCA's technology and market share to whatever companies might wish to take it, especially if those firms hailed from American allies in East Asia. In the beginning, it was the American government that gave RCA its life. And in the end—the long, protracted breakdown and breakup of the company—it was the American government that was most responsible for RCA's demise. Both acts were done, as we will see, with national security foremost in mind.

Welch repeatedly claimed during this period that his main intention was to organize General Electric for global-scale competition. "You have to be global in this business to survive," he said the day the Thomson deal was announced.[18] It was a position that put him far in advance of almost all his contemporaries in American industry. Yet the real lesson was not that Welch had figured out before anyone else how to thumb his nose at the impotent regulators and legislators in Washington. Rather, it was that Welch had learned before anyone else how to profit by embracing the world just as it had been engineered for him by forty years of U.S. government action. The reason the U.S. government did not object to Welch's redistribution of industrial activity across the face of the earth is that it so well fit the nation's prevailing national security strategy.

So there was a world hidden behind the world in which Clinton seemed to be acting in the early 1990s. When he blasted Japan for unfair competition during the 1992 campaign and when he pondered how to shape trade policy with China, he did so against a global political and economic background that had been shaped with great care by two generations of American leaders. It was a world in which the nations of the West competed much more on the surface than deep down, and in which trade was not leading these nations in different directions but binding them ever more tightly and inextricably into a sort of American empire. The history of RCA in the 1980s illustrates, as well as any company history of the era, the degree to which the U.S. government had come to accept that the nation's true security interest lay not in industrial autarky but in an extremely deep industrial interdependence with like-minded societies. Long before the panics about a breakdown of the Western economy into autonomous trade blocs in the early 1990s, American governments had felt so supremely confident that this would never happen that they let even key industries move offshore; indeed, they encouraged those industries to move away. This assumption, and the thinking that underlay it, must be understood to grasp the full significance of the Clinton Administration's actions and inactions during the early 1990s, and to comprehend the political framework of the global world into which America's companies were moving with ever-greater speed.

That laissez-faire free-trade policies were not behind the U.S. government's lack of reaction to Jack Welch's sell-off of RCA assets, or its lack of reaction to hundreds of other instances in which American firms suffered and sometimes died owing to seemingly unfair foreign competition, may seem surprising. So, too, the fact that true laissez-faire ideology did not guide any American president in the international arena until Bill Clinton. America and the concept of free trade, after all, seem to have been joined at birth, and not only because Adam Smith published *The Wealth of Nations* three months before the Declaration of Independence was completed. To make sense of this disconnect requires a short look at how American governments over the years have actually responded to and employed the idea of free trade.

It is beyond dispute that many Revolutionary-era Americans were inspired by Smith's work. It is also true that Smith's opus, the cornerstone of classical free-market economics, was very much influenced by the musings of Colonial Americans, especially Benjamin Franklin during his long London sojourns. But American attitudes toward trade in the early years of the nation are much more complex than they are often portrayed. For plantation owners like Thomas Jefferson and James Madison, and for the merchants of Boston and New York and Philadelphia, the main appeal of free trade was that it seemed to express so well their own natural interests. In the years running up to July 4, 1776, America wanted to sell its cotton and tobacco and corn for as high a price as possible, and it wanted to spend as little as possible on European-made shirts, tableware, and wine. The problem, as the American leaders of the time saw it, was that as British colonial subjects they were supposed to buy and sell only with British traders, who in turn would deal with merchants in France, Spain, Holland, China, and India. Ultimately, the independence that many Americans sought was from the British middleman.

Smith's vision of international trade appealed to Americans for reasons that had much less to do with the overall efficiency of the North Atlantic economy than with other social goals. Jefferson is often held up as one of America's great champions of free trade, yet from early on his support was based largely on his wish to promote an American society made up of free men tilling the soil. In his 1785 book *Notes on Virginia,* he closely echoes Smith in envisioning a world in which Americans grow crops, Europeans manufacture goods, and traders arrange for equitable exchanges thereof. But Jefferson did not believe such specialization was a more efficient way to arrange work. On the contrary, he thought it would be cheaper for America to import European workers rather than their products. But he considered it well worth the extra cost of buying finished goods if Europe's workers remained right where they were, in Europe. "The mobs of great cities," Jefferson wrote, "add just so much to the support of pure government, as sores do to the strength of the human body."[19]

Across the ocean, the British in the early- and mid–nineteenth century would make great strides in advancing the idea of free trade in theory and in politics. Two men especially stand out. Most important for economic theory was the work of David Ricardo. On the subject of international trade, Ricardo sketched out what is now called the theory of comparative advantage, which illustrated how two nations might benefit through extreme specialization in production. Ricardo's model, in which England traded wool for Portuguese wine, demonstrated that the "general mass" of production could be increased if both nations concentrated only on manufacturing one of the products and then engaged in unfettered trade across their border. This could sometimes be true, Ricardo showed, even in cases where one of the nations was able to produce both products more efficiently than the other.[20] To a great degree, Ricardo's theory still undergirds the thinking of most economists to this day.

Politically, the most important figure in nineteenth-century free trade was a man named Richard Cobden. The son of a poor farmer, Cobden grew up in near penury, but by age thirty-two had parlayed a tiny investment in a calico business into a large fortune. In 1839, he helped found the Anti-Corn Law League, devoted to tearing down the tariffs that protected England's grain growers. The league had two aims: to put more money into the hands of shabbily clad grain growers abroad, who would then use the money to buy wares of the Manchester mills, and to divert as much money as possible out of the hands of the English grain-growing aristocracy and thereby clear a pathway to power for the self-made men of Manchester. Cobden's impact on the history of free trade was due mainly to the fact that he pursued these domestic political goals by promoting the idea that free trade contributed to peace. This idea itself was not new. As a stated philosophy, the linkage dates at least to late Roman times.[21] It would only really flourish, however, in the hands of European and English writers of the Enlightenment. The most famous contribution was German philosopher Immanuel Kant's short essay "Perpetual Peace," published in 1795. Trade among nations, Kant wrote, was one of three factors—along with democracy within nations and international law over nations—that would greatly reduce the likelihood of conflict among nations. "The spirit of commerce," Kant had declared, "is incompatible with war."[22]

Cobden was the first man to really bring this ideal into the day-to-day politics of a nation, and his rhetoric could prove very inspiring. "I see in the Free-Trade principle that which shall act on the moral world as the principle of gravitation in the universe,—drawing men together, thrusting aside the antagonism of race, and creed, and language, and uniting us in the bonds of eternal peace."[23] Yet Cobden was never a true idealist.[24]

Soon after one of his greatest practical achievements—the landmark free-trade pact between Britain and France in 1860—Cobden made it clear that he believed free trade could contribute to the cause of peace only at the margins. Late in his life, as he beheld the horror of the American Civil War and a seemingly senseless naval arms race between London and Paris,[25] Cobden would conclude that human nature was simply too rotten to be reformed deeply by commerce alone.

Nevertheless, Cobden's message would go on to exert a huge influence on less practical men, both at the time he lived and to this day. Of Cobden's contemporaries, among the most important to fall under his spell were Karl Marx and Friedrich Engels. In *The Communist Manifesto,* published in 1848, the two were clearly thrilled and inspired by the visions of Cobden and the other free traders, which Engels would have come across certainly by the early 1840s, when he worked at his father's mill near Manchester.[26]

In the highly practical America of the nineteenth century, by contrast, the response to Cobden's rhetoric was always filtered through the lens of politics, as was all thinking about trade. In early 1846, Cobden bragged of having received a letter from President James Polk, who informed the English politician of how he was lecturing the citizens of America on the benefits of free trade. In the United States, however, when many heard such talk from the Tennessee expansionist, it would simply have reminded them of South Carolina's 1832 attempt to "nullify" federal tariff laws, which they believed favored manufacturers over planters. If anything, in America the concept of free trade had been deeply tainted by a too-close association with reckless, even treasonous, slave-state politicians.

The free-trade debate in America would remain fundamentally political in nature until well into the twentieth century. For the one hundred years between the Nullification Crisis and the election of Franklin Roosevelt, most Americans never viewed trade policy as anything more than a tug-of-war between producers who wanted protection and agricultural interests who wanted cheaper imports and bigger markets overseas. It is almost impossible to find any linking of trade to morality. Rather, Americans viewed the tariff system the way they viewed any tax system, which is as one of the means by which a victor party apportions gain to its supporters and punishes opponents. Concepts of efficiency did play some role in mitigating the more egregious acts of tariff politics, as they sometimes mitigate the most egregious proposals to overhaul today's tax system, but they never overturned the basic assumption of the average American that the tariff was foremost a political tool.

The first political step toward imbuing trade with a moral quality would be taken by the Democratic Party only in the early years of the Great Depression. It was a time when party leaders were seeking ways to drive a bigger wedge between the factory worker and the Republican Party. Northern urban labor had once been firmly in the Democratic fold, but slave-power dominance of the party eventually drove most northern workers to the new Republican party, which sealed its deal with labor by hiking up the tariff and declaring this to be good for the free worker.[27]

Although the Democrats' free-trade message attracted support among farmers in the Plains states, this was rarely enough to win power at the national level. Of the eighteen presidential elections between 1861 and 1928, only two Democrats would win office, and one of these, Woodrow Wilson, owed his victory in 1912 to a split among the Republicans. Finally, in the early years of the Depression, the Democrats at last saw an opportunity to pull labor back into its orbit in a big way. And this the party did by promising workers the most radical liberalization of labor law in the nation's history. And this it did also by carefully carving out a new position on trade, one that would allow the party to coherently weld an industrial workforce to its traditional constituency of export-desperate farmers in the South and West.

The party's new position was to blame the Depression largely on Republican protectionism. What had really done in the American economy in the early 1930s was not the stock market crash or the subsequent collapse of the nation's financial system. Instead, it was the Smoot-Hawley Tariff that had destroyed all those jobs. As a point of fact, blaming the Depression on Smoot-Hawley was a big stretch. Trade had never recovered from the effects of the First World War, nor from the remarkably shortsighted and economically destructive peace treaty crafted at Versailles (not least by Democratic President Wilson).[28] For another, Smoot-Hawley was actually a somewhat less onerous piece of legislation than the Fordney-McCumber tariff of 1922. Yet placing the onus for the economic disaster on Smoot-Hawley did prove to be an inspired way to forge a new coalition on which to base a national party that would dominate power for the next half century.

And so the idea that protectionism kills jobs became one of the central founding myths of the modern Democratic Party. And not surprisingly, this myth over time came to exert enormous influence over how Americans of both parties thought about trade, especially when the trade-versus-jobs argument finally reemerged as a major political issue in the 1980s.[29] Unfortunately, by ripping the debate over tariffs from the soil of practical politics in which it had for so long been rooted, the myth in the real world would serve mainly to help clear the ground for much more ideologically-driven views of free trade.

In his farewell address in 1796, President George Washington warned Americans not to "implicate" themselves in the "vicissitudes" of European politics. If Americans were wise enough to "avoid permanent alliances," the wide ocean would give them the freedom, Washington said, to "choose peace or war, as our interest, guided by justice, shall counsel."

Yet Washington knew true independence was a result of much more than favorable geography. For a nation that depended on others for its manufactures, this same wide ocean could prove to be a frightful barrier. During the War of Independence, severe shortages of muskets and gunpowder and uniforms had nearly destroyed Washington's own army. This was why, during his first term as president, Washington asked his Treasury secretary, Alexander Hamilton, to draw up a manufacturing strategy for the new United States. What resulted would in time provide the foundation for the single most important pillar in America's foreign policy, one that has had a much greater overall effect on the nation's trade policy than all the arguments between farmers and producers.

In his "Report on Manufactures," Hamilton sketched out what was the world's first complete plan for using state power to build up a nation's capacity to produce what was needed for war and to master new technologies. Hamilton proposed many policies, all of which have been used in some form since. Of all these tools, though, it was the protective tariff that has always stirred the most controversy, and for years after Hamilton's report, the government held off on putting his tariff policy into effect.[30] This only began to change during the Napoleonic wars, most dramatically when Jefferson imposed an embargo on all American trade with both England and France. But this was an act of desperation, in response to repeated British seizures of American ships, cargoes, and crews, and to Napoleon's effort to close off all European ports so as to create a self-enclosed Continental System of trade. Only after the Americans were again embarrassed by their inability to counter another British invasion, in 1814, would a majority in Congress finally favor a true protective tariff. The decision was made easier by the fact that by this time many New Englanders had successfully shifted their capital from trade to production.

Hamilton's thinking would now transform the world. In America, Kentucky's long-serving Senator Henry Clay used Hamilton's thinking as the basis for what came to be known as the American System, in which the goal was to create a largely closed economy whereby American farmers would feed American factory workers, who in turn would manufacture the tools and clothing needed by American farmers, and, of course, weapons. Though Clay's approach remained controversial for many years—until the Civil War support for the tariff pretty much shifted along with control of the presidency—it later shaped the thinking of Abraham Lincoln, who took advantage of the South's secession to create a much more institutionalized high-tariff development policy for the nation. And for the half century after the Civil War, American industrialists would be able to take advantage of one of the most protective economic systems in history to engage in an orgy of development, much of it paid for by British investors.

America's example in turn inspired industrialists and nationalists around the world to study America's protectionist policies. In recent years, Americans have become accustomed to viewing their nation as a fervent exporter of free-trade and free-market theories. But in the nineteenth century it was America's protectionist model that was avidly studied in Germany and Russia and Japan.[31] More than any other philosophy of the nation-state, Hamiltonianism can be viewed as having laid the foundation for the catastrophic industrial-powered wars of the twentieth century. Technology and war have been intertwined as long as humans have made tools. But in the late nineteenth century, it was Hamiltonian protectionism that helped to shape the industrial fault lines along which the truly massive wars of the last century would occur.

Naturally enough, Hamiltonianism also gave birth in time to an American foreign policy strategy premised on the assumption that the United States and its main nation-state rivals were largely autonomous industrial units. Known generally as "Realism," this way of thinking about the power of the nation-state would exert great influence over American foreign policy for much of the century. Without going into any further depth about the nature of Realism itself, it is important to look at how Realism affected American thinking about the uses and abuses of trade.

America's realist tradition can be traced to many fathers. One of the most influential was Alfred Thayer Mahan, a rear admiral in the U.S. Navy and the most influential strategist in the early stages of America's overseas empire.[32] A devotee of Social Darwinism, by 1911 Mahan had developed a thesis through which he interpreted both the arms race in Europe and what he saw as the contest shaping up between European nations (including the United States) and the rest of the world. The largely industrially driven competition to build bigger and better weapons, Mahan argued, was simply a good healthy rivalry that enabled the relatively small states of Europe to develop both the weapons and spirit to prevail against the real threat, which was posed not by other European nations but rather the great "barbarian" masses of the "non-European" world. General war within Europe, Mahan concluded, was best avoided not through international agreements or arbitration, but through the arms race itself, which created a natural "equilibrium" of power and which served as the most perfect "institution" for "maintaining peace."[33]

At about the same time that Mahan was perfecting this line of thought, the English-born Norman Angell published *The Great Illusion*, a book in which he assailed the then-common view that one nation could gain "economically" by defeating another in war. Son of a rich shopkeeper, Angell for many years edited an English-language newspaper in Paris. As the Continent drifted toward war early in the twentieth century, Angell sought to update Cobden's campaign for peace by approaching the subject less through morality and more through rational argument. And so he now argued that the domestic credit and commercial contract systems of the era were so fragile, and the national financial systems so intertwined across borders, that any major war in Europe would destroy far more wealth than it could ever transfer to a victor. Angell never said this interdependence made war impossible; he simply held it up as an excellent reason to question the then-widespread assumption that an internation war in Europe was not only inevitable but perhaps even desirable. Published in 1909, *The Great Illusion* became a huge success. Translated into twenty-five languages, the book by some accounts sold more than two million copies worldwide. Among the Americans inspired by Angell was steel magnate Andrew Carnegie, whose newly formed Endowment for International Peace paid to translate *The Great Illusion* into German.[34]

Angell's work left two legacies. The first was the fierce reaction against his writings by the Realists, who from this point on would largely define their beliefs in attacks against liberal trade "idealists." Mahan's 1911 book, for instance, devotes a full chapter to attacking Angell's theories. Angell's second legacy was a highly sophisticated and highly realistic philosophy that rejected the simplistic Hobbesian thinking of the Realists as a grossly insufficient response to the challenge of managing the modern world. And the truth was that despite a widespread effort to paint Angell as a pacifist, he was anything but. In the 1930s, Angell would be among the first to call on the United States and Britain to rearm to meet the Nazi threat, and he was one of the first to warn of the military danger posed by the Soviet Union. A more accurate label for Angell would be to regard him as a "realistic liberal" who considered trade relationships a highly effective coercive device that, if used with intelligence and tact, not only could supplement the use of military force but often make its use unnecessary.

In time, as we will see, it was just such realistic liberalism that would emerge as perhaps America's single greatest contribution to the imperial arts. In Washington, the initial development took place in the administration of Franklin Roosevelt, largely under the guidance of Cordell Hull, Roosevelt's secretary of state. Hull is famous for declaring, perhaps apocryphally, that "when goods don't pass borders, armies do." Yet in practice, Hull would manage the nation's trade not as a Cobdenite idealist but in the highly practical tradition of Jefferson. Hull believed that free-trade rhetoric could be of great political value—he was one of the authors of the strategy to vilify the Smoot-Hawley Tariff, and Hull saw liberal trade as of great potential value in attracting the support of resource-rich Latin

American nations in the coming war. Yet Hull was always very cautious in his expectations of what commerce could effect. Like Cobden in his later life, Hull believed that freer trade was a process that would soften the human heart only over the course of generations, and in the meanwhile it was a goal to be pursued only on the basis of strict reciprocity.

In 1944, America's realistic liberals would make the first of what would be two attempts to shape the world through commerce. This took place at the Bretton Woods Conference, today remembered most for the birth of the International Monetary Fund and the institution that would evolve into the World Bank. What is less remembered now is that Bretton Woods participants also drew up plans for a third institution, to be called the International Trade Organization or ITO. Whereas the IMF and the Bank were designed to regulate the global monetary and financial systems, the ITO was designed to enforce a nondiscriminatory global trade system within a multination framework.[35] But, even though the ITO was designed to foster a much more robust trade among nations, it was not truly a liberal organization. On the contrary, the ITO was the result of the Administration's firm belief that the only way to create anything like a free-trade system was for powerful states to create a global institution with the ability to sanction both national governments and private-sector corporations anywhere in the world. The ITO was a simulacrum of a liberal trade system, designed to be enforced by steely-eyed realists.

And yet no sooner was the ITO's constitution dry than the American government would decide, in the first years of the Cold War, that even this radically realistic trading system was not realistic enough. And so the United States would now develop realistic liberalism to an entirely new level, one that over time laid the foundation for today's post-trade world.

In Europe, the French politician Robert Schuman has a university named after him, and various foundations and study centers, as well as avenues and streets across much of the Continent. So, too, the French economic planner Jean Monnet. The main reason is the role the two men played in the foundation of what is now the European Community. Schuman in the late 1940s was a prime minister and then foreign minister of France. Monnet was a visionary bureaucrat who during the war worked intimately on resource-planning issues with the British and Americans. The pioneering act of these two men was to conceive of the European Coal and Steel Community, which started as an agreement by France and occupied Germany to turn control over the Ruhr Valley steel industry to an organization that existed outside the power of either nation. Italy, Holland, Belgium, and Luxembourg would all soon join, and in so doing they set into motion a process that in coming years would organize Europe into a single economic community. In the half century since, the result has been a remarkably harmonious blending together of the economies of European nation-states that for the previous half millennium had engaged in numerous and brutal wars. Viewed by almost any measure, the result of this work stands as one of the great political achievements in history.

Yet if Europeans were to tell the full story of the foundation of the EU, there would also be universities and foundations and boulevards named after Harry Truman, who was the American president at the time. This is because the desire to create a single European economic community actually originated among the Americans, who in the late 1940s still to a great extent controlled much of Western Europe. The real seed of today's ever more unified Europe was the Marshall Plan. To coordinate distribution of the American money, food, and technology being transferred to Europe, the Americans set up the Organization for European Economic Co-Operation, which almost immediately took upon itself the task of reducing trade barriers within Europe in order to ensure a more rational use of these and other available resources. Two years later, when Monnet drew up the initial plan for multination control of the coal and steel industries, it was the Truman Administration that helped convince Schuman to introduce the idea to the French. The European Union, in other words, was in its initial instances largely an American creation, and America has rarely strayed since from firm support.

In terms of postwar trade policy, the results of this new American strategy in favor of the integration of Europe would prove profound. Very soon after putting the final touches on the ITO, the American government embarked on a program in Europe that was in many ways the antithesis of all the thinking that had been expressed in the new institution. The ITO had envisioned "nondiscriminatory" trade among nations, and had envisioned penalties for any government or company that interfered in the "natural" flow of commerce. Now, however, the U.S. government devoted most of its energy and creativity instead to erecting a trade structure in Europe designed in many instances to exclude American-made goods.[36]

The reasons for Truman's radical reversal are many, varied, and complex, but two are most important. First was the desire to somehow tie the western two-thirds of Germany to the rest of Europe in a way that would allow all these nations to grow economically, while also preventing Germany from ever again developing an industrial capacity that would allow it to war on its neighbors. Second was the rapid shift of the Soviet Union from World War ally to Cold War adversary. Americans now concluded that not only did Europe need massive aid, it also needed a trade system designed to build up its industry as rapidly as possible, in part by directing production activities away from America. So at a time when the United States enjoyed enormous economic and industrial advantages, which would have enabled it to lock in permanent huge disparities in wealth and power, especially with Germany, Washington instead chose to promote active "discrimination against American goods."[37] The problem with the ITO, from the point of view of the Truman Administration, was not the integrationist tendencies built into the institution; rather, it was that these integrationist energies would act too slowly and spread the gains from integration across too wide a geography.

After the war, the United States always maintained a realistic take on the world. From 1947 to 1991, the United States devoted vast piles of treasure to building a military force always at least the match of the Soviet Union's. Balance-of-power politics continues to some degree right up to today, most obviously in the bilateral and multilateral regimes to regulate the construction and deployment of nuclear weapons. But starting with the Bretton Woods Conference in 1944 and especially after the launch of the Marshall Plan in 1947, the United States also engineered what can only be regarded as a radical experiment in the economic integration of nations. And it did so in large part by using trade policy and other economic tools to steer growth in certain directions toward certain ends, to win friends and influence peoples.

The effort was by no means entirely or even mostly selfless. The United

States, as did the Soviet Union, clearly "coveted" the "potential industrial power" of both Europe and Japan for the conflict brewing between the two superpowers.[38] But whereas the Soviets exerted control over their "allies" through brute force, the Americans sought to create a community of political interests reinforced by intimate economic and industrial ties. America, in the words of one European historian, sought to create an "'Empire' by Integration." And it did so consciously, operating with a clear awareness of how "a system of international trade" can "very easily be exploited for purposes of national power policy," as the American economist Albert Hirschman wrote in a highly influential 1945 book.[39] "Empire" is somewhat too strong a term for the world system actually engineered by the American state. By gently directing corporations to spin international webs of industry, the American state created a system still able to guarantee a great deal of personal and national liberty and that fairly shared out wealth among the member nations. That said, the international industrial web also served remarkably well to prevent the return to power of America's old enemies, and it reserved to Washington the role of spider.

America's effort to tie down Japan economically is in some senses even more clear, because it involved a series of much more dramatic compromises by the U.S. government. The goal in Europe was to force a blending of Western European nations into each other, and only secondarily was the intent to blend the resulting European economy into that of the United States.[40] With Japan, however, from the beginning the sense was not so much that the island nation had to be lashed down for the sake of others—Japan did not have nearly as long a history of acting irresponsibly as did the Germans. Rather, it was that if this industrial nation was to work with the United States and not against us, it needed a guaranteed supply of resources and an ample market in which to sell its products. Japan's economy, in other words, had to be made "viable."[41] The main challenge, after the Maoist revolution in China in 1949, was that there was no nearby market with which Japan could safely trade, at least from the point of view of the American government.

By the early 1950s, the Truman Administration had decided on a two-track approach to Japan.[42] First, the United States would increase its efforts to break up the European colonial structures in Southeast Asia and thereby open markets such as Vietnam, Malaysia, and Indonesia to

Japanese companies. The second track was much more radical, and this was to give Japan "relatively unrestricted access to American technology and the American market," while demanding no major reciprocal openings in return.[43] This policy was then pursued with increasing vigor by Presidents Eisenhower, Kennedy, and Johnson. In other words, to help ensure Japan's loyalty in the global struggle against the Soviet Union, American presidents for two decades repeatedly traded away large chunks of the U.S. domestic market to Japanese manufacturers, most dramatically in the Trade Expansion Act of 1962 and the subsequent Kennedy Round of GATT. And of all the American corporations of the era, RCA was one of the most affected by these policies. First, the Eisenhower Administration in the 1950s used antitrust power to force RCA to share its core technologies, not only with American firms but with the Japanese. Then, during the 1960s, the Kennedy and Johnson Administrations actively promoted steep tariff reductions that resulted in a surge of imports of radios and televisions. Yet despite the pain felt by RCA and many other American companies, America's leaders felt the overall gains to the nation were more than worthwhile. By the early 1970s, the Nixon Administration concluded that Japan had become so dependent on the U.S. market that there was no longer any real reason to fear Tokyo would seek its own political path. Not perversely, this lack of fear served to dampen concern about the further capture of American markets by Japanese corporations.[44]

It would be a mistake to view trade as the only tool used to tie the nations of the West together. The United States also maintained huge occupying armies, engineered tight military alliances, directed immense flows of aid, forged bilateral and multilateral ties and organizations, and exerted control over the shipment of raw materials such as oil. The scars of war and the generally pacific tendencies of democracy also have played vital roles in shaping new destinies, most especially for Germany and Japan. But the only way to understand the shape of today's global economy, and the presumptions and prejudices and habits of thought and physical interlinkages that underlie today's system, is to understand how the U.S. government put trade policy to use in the decades after the war in support of an overall integrationist effort in the West.

It would also be a mistake to believe that the American administrations that set these forces into motion were not concerned about their effects on American companies and American workers and the American economy as a whole. On the contrary, American governments fretted openly and often about the nation's balance-of-payments deficits, and as early as the mid-1960s many had begun to fear that Japan was taking unfair advantage of America's generous opening of its trade system. Later, as Japan progressed technologically, American leaders often expressed very real concern about the loss of key industrial arts to that nation. Yet the overall pattern remained clear. The U.S. government for two decades acted to foster integration, then acted for the next two decades on the assumption that the permanent subjugation of Japan through economic integration was a fait accompli.

It would also be a mistake to view economic interdependence as the only goal or even the main initial goal of America's postwar trade policy. The first aim, as mentioned, was simply to press Japanese and German industry into service in what was seen as a common struggle against the Soviet Union. From the beginning of the Korean War in 1950, the Truman Administration pushed both the Europeans and the Japanese to rebuild their defense industries, and it backed up this request with huge orders and with the transference of many advanced technologies. Yet here, too, it is clear that once the process was set in motion, the American government allowed the military industries of the United States, Europe, and Japan to continue to blend together without any significant hindrance. The government did every so often protect certain industries.[45] Yet the effect of such intrusions was never more than a minor grooming of an ongoing process of deep integration that was viewed in the aggregate as a very good thing. Even as early as the Vietnam War, the U.S. government had come to realize that American manufacturers were no longer able, by themselves, to "still develop, effectively and efficiently, all the technology needed to build modern weapons systems."[46] But by that time the U.S. state also clearly had concluded that it could get the technologies that it needed from the corporations and governments of the integrated nations of the "West."

Last, it would be a mistake to interpret even most of the specific deals by U.S. trade negotiators over the last half century as having been determined specifically by a desire to promote interdependence among nations. It is by no means clear that all or even most U.S. negotiators understood the concept, given that the policy was never made absolutely explicit or ever discussed widely.[47] By no means can today's global economy be viewed as the product of micromanagement by government bureaucrats. It was more, in the words of one of the more popular books on the issue, the result of an effort to create a "political framework" within which a particularly shaped market would "occur."[48] For that matter, it is unlikely that even the most bullishly interdependence-minded policy makers in the 1950s and 1960s ever imagined that their actions would lead to such a richly interdependent system as what actually emerged in the 1990s.

And the role of liberal free-trade theory? The concept of free trade was in fact never far from the minds of American leaders of this era, even though until the 1990s it was never pursued as an end in and of itself. Rather, free-trade theory can be viewed as having predisposed or conditioned American leaders to feel a comfortableness with the interdependent world they were engineering; that their actions were not economically unwise; indeed, that they were delivering a highly valuable secondary effect, which was efficiency. And at times, free-trade theory certainly provided these leaders with a justification, and ideological cover, for a strategy they rarely felt comfortable explaining to the public, whether in America or Europe or Japan.

Perhaps the finest depiction in film of an American multinational corporation is found in Billy Wilder's movie *One, Two, Three*. Wilder was a German director who fled to Hollywood after Hitler came to power, and in 1961 he took on the Eastern European Communists by casting James Cagney as a fast-talking Coca-Cola executive based in West Berlin. Wilder's East Berlin is sleepy, paranoid, flyspecked, and spy ridden, whereas the city's western half is a gleaming modern metropolis filled with friendly Germans eager to learn how to dress, speak, dance, think, and chew gum like Americans, all under the direction of a man who only a few years earlier had played the lead in *Yankee Doodle Dandy*.

But the American multinational corporation was in truth not some sleek young newcomer that grew to maturity only after the war. On the contrary, it was one of the oldest hands in the business of managing cross-border commerce, having arrived on the scene more than a century before.[49] In order to understand what sort of building blocks America's postwar governments used to create the new interdependent economy, and for that matter the institution to which the Clinton Administration thought it was turning over control when it began to imagine a truly laissez-faire trade policy in the early 1990s, it is vital to understand the nature of the private-sector entities that for more than a century have organized most cross-border business.

The multinational corporation was very much an American invention. In most of Europe, manufacturers wanted only to export their finished products, not the means of production.[50] The American willingness to export ideas and technologies, and to some extent capital, through the vertically integrated corporation was due to many factors, though one was paramount. In contrast to most industrialized nations of the nineteenth century, the United States was chronically short of workers, even after the U.S. government opened the border to mass immigration from Europe.

America's unique confidence in the multinational corporation was also due to the fact that the nation boasted much bigger corporations than any other country. Until the Civil War, corporations were relatively few in number and transient in nature, and they were very much subject to the will of the individual state legislatures that chartered them. In the years afterward, however, American corporations began to grow to enormous size and scope, feeding off new technologies and services like the railroad and the telegraph, and a new legal environment that aimed to regulate the corporation but actually ended up clearing a path for uncontrolled merger.[51] It was only natural that such a new and powerful institution would itself be exported. And so it was, in great numbers. By 1900, at least seventy-five American firms were producing outside the United States,[52] while other American corporations were pioneering modern methods for everything from mining and refining copper to drilling for petroleum to building railroads to growing bananas. Americans were also among the first to export services other than banking. New York Life Insurance Co. started selling policies in Canada in 1858 and in England in 1870, and by the end of that decade had spread across almost all of Europe.[53]

10:30 Friday

Mike

Lise

530 - 677-6267

Gold Hill Glass
Shingle Springs

Prunedale Storage

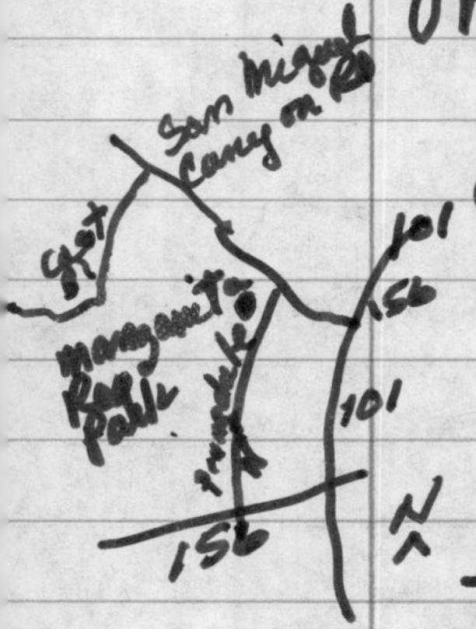

8305 Prunedale North Rd
93907 Ph: (831) 240-4018

- Every Unit is Individually alarmed
- High Security Padlocks
- Tenant Ins. Pgm.
- Off-hr. appt.

Pacheco Pass Self Storage

6600 Brem Ln

Gilroy   408 848 2 367

CROCKER's LOCKERS

7151 Crocker Lane, Gilroy

408 842 0464

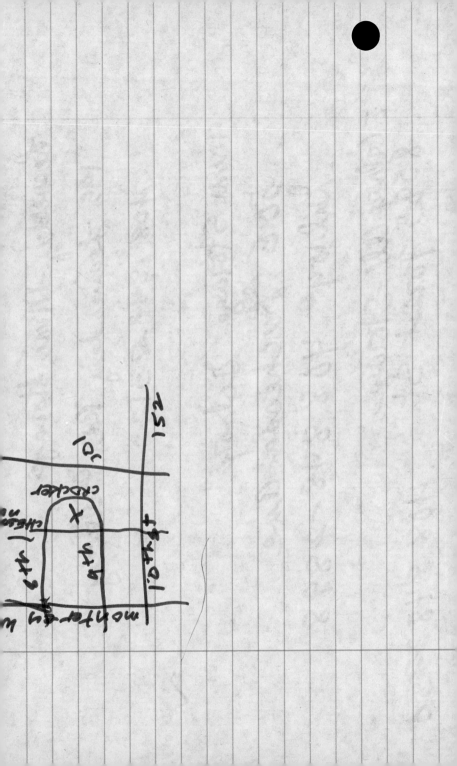

State TAXES

⬤

Leavesley Mini Storage
195 Leavesley Rd., Gilroy
408 842-7312

Mini Storage Gilroy
50 E Luchessa Ave.
Gilroy   408 848-2898

- Gilroy All-Storage
8585 Forest St.

408 848 3350

It would not take long for the American state to discover these institutions and to put them to many uses.[54] American society has rarely been content merely with controlling the political and social power of the corporation, or in simply enjoying the fruits of its laborers. On the contrary, during the first half of the twentieth century, American governments tacked onto the corporation many domestic social responsibilities that had nothing at all to do with efficient production. The most obvious such task is responsibility to collect payroll and income taxes. Much more socially significant was the reliance on these businesses to manage such social benefits as health insurance and pensions.[55]

One of the most significant instances of such piggybacking by the state on the private-sector corporation was in the management of America's foreign affairs. From the first, the U.S. government has never been shy about bending American private-sector entities to its will in managing relations with other nations. Even if we entirely ignore the extremely interventionist tariff policy, which obviously could be used to reward certain nations and punish others, from well before the First World War the American government was anything but a passive onlooker. As the liberal economist and trade historian Jacob Viner wrote in 1928, American presidents have sought from the first to "channel" foreign trade and later foreign investment in ways to "enhance the foreign policy objectives" of the United States.[56]

This often amounted to much more than merely reacting to events as they unfolded. The American state early on developed, first in the Americas and then in and around China, a uniquely interdependent relationship with American private-sector firms, one that in many ways proved more effective and efficient than most similar relationships developed in Europe or Japan. By no means did the American state intentionally engineer the multinational corporation to be its tool. Rather, it was more that the state, over the course of many decades, discovered that "the growing overseas empires of American corporations could be made to serve the larger interests of the United States."[57]

It was only in the early years of the Cold War that the U.S. government began to think strategically about how to shape and direct the actions of these enterprises. This is not to say that the government now began to micromanage the actions of these firms; if anything, the U.S. government throughout the postwar period has tended to give much more autonomy to American multinationals than governments in Japan, France, and Germany give to firms based in those nations. Rather, the goal was simply to force more of these enterprises to move more of their operations abroad, and to accomplish this Washington developed a combination of carrots and sticks. The carrots usually came in the form of generous subsidies, especially exemption from taxation of profits earned abroad.[58] The most important stick came in the form of lower tariffs, which, as we saw in the case of Motorola, prodded many an unwilling corporation to shift production abroad.[59] Although the overall goal was to make American multinationals into "instruments of American global" power, the U.S. state rarely showed much loyalty in return.[60] On the contrary, the American state over time came to think in much the same way as many of the foreign-based corporations that had invested in the United States, or that depended on sales in the American market.[61] These too, it turned out, could be made into instruments of American power.

The overall effect of U.S. multinationals in shaping the global economy can hardly be overstated. By the mid-1960s, U.S. corporations directly employed 5.5 million workers around the world, and when the many layers of suppliers and peripheral businesses are added in, the overall number was much greater yet.[62] To a large measure, it has been American corporations—in conjunction with the American state—that determined who did what where. Or, to put it in economic terms, it was these two entities that determined the "international division of labor" as well as the "distribution of gains in the world economy."[63] This is a power that American corporations are very much able to exercise even when they may seem to be in "retreat," as was illustrated by GE's dramatic reshaping of the global market for electronics in the 1980s.

Through all the years, the only constant aspect of the American multinational corporation was that it was constantly changing in nature. By the time Motorola first began to set up factories in Tianjin, the direct-investment model that firm followed was already being abandoned by many if not most of its American competitors. As we saw in the last chapter, even as Motorola was proudly cutting the ribbon on the first stage of its immense complex in the northern port city, other American companies were perfecting a very different style of entry into that same market, one that in many ways rendered Motorola's highly traditional, highly integrated, and extremely expensive strategy immediately obsolete. And as we will see in the coming chapters, it was this new strategy in which work overseas was contracted out to other companies—a strategy that was designed in no small part by managers seeking to enable their corporations to more effectively escape the ability of the American state to coerce them in particular directions—that would at last begin to spell the end of a relationship that had proven so powerful in reshaping the world.

In the 1960s, many Americans began to fear that the nation's economy and its whole society were being grossly distorted by the power of giant manufacturers like General Motors and General Electric. In our desperation first to escape the Depression, then to win the Second World War, then to out-innovate the Soviet Union, we had surrendered too much power to the managers of the great corporations, and to their allies in the labor unions and in government regulatory agencies. The result seemed to be a sort of dictatorship of the producer, in which all the other interests of American society were made to serve those of the industrial complex. Most grievously affected was the consumer, who in the words of the economist John Kenneth Galbraith had been "bound to the ends of the industrial system."[64]

At the time, the inertia of the system seemed so strong that few dared hope for any big overhaul anytime soon. But two political movements were soon set into motion. The first was the deep and widespread effort to better protect the interests of the consumer, mainly through regulation. The second, which was partly a reaction against the first, was to return more power over the corporation to the shareholder, whose interests, it was said, had been crammed far down below those of the worker, the manager, the bureaucrat, and now the consumer. The consumer revolution would play out first, in the late 1960s and through the 1970s. But with the election of Ronald Reagan, it was the shareholder revolution that would come to predominate.

Debating the economic and political wisdom of the effort to shift to the shareholder more power over the actions of the corporation is not our point here. Rather, our goal is to understand how this movement came to affect the international political and economic structures so carefully built over the course of the half century after the Second World War. Two effects, it would seem, stand out as paramount. First was to get American governments to regulate the economy with a much lighter hand. This policy was applied initially to the domestic economy, especially following the election of Ronald Reagan. Later, following the election of Bill Clinton, it would be applied, as we have seen, more and more to the international economy. The second important effect of the shareholder revolution, which we will see in coming chapters, was to reshape the institution of the corporation, most especially by shifting control from the professional manager to the investor. Together, these two changes have had an enormous impact on American society, and on the world economy. The American state, rather than absorbing and "socializing" the private-sector corporation, as Galbraith had feared, within a remarkably short period of time ceded the task of managing not only the domestic economy but the entire world economy not merely to the private sector, but to the shareholder in the private sector corporation. And, given the intricate web of interlinkages between trade and politics so carefully wrought by U.S. governments over the previous half century, the effect was also to turn over to the shareholder the task of managing our nation's security.

Nowhere is this more obvious than in the case of our recent relations with China. After Clinton lifted the hand of the state off commerce between America and China, the result was a bilateral relationship unprecedented in the history of the United States. Trade between the two nations would grow so phenomenally fast that by the end of the 1990s the two societies had been made intimately interdependent—to a degree that outstripped by far the interdependence of the United States and Japan in the 1980s, and that in some ways is as tight as the interdependence between France and Germany today. And yet, even as this was taking place, the two nations careened from one highly perilous military showdown to another, leading even to threats of nuclear war.[65]

After two centuries in which the American state had viewed trade policy as one of the most powerful tools to ensure the American nation's security, and one of the prime mechanisms for projecting and amplifying America's power in the world, the Clinton Administration simply let go.

This was a very different act from when the Reagan Administration nodded at the sell-off of RCA by GE in the late 1980s. Japan was a country that was interdependent in numerous ways with the United States, that was tied to us on many levels. In the case of China, the interdependence that was now forged was only economic and industrial in nature; in almost every other way, the two nations remained separated by deep divisions in outlook and in aim.

The assumption, it seemed, was that the human heart had somehow changed, that humankind had reached a point where such coercion was no longer needed and where the "marketplace" itself would forge harmony among peoples. It was an assumption far more hopeful than any ever uttered by such archetypal "idealists" as Richard Cobden or Norman Angell. It was an assumption that may well prove to be perhaps the single most grave error in the history of the American nation.

CHAPTER FOUR

THINKING IN LINKS

The Logistics Revolution

The first time Michael Dell nearly busted his company was in 1985, when his then-tiny business of assembling "clones" of IBM personal computers fell far behind on promised deliveries, leading to an investigation by Texas state officials. The second time came three years later when, flush with success, Dell embarked on an audacious plan to leapfrog his much bigger competitors by designing a whole new generation of PCs. Instead, he ended up with a great set of technologies built into an overly expensive product line, which didn't sell. Dell's third and most precipitous fall came in 1992, when a ballyhooed venture into retail sales sucked up so much cash that he nearly had to shut the company. Each time Dell's competitors in the PC industry chuckled and shook their heads at the upstart, who relied on catalogs and toll-free phone numbers to sell souped-up machines assembled from off-the-shelf components. After the third near crash, the razzing took on a sharper tone. The "whiz kid," it now seemed, had become the "fizz kid."[1]

But each time Dell had stocked away a valuable lesson or two about the market for computers and about the characteristics of his company. Risk, he saw, lay everywhere—in poor service, in technological cul-de-sacs, in piles of obsolete inventory, in losing track of your cash flow. Now, though, Dell seemed finally to have all the pieces he needed in place. Or, more accurately, he finally understood which pieces to leave out, and how to link together more efficiently the pieces he kept.

Dell soon ramped his business back up a fourth time, earning himself a fresh reputation as the "comeback kid."[2] But the admiration remained limited. Dell the company was still viewed as at best a brash smart outlier, a smart number-five or -six company in a savagely competitive industry. Dell the man was praised as an entrepreneur savvy enough to focus on his little niche of selling customized PCs to businesses and universities, while ceding the immense roiling consumer market to deep-keeled operators like IBM, Hewlett-Packard, and Compaq. More fundamental, whether he was a whiz kid, fizz kid, or comeback kid, the image that most always stuck to Michael Dell was that he was merely a kid. From the beginning, Bill Gates and Steve Jobs were respected as engineers and computer "scientists," innovators who brought forth something new into the world. But Dell, who had launched his company out of his dorm room at the University of Texas at age nineteen, struck people as more of a gangly adolescent armed with a screwdriver, who repackaged other people's work and stuck his name on the box. Worse, Dell was widely reported to be an overconfident and even domineering boss, a sort of nerdy Napoleon, an "enfant terrible."[3]

Given such limited expectations, the initial results of the third revamping of Dell Computer came as an astonishment. Between the second quarter of 1994 and the same period of 1995, sales grew by a phenomenal 52 percent. A year later, they had soared another 40 percent. Even more important than the gross was the net, and Dell's profits rose even faster, up 92 percent year on year in the third quarter of 1996. Now, suddenly, the tone of Dell's press coverage began to change. So, too, the tone of investors, who began to worship Dell as one of the new heroes of the decade. And why not? Between 1994 and 1999, Dell's revenue swelled by five times, to $18 billion. In the three years up to 1999, the price of a share of Dell stock soared 4,200 percent.[4]

No longer was Michael Dell dismissed; on the contrary, everyone now wanted to know all of his secrets. It had to be something more than selling directly to the buyer, because Gateway had mastered the same trick and Gateway wasn't doing nearly as well. It couldn't have all that much to do with the quality of the product or the technology—Dell always got top marks—but all the main PC makers delivered excellent machines. So Dell's competitors now strove to "reverse-engineer" his company, studying how Dell executives connected the firm's sales strategy and "build-to-order" model back through his assembly plants and into his supply chain. And the competitors listened more closely to what Dell himself said. Whereas other CEOs sang of their product's speed or ease of use, Dell enjoyed detailing seemingly mundane operational issues such as inventory and "logistics," which is the management of the movement of parts, supplies, and components into and through a company. Soon many began to discern a pattern. Dell's quantum leaps in revenue in the mid- to late 1990s coincided with a series of drastic cuts in inventory. In January 1995, Dell claimed to have slashed his company's stock down to thirty-five days, versus what he said was 110 days at Compaq. A year later, the company had cut his inventory by half again, to seventeen days. By 1997, it was down to eleven days. By 1999, it was down to six days.[5]

Competitors now scrambled to follow. By this time, though, Dell had built up so much momentum, so much knowledge about moving and integrating components purchased around the world, that he had little trouble staying far ahead even of much bigger and richer competitors. What made his production system all the more bold was that he did so with a supply base that spanned the Pacific Ocean. As other companies struggled to reorganize their internal operations, to contract out more work, to blend in more overseas sources of supply, Dell focused on using the latest in supply-chain management software to coordinate the movement of components from wherever he could get them. Almost entirely unrestrained by existing in-house component-manufacturing operations, Dell concentrated instead on developing a system that could track individual items—no matter where they were made—more tightly and efficiently than was possible even in the most perfectly integrated of old-line companies. For Dell, manufacturing was not making things, it was buying and moving and assembling and delivering things that other companies had manufactured.

One of the more observant articles on the early days of Dell was published in *Forbes* in 1992. Michael Dell, the magazine said, is "neither a retailer nor a manufacturer, but something in between." What Dell did, the reporter wrote, was apply new software management tools to integrate and coordinate the manufacturing process far up the chain of supplies that fed into the assembly plant floor, and to link more tightly than any of his competitors with his outside suppliers, especially overseas.[6]

The resulting "leanness" of Dell's inventory flow meant the company could blend newly available technologies more quickly into its products, that it was less likely to be caught with last year's components, and that it had more current information about the likes and dislikes of its customers. Most important of all was that, relative to its competitors, Dell had much less capital tied up in parts. Dell as a result was able to use available capital much more efficiently, and hence expand much faster than much bigger companies. And the result was that the company was able to jump from the number-five position among PC makers in 1996 to the number-one spot in 2001, without buying a single big competitor.

The PC industry was not exactly a sleepy backwater; companies like Hewlett-Packard and IBM and Compaq and Apple were among the most sophisticated manufacturers anywhere in the world in the 1990s. Yet Dell's mastery of low inventory, more than anything else, enabled him to deliver a better-quality product for less money more quickly. Many of Dell's competitors never knew what hit them.

The essence of Dell's success was not really all that complex, however. The company was one of the first to grow to maturity within a world that had been redefined by three new freedoms. The first two of these, as we have seen, were political. These were the freedom to do business wherever in the world a company wished and the freedom to operate only for profit, unburdened by any sense of responsibility to any community or any individual. The third freedom was technological, and it was to use modern logistics to extend the assembly line far further and in more directions than any company had ever dared before.

In the process, Dell and the other pioneering users and suppliers of logistics services would manage to hopelessly confuse the definition of manufacturer, while shifting power from the producer to the retailer and ratcheting up the speed of globalization. Over the 1990s, these companies would drive a process that forged a degree of economic interdependence among nations more intimate and more extreme than any politician had ever imagined.

The roots of modern logistics can also be traced back to the late 1940s. But it is a story that starts off with somewhat less drama than the brokering of economic interdependence among nations that was taking place at much the same time in Europe. This is because when the Truman Administration was helping to enforce a marriage of the nations of Western Europe, Sam Walton's main concern was to get across the Mississippi River to buy lots of negligees.

In those first years after the war, Walton owned a small five-and-dime in the town of Newport, Arkansas. Managing the company's supply chain meant that Walton, after work at the store, many days would drive down to Cottonwood Point to catch a ferry to Tennessee, where he would visit suppliers in the mill towns that lined the river. "I'd stuff that car and trailer with whatever I could get good deals on," Walton wrote years later in his memoir. Usually, this was on "softlines" like "ladies panties and nylons, men's shirts—and I'd bring them back, price them low, and just blow that stuff out the store."

About that time, Walton learned of a manufacturer's agent in New York by the name of Harry Weiner, who had an office on Seventh Avenue. For 5 percent of the deal, Weiner would arrange for manufacturers in the grimy loft buildings of Manhattan's midtown Garment District to ship directly to Walton's threadbare Newport store. Also about that time, Walton began to call up directly many of the companies that supplied him through his Ben Franklin franchise contract. The Ben Franklin Company required Walton to buy 80 percent of his merchandise through the corporate system, skimming off a fat premium in the process. Walton figured that if he went straight to the suppliers, he could avoid paying the middleman. Most of the time the suppliers refused, because "they didn't want to make Butler Brothers mad." But, Walton bragged, "every now and then," he "would find one who would cross over and do it my way."[7]

A pattern had been set, and when Walton began to automate and scale the process a few years later, it would change the face of retailing in America. Other store owners knew the "stack 'em high, sell 'em low" volume sales strategy. Others had better signage and smarter floor plans and brighter lighting. Others were as adept at promotions like giving out free popcorn or soft ice cream. Others were as cheap as Sam Walton, who would later famously make his executives sleep two to a room on business trips, and who shared a room himself. Other retailers were as viciously anti-union in their sentiments. A few were even as diligent as Walton at hunting down cheap merchandise, to the point of openly violating contracts with the franchiser. But what grew Wal-Mart into the biggest of all retail leviathans is that no competitor proved as precocious in using computers to track and control the processes of buying merchandise and getting it onto store shelves.

One of the secrets of many of the more successful manufacturers of the 1990s was that they adapted Sam Walton's supply-management system to their own "production" operations. Wal-Mart's logistics strategy has long been one of the key case studies for students of the supply chain, and Walton's deceptively folksy memoir, *Made in America,* though thin on detail, remains one of the inspirational texts of the logistics industry. One early article about Michael Dell compared the young computer assembler to Ray Kroc and Charles Schwab.[8] But the much more powerful influence on Dell was Sam Walton. In an interview, Dell named Walton as his most important guru, specifically for Walton's mastery of logistics.[9]

Not that the basics of Walton's management of the Wal-Mart supply chain was entirely new. Logistics is a term borrowed from the military, where it is used to describe the art of supplying troops in the field. The term entered English from the French, mainly through the writings of one of Napoleon's generals, Antoine Henri Jomini. Napoleon was perhaps the first gifted practitioner of large-scale logistics since the Romans, though this system would fail him once he reached the outskirts of Moscow. In America, the study and application of new logistics arts tended to take place first in the military and then move quickly into the private sector. The U.S. Army first demonstrated a mastery of logistics after it landed a 12,000-man invasion force in Veracruz, Mexico, in 1847. A decade and a half later, its feats in equipping and supplying the massive Union forces of the Civil War were without parallel in the nineteenth century. By 1918, the U.S. Army was able to maintain a two-million-man force in high style across the Atlantic in Europe, while during the Second World War the American military organized the most spectacular logistics operation of all time, feeding, arming, clothing, and transporting more than ten million soldiers fighting on multiple fronts. In the private sector, the first complex supply chains in the United States date to the 1870s, when companies began to integrate telegraphed information with transport services provided by fast, predictable railroads. Among the first experts were the retailer Macy's and the catalog company Sears, which used the new techniques to speed up the turnover of their stock.[10] Another burst of innovation came with the rise of trucking systems in the 1920s, and yet another in the late 1940s following standardization of the shipping pallet.

What Sam Walton did do was to apply computerized management tools earlier and more effectively than most of his contemporaries. Writers on Wal-Mart often focus on the physical aspects of the company's logistics system, especially the wide array of massive distribution centers. These are not so much warehouses as giant sorting machines that quickly redirect supplier shipments onto trucks destined for individual stores, within hours pushing boxes unloaded at one end of the center onto trailers at the other end. Wal-Mart handles some 85 percent of its supply work in-house, and the massive system gives the company a huge cost advantage versus most of its competitors. In all, Wal-Mart operates more than sixty of these centers around the country. The company expands not so much store by store, but distribution center by distribution center.[11]

The real key of the Wal-Mart system is not these physical sorting operations, however, but how the whole system is managed. As Walton tells the story, he took his first step to computerizing the system in 1966 when he enrolled in an IBM course on using punch cards to track information. Walton, who died in 1992 at age seventy-four, never made any claim to any particular personal expertise in computer technologies. But he was eager to depict himself as a pioneer in putting computers to practical use in managing a retail business. And what Walton claimed to have learned in IBM's school was how to track his merchandise to ensure that the right goods arrived at the right store in the right quantity at the right time. This meant fewer missed sales due to empty shelves, less handling of products in the warehouse and in the store, less need to check inventory physically, and fewer returns to the warehouse or the manufacturers. From the start, Walton understood that automating the management of inventory was a great way to save money. Over time, he learned that his stock-tracking system also gave him power over his employees and over many of the manufacturers that sold to his company.

Walton's own experience cheating the Ben Franklin chain made him very aware of how hard it could be for a big company to control local managers. But by enabling him to track the sales of every good in every store on an almost day-to-day basis, Walton discovered that his computerized system allowed him to see exactly when and where any of his retail managers was failing. To emphasize just how important such tracking was for the company's bottom line, Walton in his memoir quotes an old friend in the retail business. As he has his buddy explain it, Walton "became, really, the best utilizer of information to control absentee ownerships that there's ever been." The close tracking of sales of individual items is what gives Walton "the ability to open as many stores as he opens, and run them as well as he runs them, and to be as profitable as he makes them."[12]

The facts gathered by the information system proved almost as powerful for Walton in his dealings with suppliers. In retail, the traditional relationship between the store owner and the distributor or manufacturer was pretty simple—manufacturers would manufacture, and retailers would adapt to the shipping cycles, distribution points, packaging and size decisions, and inventory flows of the manufacturer. Very early in his career, Walton realized he was largely at the mercy of such giant suppliers as Procter & Gamble and Kodak. Even after he had built Wal-Mart into a big business, he often found it hard just to get such companies "to call on us at all, and when they did they would dictate how much they would sell to us and at what price."

But now Walton finally had an equalizer. The information his system gathered about what was selling where and how was of value not only to Wal-Mart, but also to the big manufacturers. Especially as Wal-Mart grew into a nationwide operator, the information the company gathered could be packaged to give the suppliers a much better sense of their end customers, which could help in reengineering everything from product packaging and content to the manufacturing process itself. Walton claimed to be particularly proud of a deal he made in 1987, while on a canoe trip with a vice president of Procter & Gamble. By then, Wal-Mart had become P&G's single biggest customer, yet purchasing was still handled by low-level regional buyers, who still wrangled over prices just as they had thirty years earlier. As the two men floated down the Spring River, Walton says, a vision emerged of a "partnership" between supplier and retailer based on the sharing of sales information. Such a system would result in better coordination of production and shipping and warehousing. In essence, it would allow Wal-Mart and P&G to manage their businesses together, to plan in tandem, to reduce inventory jointly, to speed the flow of goods from factory line to shopping cart, to cut drastically the stretch of time that existed between raw material and ultimate consumption.[13]

For Wal-Mart, the 1987 deal also gave the company its first real wedge into the operations of Procter & Gamble. And soon Wal-Mart was using the same wedge to bust into the operations of many other suppliers as well. What was first touted as a loose network of partnerships forged around the fair exchange of information soon evolved into a tight system in which Wal-Mart served as central broker and director not only of information but of the processes themselves. This was not simply a matter of Wal-Mart's size, though the company's sheer bulk was becoming an ever-bigger factor in its favor. Much more important was that Wal-Mart's masterful management of information about its operations enabled it to force its suppliers to adopt its information systems, and to adapt to its processes and methods, rather than vice versa. This was a reversal with dramatic ramifications. Once the age-old divide between manufacturer and retailer had been thus bridged, the power in the relationship shifted very rapidly toward Wal-Mart, as it would later to the dominant retail-oriented company in sector after sector. After all, in a system in which all parties are tightly integrated, it is logical, at least in the short term, for the central party to coordinate how suppliers pack their products, how often they ship them, how they deliver them and where, and how they manage and package information. Not all manufacturers adapted gladly to Wal-Mart's rules. Some even refused to play. Most of these, however, had to find other outlets for their products.

Once set in motion, the shift of power and initiative from manufacturer to retailer tended only to accelerate. The more Wal-Mart learned about the operations of its suppliers, the more it was able to compare one supplier to another, to spot inefficiencies and demand fixes, to zero in on profit centers inside its suppliers. As time went on, Wal-Mart was able to dictate not only how its suppliers packaged and distributed their products, but what they manufactured, how they manufactured, how much money they made on their businesses, and indeed whether they would remain in business at all. Wal-Mart became not merely the market leader; in many senses, it became the market itself.

Few companies have the wherewithal to invest tens of millions of dollars into an information system, as Wal-Mart did in the 1970s and 1980s. Which means the great logistics revolution that helped to reshape global manufacturing in the 1990s would have spread a lot less quickly if not for development of powerful software management systems, and especially the rise of companies designed to sell logistics services to all comers.

To most people, FedEx is a name that conjures images of the overnight delivery of documents and books, a company that helps an operator like Dell to sell direct to customers. One of the very first articles about Michael Dell, back in 1985, mentions his reliance on FedEx to deliver to his buyers. But for us, FedEx is important not for how it revolutionized the delivery of finished products to the customer, but for how it revolutionized the delivery of components to the assembly line. FedEx for many manufacturers was the company that enabled them to globalize their supply lines, allowing them to rely on a supplier in Asia or Europe just as intimately as on a supplier located twenty miles across town. The FedEx model—supplemented and oft times improved by competitors like UPS—was one of the key factors in the rise of the complex multi-country production line in the 1980s and especially the 1990s.

Like Dell, the story of FedEx involves a dorm room legend. In the mid-1960s, Fred Smith stayed up late working on a paper for an economics class at Yale. Smith, whose father had built up a bus company in West Tennessee in the 1920s and later developed the Toddle House restaurant chain, wrote up a plan to buy a fleet of jets, to fly out of a single hub, to operate only at night, and thereby to provide door-to-door next-day delivery service across the nation. But Smith, who claims to have received a C on this paper, would never run into the same image problems as Michael Dell. This is because before he was able to try out his vision in the real world, he spent two tours of duty in Vietnam. First he served as a Marine infantry commander and then, after being wounded, he re-upped as a pilot and flew 200 missions providing forward support for troops on the ground.[14]

FedEx finally got off the tarmac in 1972, working out of a base in Memphis. The business was the biggest venture capital project of the era.

Only twenty-seven at the time, Smith stuck in $8 million of family money and raised another $91 million from investors. Unfortunately, he also lost $29 million in the first twenty-six months of operations, and almost went bust twice. The trouble lay not so much in Smith's initial business model—which was to speed replacement electronics and industrial parts to big corporations—as in the regulatory software of the era. Because of strict rules set by the Civil Aeronautics Board, FedEx was not allowed to fly big 727s but had to rely instead on much smaller planes, especially French-built Falcon jets. This meant that on busy routes the company often found itself dispatching five planes per night to a single destination, resulting in a huge waste of labor and fuel. Relief finally came in the form of what came to be known on Capitol Hill as the Federal Express Bill, which was approved by the Carter Administration in late 1977. Almost immediately, the company's revenue began to surge, from $72 million per year to more than $1 billion in 1983.[15]

Smith was not the only man who was inspired by visions of airplane-based super-rapid distribution, or even the first. By the late 1960s, logistics was emerging as a distinct subject of study in a few universities. Other early ventures included DHL and TNT. But especially after the overhaul of CAB regulations, FedEx grew much faster than its competitors. The big breakthrough came when the company opened storefront shipment centers in cities across the United States and expanded into the document and small-package business. By the late 1970s, FedEx had a big presence in Europe. In the 1980s, its purchase of Flying Tigers cargo airline gave it a dominant position in the air cargo business in Asia.

For manufacturers, one of FedEx's biggest innovations dates to 1975, when the company set up a "Parts Bank" in Memphis, where it warehoused replacement components for twenty-five companies, including Xerox and Burroughs. The next real quantum leap wouldn't come until 1990, when FedEx introduced a service wherein it would manage the logistics of other companies, not only on an emergency basis but as part of the day-to-day routine. The first big contract was with the clothing retailer Laura Ashley, for whom FedEx managed all warehousing and merchandise delivery. Next came National Semiconductor in 1992. "The goal," said one executive at the chip manufacturer, "is to get National Semiconductor out of logistics business" altogether. And so FedEx did.

Before signing the logistics deal, National Semiconductor had managed relationships with forty-two freight forwarders and thirteen transport carriers to deliver products out of a myriad of facilities. FedEx replaced this with a single global distribution center in Singapore. Costs were cut in half, and delivery times were cut from as long as eighteen days to a maximum of two.[16]

Up to this point, most operations involved manufacturers using FedEx to manage delivery to their customers. But already in the early 1990s, the relationship was beginning to invert. More and more companies came to view FedEx not only as a way to deliver their products but as a tool to organize and rationalize the supplies and components flowing into their company through their supply chains. Nor did the use of such services result only in new efficiencies; increasingly, it resulted in new power. As Wal-Mart had discovered on its own, more and more manufacturers came to realize that the close tracking of inbound shipments was a way to more closely manage the companies that did the actual work for them. FedEx's information-management system enabled many American manufacturers not only to operate more efficiently, and far more widely, but also to expand their leverage over their suppliers.

Logistics would finally reach the mainstream in 1994, when *Fortune* magazine declared the art to be "strategic." Logistics, rather than product design or quality or technology, was more and more seen as the real source of value in a company. "Frankly, the cost of making a product is almost irrelevant," one U.S. chemicals distributor said. "You have far more opportunity to get cost out of the supply chain than you do out of manufacturing. There's so much duplication and inefficiency."[17]

And now any company could hire the very best systems and infrastructure in logistics. FedEx and companies like UPS, BAX Global, and TNT had packaged the secret of Wal-Mart and made it available to the mass manufacturers. Any company could now enjoy much the same efficiencies as that huge retailer, without having to develop its own software or build its own warehouses or buy its own trucks. As an executive at National Semiconductor put it, to develop the sort of service the company had originally envisioned, "we would have had to make our company into Federal Express." Much easier and cheaper was simply to hire FedEx.[18]

The emergence and perfection of modern logistics systems was one of the prime factors in the rise of the global assembly line. At a time when dozens of long-protected economies were opening in the early 1990s, and when the U.S. government was all but abandoning any effort to shape the world economy, and when the corporations were rooting themselves up and cutting themselves into little pieces, logistics was the final factor necessary to remake the production system on a global scale. The Japanese model of just-in-time production called for geographic clustering. But now global-scale logistics service companies gave manufacturers an entirely new center of gravity, one that they could shift from day to day. Similarly, the FedEx model, for many companies, also proved to be the main tool that enabled them to rationalize their supply base for the first time on a truly global scale, and to abandon their strategy of maintaining distinct, vertically integrated industrial complexes in Europe, North America, and Asia. The mere existence of air express services gave managers the courage to cut much deeper into their supply lines and to reduce inventory to a much greater degree. If a ship got caught in a storm, or a port was closed by a strike, it didn't mean that their assembly line went down. Though flying was expensive, managers knew that replacement parts could easily be loaded onto a plane to keep the lines moving.

In 1994, Compaq Computer's CFO, Daryl White, said his company had finally and fully mastered the business of making personal computers. And a little bragging certainly seemed excusable. Compaq was, in the words of the press, "white hot," having just passed IBM and Apple to become the number-one PC maker in the world. "We've changed the way we develop products, manufacture, market, and advertise," White said. Only one basic piece of the puzzle remained to be mastered. "We haven't addressed logistics," he said. This was next on his agenda, though, and White figured it could mean savings of between $500 million and $1 billion per year.[19]

What White didn't realize is that logistics was no longer the final step in a company's rise. No longer was logistics simply the management of supplies flowing into a company, on one side, and the management of the flow of finished goods out the other. Rather, logistics had become the core activity of the manufacturer, the glue that held the modern manufacturing corporation together. And unfortunately for Compaq, one of the true pioneers in the use of logistics happened to be a direct competitor. Dell, which had grown up depending on FedEx almost from day one, and which had shaped itself entirely to thrive within a FedEx world, was fast catching up to Compaq. White, in finally focusing on logistics, was just starting down the path that Dell had long been on. Not surprisingly, Compaq's stay atop the PC world, and its very existence as an independent company, would prove fleeting.

In 1980, James Harbour quit his job at Chrysler to set up his own consulting firm. Harbour, who had been director of corporate manufacturing, was convinced that Japanese production methods were much superior to American methods in terms of both productivity and the quality of the resulting product. Yet even though Harbour's concerns were based largely on direct observation—Chrysler's 15 percent share of Mitsubishi gave him a unique window into the workings of a Japanese manufacturer—Harbour's bosses at Chrysler didn't share his concerns and wouldn't give him the time he needed to study the issue in detail. So Harbour set out on his own to get a better understanding of the many differences between how Japanese and American car companies approached manufacturing. What he found was an entirely new production system, one that at first inspired fear and loathing among Americans. It wasn't long, however, before the U.S. firms began to counterattack the Japanese by combining Japanese production techniques with an American sense of space.[20] One of the secrets of Dell's success is that it would later use modern logistics to re-create the Japanese manufacturing model on a global scale.

At the time Harbour began his quest, the Japanese sold mainly small cars on the U.S. market, but in this niche their products were generally regarded as much better and cheaper. Not that the Americans had any shortage of good excuses at hand. One popular rationalization was that Americans were new to the business of making small cars, having been pushed into this somewhat distasteful task by the 1973 oil embargo and the resulting U.S. government effort to promote better gas mileage. For decades, Americans had built big cars for big roads. They were especially proud of such two-ton behemoths as the Cadillac Deville and the Lincoln Continental, and of gas-guzzling hot rods like the Chevrolet

Corvette and Dodge Charger. Japan, by contrast, had spent the previous quarter century building tiny and economical cars for a small and resource-poor island populated by undemanding workers. Another popular excuse of the time was Ralph Nader, whose campaign for safety had led GM to shut down its main small-car unit, Corvair, and whose work contributed to the demise of Ford's main small-car effort, the Pinto. The most popular excuse of all, however, at least in the boardrooms of Detroit, was the high cost of American labor, in terms of both wages and restrictive work rules. For the average American automotive executive of the early 1980s, the main reason their companies couldn't compete head-to-head with the Japanese was that their unionized workers demanded so much more than their immaculately groomed, calisthenics-performing counterparts across the ocean.

Harbour, after a half year spent studying Japanese and American automotive plants as a freelance consultant, thought he had a fairly good idea of the problem, and he presented his findings to senior executives at GM, Ford, and Chrysler. The real reason Toyota's Celica and Nissan's Datsun 260C were clobbering the Chevette and the Pinto in gas mileage, performance, and quality had nothing to do with the conventional rationalizations. Rather, Harbour said, the problem was much more fundamental and much scarier—the Japanese companies were simply better than the Americans at manufacturing. Not only did they deliver higher-quality products, which was self-evident, but they did so much more efficiently. American car companies, Harbour reported, required twice as many man-hours to build the same car, resulting in a cost differential of more than $1,700 per vehicle, even in the cheap compact segment of the market. The problem, he concluded, was not shortages of gas, or government safety regulation, or overpaid unionized workers, or even Japan's protected market, but simple bad management. The executives thanked Harbour for his report, asked him to keep his findings quiet until they had time to review the issue more fully, and promised to call. A year later, the phone still hadn't rung, so Harbour began to hawk his study to other manufacturers and to use the press to help advertise his findings.

Harbour was not the only American manufacturing expert to notice that the Japanese were doing something different. Right at the beginning of the 1980s, numerous articles began to appear celebrating the Japanese achievements in manufacturing and offering explanations. Americans began to hear the first mentions of Japanese production terms like "kan- ban" and "jidoka," and the first explanations of production concepts like "just in time" and "defect prevention." Many of the stories pointed to Toy- ota as the source of the key innovations, and Americans now for the first time learned of Toyota's "production philosophy." The world of manufac- turing, it was now clear, had not stopped evolving in the 1950s. American corporations, in the thirty-five years since the end of the war, had grown increasingly convinced that they had largely perfected the manufacturing arts. Rather than continue to fret over how production was organized, many had shifted their energies and engineering efforts to the develop- ment of new products, or to bulking up their brands through television advertising and community philanthropy, or to developing in-house credit operations, or simply to managing the status quo. Fewer and fewer American corporations engaged in energetic efforts to recalibrate the equi- librium between man and machine on the factory floor or the manufac- turing campus. American producers had settled into a sort of steady state, marked by relatively comfortable balances between labor unions and man- agement, between Wall Street and management, and between manage- ment team and management team in the highly polite oligopolism that prevailed in most industrial sectors. Now the balances had been upset. The Japanese had figured out a much better way to make things.

More embarrassing yet was to discover that the Japanese had to a large extent learned their tricks by studying such manufacturers as Henry Ford and the writings of American consultants, including W. Edwards Dem- ing and Peter Drucker.[21] While many American manufacturers tended to regard Ford as something of an eccentric, whose massive operation was so far out of the ordinary as to offer few real lessons, the Japanese found a variety of traits worthy of emulation, not least Ford's never-ceasing search for better ways to organize production. Ford was famously horrified by unnecessary motion in production, not least in the loading, unloading, and storing of inventories of parts. At the immense River Rouge facility, he had solved the problems in his typical outsized fashion, decreeing that the railroad cars that carried raw material and parts on River Rouge's in- ternal loop would double as warehouses. Similarly, much more than most American manufacturers of the era, Ford strove mightily to keep that inventory to a minimum. During a 1920 recession, Ford demanded a better scheduling of the railroad he owned and thereby cut his inventory of raw materials like iron ore and timber—including those in transit from the mines and forests—down to a phenomenally tight fourteen days total.[22]

Of course, few companies anywhere in the world could even dream of replicating the huge-scale efficiencies of Ford Motor circa 1926, least of all manufacturers in postwar Japan. According to the book *The Machine That Changed the World,* one of the most in-depth studies of Japanese manufacturing techniques in the automotive industry, Toyota's managers never even tried. Instead, they spent years developing an entirely new approach to manufacturing. The book's authors, who at the time were members of an MIT industrial research project, distinguish among three general ways to manufacture complex products like automobiles. The first to develop was what they call "craft" production, in which manufacturers use "highly skilled workers and simple but flexible tools to make exactly what the customer asks for—one item at a time." These products are generally of a very high quality, but they also are very costly to make. Next to develop, most famously with Ford and the Model T's moving assembly line, was the mass producer, which "uses narrowly skilled professionals to design products made by unskilled or semiskilled workers tending expensive, single purpose machines." At Toyota, managers took production to a third stage, which combined much of the quality of craft production with the efficiency and scalability of mass production.[23]

Toyota up through 1950 was essentially a craft producer. Over the previous thirteen years, the company produced a total of 2,685 automobiles, compared with the roughly 7,000 vehicles that Ford churned out on any given day. Toyota's managers, however, wanted to produce on a much bigger scale, and the Ford assembly line model—which relied on the work of hundreds of machines and tens of thousands of workers—was obviously of little or no use. Toyota simply lacked the capital to outfit even one assembly line in the American manner. So the company instead set to work experimenting with new ways to run the machines and new ways to organize the workers around the machines. At a company like Ford, managers would usually devote one machine to the making of one part for months at a time, if not for the entire production run of a model. Stamping out the same exact piece over and over and over seemed the most efficient way to run a machine, especially since it could take days to change the stamping dye in order to make a different part. Toyota, however, devoted years to experimenting with ways to make the machines themselves more flexible, concentrating especially on cutting the time it took to change a stamping dye. The single most revolutionary change was that Toyota's managers eventually got the process of switching out a dye down to as few as three minutes, which meant that a single machine could turn out many different parts in a single day, in much smaller batches. The machines of mass production, in a sense, had been harnessed to craft.

It wasn't long until Toyota realized that their new system delivered a couple of unexpected but huge benefits—a big reduction in the cost of inventory and a reduction in the number of defects. Inventory must be handled, stored, and owned, all of which costs money. American mass manufacturers have long been wary of holding too much inventory—for instance, it was widely known that "uncontrolled purchases" of supplies almost killed General Motors in the depression of 1920.[24] But American managers also tended to accept large inventories because this meant never facing any shortages of parts, which at least in theory meant that the assembly lines themselves would only rarely go down and that their highly expensive machines would almost always hum along at a proper speed.

The Japanese, however, by altering this balance, by making machines so much more flexible, were able to produce only the exact number of parts they needed, very close to the exact moment when these parts were needed. Such low inventory, in turn, meant that when a defect was spotted—say, if a radiator did not fit right—the problem had to be fixed almost immediately. Such a temporary shutdown of the line would violate the number-one rule at most American companies, which was never to stop the machines. But the Japanese knew that most problems could be quickly fixed. And any immediate costs in terms of downtime were balanced out by the fact that defective parts weren't being stamped out by the thousands, and then weren't being built into cars by the thousands. This meant much less money spent on fixing defects after assembly (or even after sale), and much happier customers.

Toyota did something else as well, which was to establish a network of captive, single-source suppliers near its factories. In Chapter Six, we will look more closely at how the American version of Toyotaism hugely magnified the dangers of such single-sourcing relationships. But it is important to look here at how Toyota stitched these networks—which were often made up of dozens of little suppliers—together using the same basic just-in-time principles it applied within the main factory. Later, Toyota's master manufacturing engineer, Taiichi Ohno, likened the resulting network to "a human body" in which "autonomic nerves" are able to react automatically to any distress. By connecting Toyota so closely to outside suppliers, Ohno had turned the factory into a sort of superfactory and, to a degree, he had made this superfactory self-aware.[25]

In the event, American manufacturers, though often initially horrified to realize just how much more advanced Japanese manufacturing methods had become, were also often electrified by reports of Toyota's revolutionary approach, and many rose quickly to the challenge. Within months of the first newspaper and magazine stories about the Japanese production techniques, many American companies had begun to experiment. The Ohio Bicycle division of Huffy Corp. began to reorganize relationships with suppliers. General Electric announced that four of its manufacturing divisions were testing *kanban* production techniques. Westinghouse was one of the first to report real results, as what it called a "partial *kanban*" system cut inventory by half and reduced line-paralyzing "stock-outs" by 95 percent. Even Sam Walton traveled to Japan to study supply chains and Japanese-style company-worker relationships.[26]

Soon an entire mini-industry was in bloom. Academics, consultants, and journalists flocked to Japan to study Toyota and other companies, much as Japanese and other engineers had sought inspiration in Detroit in the 1920s and early 1950s. Executives who had seen the light—and had racked up the numbers at their own companies to prove it—quit to write books, open institutes, and work as consultants. The most valued of the new experts were the growing legion of Japanese freelancers who crisscrossed America hawking their manufacturing bona fides. Standard operating procedure for these knights of production was to arrive at their American customer early one morning and start shoving machines around the factory floor, reordering workers into teams, demanding that the members of these teams be "cross-trained" to understand and perform one another's jobs. The enemy, the freelancers declared, was *muda*, the Japanese word for "waste." Their starting point for battling *muda* was often the stockroom, where they would demand that shelves immediately be cut down, or removed entirely, to physically eliminate most or even all places to store the hated inventory.

Even many of the oldest and seemingly most ossified of American manufacturers began to catch on fast. Automotive supplier TRW was an early convert to JIT, as was motorcycle maker Harley-Davidson. By late 1982, even General Motors told stockholders that it was trying to learn, aiming first at cutting its $9 billion inventory of parts by 25 percent. By mid-1983, Chrysler claimed to aim at a 50 percent cut in inventory. And soon the companies were actually delivering results. By the late 1980s, General Motors was running some of the most efficient production lines in Europe. A new Ford plant in Hermosillo, Mexico, was reported to be among the most advanced in the world. The Americans not only soon proved themselves capable of matching the Japanese at their game, but many began to surpass their erstwhile teachers.[27]

Americans had picked up the gauntlet. The race, it seemed, was on.

Postwar America was largely a self-contained America. Although for much of the late nineteenth and early twentieth centuries, the nation had relied on immigrants to man the machines of mass production, in the 1950s this no longer seemed politically acceptable. The combination of strong labor unions, and the growing conviction that productivity could be increased through a slow and orderly increase in the automation of factories, all but headed off any calls for a resumption of large-scale immigration. Although "the world contains a great many potential recruits for [America's] labor force," the economist John Kenneth Galbraith wrote in 1958, "nothing is viewed with more suspicion than this method of expanding production."[28]

Yet in point of fact, the U.S. State Department was at this very time promoting policies that would result in a de facto expansion of the size of the labor force available to American manufacturers serving the American market. As we saw in the last chapter, in the late 1950s and early 1960s a combination of new trade agreements and subsidies for overseas investment led many American manufacturers into new ventures overseas, especially in Asia. The basis for what decades later would emerge as a truly global workforce in the employ of American capital was being laid. Although we looked at this issue from the point of view of the U.S. government, it is also worth looking at it from the point of view of the companies that were affected, to understand how in many of their initial actions they were in essence doing nothing more than adjusting, as best they could, to a world that was continuously evolving, and that was being continuously reengineered by the action of governments. How these companies actually adjusted is, in turn, worth understanding, because quite apart from any government policy, many of these American firms approached the task of investing in East and Southeast Asia very differently from their Japanese or European competitors, creating much more open, collaborative, and multinational systems. And it is important because in the process they laid the industrial foundation that years later would enable the rise to power of such firms as Dell and Cisco.

From the late 1950s into the 1970s, dozens of U.S. companies, responding to the wide array of carrots and sticks used by the U.S. government, moved operations to Asia far faster than they would have if responding only to market signals. One good example is General Electric's response to the reduction of tariffs on radios made in much of Asia, set out by the Kennedy Round of trade concessions in the mid-1960s. GE managers, suddenly faced with a choice between ceding much of the U.S. market for radios or restructuring to exploit the same pools of labor available to their new competitors, opted for the latter. GE opened its first radio plant in Asia in 1967 and brought a second online in 1970. But the company clearly did not relish the task, with all the expense and effort. As GE executives later made clear to the U.S. Tariff Commission, the company "would not have moved its radio-manufacturing operations offshore" had it "not been" for the trade concessions. In other words, it acted mainly to stay competitive with manufacturers located in these now-privileged production sites, by blending the same low-cost labor into their U.S.-bound products.[29]

Yet over the years, the comfort of the Americans in producing in these nations for the home market would grow quickly. So, too, their appreciation of the benefits of manufacturing in these nations as the ranks of local engineers swelled, as more local companies mastered advanced production work, as local governments became more adept at working cooperatively with American investors. In 1977, Hewlett-Packard set up a small operation in Singapore to assemble calculators; within a decade, the company had built up on the island one of its most important production centers for printers and PCs, and it had come to rely on Singapore-based engineers to design manufacturing processes, to develop manufacturing tools, even to design semiconductor chips. In 1981, Apple Computer opened a line in Singapore to assemble printed circuit boards for the Apple II personal computer, flying the boards to San Francisco and then trucking them to the company's assembly plant in Dallas. By 1985, Apple had upgraded the Singapore facility to serve as final assembler for the entire world, including Japan's highly demanding consumers.[30]

The willingness of these American companies to engage in advanced manufacturing work in Asia is very different from that of Japanese manufacturers that invested in the same nations. Japanese multinationals were even more active than the Americans in the countries of the region. But the Japanese were much less interested in using these factories to serve their home market, instead generally limiting them to the assembly of products destined for sale on the local markets. Compared to Americans, Japanese firms tended to adopt a much more mercantilist, top-down structure for their Asian production operations, with research and engineering handled mainly at home in Japan by Japanese, and with most advanced components built in Japan by Japanese and then exported to the overseas assembly lines. For many years, the Japanese government preached a vision of economic cooperation to its neighbors in Asia. If all the nations worked together, like geese flying in a tight formation, everybody would get to the same goal at the same time. Japan, however, very much expected to be the lead goose.

The approach of American industry in Asia, right from the first major investments in the 1960s, tended much more toward cooperation and openness. Whereas Japanese corporations tried to keep even remotely strategic activities in the hands of Japanese engineers, Japanese workers, and Japanese suppliers, American companies were often eager to enter into highly interdependent relationships with foreign-owned companies from Taiwan, Korea, and Malaysia. Most of the American companies operated as a sort of open industrial platform in which almost any company could in theory take part, and the system that emerged was characterized by highly cooperative relationships marked by a great and growing degree of specialization among the participants.[31]

The biggest difference between the American and the Japanese models of production is that right from the start the Americans focused not on using the local facilities to serve the relatively poor local markets, but instead blended this local production into a system designed to serve the rich and demanding U.S. market. This meant that American-invested production in Asia tended to advance technologically at roughly the same pace as the U.S. market, and that American companies were much more apt to transfer key technologies to offshore plants and offshore suppliers.[32]

By the late 1980s, many American manufacturers had begun to realize that they had, however unwittingly, developed a highly valuable strategic asset in their competition with the Japanese. American electronics companies, which at the time were increasingly fearful of following RCA and the other American consumer electronics firms into an ultimately deadly dependency on their Japanese competitors for memory chips, displays, and other precision components,[33] now realized they had developed a codependent industrial system that served as a source of vital support in their battle to keep firms like Sony and Fujitsu from capturing their markets.

Starting in the late 1980s, the American corporations began to use the emerging logistics services of companies like FedEx to interconnect this multination production network ever more tightly and efficiently. For years, even as American corporations had developed ever more specialized supply bases in Asia, the fear of disruption in the production line meant that most kept inventories large. Now, however, American corporations that had begun to attack *muda* within their domestic production lines realized they could do so also on the scale of their cross-border production systems in Asia. Armed with newly powerful software and more efficient and cheaper transport services, these companies could now aim to manage production spread across a whole multination region, much as Toyota had organized production in a single neighborhood around one of its plants in its hometown of Toyotashi.

By contrast, few of the Japanese companies in the region made much of an effort to match the Americans in developing such regional cross-border production networks, or to cut out waste and duplication within their manufacturing operations at any sort of global level. On the contrary, the Japanese production networks, in the words of one study, "boasted redundant investment and remained relatively closed."[34] Japanese firms usually continued to insist on working in very close proximity to their suppliers.

In the 1990s, it became clear that a highly important subset of American producers had figured out how to turn Japan's just-in-time production philosophy against their competitors, not least those from Japan. Whereas the Japanese continued to organize their operations mainly on a national scale and in hierarchical multination networks, more and more Americans now organized their operations as a single interdependent global system. This, at bottom, is what enabled Dell, and not another Japanese or Asian firm, to emerge in the 1990s as, in the words of the consultant Kenichi Ohmae, the most "incredible incarnation of the Toyota system."

When America's mass manufacturers of the early twentieth century took over the job of distributing and marketing their own products, they did so largely to be able to "push" their products onto the market with greater consistency and control. The goal of managers at these companies was to run their great banks of machines as much as possible according to the logic of the machines. If an assembly line was capable of turning out 100,000 sewing machines per month, but if demand originally was for only 50,000 units per month, it was regarded as much more efficient to somehow find a market for the excess production than to operate the expensive machinery at half capacity and wait for the market to grow organically.

Hence the rise of modern advertising, of modern franchises and dealerships, of in-house credit divisions, of all the tools designed to convince a consumer who may not need a product that he or she did in fact want and could afford to buy that product. In the 1890s, fear that the U.S. market had become saturated with the output of the nation's vast new factories was partially responsible for America's fascination with China's market. When China and other nations ultimately proved incapable of absorbing America's surpluses, American corporations mastered the arts of cramming that product onto the U.S. consumer. In perfecting mass marketing in the early decades of the twentieth century, Americans in essence perfected a sort of internally directed mercantilism. In the 1990s, Dell would take this art to a new level and into new realms, learning how to cram Asian-made product into the American market more effectively than any other firm of the era.

Toyota's production system, by contrast, was often hailed by its adherents as eliminating the need for a corporation to push products onto the market, being designed more to "pull" those products out of the factory only when demanded by an eager buyer. The Japanese term *kanban,* for instance, derives from the original version of the system when a card was physically passed back along a production line from workstation to workstation, as a way to signal workers at each point that it was time to begin their task. By starting work only when a card reached their station, the employees would do work only when there was need for that work.

In the 1990s, especially as more American companies adopted Toyota's production system, many people felt the practice of pushing product onto the market had finally given way to a more efficient and sustainable system in which products would be built only as desired. Toyota's much more flexible method of production, so the thinking went, had finally shifted the power in the producer-buyer relationship from the manufacturer right through the retailer all the way to the end customer. No longer would there be any need to fret about the relative power of the lead producer or the lead retailer or some well-entrenched supplier; all were now directed by the individual buyer. The invisible hand of laissez-faire economics seemed to have morphed at last into the lazy hand of the American consumer, clicking away on a Web site or flipping through a catalog.

At first glance, Dell's manufacturing operation appears to be one of the highest perfections of such "pull." According to company lore and marketing copy, Dell builds its products "to order." Customers are given the sense that when they go online or pick up the phone to make an order, the array of components they choose for their PC then immediately starts moving down the assembly line toward the cardboard box in which it will travel to their home. And to some extent this is true, as a gray plastic tote tray loaded with the specific components for the specific computer will soon begin to wend its way through the maze of tubing and conveyors that connect the individual work cells of a Dell assembly line. Up and down the tote will travel on dumbwaiter-sized elevators to cell after cell, from person to person, each plugging in a different object or making a particular connection, until the finished PC or laptop reaches the packing station, where it is wrapped, boxed, and handed over to UPS or FedEx for final delivery.

Yet Dell assembly lines like those in Austin or Nashville are in some ways little more than Hollywood storefronts. But rather than hide nothing, they are actually designed to help hide something that is very real— the extremely complex supply system that stretches out from Dell's delivery docks all the way around to the other side of the world; in the case of a simple desktop, Dell receives some 4,500 parts from some 300 suppliers. On the inside, a Dell assembly plant looks much like its Japanese precursors; over each work cell a set of lights flicks from green to yellow to red in the modern version of the *kanban* system. If a worker falls behind, a yellow light signals that the next station should wait. If a key part is missing, or if a machine breaks, the light turns red. Given the complexity and leanness of the process, it is not surprising that the light turns red many times each day, to the point where workers are trained to take advantage of the shutdowns to clean their workstations and, if the problem persists, to head upstairs to watch training videos and take ad hoc classes. Yet as hard as it is to manage such a system even in one factory or in one locale, it is important to realize that Dell's actual assembly line stretches far beyond the factory walls to hundreds of points often more than ten thousand miles away. A company logistics engineer in Austin must keep a watch out for red lights not only on the line at Austin but at literally hundreds of potential bottlenecks, for an almost inconceivably vast array of reasons, ranging from South Seas typhoons to West Texas dust storms.

Most problems are quickly solved. Yet in such a complex network of activity, others can take days or even weeks to smooth out. Dell, however, is no more eager than was Ford three quarters of a century ago to idle its system and thereby cut off its flow of cash. The rules of running an industrial enterprise are the same as always. The best way to ensure a healthy return on invested capital is to work that capital as efficiently and as ceaselessly as possible.

So what Dell does besides building its products "to order" is something the company calls "demand management." To ensure a steady flow of work along a line that relies on such slim inventories, Dell has developed a number of techniques to lure consumers into buying what it has on hand to sell. Dell customers don't so much choose what they want from the full array of products that Dell handles. Rather, they choose what Dell wants them to choose from a very finite and yet constantly shifting set of possibilities. Dell, in other words, engineers demand just as it engineers supply. If there is a shortage of a certain video card or of a certain type of terminal, Dell will cut the price on other configurations and other components until any imbalance has been righted, until production and supply and demand are all back into the forecast equilibrium. Sam Walton, back in Newport, Arkansas, mastered the art of "blowing" his "stuff out the store." Dell has mastered the ability to shape its customers' desires to the momentary capabilities of the company's assembly machine. When a customer wanders into Dell's reach, whether by browser or phone, the company wants to make sure the customer buys whatever happens to be available. Ultimately, not only has Dell mastered the art of making a sale no matter the perturbation in the flow of components (if not too great), it has also mastered the use of sales to actually help smooth out any perturbations in that flow of product through the company. It is a retail philosophy not much different from that of the French grocer who stocks his shelves with only seasonal fruit.[35]

Dell in the 1990s was one of the first manufacturers to come of age in a world fully familiar with Toyota's just-in-time production system, very much at ease with the idea of employing workers and engineers and managers in many nations in a single common effort, fully able to take advantage of highly advanced logistics services managed by others. Blended together, the result was that Dell learned how to coordinate manufacturing done in its name by hundreds or even thousands of companies around the world, thereby commanding the labor of tens if not hundreds of thousands of workers, and then choreograph the overall operation as neatly as if it were all happening under the same roof.

And Dell went yet further. Like Wal-Mart, the company gained ever more power as it became ever more adept at managing its supply chain. Unlike Wal-Mart, which of course loses its hold over its customers at the checkout scanner, Dell figured out how to extend its reach right into the customer's living room. By engaging in "direct" sales, whether via the Internet or over the phone, Dell managed to stretch its system to link directly to the customer, then connect that customer back almost directly to the most distant supplier. In essence, even without any vertical integration of physical production, the company has managed to internalize every marketplace that existed between most of the companies engaged in the manufacture of computer components on the other side of the world and the end buyer in America. Dell's system, for all intents, is a sort of private road that stretches from the factories of Taiwan and China straight to the American sofa, cutting out not only all the middlemen but also most of the managers.

Taiichi Ohno's innovation was to make Toyota's factories "feel" any problem in their production systems, and then to extend this nervous system from the factory to nearby suppliers. For companies like Dell, complex modern logistics is what has enabled them to extend this nervous system vastly further, to a point where the company now feels every breath, every hiccup, of every creature within its reach. And increasingly, Dell is able to reverse the flow of energy to these nerves, to adjust with magnificent precision not only the levels of hunger in the system but the objects of that hunger, fitting the appetite of the end consumer to the food supply while skimming off all the fat in the process.

Of course, the whole system works only as long as there is food within reach. Which means that modern logistics is much more than a matter of sharing a nervous system. It is also the tool that has allowed private-sector companies to create a much more visceral connection among the industrial nations of the world than any politician today dares to admit.

CHAPTER FIVE

ASSETS BACKWARDS

Outsourcing and the Arbitrage Firm

In September 2000, Belgian prime minister Guy Verhofstadt flew to California to meet John Chambers, the CEO of the pioneering Internet hardware manufacturer Cisco Systems. Verhofstadt had first invited Chambers to meet him in Brussels, and when Chambers had demurred the Belgian suggested instead a tête-à-tête in New York, where he planned to attend the United Nations Millennium Summit along with some 160 other world leaders. But a transcontinental flight didn't fit Chambers's schedule, so Verhofstadt—who while in Manhattan was also busy negotiating long distance with truck drivers who had blocked key roadways at home as well as squiring around Belgium's crown prince— agreed to Chambers's invitation to dine with him in San Jose.[1]

It may seem surprising that the prime minister of a European nation would travel across the United States to meet with a man whose main job is to sell electronics products. But Cisco is a special company. Over the six previous years, the company had grown its revenue by twenty-six times, from less than $714 million to nearly $19 billion, and by March 2000 Cisco's stock valuation had hit $531 billion, far higher than that of ExxonMobil or General Motors or General Electric. And Verhofstadt was hardly alone among world leaders in making an effort to meet the Cisco CEO. During the crazed Internet boom of the late 1990s, Chambers was perhaps the most sought-after corporate leader in capitals around the world. In the single year leading up to September 1999, Chambers met with more than thirty heads of state, including Bill Clinton, Tony Blair, and Chinese president Jiang Zemin.[2]

Nor was Chambers just any old salesman. On the contrary, he was a true virtuoso of the razzle-dazzle, one of the finest modern practitioners of an American tradition that wends back through Jim Baker to Ron Popeil to Huey Long to P. T. Barnum. In the mid-1990s, when Chambers was first perfecting the patter that would help propel his company into the stratosphere, he knew that few members of his audiences had any real idea of how the Internet worked, and that fewer yet really cared about the actual technical details. So rather than talk about Cisco's routers and switches and software, Chambers spoke instead of what the Internet could do for people, how it would revolutionize their lives and businesses. His mantra in speech after speech was that "the Internet will change everything."[3] Often it seemed that what Chambers was selling most was change itself. In one 1999 speech at a government technology show, he stated the word "change" fifteen times in only a few minutes.[4]

And Chambers delivered his sermons with an evangelical fervor. Sandy-haired, of moderate height, with pale blue eyes, Cisco's boss is anything but imposing physically.[5] Yet at the height of the Cisco craze in the late 1990s, once Chambers started speaking, he had a way of impressing himself deeply into the minds of his listeners. A son of Charleston, West Virginia's, upper classes, Chambers has an accent that still betrays a trace of the courtly southern gentleman. But he speaks with such speed and such passion that he has more than once been compared to a televangelist. One British paper noted his "preacher's eyes" and how listeners often "feel as though he is trying to save you from damnation."[6] A journalist watching him in action in Hong Kong wrote that it "would not have seemed too strange for him to have called up a member of the audience" and performed a "miracle healing."[7]

Whether he met world leaders in their palaces or waited for them to come to him, Chambers's purpose was never to promote the Internet as an Esperanto-like forger of global togetherness and understanding. Rather, his aim was simply to grow his company fast enough to dominate an industry that was expanding far more rapidly than almost any industry ever before. Like General Electric with its lightbulbs and wires and turbines more than a century previously, Cisco's challenge was to get its new technology into as many markets as possible before any competitor could launch an attack. In the new global marketplace of the 1990s, however, Cisco's challenge was only that much bigger. No longer could a manufacturer aim first to capture the American market and then march from this secured position to battlegrounds overseas. Rather, a "first mover" technology pioneer now had to win all the world at once.

Depending on his audience, Chambers's salesmanship served alternately to obscure and celebrate the two great innovations that enabled Cisco to expand so phenomenally fast. As we will see in the next chapter, Cisco early on developed an audacious acquisition strategy, gobbling up smaller companies filled with technologies and engineers and skilled managers with an astonishing voraciousness. Second, Cisco developed an approach to manufacturing that, for a company that sought to hone an image as a tech leader, was in many senses more profoundly revolutionary than Dell's. Cisco outsourced manufacturing more fully and more rapidly and at an earlier stage in the development of the firm than almost any previous company. At first Cisco developed this outsourcing strategy mainly as an effort to make use of the capital investments of other firms while devoting its own resources to buying and integrating and marketing. But Cisco's whole-hog approach to outsourcing soon developed into a key factor in the company's success. Whereas at General Motors Lopez de Arriortua accelerated an already ongoing process of cutting the company loose in order to protect market share, Cisco turned the task of manufacturing over entirely to others so it could concentrate more single-mindedly on capturing near-absolute control of a brand-new market.[8]

The key decision in Cisco's manufacturing strategy came in early 1994. At the time, company managers knew Cisco was staring at a huge market for its products, which direct the flow of information on the Internet and other networks. Sales of routers were surging, and executives were certain of much more business to come. At the time, Cisco did most of its own manufacturing, mainly in California. But executives were quick to identify manufacturing capacity as one of the main factors likely to constrain the company's growth. Ramping up production cost capital, engineering talent, and management time, and compared to many of its potential competitors Cisco was still a very small company. Further, no matter how many resources the company could round up, there is always an absolute limit to how fast any firm working on its own can expand output. To complicate matters, Cisco had recently purchased another firm that manufactured network switches, and executives now planned many more such acquisitions. This meant the challenge for Cisco's manufacturing team was not simply to multiply the production of routers but also to figure out how to radically expand the output of many other types of devices they had no experience making.

More out of desperation than conviction, Cisco began to look for outside help, especially among the many small companies that specialized in building electronic components on a contract basis for bigger companies. After a pilot project to manufacture routers proved highly successful, Cisco's use of these contract manufacturers, in the words of one senior manager, "just snowballed."[9] Within two years, Cisco had offloaded nearly 75 percent of its manufacturing and soon the company was contracting out even final assembly of its products. By 2000, some 90 percent of Cisco's subassembly work took place outside the company, as Cisco managers kept control only of high-end, developmental production work. This work took place in thirty-four plants around the world, only two of which were owned by Cisco. Of all the people who worked to build Cisco-branded products, only 15 percent were Cisco employees.[10] The reason for such a wholesale outsourcing was not hard to figure out. In 2000, Executive Vice President Carl Redfield estimated that turning over manufacturing to outside contractors each year cuts Cisco's production costs by between $900 million and $1.3 billion.[11]

It would be wrong to think that Cisco thrived only by doing business in unorthodox ways. The management team mastered many traditional business practices, including the carefully managed obsolescence of products, the exploitation of brand and pricing power, and a fanatical focus on keeping customers happy.[12] It would also be wrong to give too much credit for these strategies to Chambers alone. The extreme adaptability that allowed the company to adopt such new approaches was visible in the firm's makeup long before Chambers took over the top spot in early 1995. If anything, the company's core flexibility was evident in the hiring of Chambers in the first place. When the Cisco board began in 1991 to search for someone to run the company over the long term, many on the search team wanted a manager with a background in building things. Instead, they hired a charismatic salesman.

But once he was inside Cisco, Chambers's attitude toward manufacturing did matter, and it only reinforced Cisco's willingness to abandon standard operating procedures. On almost any question about technology and manufacturing, Chambers was a raving agnostic who went beyond even GE's Jack Welch in his refusal to bend his knee to any engineer or operations manager. It wasn't that Chambers was diametrically opposed to manufacturing. It was more that—having spent years hawking products for IBM and Wang—he just didn't care anymore about the building of things. When it came to manufacturing, Chambers had therefore developed two main rules, and both were negative.

First, he hated the "not invented here" mentality of many engineering-driven firms, like IBM, which for years insisted on making almost every piece of every product they delivered.[13] Second, Chambers didn't want to invest any money in China-based production. At both IBM and Wang, Chambers had traveled extensively in Asia and had concluded that it was better to put "your money in a safe deposit box" than to risk it building and operating factories on the Mainland.[14] On the other hand, Chambers had no qualms whatsoever about taking advantage of someone else's decision to risk their capital there, and he saw no reason not to contract for use of a good factory, no matter where it was located.

At the beginning of the decade, General Motors proved that a manufacturer could learn how to survive by outsourcing, and by the middle of the decade Dell had proved how to rise to power by repackaging the work of others in its name. Now Cisco took outsourcing a step further and showed how with remarkable swiftness a company could use the manufacturing capacity of others to—cuckoo-like—dominate an entirely new industrial activity. In the process, Cisco validated the idea that, more than the holding of patents, more than an understanding of process, more than the creative use of cartel and oligopoly power, the key to capturing control of a global market was to focus as little as possible on making things.

Cisco's manufacturing model was new mainly in relation to what had come in the decades immediately before. In many respects, Cisco's strategy was more a rediscovery of an approach to manufacturing tried many times before in many other industries.

How to organize productive work is a subject that has been debated for centuries, not least in the opening chapters of Adam Smith's *The Wealth of Nations*. "The greatest improvement in the productive powers of labour," Smith wrote in Chapter One of the book that would become the fountainhead for the modern study of economics, "and the greater part of the skill, dexterity, and judgment with which it is any where directed, or applied, seem to have been the effects of the division of labour."[15] Smith's purpose in writing about the division of labor was to lay a foundation for a philosophy of economic organization, not to debate different ways in which productive work might be set up more efficiently. That, of course, is the business of business. It is up to the owners of the productive enterprise, or their hired managers, perhaps in concert with the workers, to identify the most efficient way to organize production. Success, for a new business, is measured by the return on the initial investment, and for a more mature business also by its ability to compete. It is ultimately the responsibility of owners and managers to decide how to structure the work and what is the optimal degree of specialization. It is also their job to decide which products and services to make and which to buy—in other words, how much activity to integrate "vertically" into the firm.

There are many ways to define vertical integration within a manufacturing firm. The business historian Alfred D. Chandler focused especially on the efforts by American manufacturers of the late nineteenth century to add marketing and distribution abilities to the basic activity of mass production.[16] The ability to manage the flow of product to the end customer is much more important to the ultimate success of a company, Chandler felt, than whether it made all the components that went into the physical product. Integration can also be horizontal, as when companies buy up their direct competitors. And integration can take place across categories and product lines, in the hope that such amalgamation will allow a more efficient management of the whole. Famous models of this type of integration include General Motors, General Electric, and General Foods.[17]

In the popular mind, however, vertical integration is dominated by the image of the factory. To a large extent, this is due to the outsized shadow cast by Henry Ford, whose immense carmaking business came to define mass manufacturing during the 1910s and 1920s. Ford didn't start off with vertically integrated production, but he did seem to move inexorably in that direction. During his first car-building venture, in 1903, Ford ran into trouble with his investors because he kept fiddling with the manufacture of components like transmissions, rather than simply buying products available on the open market. In his next venture, Ford did compromise and accepted outside sources of supply, as long as they were built to his exact specifications.[18] But this was only temporary. From 1904 to 1926, Ford steadily brought more and more work into the direct control of his corporation. So set was he on absolute control that his main outside supplier, run by the Dodge brothers, broke with him and began assembling its own vehicle in 1914, largely to guarantee itself a long-term outlet for the parts it manufactured.

The culmination of Ford's vision of vertical integration came at the River Rouge industrial complex, built on 2,000 acres three miles outside Detroit. By 1926, when Ford launched his Model A, the Rouge had grown to ninety-three buildings and 75,000 employees, and was able to turn out 4,000 cars per day. The operation was linked together by 120 miles of conveyors, thirty miles of internal roads, and ninety miles of railroad track, including an elevated railway that ran from factory to factory on the complex. Steel emerged from Ford's foundry and passed into the stamping presses and machine shops, then out into buildings that made most of the components, before wending back toward the final assembly line. The Rouge was the single greatest manufacturing complex the world has ever seen. Iron ore and coal were off-loaded at one end; finished automobiles drove onto railroad cars at the other.

Ford's distaste for relying on outside suppliers was extreme. At the Rouge he made his own steel in what was then the largest foundry in the world. He made his own electricity in a power plant able to light a city of 350,000. He sorted his own coal in a facility as big as any upstream near the mines of West Virginia or Pennsylvania. At its peak, Ford's integrationist urge reached far outside the confines of the Rouge itself. He bought up timberland in Michigan, iron ore mines in Minnesota, and for years sought to develop ways to replace petroleum with ethanol made from corn and other farm products. In 1928, angered by a Dutch-Asian rubber cartel, Ford talked the Brazilian government into awarding him a

2.5-million-acre concession on the Tapajos River in the Amazon, where he tried to set up the world's biggest rubber tree plantation.[19] Nor would Ford abide outside transport providers. Ford bought a railway—the Detroit, Toledo & Irontown—and a fleet of Great Lakes ore carriers.

There are many good business reasons to integrate production vertically. Ford did so to grow fast,[20] to ensure greater flexibility in production,[21] and to reduce exposure to the markets for commodities, components, and services. Sears integrated to ensure sufficient supply of certain manufactured goods.[22] GM did so at times to capture the high profits from especially innovative support activities.[23] Sometimes a company will buy a key supplier to make it harder for a new competitor to enter the market.[24] Sometimes companies merely like to advertise their manufacturing macho; well into the 1990s, electronics firms including IBM and Nortel famously manufactured their own screws.

But there are also many good reasons to avoid vertical integration of production.[25] At the time that Ford was striving to encompass as much as possible, no other auto company followed his lead. GM in the 1920s never integrated more than half as much activity as Ford,[26] while the rest of the industry on average manufactured only about a third of its components. When Chrysler was launched in 1924, managers chose to buy almost all their components from outside suppliers.[27] Like Dell and Cisco in the 1990s, Chrysler wanted to avoid tying up capital in buildings and real estate and machines. And like Dell and Cisco, the company was able to innovate faster than its more integrated competitors.[28] So successful was Chrysler's decision to rely on outside suppliers that within a decade the company had surpassed the immense Ford in sales.[29]

Even Ford continued to rethink integration on an almost day-to-day basis. While the company grew in-house content from 45 percent in 1922 to 74 percent of the average car in 1926, Ford reversed course in 1927 almost as soon as he got his Model A into production.[30] Over the next few years, the company farmed more and more work out to suppliers. Finally, during a financial crisis in the early 1950s, a new generation of Ford production engineers overhauled the whole operation, settling for a balance roughly the same as General Motors, with about half of all work taking place outside the company.[31]

The last important model of vertical integration—and the one that would be most in the minds of American manufacturers in the 1990s—was developed in Japan by Toyota. Beginning in 1949, the automaker began to reorganize the ownership and organization of its manufacturing operations, spinning off internal parts-making departments such as Nippondenso, Aisin Seiki, and Toyoda Gosei as separate companies. In less than ten years, the percent of the value added to a Toyota vehicle by Toyota's own workers fell from 75 percent to 25 percent of the total. It is not clear exactly why Toyota chose to do this, though some studies speculate the company was trying to adapt to the U.S.-run occupation government's ultimately doomed effort to break up Japan's large enterprises. But for Toyota, the result was a unique semicaptive supply base. The newly created tier-one suppliers were prohibited from selling to Toyota's archrival Nissan, but they were allowed to scout up business from many other Japanese manufacturers and thereby realize big efficiencies. In this way, Toyota was able to spread the costs and risks of its supply base over a much larger set of customers, while also managing to sever much of its workforce from any direct connection to its main stream of revenue.[32]

In 1937, economist Ronald Coase wrote an article titled "The Nature of the Firm," which was the first important attempt to accommodate economics to the rise of the vertically integrated company. The gist of Coase's argument was an attempt to make sense of the fact that twentieth-century firms like Ford, in the very process of integrating vertically, were internalizing markets and thereby breaking out of the confines of classical economic theory and its reliance on a freely operating "price mechanism" to determine the ideal allocation of resources in an economy. Like Smith, Coase made no attempt to critique how any particular company was organized—what, for instance, any firm might choose to make rather than to buy. What Coase did attempt was two things: First, he believed that since the modern corporations were in effect internalizing marketplaces, it would be valid to extend the tools of classical economics right into the firm itself. Second, Coase sought to make some general observations about what factors tended to limit the vertical integration of a firm and what factors tended to favor such expansion. He singled out three for special mention: new communications technologies, new transportation services, and new management techniques.[33]

In the 1990s, for Cisco and dozens of other companies, every one of these factors was present. Modern logistics and transport services had brought factors of production even on the other side of the world to within twenty-four hours of the home-country assembly line. The Internet and the collapse of telecommunications costs made it much more practical to organize tightly over much wider spaces. And finally, new software tools had radically altered managerial techniques and was shifting power upward within the organization.

Cisco managers responded to this environment with a strategy that was essentially a hybrid of two approaches to integration, both with ample historical basis. Given the existence of a robust base of suppliers and small innovators, Cisco decided to cut loose from the parts of its business that were most difficult to expand organically—namely, manufacturing and R&D. At the same time, Cisco adopted a strategy of acquiring a closely related set of products, much like General Motors in the 1910s or General Foods in the 1920s. The result was that managers, over the course of five years and on a global scale, were able to capture for their company the de facto title of General Internet.

Competition, in both the popular culture and in politics, has traditionally been viewed mainly as a battle that takes place among companies selling the same basic product. But business managers have long known that competition takes place along many other planes as well. The world's best-known business professor, Harvard's Michael Porter, has long held that there are five "underlying forces of competition." In addition to the "intensity of rivalry" among existing competitors, there is the threat posed by the potential entry into the market by new competitors, the threat posed by the potential introduction by other companies of "substitute" products or services, the bargaining power of the people or companies that buy from you, and the bargaining power of the companies that supply to you.[34]

To understand what Cisco achieved with outsourcing, it is important to focus on this last area of competition. The one thing that a manufacturing corporation never wants to do when hiring someone else to produce key components is to give that supplier real pricing power or, worse, the ability to emerge as a direct competitor. For Cisco, the decision to off-load even the final integration and assembly of its products presented many challenges, not least being how to control its suppliers. Whereas a company like Dell sells products developed and manufactured by others, and seeks mainly to stay in position to exploit (but not drive) technologi-cal advances, Cisco still wanted very much to control both the pace and path of technological progress in its industry. This required a new set of strategies and tools for organizing the work done in its name by others.

Economists recognize the ability of a supplier to "hold up" its cus-tomer, in the sense that a supplier can sometimes jack up prices. One of the more notorious such incidents in recent years came when Japanese suppliers of DRAM memory chips—soon after capturing control of the market from American companies in the 1980s—simultaneously cut pro-duction and quickly turned a glut into a very lucrative shortage. Yet in-stances of true holdup are relatively rare in business, mainly because the benefits tend to be fleeting. Customers usually adjust relatively easily, ei-ther by seeking out new suppliers—in the case of the DRAMs, for in-stance, American buyers responded by building up alternative sources in South Korea and Taiwan—by engineering around a particular technol-ogy, by doing the job itself, or by invoking antitrust.

Although it's not a phenomenon recognized in economic theory, the idea that a supplier will somehow evolve into a competitor tends to be a much deeper fear for the average manufacturer. Almost nothing maddens managers more than the prospect of a company they have trained and en-riched, and to which they have transferred technology and knowledge, suddenly taking direct aim on their end customers. It is akin to the fear of Laius, the king of Thebes, upon hearing from the oracle that he would one day die at the hands of his own son.

Instances abound of such "betrayals." In the 1970s, RCA and other American television makers lost their business to the Japanese companies to which they had turned for parts and components.[35] In the 1980s, American bicycle manufacturer Schwinn farmed out most assembly work to Taiwanese bicycle maker Giant, then had to fend off an effort by Giant to buy Schwinn's name and distribution network when that company fell on hard times. In the 1980s, Intel and Microsoft wrested control of the PC market from erstwhile patron IBM. In the 1990s, Taiwan's Acer Corporation succeeded for a few years in competing against its former customers in the U.S. PC industry.

In mature, asset-heavy industries, size provides a lot of protection. Any auto supplier looking to reprise the launch of Dodge by vertically integrating up to the status of lead firm must raise huge sums of money just to get to a point where it can compete with a niche manufacturer like Kia. Not that there have been no recent efforts, as we will see in Chapter Seven. But in the electronics industry, the rise of a new competitor is both very common and potentially very dangerous. The speed at which many technologies evolve means that status as an industry's "first mover" does not guarantee a dominant share of the market for long. The same constellation of contract suppliers that enabled Cisco to grow so rapidly, after all, can be exploited just as easily by any other company.

To counter such dangers, manufacturers over the decades developed a number of strategies to keep themselves in the "command and control role" in the production process. Traditionally, the most important tactic has been to divvy up labor in such a way as to ensure that suppliers cannot learn too much about the core business, and to make sure they never talk directly with the end customer.[36] Lead firms can also always sue suppliers for patent infringement or other violations of their contract.[37] But there are very real limits to what a manufacturer can protect. As Laius found, a baby's feet can be tied, but short of killing the child outright, there's no guarantee you won't meet again one day at the crossroads.

But starting in the mid-1980s, the rise of new information technologies resulted in two changes that over the coming years would give lead firms in the electronics industry much more direct control over their suppliers, and which would go a long way toward eliminating many of the traditional fears of outsourcing. First was the growing conviction among executives that the real value in many products lay not so much in the ability to manufacture the hardware but in the software that tells the hardware what to do. Value, as one seminal article put it in 1991, lay in defining "how computers are used, not how they are built."[38] The second change was the rapid integration of new information technologies into the manufacturing process itself. This gave lead firms the ability to manage their suppliers much more closely, in much greater detail, and with much greater power over day-to-day operations.[39]

For any manufacturer, the ideal is to reach a point where their company not only is able to affect the pace of change of the key technologies within its industry—which gives it more ability to manage its own cash flow and profits—but to determine the direction in which the technologies evolve. In the late 1990s, Berkeley professors Michael Borrus and John Zysman coined the term "Wintelism" to describe how some companies win control over the setting of standards in an unregulated and open system. Based on a common conflation of the words Windows and Intel, Borrus and Zysman defined Wintelism as a standards-setting strategy pioneered by Microsoft and Intel in the mid-1980s, after the two firms had been awarded de facto monopolies from IBM to develop the operating system and key semiconductors for IBM's personal computers. The two upstarts moved first to seize "control" over the "evolution" of the PC's key standards, which they did in alliance with the legions of hardware companies that IBM had licensed to manufacture IBM-compatible products. Once that was accomplished, Microsoft and Intel shifted to a more defensive game, in which they developed "strategies to set and control the evolution of de facto standards," both to prevent IBM from bringing the key PC technologies "back in house," and to fend off all the other upstarts seeking to carve away a chunk of the new business.[40]

In the case of Cisco, the company's key tool for grabbing and keeping control of its industry was its "Internet Operating System," or IOS. This was a Windows-style program that functioned as a sort of electronic railroad track to connect all Cisco's various products to each other, and to any product manufactured by a company that agreed to pay a fee to run on Cisco's track. By 1997, Cisco had awarded licenses to companies ranging from Hewlett-Packard to NEC to Alcatel to Ericsson. And with its market position always under siege, Cisco continued to churn out generation after generation of its operating system, to make it harder for any potential competitor to pry Cisco's customers away from Cisco products.[41] Rather than focusing on manufacturing, Cisco focused on becoming the company that decided what its suppliers manufactured *and* what its competitors manufactured. Cisco became, in the words of Borrus and Zysman, a "pure product definition" company.[42]

Obviously, such a strategy is most possible in electronics-related industries. But as more and more products come to be dominated by electronics controls, such a strategy comes within the reach of more companies. And the effects can be profound. Using such a strategy, lead firms are able to keep a much tighter control over their suppliers, even at times to the point where they feel comfortable relying on single tier-one suppliers.

In recent years, as vertically integrated companies off-loaded more and more of their manufacturing activity, and as new companies grew up amid an ever-wider and -brighter universe of suppliers, we have for all intents witnessed the formation of a new type of system. In the past, competition at the level of the product took place between companies arrayed in a line, between companies that directly managed (if they did not directly own) every stage in bringing their products to market, whether it was the manufacture of screws or the design of the operating system or the marketing of the end product. But with Cisco, as to a lesser degree Microsoft and Intel, we have witnessed the ascension of what can be thought of as the "hub" firm. These are companies that, by becoming the first to truly dominate a sector, emerge as the center of their own systems, with even competitors reduced to the status of satellites.

In the 1950s, General Motors and Ford, in a series of negotiations with the United Auto Workers, agreed to a basic distribution of power and profits within the automotive industry. Roughly half of the value of the average car would be produced in-house by unionized employees at GM and Ford, while half would be produced by outside suppliers where the workforce might or might not be unionized. For more than thirty years, this balance was almost perfectly reflected in the overall employment levels in the industry. Even in hard times, the nearly perfect fifty-fifty split remained intact, as the Big Three and their suppliers tended to lay off and hire workers in almost exact tandem well into the 1980s.[43]

This manager-centered system only began to break down under pressure from Japanese competition. As noted earlier, when the Japanese assault really began to draw blood, managers in the U.S. auto industry were convinced that the main reason their companies kept losing market share to Toyota and Nissan was the high cost and high rigidity of their unionized workforce. Now, with market share and profits both falling, the automotive firms for the first time in decades launched a real assault on the

UAW. Unions had always fought on two main fronts. One battle was for decent wages and benefits for the workers employed directly by the lead manufacturers. The other battle was to maintain the percentage of the overall jobs that were kept in-house, under the direct protection of the unions. But in contracts negotiated in 1987 and 1990, the UAW finally ceded on the outsourcing question. In exchange for a commitment to protect all existing assembly workers from losing their jobs through outsourcing, the union traded away the fifty-fifty division of work between the lead firms and their suppliers. This meant that as the workforces of GM, Ford, and Chrysler shrank through retirement and attrition, the companies now had more freedom to buy more of their parts from outside companies.

When a company like Cisco accelerates the disintegration of manufacturing activity within the lead corporation, the result means very different things for the shareholder and for the worker. For the shareholder, one of the prime benefits of off-loading work from the lead firm onto other companies is to transform fixed costs into variable costs. Any firm able to slough off plants and workers in bad times is better able to protect its margins, and hence its return on investment, and highly outsourced companies are obviously much more able to do this. Such flexibility often runs counter to the instincts of the engineers and scientists who once dominated the ranks of corporate leadership, and who by nature tend to value stability and loyalty. But such flexibility is one of the oldest and most enduring dreams of capital, and it has been pursued often with great vigor by the salesmen and financial experts who dominate the ranks of CEOs today.

For the average employee, however, such disintegration usually tends to mean less stability in the day-to-day workplace. As more and more of the functions once performed by the lead corporation are converted into commodities that can be purchased easily from outside suppliers, more people find themselves working for contract manufacturers and contract accounting firms and contract programmers. This means that fewer people have any ability to tap directly into the stream of revenue generated by the lead firm.

It's not surprising that American companies were the first to embrace outsourcing with such gusto. The American social system is neither as robust nor as universal as that of most other industrial nations, and American employers have much more cultural and legal leeway to seek out less formal relationships with their workers. In Europe, where the modern social benefits system dates to the government of Otto von Bismarck in Germany in the 1880s, most nations offer a generous set of social "guarantees." In Japan, the basic benefits are not nearly as robust as those in Europe, but most workers still enjoy a near guarantee of lifetime work.[44] In the United States, by contrast, until well into the twentieth century there were very few cultural norms or laws that required businesses to provide anything more than a day's pay for a day's work.

This finally began to change three years into the Great Depression, with the election of Franklin Roosevelt. Working with progressive members of Congress and labor unions, the new Administration cobbled together a rather ad hoc benefits system, made up mainly of state and local programs combined with federal incentives to employers. To this day, with the exception of Social Security and Medicare, no social benefit in America is truly national in nature.[45]

This patchwork nature of the American social system meant that individual companies often faced very different sets of obligations, depending on where they were located. And it often meant that even though American corporations were more free to fire employees than were most of their overseas competitors, they were often expected to manage and pay for health and pension coverage that elsewhere was borne entirely by the state.

As a result, the average big American business has always been forced to view its social responsibilities as a line item that at times might prove a big liability in competition, both at home and abroad. Even so, from the 1940s through the 1970s the average American worker enjoyed a steady ratcheting up of protections, benefits, and purchasing power. Well into the 1980s, big manufacturers generally didn't fret about rigid work rules or benefits packages that seemed overly generous, regarding these as the inescapable costs of ensuring that the continuity of their business was never in danger. Keeping a few surplus workers on the payroll was, after all, not much different from the then-common American practice of maintaining big piles of excess inventory.

The big turning point came in the early 1980s, especially in industries under direct assault by the now-unfettered Japanese. General Electric

CEO Jack Welch was one of the first to upset the old social balances. Within a year and a half of taking over GE in April 1981, he had cut 35,000 employees from a payroll of 404,000, and over the next year he would carve away another 37,000.[46] Other industries were not far behind, and the automakers in particular would soon take up the machete with a vengeance. Beginning in 1987, for the first time in decades more autoworkers labored for suppliers than for the Big Three. Over the next ten years, this differential grew fast, to a point where in 1996 there were only some 350,000 workers still directly employed by the big auto manufacturers, while 500,000 labored for outside suppliers.[47] During the same period, the average wage in the industry fell, and the difference in pay for in-house and contracted workers grew wider. In 1987, employees at the assemblers earned about $18.50 per hour, versus $15 per hour for workers at the outside suppliers. By 1996, pay for the assembly workers had risen slightly, to about $19 per hour, but pay at the average outside supplier had fallen to roughly $14 per hour.

Nor was this phenomenon limited to heavy industrial firms. The decline in employment extended throughout the U.S. economy, with the workforce at the average Fortune 500 corporation shrinking dramatically from the 1970s onward. Between 1973 and 1993, the median number of employees in Fortune 500 U.S. industrial firms fell from 16,018 to 10,136, or some 37 percent.[48] Big unionized firms were among the most aggressive at shedding jobs. Between 1980 and 2002, General Motors cut direct employment by 53 percent, Xerox by 44 percent, and DuPont by 42 percent.[49]

Yet once set in motion, the process of shifting work to outside suppliers tended to quickly spread far beyond the unionized employee and the assembly line worker. By its very nature, the disintegration of the modern vertically integrated corporation also had to fall hard on middle management, which had arisen in the first place to serve as the information system of the integrated enterprise.[50] In the 1980s and 1990s, companies discovered that many of the routine tasks of middle management were ideally suited for automation and for outsourcing.[51] In 1912, widespread fear that new "scientific management" methods promoted by the manufacturing consultant Frederick Winslow Taylor were "deskilling" American workers led to hearings in Congress. In an appearance before the House Labor Committee, Taylor did little to help the matter, declaring that the main job of management was the "deliberate gathering in . . . of all of the great mass of traditional knowledge, which in the past has been in the heads of the workmen, and in the physical skill and knack of the workmen, which he has acquired through years of experience."[52] In the 1990s, the emergence of advanced software systems seemed to have at last enabled such a "gathering in" of the work of management itself.[53]

For years, John Chambers at Cisco worked to cultivate a reputation as a man loath to lay off any employee. Time and again, he told the story of his experience at Wang Computer, where he was bumped up to CEO in 1990 just in time to lay off the last 5,000 workers and close down the firm, which had run out of cash. At the very height of Cisco's ascension in the late 1990s, in interviews with reporters, in presentations to investors, Chambers spoke repeatedly of how terrible it had been to fire so many people, and of how he never wanted to repeat the experience. The message, of course, was that Cisco was a different sort of company, that it somehow had found a way to be much more fair to its workers. To underscore his conviction, Chambers even hinted that upon retirement he would dedicate himself to the teaching of "business ethics."[54]

As it turned out, Chambers did have to eat his words. After the sudden brutal economic downturn of early 2001, Cisco for the first time ever cut its direct payroll, from 38,402 employees down to 34,446 over two years. But the reason Chambers even dared to make such a claim in the first place was that Cisco's core employees were cushioned by vast legions of temporary workers. At the height of the market, only one in seven of the people engaged in the manufacture of Cisco products worked directly for the company.[55] Most instead labored for contractors that Cisco could cut off at will. And not surprisingly, many of these contract manufacturers tended to keep half or more of their employees as temporaries. During Cisco's slide in 2001, many tens of thousands of workers did lose their jobs, at least for a while. But unlike with GE in the early 1980s, the slaughter took place far out of sight of the CEO, or the board, or the business press, or even the employees at the core company, being spread instead out over an array of small contractors located throughout the United States, and in nations like Mexico, China, Brazil, and Hungary.

The shape of a world remade by outsourcing had become clear as early as 1994, when Manpower surpassed General Motors to become America's largest employer, with some 650,000 people in its temporary work system. (Both Manpower and General Motors have since been passed by Wal-Mart.) The Japanese, through the Toyota model, taught the Americans a few things about how to make the supply chain more flexible, not least as a way to cut back radically on the cost of inventory. In the 1980s and 1990s, American companies—inspired to no small degree by Cisco—got back into the game in part by teaching the world a few lessons about how to use Japanese tricks to make the American workforce—indeed, the global workforce—more flexible and far less expensive.

In the early 1990s, when Cisco had yet to register a $1 billion year and when Dell was recovering from one of its various near-death experiences, a lot of manufacturing experts were busy talking about what they called the "virtual" corporation and "virtual" manufacturing. One of the more influential descriptions came from a former Intel vice president, William H. Davidow. The "ideal" future corporation, he wrote, is one able to "instantaneously" make products "customized in response to customer demand."[56]

By this time, many U.S. companies felt they had mastered at least the rudiments of the Toyota system, and a number of these firms were now looking for ways to somehow out-Japanese the Japanese. Few American manufacturers doubted that their future success lay in somehow further improving the operations of the factory itself. As one article put it, "the factory will be the hub of their efforts to get and hold customers."[57] The idea was not merely to match the Japanese at their game but to leapfrog right past them to a form of production that was vastly more lean and flexible than anything Taiichi Ohno had ever imagined, to a sort of Jetsons-like ability to form almost anything instantaneously out of whatever random collection of atoms happened to be lying about.

Sure it was getting ever easier to locate factories anywhere in the world and to tap into far-off suppliers of inexpensive labor. But it was exactly this distance, many of the gurus of virtual manufacturing felt, that was likely to prove deadly to the manufacturer of tomorrow. A virtual corporation, Davidow wrote, will "abhor distance. If it can find a friendly environment close to customers, it will want to locate there. Being close will enable it to be more responsive."[58] To emphasize his point, he wrapped his vision in the American flag, decrying America's loss of its "production skills," inveighing against those who preached "deindustrialization" in favor of becoming a pure service economy.

Yet like so much in America's ever-churning sea of business, this vision of virtual manufacturing as a more perfect production technique would soon be inverted completely. The key factor in the sudden reversal was that many American companies were discovering that their products were once again highly competitive, both at home and overseas. Years of Japanese-influenced efficiency campaigns had cut production costs, often drastically. So, too, the rapid increase in sourcing from factories located in places like Mexico and China. So, too, the massive readjustment of the dollar-yen exchange rate engineered by the Reagan Administration in 1987. With surprising abruptness, the cost gap that had long existed between American and Japanese producers had all but disappeared. This meant that Americans now found themselves with not one but two options. They could push on in a never-ending effort to out-Japanese the Japanese in the business of making things. Or they could revert to the more American tradition of regarding manufacturing as only one of the many pieces that make up a successful enterprise, a piece that is by no means the most important. American executives have for most of a century believed that competition rarely takes place solely on the product-versus-product level, but rather more on the level of management team versus management team.[59] As Alfred P. Sloan Jr. wrote in 1963, the "elementary functions of a manufacturing *business*" were "engineering, production, sales, *and* finance."[60]

Many American companies did try earnestly to take manufacturing to some next level. But many of these firms soon found themselves bucking ever-stronger countercurrents, the fiercest of which came from the growing reliance on outside manufacturers by companies like Dell and Cisco. By its very nature, outsourcing tends to mean that once one competitor in any industrial sector turns to cheap outside suppliers, the resulting pricing pressures will usually force even the most powerful of its integrated competitors to follow. Michael Porter put it well, in an article in which he warned companies not to unleash the genie of outsourcing if at all possible. Outsourcing, Porter wrote, has a "dark side when it comes to industry structure." By forcing competitors to rely on the same vendors for many components, outsourcing lowers the market barriers that keep out new entrants and shifts competition from quality and service into the realm of prices. Ultimately, Porter concluded, outsourcing can cause all companies in a sector to lose much of their control over their own businesses.[61]

However dangerous outsourcing might be for already established companies, for upstart firms like Cisco it was viewed as perhaps the only path to riches. And the fact that Cisco proved to be a phenomenal success helped in turn to revolutionize the whole image of outsourcing. Before Cisco, hiring other companies to manufacture for you was widely viewed as a sign of weakness, an indication that your engineers were somehow not up to the task of production. Most companies that regarded themselves as manufacturers therefore tended to hide the fact when they outsourced production work, especially of any key component or final assembly. And at first, Cisco's outsourcing strategy was in fact widely derided by managers at many other companies. As one editor at *Forbes,* in a book on the company, summed up such thinking, Cisco had become "simply an empty vessel for selling products created by others, manufactured by others, and installed by others."[62]

Yet it wasn't long before Chambers and Cisco's other top executives began to redefine manufacturing fashion. Armed with one of the hottest stocks of the decade, he no longer needed to use his sophisticated shtick to misdirect potential customers away from too close a look at Cisco's manufacturing techniques. On the contrary, Chambers now began to use Cisco's outsourcing strategy as a prime selling point. The very best example of all the glorious things a company could accomplish by embracing the Internet was right here, in Cisco's own outsourced manufacturing system.[63] The Internet, so the story went, was what had enabled Cisco to off-load the dirty business of making things, and once free of this weight, to explode in size and scale and power.

So of all the companies that pioneered new outsourcing arrangements in the 1990s, it was Cisco more than any other that made a concerted effort to redefine "virtual" manufacturing to mean not a much more intimate coordination among designers and engineers and workers on a nearby factory floor, but instead a near-absolute divorce of the lead firm from the actual job of making things. When Cisco vice president Don

Listwin called Cisco's approach "not-at-all manufacturing," or when the company's top logistics manager said "the ideal is for Cisco not to touch that product ever," they very much helped to set the tone for how Wall Street came to view manufacturing during the latter years of the decade. And this was as something to off-load as fast as possible.

Rather than being celebrated as one of the great competitive arts, indeed as one of the great human arts, manufacturing was ever more loudly dismissed as a business dead end, a sort of junkyard inhabited by the greasy kids who took high school shop class and raced unmuffled cars. "Suddenly, factories, trucks, salespeople, and other assets that once defined most companies' competitive edges [have] become a liability," one reporter wrote. The advanced machines that only a few years ago had seemed the basis for the future were now judged as no more attractive than an "outdated power plant" or some other "near-worthless stranded asset." In the age of the Internet, thanks largely to the sales effort of the company whose business was to vend the hardware of the Internet, capital had come to believe that "speed trumps mass almost every time."[64]

Of course, no matter the rhetoric, somewhere someone must actually spin raw materials into a finished physical product. Someone somewhere must oversee the design and configuration of what the lead firm sells. Someone must stamp and press and mold, someone must plug and assemble and test, someone must load the software and box up the product. "Not-at-all manufacturing" ultimately means only that you have hired someone else to do the work.

At the time when Cisco first began to experiment with the radical outsourcing of production in the mid-1990s, Flextronics was still a little-known contract manufacturer based in Singapore. With only three small factories and some $100 million in revenue, the company was a distant number twenty-two in what was then a small and inchoate industry, in which a scattered set of relatively low-tech firms produced commodity components for big companies and managed some assembly work for smaller firms. Yet over the next decade Flextronics' growth, and that of a small cohort of similarly aggressive and creative contract manufacturers, not only directly paralleled the rise of Cisco and other lead manufacturers, it at times far outpaced even the most successful of the bigger firms. In the ten years starting in 1993, Flextronics multiplied its revenues more than 100 times, or about four times as much as Cisco over the same period.

Any company like Cisco that chooses to outsource large segments of its production operation has two real choices to manage the resulting network of activity efficiently. First is to handle the process in-house. For years, this was the practice at such early masters of contract manufacturing as Hewlett-Packard, which farmed out work to hundreds of distinct suppliers while keeping overall control for integrating the work. The second option is to outsource as much as possible the responsibility for managing the outsourced system to a few trusted companies. This, in essence, was the model that Cisco adopted in the early 1990s, when it turned to Flextronics and the other top contract manufacturers. In many senses, Flextronics and top competitors like Jabil Circuit and Solectron[65] rose to power not because they were especially adept at manufacturing but because they promised to take over the task of managing the entire production operation for firms like Cisco.

To understand what Flextronics provides to a company like Cisco, it helps to look at the vision that animated company CEO Michael Marks even before he took over control of the company in January 1994. A student of Ford's River Rouge strategy, Marks says that from the first he dreamed of growing Flextronics into a vertically integrated producer, able to handle multiple steps in the production chain, as well as some distribution. Marks believed that no matter how good a company became at managing its logistics, there were still real long-term efficiencies available for anyone who could afford to locate multiple production facilities close to one another. In the short run, Marks figured that simply being able to integrate the still-scattered activities was itself a service he could sell.

As it proved, Marks would achieve his dream of a coherently integrated company only after a very roundabout journey. In the early 1990s, Flextronics and the other contract manufacturers were still small companies with a very urgent need to build up revenue in whatever way they could. As a result, all of these firms for years focused almost entirely on bulking up, by signing as many contracts as possible with the Cisco-like upstarts of the era, and by scooping up whatever manufacturing operations the big, vertically integrated companies tossed off in their ever more desperate efforts to keep up with the upstarts. As a result, by early in the new century, Flextronics was able to boast a highly diverse customer list. For the once proudly self-sufficient telecommunications manufacturer Nortel, Flextronics handled all manufacturing. For Microsoft, Flextronics managed the design and building of Xbox video game consoles. For cell phone maker Ericsson and its partner Sony, Flextronics handled all manufacturing and logistics. Other important customers included onetime manufacturing pioneers Xerox and Casio. The customer lists at the other leading contract manufacturers were just as varied and just as studded with the names of the industrial stars of generations past. In less than a decade, each had accumulated dozens or even hundreds of electronics plants, sometimes in more than twenty nations, usually with little seeming pattern, purpose, or coherent internal organization.

For any manufacturing traditionalist, the contract manufacturing model can seem shockingly polygamous. At many of Flextronics's plants, the company has set up multiple assembly lines to serve multiple customers, locating the product runs of even vicious rivals right next to each other on the factory floor. A telecom product stamped with the Cisco brand may be assembled within a few feet of a product stamped Nortel, in a process overseen by a single group of workers and technicians. But even the most paranoid of the big branded companies have learned quickly to accept this arrangement, as such pooling of people and machines reduces the cost of manufacturing by between 10 and 20 percent compared to dedicating a plant to a single company.[66]

Not surprisingly, contract manufacturers have emerged in many other industries, including clothes, toys, shoes, pharmaceuticals, and semiconductors, even brewing and the processing of food.[67] The model is increasingly common in aerospace, and it is growing especially fast in the automotive industry. In 2000, the five biggest North American automotive suppliers—Delphi, Visteon, Lear, Johnson Controls, and TRW—registered more than $85 billion in sales, up by more than half in only five years.[68]

In the case of Flextronics, the company still appears in many ways to be highly scattered, having to coordinate management of production operations located in more than 100 separate sites in twenty-seven nations on four continents. Yet it is increasingly clear that Marks's original vision continues to shape Flextronics, especially as the company shifts more and more of its new business to six highly vertically integrated industrial parks, in Shanghai and Doumen in China, and in Poland, Hungary, Mexico, and Brazil.

Not all Flextronics competitors follow this same strategy, but in general the trend among contract manufacturers is toward ever bigger, more global suppliers capable of ever more complex integration of manufacturing activity.[69] Cisco may have revolutionized how people perceive and value manufacturing as a human activity. Yet Cisco's freedom to embrace and preach "virtual" production was made possible almost entirely by the emergence of companies able to do the real work of manufacturing while posing no real competitive threat. In many senses, Flextronics and the other contract manufacturers are the powers that made possible Cisco's power. But theirs is a limited power, that of a valued but always expendable employee. In a new global economy populated by ever more aristocratic and even dilettantish lead firms, Flextronics and its colleagues have come to serve increasingly as the foremen, responsible for rounding up the workers and getting them to work.[70]

B y the end of the 1990s, it was clear that an entirely new industrial hierarchy had been created, mainly by American corporations. It was, as one expert at MIT's Industrial Performance Center put it, "a new American model of industrial organization."[71] This was not the web of largely independent and largely equal companies imagined a decade ago by Robert Reich. Instead, it was a system that increasingly tended to center real power in a single first-mover company in each industry. It is a system that is not "American" in any geographic sense; on the contrary, it very much depends on a global scale. But it is a system designed to be especially amenable to American capitalized companies, with their overriding desire to protect their own profit margins at the expense of other people's capital.

From the point of view of American shareholders, the new model delivers many very real benefits. Initially, the new hierarchical network model of production helped many U.S. firms—especially in the electronics industry—to counter efforts by Japanese companies to monopolize more industrial activities. Second, at least temporarily, this new model of net-worked outsourcing has eliminated the fear that the suppliers on which the lead firms depend will grow into potential competitors (unlike Tai-wanese suppliers like Acer and Mitac, which tried to go head-to-head with their erstwhile patrons).[72] Third, the new global production hierarchy helps to make the world a simpler place for America's big electronics firms by enabling them to quickly order up manufacturing services in almost any region of the world, be it in response to political or economic pressures. Fourth, and in the long run most important, the new system has proven to be very effective at enabling lead firms like Cisco to consolidate and better concentrate their power over supply networks. By placing erstwhile inter-nal operations on the other end of a contract or a series of contracts, these lead firms gain much greater overall leverage vis-à-vis the individual sup-plier, worker, and government. This in turn gives these firms much more leverage to use against their slower-moving direct competitors.

When the modern American corporation first took shape between the 1870s and the 1920s, many firms vertically integrated their supply and manufacturing operations as a way to exert much more direct control over the markets for the materials and services (including manufacturing services) on which they depended. The general goal was to dampen fluc-tuations in prices and to create more predictability in the flow of cash within their internalized system. In the 1990s, by contrast, Cisco led the way in undoing this process, not least so as to be able to take more advan-tage from these same fluctuations. Indeed, a growing number of large firms today view the rise and fall of prices for inputs like labor and raw materials not as a problem to be smoothed out by shelling out capital to bring more activities under the direct control of the firm's management, but rather as a never-ending opportunity to ratchet down costs and hence perpetuate profit margins. And so today's top firms are increasingly de-signed to play country against country, supplier against supplier, and worker against worker. General Electric CEO Jeffrey Immelt put it suc-cinctly in a recent annual report. The "most successful China strategy," he wrote, "is to capitalize on its market growth while exporting its defla-tionary power."[73]

We tend to view outsourcing as either a win-win situation in which a rich country off-loads low-skilled work onto a poorer one, resulting in a more efficient overall economy, or as a zero-sum win-lose situation in which one nation's workers gain at the direct expense of the workers in another nation. But in a growing number of instances it appears that outsourcing may well be a lose-lose situation, at least for the workers and suppliers in the industries directly affected. As we will see in more detail in Chapter Seven, American workers are by no means the only ones caught in these downdrafts.[74]

The "business of manufacturing," to borrow the phrasing of GM's longtime president Alfred Sloan, for the fastest-moving firms in the 1990s ceased to involve the actual transformation of matériel into product. Rather, for Cisco and the other most successful firms, the business of manufacturing became to structure a system of sourcing that enabled the lead corporation to exploit differences in wages, skills, regulation, tax policy, subsidies, and infrastructure in nations around the world more effectively than its direct competitors. One result was a huge but one-time leap in efficiency. Another was a phenomenal shift of power—away from individual workers, and small firms, and slower-moving big firms, and the state—to the companies with the most nimble management teams and to the capital that backs them.

A third result, which for our purposes is most important, was a phenomenally fast extinction of the traditional vertically integrated producer, and of that producer's traditional focus on mitigating risk and planning for the future. To some extent, the old "modern" twentieth-century manufacturers have now been replaced by newly reintegrated manufacturing services firms like Flextronics. But for the foreseeable future, these contract manufacturers will likely remain very much subservient to the lead corporations, which have the power and scale to keep them constantly off balance, and constantly focused only on delivering the goods as cheaply as possible, and constantly distracted from the producer's traditional role of caring for the system as a whole.

CHAPTER SIX

THE GREAT CONSOLIDATION
Of Scope & Scale

Jurgen Schrempp was back. Less than two years after his border-busting deal for Chrysler, the Daimler-Benz CEO was looking for another automaker to buy. Almost unknown in the United States before he gobbled up the country's number-three car company, Schrempp had since been puffed to near-heroic proportions by journalists on both sides of the Atlantic. Whereas Lopez de Arriortua at General Motors was welcomed as an eccentric who promised to transplant hybrid European production techniques to America, Schrempp was embraced precisely because he seemed so utterly American, in his audacity and in his spirit, if not entirely his personal style. Yes, Daimler had purchased an American icon, but the goal seemed not so much to impose German order on the Yanks as to transfer some American spunk and audacity to an old-style European firm. The only real question, it seemed, was whether the world was "big enough" to contain the energy and vision of this self-made tycoon.[1]

Not that Daimler was yet done digesting Chrysler. The 1998 deal had set a new record for industrial mergers, and it was one of the biggest cross-frontier deals ever. It lashed together one of Germany's "national champions," a firm renowned for precision and conservatism, with a company known for daring, dash, efficiency, and, at the time the deal was struck, profitability. Laws and customs in both nations had been challenged, but in this the deal seemed not so much revolutionary as pioneering, even necessary. The automobile industry, which only a decade before had boasted some forty players around the world, was down to half that and by most accounts was fast coming under the control of six dominant players. Schrempp wanted newly formed DaimlerChrysler to be one of those six, and the way to do that seemed to be to gobble yet another firm now and digest the consequences and debt later. Chrysler and Mercedes together still ranked only a distant fifth in the number of cars built each year, far behind General Motors, Ford, Toyota, and Volkswagen. With all of these now scoping out their own acquisition targets, Schrempp felt a need to stay in the game and get what he could. Top among his targets were France's Peugeot, Italy's Fiat, and Japan's Honda.

Lean, tanned, and tall, his face made sharp by square wire-rimmed glasses, Schrempp exuded an almost manic energy and strength, both inside the office and out. He loved being hailed as the "man who swallowed Chrysler," and he acted like a real-life mogul with outsized appetites. He chain-smoked Marlboros, worked from dawn until well past dusk, washed down plates of sausage and potatoes with fine red wine, and not infrequently partied past midnight with his personal secretary, Lydia Deininger. Still in his mid-fifties, Schrempp clambered up mountains, hunted game on his own reserve in South Africa, played jazz trumpet, and installed a bar in his new office in Chrysler's Detroit headquarters. America boasted a surfeit of feisty, quirky, brilliant, driven CEOs, but Schrempp was one of the few foreign corporate leaders who had ever earned a real rock-and-roll reputation. A born iconoclast, Schrempp had to master his skills far from the stultifying corporate corridors of Stuttgart, spending more than a decade outside of Germany, first as a salesman and then chairman of Daimler-Benz's South Africa division, then as head of a Cleveland-based trucking unit. Now he seemed intent on smashing Germany's staid corporate culture, and at home he was widely reviled for firing workers, abandoning lagging projects, even pulling the plug on Daimler's aircraft-manufacturing division, the once-famed Fokker. In the process, he had earned such un-German nicknames as "Gravedigger" and "Rambo." Most flattering, perhaps, for a CEO on the move was to be called "Neutron Jurgen," after that most macho of all CEOs, "Neutron Jack" Welch.[2]

Schrempp liked to move fast, light, quietly, then hit hard. And nowhere was this MO on better display than in the Chrysler takeover. Yet however stealthy and dramatic that deal might have been, in retrospect it is most notable for the lack of any strong nationalistic reaction in America once it was revealed. Sony's purchase of CBS Records in January 1988 and Columbia Pictures in November 1989 had brought out the long knives. Now, less than a decade later, the sell-off of an actual industrial jewel elicited not panic but, on the contrary, a sort of excitement about the promise of a more perfectly and efficiently "globalized" world. Heralded by the *Wall Street Journal* under a banner headline as the beginning of a "New World Order," the takeover more gaudily than any other event of the decade signaled to Americans that business was now truly global in scale and scope.[3]

Not that there was no sadness. Chrysler had been a firm for which many Americans actually felt a certain fondness. Much smaller than globe-spanning General Motors and Ford, Detroit's number-three company had evolved into a sort of de facto flag carrier, especially after American taxpayers helped to bail the company out in 1980. Despite relying on such government largesse, Chrysler managed to retain the image of a plucky challenger that it had developed in the 1950s when it alone had stayed the course while such icons as Packard, Studebaker, Nash, and Hudson were disappearing from the American road. The spirit of the company seemed best captured in the bluster of former CEO Lee Iacocca, if not in his sometimes crude anti-Japanese rants, at least in his 1980s campaign to raise the funds to refurbish the Statue of Liberty. It was a spirit evident in the great glittering spire soaring up from the firm's famous former headquarters in Manhattan, where rays of light shoot from a fresco of hubcaps and hood ornaments, all stamped of stainless steel. It was a spirit that seemed to live on now in the vehicles themselves; at the time of the takeover, Chrysler was building some of the smartest and sexiest cars on the road, including the PT Cruiser and the Plymouth Prowler.

Americans were not alone in assuming a more cosmopolitan attitude toward global-scale business. Much more striking in this respect was the lack of nationalistic reaction in Japan to Renault's purchase that same year of debt-debilitated Nissan. For years Tokyo had battled viciously to keep foreign firms even from selling car parts in Japan, but now the country had quietly resigned itself to the naming of Brazilian-born Carlos Ghosn, an executive known as Le Cost Killer, as Nissan's chief operating officer and de facto head. This reversal was so dramatic that many Americans, despite their own carefully affected nonchalance about the takeover of Chrysler, couldn't help but gloat. Only a decade earlier, as one article in *Time* put it, Nissan's success had given "weight to the myth that Japanese companies were run by enlightened executives who worked in frictionless synchronicity with workers to produce superior cars."[4] Now that myth seemed finally and absolutely smashed—by, of all people, the French.

One reason for the lack of a nationalistic reaction in America and Japan and elsewhere was the growing belief that the globalization of industry had at last proven its ability to grow and spread wealth in the real world. Nowhere did this seem more evident than in auto manufacturing. For years, no other industry was regarded as more fundamental to the wealth and health of the nation. For much of the twentieth century, the ability to build cars had been regarded as the keystone of any industrial base, the foundation for all other production-oriented activity. As Chalmers Johnson put it in his book on Japan's industrial policy, automobile manufacturing was "economically strategic," equaled in importance only by petrochemicals and steel.[5] Beginning especially in the 1950s, many nations that had never had any real automobile industry nurtured their car builders in the hope that a whole cluster of other industrial activities would grow up around them.[6]

But now proof seemed to be piling up that such nationalistic policies actually restricted growth more than they promoted it. *The Economist* eagerly pointed this out in an article published two days after the Daimler-Chrysler tie-up was announced, highlighting especially how Britain's own auto industry had fared since London had abandoned efforts to protect domestic automakers in 1980. The British then watched foreign buyers gobble up every one of the country's big manufacturers, yet nearly two decades later British workers in British plants actually produced twice as many cars.[7] Then there was Portugal. Though this country had never been an automotive power, integration with Europe had paved the way for robust investment, and the tiny nation now exported some 200,0000 cars per year, built not by any Portuguese carmaker but by Volkswagen, Toyota, Citroën, and others. What better proof could there be of Ricardo's theory? Only now, rather than trading wool for wine, the nations of Europe—under the direction of global-minded companies—were trading engines for transmissions and alternators for axles.

By the time Schrempp wandered back into the market for another car-maker, the dealmaking mania in the automotive industry had already peaked. The very height of the frenzy had been reached in the spring of 1998, when his own play for Chrysler, coming in the midst of Asia's deep financial crisis, had unleashed one of the most mad scrambles for new footing ever seen in a mature industry. At once terrified by the seeming surfeit of capacity in the global market, and made ravenous by the image of Japanese and Korean carmakers pleading desperately for loans, auto-motive executives in America and Europe seemed to revert to a more primitive state of existence. Rather than dignified masters of a century-old business that had remade the face and pace of the world, they now at times appeared more like members of the Donner Party. No one knew who was buying whom, but every few weeks there was one less soul sit-ting next to the fire. Schrempp, even as he was laying his plans for Chrysler, was approached by Ford CEO Alex Trotman, who wanted to buy Daimler-Benz.[8] Ford was also known to be keen on Honda and BMW (which had weakened itself by purchasing Rover).[9] Of the hunters, Trotman looked especially dangerous, as his company had socked away $23 billion in cash. Yet sometimes even Ford was mentioned as a poten-tial target.

There were still some real limits to how much the automotive industry could be consolidated, and where. Even at the peak of the delirium, no one really imagined Tokyo or Washington or Paris allowing a total takeover of their carmaking companies. At least for the moment, a cer-tain Triadic sentiment lingered, and of the six global combines that were expected to emerge, it was widely believed that two would be based in North America, two in Europe, and two in Asia. And to the surprise of many, the Korean government managed to keep most of its car industry under national control. Although it ultimately was forced to sacrifice number-three automaker Daewoo to GM for $400 million,[10] Seoul man-aged to orchestrate a buyout of the country's anemic number-two car-maker Kia by number-one carmaker Hyundai.[11]

But Schrempp did get himself one more important scalp, which was Mitsubishi's car division. The Japanese conglomerate that only a decade earlier had raised the ire of Americans by taking over Rockefeller Center now sold off a controlling stake in its automaking unit to Daimler-

Chrysler for $2 billion. Right at the dawn of the new millennium, Jurgen Schrempp was finally able to boast that he had at last transformed his company into a true global player. "We have closed the circle," he said. "We have covered all the markets of the world."[12]

As big as the Daimler-Chrysler deal loomed within the automotive industry and in the eyes of the press, it barely registered on a list of the top acquisitions of the 1990s. Of all the deals in 1998, for instance, the takeover of Chrysler ranked eighth, far behind Exxon's purchase of Mobil, or the Travelers Group acquisition of Citicorp, or any of a number of fat deals in telecommunications.[13] By the time the M&A fever finally broke halfway through 2000, scores of industries in dozens of nations would be entirely reshaped. And by this time the numbers made it amply clear, if there were still any doubters, that the world had just witnessed "the greatest merger and acquisition boom in history."[14]

It was also clear that this M&A boom was different in nature from previous booms. In the 1960s, the main goal was to make conglomerates; in the 1980s, the main goal was to break up those conglomerates. In the 1990s, however, the goal was to rationalize world industry on a global scale, to organize as much as possible along truly global lines. After all, the boom had been set in motion by three separate political events at the beginning of the decade: the collapse of Communism, the creation of the European Union, and the signing of NAFTA. Then, even before manufacturers had completed adjusting to the world's new tri-regional structure, the process was reshaped entirely by another political event—the signing of the Uruguay Round of the GATT—which suddenly seemed to render much of their recent investments somewhat redundant.

The roots of the effort to rationalize industry on a global scale actually dated to the early 1980s, especially Jack Welch's famous speech in December 1981 when he laid down the rules that would guide his company's investments. General Electric, he said, would henceforth occupy either the "number-one or number-two" position in all of its hundreds of individual businesses. In cases where this was not already true, GE would either grow or acquire its way quickly into one of the top two positions, and if it couldn't the company would simply get out of the business.[15]

Most immediately and practically, this meant that GE intended to steer clear of any direct competition with Japanese mass producers, which Welch regarded as "virtually invincible in high-repetition, precision man-ufacturing."[16] Within only a few years, however, such thinking had helped the company to develop a truly global vision of industrial marketplaces. In 1986, Welch created a powerful new vice president to oversee GE's inter-national strategy, dubbing his new executive "Mr. Globalization." In 1989 he began to develop what would come to be known as GE's "boundary-less" philosophy.[17]

Though Welch's thinking was highly influential around the world, it wouldn't be until nearly a decade later that efforts to rationalize industry at a global scale would finally shift into overdrive. The immediate cause was a cascading collapse of Asian economies in 1997 and 1998, known popularly as the Asian Contagion. Thailand and South Korea were hard-est hit, but even once mighty Japan was left tottering. In reality, the Asian financial crisis had little to do with industrial overcapacity and lots to do with the weaknesses inherent in the overly indebted but largely nontrans-parent financial systems of these nations. Even so, by this time industrial-ists in dozens of sectors were ready to make dramatic moves. After all, even the most audacious of takeover strategies could now be deemed as no more than a prudent effort to remove excess capacity from the global economy, and thereby help lessen the severity of the crash.

For the last couple of years before the millennium, the buying and sell-ing would continue at an almost insane clip. Dealmakers did often dress up their moves in scientific-sounding terminology. The term "roll up" was especially popular; this meant buying a lot of small related compa-nies and transforming them into one big company. Dealmakers also liked to rattle on about "synergy." Originally a biologic term to describe what happens when two organisms combine to achieve an effect neither could achieve alone, when used by an acquisition-minded executive "synergy" meant a new form of mathematics in which adding one to one yielded three when it came to revenue and one when it came to cost. Yet as the boom continued, it became ever more obvious that there was often very little that was scientific—or even economically intelligent—about the in-dividual deals themselves. Everyone everywhere every day was out only to grab or get grabbed (for the right price). Especially in mature industries, the business of big business became, for these few years, to buy and sell business.

And so the deal total in 1998 was half again the record set in 1997. And 1999 proved even more manic, as some $3.4 trillion in mergers shattered the record yet again. Typical was the consolidation of the world aluminum industry. In the world's first three-way cross-border deal, Canada's Alcan jumped into the number-one spot by purchasing France's Pechiney and Switzerland's Alusuisse. It took only a week, however, for Alcoa to counter with the purchase of Reynolds Aluminum, allowing the American company to reclaim the top spot it had long held. Big deals also remade publishing, logistics, supermarkets, even the accounting and consulting business, leading at one point to the ridiculously monikered Pricewaterhousecoopers, soon mercifully shortened to PwC. Increasingly, the deals seemed to be remaking cultures as well. Olivetti's play for Telecom Italia in 1998 was Europe's first-ever attempt at a large-scale hostile takeover.[18]

Though some nations still resisted the complete globalization of their economies—despite Schrempp's example, German and French companies for all intents remained off-limits to overseas suitors—the boom left the world a very different place. In some industries, there was still a great deal of diversity. Eight to ten big players might be distributed worldwide; a leader might be lucky to control a 25 percent share of the global market. But in a growing number of other industries, the world market had in the words of the *Wall Street Journal,* "become dominated by a few big companies."[19] Some of these were well-known branded firms like Intel; others lay many layers below the view of the consumer. Some had rolled up their power through aggressive acquisition; others had grown organically and then benefited from the increasing reluctance of big companies to challenge one another once entrenched.

The list goes on and on. Japan's Sharp captured 60 percent of the market for flat screens, while Corning captured 60 percent of the market for flat-screen glass. General Electric delivered 60 percent of the world's gas-powered turbines, while first Boeing and then Airbus delivered 65 percent of all airliners. Samsung controlled 60 percent of the market for DRAMs, Cisco 85 percent of the world market for Internet routers and switches, Japan's Polatechno 80 percent of the world market for liquid crystal display polarizers, ARM Holdings of Britain 80 percent of all central processing units in cell phones. Nor were such roll-ups limited to high-tech industries. By 2004, bottle and package maker Owens-Illinois had captured well upward of 50 percent of the world market for packaging products, including the commanding position in North America, Europe, Asia, and South America.[20]

America had, of course, experienced such industrial gigantism before. Early in the twentieth century, U.S. Steel controlled as much as 80 percent of America's market for the metal, International Harvester sold 85 percent of all mechanized farm machinery, Standard Oil controlled as much as 90 percent of petroleum-refining capacity, Alcoa enjoyed a 100 percent monopoly in the production of aluminum.[21] It was around this time that Arthur Moxham, a top manager at DuPont, formulated a rule remarkably similar to Welch's dictum of 1981. A big company, Moxham said, should aim not at monopoly but rather at controlling only about 60 percent of the market for any product, and to maintain the ability to price "that 60 percent cheaper than others." In this way, Moxham concluded, the market leader would always, even "when slack times came," be able to "keep *our* capital employed to *the full*."[22]

Of course, in 1903 Moxham spoke only of a 60 percent share of the U.S. market. A century later, GE and its followers would speak of 60 percent shares of the world market.

Which is a big difference.

The 1998 case against Microsoft was by far the most high-profile antitrust action in the United States in decades, and Clinton Administration officials would later hold the case up as proof they had taken a much more "activist" policy than either the Bush or Reagan Administration before them.[23] During his first term, Clinton had bulked up the staff of the Antitrust Division and had approved a few huge cases against price fixing by giant commodities traders such as Archer Daniels Midland. Now his team seemed ready to stalk other big game. And, in relatively short order (as antitrust cases go), the government would bag its quarry, winning a dramatic order to split Microsoft in two.

Yet the real lessons of the Microsoft case are more complex and more muddled than they were presented by the Clinton antitrust team. If any-

164 — END OF THE LINE

thing, what was certainly one of the most high-profile antitrust cases since the breakup of Standard Oil did more to illustrate the weakness and lack of coherence of government efforts to regulate big business in the 1990s than it did to clear a new path for other governments to follow as a truly global economy took shape.

One problem with viewing Microsoft as a model stems from the choice of target itself. Although there is little doubt that Microsoft abused its market power to protect its operating system and its Web browser, the fact that its software was already so widely entrenched meant that the arguments both for and against breakup would naturally be highly complex and at times highly confusing. By the end, the case would be widely perceived as underscoring the difficulties and even dangers of using antitrust power at all in the new era of networked economies and networked production systems. This was nowhere more evident than in the thinking of the judge who actually ordered Microsoft to be broken up. Initially, he had intended to leave the company intact, because he feared that slicing apart such a complex entity might somehow throw the American economy out of balance. The judge later admitted to changing his mind, but this was not due to any rational government argument. Rather, it was because he felt Microsoft head Bill Gates had shown too little contrition and had acted in too arrogant a manner.[24]

The second main problem in viewing the Microsoft case as a model stems from the Clinton Administration's claim that it was in fact pursuing a more activist antitrust policy than its predecessors. This was true, but only when the radical increase in the number, size, and scope of the deals that took place in the decade is ignored entirely. On the contrary, despite the absolutely unprecedented global M&A boom that was taking place around the world, the Microsoft case proved very much to be the exception to the Clinton Administration's rule. The U.S. government has very clear authority to reject or reshape any deal that affects the American consumer even when the deal is made by two foreign firms. Yet the Clinton Administration challenged remarkably few of the big cross-border mergers of the 1990s. Although blocking the tie-up of Daimler and Chrysler was probably not warranted—in the world automotive industry, there was still lots of competition—other deals were clearly creating global-scale oligopoly or even monopoly. Yet Clinton's antitrust team acted only rarely, and in the rare instances when they did block a takeover, they often backed off quickly. In 1997, the government rejected an attempt by Alcoa to purchase Reynolds Aluminum, but two years later it raised no objection to the same deal. Even the great win in the Microsoft case was due more, as we have seen, to happenstance than to any well-leavened new strategy. And as it proved, Microsoft was able to avoid any real penalty by simply dragging on its appeal until the Bush Administration—which didn't even have to reject a well-wrought argument in favor of an overall more activist policy—simply dropped the case.

It is important to understand why the Clinton Administration did not adjust U.S. antitrust enforcement or policy in response to the radical reorganization of the global economy that took place in the 1990s, and what the effects of this failure have been and will continue to be. To do so, it is useful to distinguish between the popular perception of the government's antitrust power and the ways in which U.S. federal governments have actually put that power to use since the Sherman Antitrust Act was passed by Congress in 1890.

Sketching the popular perception is simple: The American public has always tended to strongly oppose any major consolidation of economic power by either the private or the public sector. Distrust of monopoly and oligopoly traces back in the common law at least as far as the fifteenth century. To a degree, the War of Independence was a war against monopoly—the resentment against the English East India Company, for instance. Decades later, Andrew Jackson transformed opposition to monopoly into a sort of touchstone of popular democracy, most dramatically in his fight over whether to grant a monopoly to the Second Bank of the United States. The antimonopoly rhetoric of that era—which itself traces back to Jefferson's conception of the ideal citizen as a self-sufficient yeoman farmer whose political voice would be threatened by any concentration of power—lives on in American politics today.

Sketching the actions of the federal government since the passage of the Sherman Act is a more complex task. This is because American politicians, even those who regard private-sector economic power as primarily a political problem, have from the first sought to pursue their goals in ways that are not economically counterproductive or outright destructive. From the beginning, most politicians have approached antitrust not as a matter of breaking up big corporations simply because they are big, but as a challenge to somehow regulate the power of these big entities while making sure not to kill off any of the golden geese of mass production. Governments have approached this task in two ways. First, in instances of what are sometimes called "natural" monopolies, like railroads and utilities, they initially tended to respond with direct government regulation of rates and routes, such as through the Interstate Commerce Act. The second approach, expressed in the Sherman Act, is wherever possible to avoid such direct regulation by finding ways to keep the big corporations somehow subject to regulation by the forces of the marketplace.

In the popular mind, Theodore Roosevelt stands tall as the man who finally put antitrust to use as intended.[25] In the first decade after the Sherman Antitrust Act was passed, the vagueness of its wording had allowed investors to use the law in ways that most of its authors had not expected, such as to break up unions and to replace inherently fragile cartels with giant, fully integrated corporations.[26] Yet despite Roosevelt's reputation for battling big business, not least the fearsome Standard Oil, the fact was that he busted very few trusts. On the contrary, Roosevelt tended to view government's role as more that of a conservation-minded hunter, charged with culling out the few rogue actors from the great herd of "good" corporations that delivered "fair prices" to the consumer and "fair" return to the investor.[27] And this would remain the attitude of most administrations for the next three decades, right into the second term of Franklin Roosevelt.[28] This can be viewed as the first of the three basic consensuses that governed U.S. antitrust policy in the twentieth century.

Just before and during the Second World War, a new consensus began to take shape. This consensus, which can be viewed as the "modern" era of antitrust policy, was characterized by a major expansion of the goals of regulation. The government now sought wherever possible to ensure that at least three big players remained in any national marketplace. Monopoly, in other words, was now viewed as bad, even when it clearly seemed to be efficient in the near term. But oligopoly, among giant, stable, vertically integrated corporations, was fine.[29] The result was an industrial landscape that remained remarkably stable for four decades and that was notable for its many groups of three. In steel, there was Bethlehem, U.S. Steel, and Republic; in chemicals, DuPont, Union Carbide, and Allied;

in aluminum, Alcoa, Reynolds, and Kaiser; in food processing, Quaker Oats, General Foods, and General Mills; in automobiles, GM, Ford, and Chrysler.

This consensus began to fray in the 1970s, for two reasons. First was the rising influence of a group of economists—centered at the University of Chicago—who held that government management of these market-places was not only unnecessary but often counterproductive. Capitalism itself, they claimed, was such a vibrant force that it naturally created the market conditions that kept even a pure monopoly in check. The second argument in favor of relaxing the regulation of competition was the rapid and very evident increase in competition from foreign firms, especially from Japan.[30] As early as the 1960s, many of those who argued in favor of opening U.S. borders defended their position at least in part as a way to further counterbalance the power of the American oligopolies. The result, early in the Reagan Administration, was the third major consensus on antitrust policy. No longer would government focus on maintaining a particular market structure, but rather it would simply watch out for abuses of pricing power. To a degree, the Reagan policy marked a return to the policy formulated by Theodore Roosevelt. But it was also based very much on the expectation that new competition from abroad would only continue to grow for the foreseeable future.

Viewed in this light, it is not surprising that the Clinton team did not adjust the basic antitrust policy that it inherited from the Bush and Reagan Administrations. After all, by 1994 Clinton had adopted a radical laissez-faire trade policy, so it would be only natural for top officials to assume that global competition would only increase and would in turn continue to obviate any major need for the government to engineer more competition among giant corporations. Well into the decade, even as sector after sector was in fact consolidating into global-scale oligopoly or de facto monopoly, most policy makers nursed an image of the American corporation as a somewhat brutalized victim of international competition. As one of the main books on the subject of the corporation in the 1990s put it, the average big American manufacturer was still a "sweating and not-always-successful competitor," a long way from regaining its stature as a "powerful actor" in society.[31]

This attitude can be attacked for two reasons, though. The first, which is the harder to excuse, is that any conviction that global competition somehow automatically absolves the government of any need to manage competition requires the beholder to view the global marketplace as highly static. One of the great contributions of the famous Austrian economist Joseph A. Schumpeter more than a half century ago was to illustrate just how dynamic most capitalist economies tend to be. Yet now the same attitude that he had attacked in overeager New Deal–era regulators had reappeared in a sort of mirror image, in the belief that globalization meant never having to regulate again.

The second problem with Clinton-era antitrust policy was the antitrust division's failure to significantly expand what is considered to be pricing abuse, to consider the effects of pricing policy on interest groups other than the consumer. Given that at the time no one really had a clear understanding of how the new disintegrated, arbitrage-oriented corporations were evolving so as to be able to manufacture their profits in an imperfectly globalized economy, this failure is perhaps excusable. But the results were no less dramatic. Given that the only real trip wire in antitrust policy continued to be abuse of pricing power as turned against the consumer, many of the smarter corporations of the 1990s simply turned this power away from the consumer and applied it to their suppliers and the workers within their production systems, only to then deploy an ever-falling price at the consumer end as a weapon to keep their direct competitors always off balance. In some cases, the overall effect of such a policy on the economy was far worse than had they targeted the consumer.

In going after Microsoft, the Clinton Administration's antitrust team did have to stretch the Reagan-era consensus on competition policy somewhat. This is because not only was Microsoft not accused of raising prices unfairly, the firm on the contrary was widely condemned by its competitors for lowering its prices to a point where it was able to crush their ability to compete effectively. Although such aggressive pricing by a market leader has often over the years been held to be illegal, the narrowness of the Reagan-era focus inherited by Clinton's team required them—in going after Microsoft—to dust off the issue of how competition within a particular industry affects the pace of innovation.

Innovation is one of the more mysterious subjects in human life, at least when looked at through the lenses of the sociologist or anthropologist or theologian. But over the last century, Americans have learned a great deal about how government regulation of competition can foster private-sector innovation, at least in the form of new technologies and products. Two links especially are important to any understanding of how the consolidation of many industries in recent years has affected the pace of innovation, and what if anything the government can do about it. This in turn raises the issue of whether government actions that aim to lessen the overall fragility of today's hyper-interdependent and hyper-specialized global production system may actually be shaped so as to simultaneously promote these forms of innovation.[32]

The first key link between antitrust law and innovation dates to the early years after the passage of the Sherman Act, when many big corporations began to search out new ways to protect their market shares. One of the more enduring and socially important responses is often credited to George Eastman. In order to develop new and better products, Eastman in the 1890s set up an in-house laboratory at Eastman Kodak and forged a close relationship with researchers at the Massachusetts Institute of Technology. By the first years of the twentieth century, similar strategies of "continuous innovation" had been adopted by General Electric, Westinghouse, DuPont, Corning Glass, and Parke Davis.[33] Later, under Thomas Watson at IBM in the 1930s, and at GE, AT&T, and Xerox in the 1940s and 1950s, the lab would morph into the research complex, where huge staffs of tenured scientists and engineers were showered with immense budgets.

The second major link between antitrust law and innovation is the dramatic economic growth that seemed to result from the postwar policy of using antitrust power to force big corporations to share out their technologies. Business historian Alfred D. Chandler has written that the Antitrust Division's hard line against market-dominant high-tech firms in the 1950s and 1960s was among the most significant economic events of the twentieth century, and that the scattering of technologies that resulted essentially set the stage for much of America's growth in the years since. It was from the technological seeds shaken out of corporations like

AT&T and IBM, Chandler has shown, that many of the biggest names in the U.S. computer industry would grow.[34]

Over the years, many other factors have influenced thinking on the interplay of antitrust policy and innovation, but none has been more important than the writings of Joseph Schumpeter. Composed mainly after he immigrated to the United States from Austria in 1932, Schumpeter's main works would help shape the policies of the New Dealers who developed the more activist, technology-centric orientation of postwar antitrust. And two generations later, interpreted quite differently, Schumpeter's writings provided much of the theoretical foundation for the Reagan era's hands-off antitrust policy.

Much of the key thinking is found in Schumpeter's book *Capitalism, Socialism and Democracy*, published in 1942. This is where Schumpeter first set down what is one of the finest distillations of a complex idea, which was the oxymoron "creative destruction." In these two words, Schumpeter seemed to capture the soul of the American capitalist system. For our purpose, the main importance of Schumpeter's book derives from his depiction of the capitalist system as being always in a state of disequilibrium that results in such perpetual and extreme change as to constantly challenge almost all status quo economic powers.[35] This led Schumpeter to make three interlocking points that would hugely influence America's antitrust policy.

First, oligopolies and monopolies perform a social good by limiting competition. In markets where many similarly sized companies exist (in what is sometimes called a state of "perfect competition"), Schumpeter believed that the resulting battles to the death over market share often destroy more wealth than they create. Oligopolist companies, by contrast, while still keeping their skills sharp by competing at the margins, also tend to avoid disastrous Marne-like frontal assaults on one another's core businesses. Schumpeter used America's Big Three automotive firms as an example. These, he said, engaged in "corespective rather than competitive" contests of strength, in which they maintain their edge by "play[ing] for points at the frontiers."[36]

Second, even pure monopolies are often much less dangerous than people think. Schumpeter did not dispute that monopolization existed.[37] But he felt that all monopolies were inherently transitory, at least in a technological sense. Every company that captures a monopoly will in time be forced to entirely renovate the technologies that underlie that monopoly or risk finding itself outflanked by other companies bearing newer or better products or processes.[38] Whether a monopoly business withers away or whether it rejuvenates itself, society benefits, Schumpeter said, usually in the form of another "avalanche of consumers' goods that permanently deepens and widens the stream of real income."

Third, monopoly profits are themselves the single most important private-sector source of support for investment in innovation. To avoid being overtaken by an entrepreneurial upstart offering a better product, firms that have captured monopolies will tend to apply a large portion of their naturally fat profits to improving their existing products and processes, and to developing entirely new products. In essence, Schumpeter held, once ensconced atop a monopoly position, any smart modern manufacturer will transform itself almost immediately into a sort of innovation machine.[39] In the end, he concluded, in another brilliantly concise phrase, monopolies "largely create what they exploit."[40]

It is easy to see why Schumpeter became a favorite of the antiregulatory economists who in the 1970s would develop much of the thinking behind Reagan-era antitrust policy. But a more full reading of Schumpeter also shows he was by no means a true laissez-faire economist. On the contrary, Schumpeter admitted that many monopolies and oligopolies "no doubt" have an "injurious effect on output" and that it is "not difficult to find examples" of the "soporific effect" of monopolization. And Schumpeter went out of his way to emphasize that his argument "does not amount to a case against state regulation." On the contrary, he took up his pen mainly out of a fear that radical New Dealers[41] would institute a policy of attacking big companies merely because they were big. This, Schumpeter felt, would be as wrongheaded as any doctrinaire laissez-faire policy,[42] but not necessarily more so.

After the war, government antitrust policy makers would follow a recipe largely concocted out of Schumpeter's work, at least as regarded high-tech market leaders. Regulators during this period sought wherever possible, as we saw in the last section, to keep America's industrial oligopolies from consolidating into duopoly or monopoly. But in cases where a firm had captured a de facto monopoly by being the first to introduce a new technology, the government did not seek to split that firm into multiple parts. Rather, officials tended to use their antitrust power to force these firms to more rapidly license the technologies they developed by reinvesting their monopoly profits. The basic goal was to make the new technologies available to as many potential users as possible. In turn, it was felt that the high-tech firms that had developed these technologies in the first place, as they saw their own ideas rising up about them in new and threatening forms, would naturally respond with yet greater feats of innovation.[43]

And so starting with a 1945 case in which the aluminum maker Alcoa was forced to license key patents,[44] the U.S. government went on to target more than 100 corporations over the next fifteen years. Not only were these firms forced to make their technologies available to competitors under "compulsory licensing" agreements, they had to make them available for free. So powerful and relentless was the government's assault that of 107 cases, the targeted corporations challenged the government in court only thirteen times.[45] The process reached a sort of peak in January 1956 when both IBM and AT&T agreed to "consent decrees" that resulted in the licensing of more than 9,000 patents.[46] In the case of AT&T, the consent decree greatly sped up an already ongoing process of sharing out semiconductor technologies.[47] In the case of IBM, it led the firm to alter basic strategy and move much more swiftly away from tabulating card machinery into computers.[48] Other highly important consent decrees include the one signed by RCA in 1958, which led to the licensing of basic radio and television technologies, and another signed with IBM in 1969, in which the company agreed to unbundle its software.[49]

A generation later, when the Clinton Administration decided to take on Microsoft, it's not clear that anyone in the Antitrust Division had studied in depth how the postwar antitrust policy had promoted innovation.[50] The important fact, though, is that it appears highly unlikely that the Clinton antitrust team could ever have revived the earlier model, even if they had aimed to do so.

The main reason here is that Schumpeter's view of how monopolist corporations innovate in order to protect themselves from upstart challengers no longer holds in many, if not most, industries. If anything, the ever more disaggregated structure of today's lead firms would seem to make any effort to use antitrust power to pry out technologies counterproductive. Firms that have already off-loaded much of the responsibility for development and research onto their suppliers, or onto no one at all, are not likely to spend money on developing technologies if they expect they will have to turn these over to competitors.

That said, the Microsoft case may still provide a valuable model, which came when the government stumbled into the path of calling for the company to be broken into two or more pieces. The robust yet controlled rivalry that characterizes oligopolist competition may not re-create America's great industrial laboratories of midcentury. But such a market structure would increase the rewards for innovation while also reducing the ability of a market leader to slow the overall pace of innovation in a particular innovation.

Ultimately, though, what remains most clear is that the structure of today's highly specialized and networked production system truly seems to slow the overall pace of introduction of new technologies in many industries. And, the Microsoft case aside, governments have yet to begin to experiment with ways to perpetuate and promote private-sector innovation. The vertically integrated producers that dominated the American economy for most of the twentieth century tended to view technological leadership as core to their long-term survival, and they responded with a variety of investments, many of which they knew would bear fruit only over the long term. Today's arbitrage-oriented firms, by contrast, are designed to focus much more on using their power over their production systems to wring out wealth immediately, rather than to devote resources to technologies that might create wealth years from now. Increasingly, these firms view development of new technologies and new products, rather than an investment in the future, as no more than an unnecessary and probably unwise cost.

In the television show *Star Trek: The Next Generation*, the most advanced of all alien species is known as the Borg. A race of humanoids, the Borg have evolved a hive-based social structure and a "singular goal," which is the "consumption of technology," and this they accomplish by assimilating other species into their community.[51] In the 1990s, many in and around Silicon Valley began to refer to Cisco as the "Borg," owing to the company's "innovation through acquisition" strategy. Between mid-1993 and mid-2001, Cisco purchased 71 firms in one of the most extravagant buying sprees in high-tech history.[52]

There are many forms of corporate assimilation, and most have long existed. Daimler's purchase of Chrysler and Hewlett-Packard's purchase of Compaq lie clearly in a tradition that stretches back to Pierpont Morgan's rationalization—or "morganization"—of America's chaotic railroad system into six huge systems and to Morgan's brokering of the creation of U.S. Steel in 1901.[53] Even Microsoft's growth model has elements in common with Ford Motor at the height of its power; the company does not so much buy new ideas as assign in-house engineers to replicate them.[54] And like Ford, Microsoft then supplements this strategy with a brutal pricing strategy that serves to limit what competitors can spend on further innovation. As Oracle's Larry Ellison complained in court in 2004, "the second Microsoft enters a market, prices drop like a rock."[55]

Cisco's strategy for buying up technology also has its precedents, and in many respects harks back to the strategy pursued by DuPont in the 1920s and 1930s. DuPont abandoned the strategy only after the Second World War, when it came under attack by the Antitrust Division and company managers responded by building up in-house research capabilities.[56] Cisco, however, took the old DuPont model to an entirely new level. In part this was because, being so much relatively smaller than DuPont, Cisco knew that success lay in moving very fast to capture control of its marketplace. And in part, the strategy emerged simply because the company could afford to do so. Not coincidentally, Cisco launched its acquisition spree not long after management paid $170 million to buy out the stakes of founders Sandy Lerner and Len Bosack, who had held about two-thirds of all equity in the firm. As the price of this stock soared, Cisco's top managers found themselves atop a vast pool of "capital" for acquisition.

Cisco perfected its innovation-through-acquisition model the first time out. Field managers had learned that one of the company's customers, Boeing, was about to place a big order for switches made by a fast-growing firm named Crescendo. Ford also told Cisco that it was interested in buying switches in addition to routers. This meant that if

THE GREAT CONSOLIDATION — 175

Cisco wanted to keep control of the Internet hardware market, it had four options. It could develop switching technology in-house, it could license the technology from another firm, it could merge with a company that controlled switching technology, or it could acquire a firm that controlled such technology. Cisco swiftly opted for the last course, exchanging a whopping $95 million worth of stock for Crescendo, which at the time had only $10 million in revenue.[57] Within eighteen months, though, the price would seem cheap, as Cisco by then had ramped up the run rate on the switching business to $500 million per year.

The strategy Cisco would henceforth follow was simple. Sales managers would listen closely to their customers, then the company would go out and buy the technologies the customers identified as important. Viewed from a technological perspective, the strategy allows Cisco to assume a sort of "chameleon-like quality" as it adapts almost instantly to the technology marketplace.[58] Viewed from a financial perspective, this strategy is not dissimilar to how a venture capital firm places its bets. "Out of a mix of companies, the firm expects that 40 percent to 60 percent will maintain their own and stay afloat," one chronicler of the company has written.[59] "Another 20 percent to 40 percent will be dismal failures, and another 20 percent to 40 percent will be whopping successes." Viewed from an innovation system perspective, this strategy helps to maintain Cisco as the keystone predator within a venture capital ecosystem. Indeed, Cisco more than any other company in Silicon Valley in the 1990s fostered what became an entirely new model for identifying, incubating, and introducing new technologies. Small firms supported by venture capital took the hard initial steps and incurred the initial risks. In exchange, Cisco provided the "exit," rewarding founders and funders at the small companies with rich chunks of Cisco stock and sometimes lucrative jobs inside the firm. In other words, not only has Cisco mastered the art of relying on others to care for the orchards, it has also figured out how to rely on others to plant the seeds, concentrating its own efforts on building up sufficient market power to be able always to pluck the ripest fruit.

Viewed from the perspective of society as a whole, however, Cisco's innovation model is perhaps less innocuous than it first appears. For one, it is one of the more clear inversions of Schumpeter's conception of how rich firms stay ahead of upstart competitors. The company's "monopoly profits"—amplified astronomically by the stock market—are not channeled into a robust in-house R&D operation charged with developing new technologies and new applications that aim to keep Cisco a step or two ahead of the entrepreneurial hounds nipping at its heels. Rather, the wealth simply enables the firm's managers to buy up useful technologies in the very process of buying up potential challengers, and thereby shift to the firm ever more of the power to direct the pace at which technology is introduced in its core markets. Intel, by contrast, is still mainly devoted to in-house innovation; the semiconductor firm is still a highly vertically integrated manufacturer, and it devotes vast amounts of its resources to innovating fast enough to keep the market for its products from shifting onto alternative pathways. Cisco, however, is a naturally amorphous, even protean firm, and it functions not so much as a traditional market leader or market maker, but more as the market itself.

The other reason the Cisco model is important is its influence over the innovation policies at a growing number of more traditional technology-centric firms. Not surprisingly, GE under Jack Welch had begun to rethink the corporation's role in developing new technologies long before Cisco came along. But it took Welch years to settle on an acquisition-centered strategy. Initially, Welch, who had earned a doctorate in chemical engineering, remained enamored of tech-driven growth. In the early 1980s, even as he shoveled workers out the door by the tens of thousands, Welch also eagerly shoveled $130 million into a new research-and-development center for GE. It was only after GE had to book a $450 million loss after a crash program to develop a new refrigerator compressor failed that Welch finally took up his ax against GE's engineering and science work.[60] When these cuts not surprisingly resulted in an immediate and steep fall-off in patent applications, Welch drifted more and more toward a Cisco-like acquisition strategy.[61] The story is similar at many other of America's once vertically integrated, R&D-driven firms. Take 3M, especially after one of Welch's acolytes at GE, James McNerney, took over as CEO.[62] Take also Johnson & Johnson, especially in their medical device and pharmaceutical divisions.[63]

Yet in many of these cases, it wasn't long before the limits of such an innovation-through-acquisition strategy became clear. Though such strategies can work well when there's a rich crop of upstarts watered by the venture capitalists, as was the case in the late 1990s, growth is much slower during normal, nonboom times. Unfortunately, it usually proves a lot harder to rebuild an in-house R&D operation than it was to take it apart in the first place. The challenge now was not simply a matter of money. In 2004, for instance, Welch's successor atop GE, Jeffrey Immelt, sought at least to halt the decline in the company's research capabilities. Yet he soon found himself battling a bureaucracy that had forgotten how to drive growth through internal initiative. "I don't want GE managers to think we can just buy our way into every new idea," Immelt complained. "It's something I'm trying to fight against culturally."[64]

The 1990s saw many forms of consolidation. There was the "traditional" merger strategy of a company like Daimler, which sought to maintain leadership within a quickly shrinking rank of competitors in a mature industry. There was the strategy pursued by Cisco, which sought simultaneously to consolidate power and "innovate" by buying dozens of smaller, tech-laden firms. There was the strategy pursued, as we saw in the previous chapter, by Flextronics and other firms down the supply chain, which sought to rationalize the service and supply activities they provide. Last of all there was the rise of the "single-sourcing" relationship, which is when individual buyers and, ultimately, whole industries come to rely on a single outside supplier even for a highly important component, whether they do so knowingly or unknowingly.

To understand this last form of consolidation, it helps to turn to the experience of the executives at Dell Computer who, after watching their American assembly lines shut down within days of the September 1999 earthquake in Taiwan, set out to better understand why this had happened. To do so, the Dell executives studied where their tier-one suppliers did their shopping, and this in turn soon yielded the first important answer. As Dell's vice president of manufacturing, Dick Hunter, would say later, all arrows kept pointing back to a firm named Taiwan Semiconductor Manufacturing Corporation, or TSMC. Up to this time, this was a company with which Dell had maintained no direct relationship; in fact, it was a company that Dell managers "had never really heard of" before. Now, however, Dell's executives realized they were in fact buying hundreds of millions of dollars of chips each year from TSMC indirectly. The news, Hunter says, "really opened our eyes."

What Dell found also illustrates how a system of outsourced production tends toward an ever-higher degree of specialization and concentration, with related effects on innovation and on risk. Indeed, one of the best illustrations is the rise and evolution of TSMC itself. Traditionally, the semiconductor industry was dominated by more than a dozen fully independent companies known as integrated device manufacturers, or IDMs. Most were household names, established American firms like IBM and Texas Instruments and Motorola, and Japanese followers like NEC and Hitachi. No matter where they were from, however, all the big semiconductor manufacturers sought to master every step of turning out a chip. This meant that all cooked their own silicon, sliced their own wafers, designed their own circuits, assembled and tested and packaged their own chips. In almost all instances, the companies also designed, manufactured, and marketed products that contained these chips, such as IBM's mainframes and PCs or Motorola's communications gear or Hitachi's consumer electronics. All the companies also sold chips, both as standardized commodities and in highly specialized designs, to manufacturers that did not own their own semiconductor factories. When Ford needed a chip for a sensor inside a new car, it would turn to one of the IDMs.

Though little noticed at the time, an event that would revolutionize the IDM production model took place in Taiwan in 1987, when a man named Morris Chang set up the world's first "pure play" wafer foundry, TSMC. Chang's idea was that his company would manufacture only semiconductor wafers, which it would supply to all comers. Customers would have to provide the design for the chips or arrange for a third party to design the chip for them. In essence, Chang applied a printing press model to semiconductors. In the same way that independent printers sold time on their presses to independent magazines and newspapers, Chang would rent out his machinery to anyone who came along with some "content" in the form of a chip design. In the same way that independent presses freed small publishers from dependence on the machinery owned by big newspapers, Chang's foundry would free up designers from dependence on the IDMs, who naturally gave precedence in their production systems to chips destined for their own branded products, and who also charged premium prices for their all-in-one services. Chang, who had studied at MIT and Stanford and who had worked for decades in the United States, mainly for Texas Instruments, decided early on to build a state-of-the-art facility. At a time when a basic foundry cost as little as $15 million, he wrangled more than $200 million in funding from the Taiwanese government and from the Dutch firm Philips.[65]

At first, Chang's new model was derided by many in the industry. "Real men have fabs" is how W. J. Sanders III, the chairman of Advanced Micro Devices, put it, using a common term for foundry.[66] But TSMC over the next decade would simply keep growing, and Chang and his managers and engineers would continue to build up not only their capacity but their knowledge, their support system among local machinery suppliers, their long-term business relationships, and, most important, a rich collection of "front-end" business partners who designed highly specialized chips to be cut into silicon by TSMC. Hundreds of such "fabless" design firms have formed over the past fifteen years, and many, such as Xilinx and Altera, have grown into powerful players.[67]

By the turn of the century, TSMC had developed so much momentum that it was one of only a handful of companies able to round up the $3-billion-plus investment necessary to mount the latest in plant equipment, designed to turn out twelve-inch-diameter wafers. TSMC and its across-the-street rival UMC became so renowned for their technological prowess that even erstwhile semiconductor leaders like Motorola began to rely on them for top-of-the-line wafers, while companies ranging from IBM to Philips to Hitachi to Infineon have eagerly entered into technology-development joint ventures. Even AMD has begun to farm out work to the Taiwanese foundries.[68]

Here as clearly as anywhere can be seen the result of the global industrial revolution of the last two decades. The whole history of mass manufacturing in America until the appearance of the Toyota model was characterized by efforts by managers at vertically integrated firms to foster and maintain multiple sources of supply. One goal, as we have seen, was to use competition among suppliers to keep costs under control.[69] The other goal was to assure continuity of supply.[70] But the invasion of the Japanese changed this calculus. When Americans tried to understand how Toyota was able to sell better-quality cars at lower prices, many concluded that one big reason was the Japanese firm's reliance on single-source relationships. Suddenly, the American approach to sourcing began to be attacked as shortsighted and wasteful.[71]

Experts in Toyota-style production have long cautioned that single sourcing should be viewed more as a by-product of a well-crafted cooperative partnership with suppliers than as the main goal for a company reengineering its supply chain.[72] Yet starting in the 1980s, many American corporations came to view single sourcing, in and of itself, as an absolute proof of efficiency. As early as 1988, both Ford and GM would boast that some 98 percent of the parts they purchased from outside suppliers were "single-sourced." This was a radical change from a decade earlier when, as one vice president for materials management at GM put it, "our practice was to double- or perhaps triple-source every part."[73] Yet this initial round of single sourcing would seem almost conservative compared to what would emerge in the 1990s. If Ford ran into trouble in the production of steering wheels for its Taurus, managers could turn quickly to the company that manufactured steering wheels for its Escort. Even in less complex industries, the supplier base remained highly diversified well into the 1990s. If a deal went sour or a production line went down, most buyers could soon scout up an alternative or a replacement.

By the end of the 1990s, however, the perfect storm of laissez-faire trade policy, outsourcing, and advanced logistics began to enable true single sourcing at the global level, not merely for a particular lead firm but at the level of an entire industry.[74]

Although such extreme dependence would have appalled previous generations of American production managers, growing numbers of big corporations in the 1990s began to realize that, at least as it affected their ability to set prices, such consolidation did not in fact shift much if any power to the supplier. On the contrary, more and more corporations realized that if integration with a supplier was deep enough, power in the relationship often actually tended to shift further toward the buyer. The basic difference was that whereas the supplier had even less ability than before to threaten to walk away from the relationship, the lead firms maintained the power to threaten to shift future purchases to a competitor of the supplier. Even in cases where a top supplier controlled 60 percent or more of production, the mere existence of potential alternatives usually gave the lead firms all the pricing power they needed.

Big American companies had at last discovered one of the main pillars of the Toyota system, which was that an outsourced production network could be structured so as to re-create all the power of old-fashioned vertical integration without the cost or responsibility of true ownership. The Americans had also discovered something even better, at least from the point of view of the lead firm. Whereas in Japan the buyer-supplier relationship was based on an almost feudal sense of mutual interdependence and mutual loyalty, American single sourcing was still premised on the idea that once a supplier had "freely entered into" a contractual relationship, there was no moral responsibility to fret about whatever suffering was necessary to meet the terms of that contract, whether that suffering was meted out to that smaller company's investors, managers, employees, or onward to yet-lower-tier suppliers.

Pricing aside, the physical result of this new embrace of single sourcing was something else entirely. In industry after industry, the result was that the supply base for many activities was often consolidated down to three or two (or even one) companies often located in a single region or city. Nowhere is this more true than in production of advanced semiconductors, as the global industrial system has evolved to a point where the keystone chips for thousands of companies now take shape on only a few production lines in a single industrial park in Taiwan.

Although such relationships obviously very much violated the second rule of America's old production managers—which was to dual-source to ensure supply no matter the contingency—their modern counterparts often did not seem to care. This was, usually, simply because the very process of outsourcing so much work had left so many of today's production managers blissfully ignorant of the true extent of their firm's dependence on a few key suppliers, as Dell's experience proves.

In 1967, when John Kenneth Galbraith wrote that the capitalist and Communist industrial systems were "converging,"[75] he was thinking mainly of the cultural and social effects of allowing an economy to be directed almost entirely by the producer, in the interest of the producer. Galbraith, obviously, was wrong. The two systems did not converge either culturally or socially. Yet the global production system of today—as it evolves toward an ever more rational organization of activity in a disintegrated global networked system—is not, it would seem, all that different from the production system that took shape in that most rational of all twentieth-century states, the true single-source society, the Soviet Union.

In the end, no deal of the 1990s would spark more disillusionment than the Daimler-Chrysler tie-up. The first to sour on the takeover were the American managers and workers. Though Schrempp had originally vaunted the deal as a "merger of equals," within a year of closing it was clear that he and the Germans were in full control, and many of the Americans increasingly felt they had been played for suckers. Daimler had lassoed a fat American manufacturer, then performed most of the butchery of rationalization in the offices of Detroit and along the assembly lines of Michigan. Less and less did Schrempp appear the star-spangled cowboy, and more and more did he seem the academy-trained Prussian cavalry officer carrying home bags full of spoil. Confirmation came at last in an article in the *Financial Times* in which Schrempp claimed he had always viewed the Chrysler deal as an outright acquisition, and had simply played a game of "chess" designed to mislead the Americans.[76] It "seems," *The New Yorker* concluded, that "we were fooled by his affable ich bin Amerikaner manners."[77]

Yet it wasn't long before Schrempp discovered that the walls of his own Stuttgart fortress were not as protective as they had only recently seemed. As time passed, the Germans began to see Chrysler ever more as a sort of Trojan horse out of which were pouring legions of American investors, infuriated by what the *Wall Street Journal* was now declaring to be a "megaflop" rather than a "megamerger."[78] One low point came when billionaire investor Kirk Kerkorian sued DaimlerChrysler for $8 billion in damages only a few days before lawyers filed a class action suit on behalf of the more common shareholders. By 2004, a sort of "fear and loathing" had spread throughout the Daimler headquarters. Having watched the market capitalization of the combined firms fall by a phenomenal $35 billion,[79] it was now the Germans who felt they had been suckered—into overpaying for a fragile company that had artificially pumped up its profits.[80]

Though the great merger wave was often depicted as demonstrating the power of managers, it was really much more notable in the end for underscoring the rising power of the shareholder, especially those in U.S. model corporations and those who became subject to U.S. shareholder power. For Schrempp, one highly personal sign of the growing power of American investors came when in late 2003 he was hauled into court in Delaware amid growing calls on both sides of the Atlantic for his head.[81] It was only the beginning of a trial that, including appeals, would likely go on for years. But already one verdict was in. *BusinessWeek,* which in 1998 had named Schrempp one of the "top executives" anywhere, now declared him to be one of the "worst managers" in the world.[82]

So in the end the great merger wave of the 1990s did truly bring the peoples of the world closer together. In some cases, as we will see in Chapter Nine, they were brought together by mutual dependence on immense oligopolies that generate profits ever more through the exercise of power. In other cases, however, they were brought together mainly in mutual loathing, at least when they had to face the evidence that, as in the merger of Daimler and Chrysler, the real mathematics of M&A is that when you add one to one you often get only one.

CHAPTER SEVEN

THE VIRTUAL MOMENT

The Snap-Together World

In June 2000, the Indianapolis-based insurance and finance company Conseco offered Gary Wendt a $45 million signing bonus to take over as CEO of the debt-shackled firm. The prospect of running the nation's biggest holder of mortgages on mobile homes may have seemed a come-down to Wendt, after his heady days as chairman and CEO of General Electric Capital Corporation, but this was a mean chunk of change. It was more than double the previous record bonus paid to a CEO, which was the $20 million Alex Mandl received to take over Teligent in 1997. It was nine times what Louis Gerstner was paid when he took over IBM in 1993, fifteen times what Carly Fiorina was paid in 1999 to run Hewlett-Packard. And it was in cash.

In *Leviathan*, the English philosopher Thomas Hobbes declared the individual to be subject, in the most fundamental sense, to the market. "The value or worth of a man," he wrote, is "his price, that is to say, so much as would be given for the use of his power." Now, three and a half centuries later, the market had declared in spectacular fashion that Gary Wendt was a singular human being. Not that there was anything strange in the workings of this market. Conseco's need was great, and the corporation's board had judged Wendt worthy of a big investment. Nor was there anything remarkable about the scale of the payout, as would soon be proved by the actions of another market. On hearing news of Wendt's hiring, investors pushed the price of a share of Conseco stock from $6 to more than $9. In the process, they more than ratified the decision of the

Conseco board. After all, what's $45 million if what you get in return is a "Billion Dollar Man"?[1]

And what was Wendt to perform in exchange for his bonus? Exactly what he had done at GE Capital, which was to tear into one of the last bastions of the traditional corporation and to outsource activities that heretofore had been regarded as inherent to the firm itself. Even at companies that had long since cast off manufacturing—along with the middle managers whose job it was to watch over manufacturing, and the R&D designed to feed into future manufacturing—most top executives had dared not disturb their accountants and information managers and programmers. Once production had been off-loaded, such "business process" activities often seemed to be the last essential glue holding the corporation together.

But then Wendt and a few other pioneering executives began to treat such "back-office" activities as little different from coiling the steel of a spring or molding the plastic of a handset. Such simple services, they felt, were little different from most manufacturing work. They, too, were commodity activities that could be purchased easily on the open market, often at a higher quality and a lower cost than from in-house sources. At GE Capital, Wendt had focused much effort on developing companies able to provide such services to internal GE units as well as to outside companies that would pay GE for such services. Such work could be located almost anywhere, but Wendt was especially attracted to India, where legions of English-speaking, college-educated workers could be hired on the cheap. Soon after leaving GE Capital in 1998, Wendt launched his own back-office service provider, named ExlService.com Inc., in the New Delhi suburb of Noida. And he set up his own investment fund to help launch other new companies that aimed to provide back-office services. This he named GW Capital, and he graced it with a logo highly reminiscent of GE's "signature monogram."

Many events during the great boom of the 1990s symbolize the radical changes that took place in the nature of the corporation, as America's firms evolved toward an ever more "virtual" character, snapped together of ever more generic off-the-shelf parts. Yet it is the apotheosis of Gary Wendt that perhaps best captures the new role of the CEO, the new scale of the rewards, and the new distribution of power within the corporate world. Wendt occupied the spotlight at the moment when the reconception of the corporation had reached its final stage, a time when executives were overseeing the breaking down of the enterprise into the most minute of individual pieces. And this atomization of the firm in turn allowed for a much fuller expression of the power of certain individuals within the organization vis-à-vis the other factors that made up the enterprise. Globalization plus new information technologies plus the latest theories of corporate organization were combining to unleash nothing less than a new "Copernican Revolution" in business, a reordering of the basic bodies of the economic universe.[2] In the afterglow of this Big Bang, Wendt glittered especially bright because he had proved himself so skilled at tearing big bodies into little pieces. And because, having once set himself free of baser compounds, he proved so adept at attracting such a greater mass of the profit.

Not that shifting GE's back-office work to India was Wendt's only accomplishment at the conglomerate, or even his premier success. Wendt's initial street value after leaving GE was derived much more from the fact that he had multiplied the assets of GE Capital by more than twelve times in the 1990s, from $24 billion to more than $300 billion, via both organic expansion and a phenomenal acquisition binge.[3] GE was the old-line company of the decade, the firm that had perfected "continual revolution," and GE Capital was the most powerful engine of that revolution. Spun off from GE, the Capital Corporation at the time it was run by Wendt would have ranked twentieth on the Fortune 500. Nor was GE Capital under Wendt simply a bank hiding inside a conglomerate. GE Capital did provide asset-based financing, like most banks, but when a borrower went south, GE Capital didn't simply auction off the repossessed assets as distressed merchandise, as would the average lender. Rather, the company often took over direct management of these businesses in order to nurse them back to health, sometimes applying regimens perfected elsewhere in the sprawling conglomerate. Over the years, Wendt personally had played a direct role in running firms ranging from Macy's department store to an electricity plant in Maharashtra to a satellite communications network to a bank in Gdansk.[4] In the 1970s, he even helped to manage the finances of the Houston Astros after the previous owner went bankrupt. Wendt later claimed some of the credit for pioneering "promotion" nights in baseball, and reminisced about giving away hats, shirts, and kazoos to lure fans to watch a lousy team.[5]

Wendt was a quintessential top corporate executive. After studying civil engineering at the University of Wisconsin, he rose fast, earning an MBA at Harvard and then throwing himself into the fast-talking, pell-mell world of real estate sales in Texas and Florida. A hard worker, the round-faced Wendt was also a natural and "brilliant deal guy,"[6] and soon found himself recruited by GE Capital. There his climb through the ranks was swift, and this was not due mainly to his charm. Wendt was once described as being "as close to the embodiment of the General Electric Co. ethic as one can get." This meant being "extremely demanding" and, apparently, yelling a lot.[7] Wendt showed little fear, at one point gaining fame as the only GE executive ever "to have shouted back" at Welch himself, at least in public.[8] In his autobiography, the robustly confident Welch has little but good things to say about Wendt, calling him the "high priest of growth inside GE Capital."[9] Yet Welch was sufficiently worried about Wendt's ability to jibe well with others that in 1998 he cast his star from the GE firmament. Welch feared Wendt would overawe whoever Welch chose to succeed himself as GE's top man. Wendt's own epitaph for his time at GE put it well. Near the end of his reign, reflecting on why he had been bypassed for Welch's job, he speculated that it was because he was "too old, too fat, too smart."[10]

None of which did anything but burnish Wendt's value in the eyes of a company like Conseco. Nor was his reputation harmed by the fact that he came complete with a bit of celebrity, or rather its more valuable cousin notoriety. This was thanks to a spectacular divorce after thirty-two years of marriage to his wife Lorna, who had been his high school sweetheart in Rio, Wisconsin. In papers filed in 1995, Lorna demanded half of Wendt's net worth, which she estimated would yield her some $50 million. Wendt countered with an offer of $8 million cash. Though no one was about to be left homeless, the divorce fascinated the public, becoming a staple in the *New York Post*, while Lorna emerged as perhaps the world's richest "feminist symbol," the long-suffering "GE wife" whose job was to "raise two Wendt daughters, to keep a nice house, and to be ready to entertain" at a moment's notice.[11] The trial offered a rare peek at life near the top of one of the world's biggest corporations. There were the rafting trips in Colorado, the elephant rides in Nepal, the climbing of Mount Kilimanjaro in Kenya. There were the Christmas parties illuminated by the performances of Marvin Hamlisch and José Feliciano. There was dinner with Rupert Murdoch. And there was the invitation to Malcolm Forbes's grand seventieth-birthday bash in Morocco, there to hobnob with Walter Cronkite, Oscar de la Renta, and Henry Kissinger.[12] Toward the end of their battle, the squabbling couple were interviewed, separately, by Barbara Walters on the ABC show 20/20. "I've worked hard," Wendt said in explaining his hard line. "She didn't." Whatever, Lorna walked away with $20 million.

At Conseco, Wendt's task was not to replicate GE Capital's acquisition strategy. Wendt was not brought in to grow the company by bulking up, at least not yet. After a poorly thought-out spree in the 1990s, Conseco was a graceless and gormless GE Capital wannabe, a bloated mass of assets and debt that now had to be chopped up and restructured. As one Conseco spokesman noted early on, it was Wendt's past "success" at "moving" jobs to India—not at buying other companies—that the board wanted him now to replicate.[13] And as it proved, Wendt's first dramatic act at Conseco was to cut nearly 20 percent of the workforce in a single blow. A third of the jobs Wendt simply eliminated; the bulk he dispatched to India. This alone was expected to save the company $60 million per year, and managers claimed the quality of the work performed there would be "equal or better" than what the American employees had provided.[14] Wendt was in a position to know exactly what the savings would be, since much of the work was transferred to his own company in India, ExlService. Not that he worked both sides of this deal for long. Soon after the outsourcing deal was announced, Wendt convinced the Conseco board to purchase ExlService outright for $53 million. His cut of this sale? Another $10 million.[15]

And so played out one of the more spectacular efforts in the final campaign to disintegrate and reconstruct the large firm. Assembly had been exploded, middle management vaporized, innovation revealed as a commodity to be purchased. All that remained were the basic processes of running a business—the financial administrators, the programmers, the information managers, and the C-Suite itself. But now Wendt, at the vanguard of a movement that was sweeping corporate America, had proven that most such work could be outsourced just like the manufacture of any component. Here at last was the final proof that the modern company really had no physical core at all, not even a traditional headquarters building. On the contrary, it seemed that the modern corporation could be assembled any day, anywhere, of anything. No longer was the challenge to design or assemble products, but to design and assemble companies. And so only the CEO might command unprecedented rewards—as long, of course, as that CEO had perfected the art of reducing all other employees into plug-and-play components.

By the time Wendt arrived in Conseco's Indianapolis headquarters, the long boom of the 1990s had passed its apogee and begun its ineluctable fall back to earth. It was on March 10, 2000, that NASDAQ topped the 5,000 mark, but by the end of the month the market would be down more than 10 percent, and from there it would just keep falling. Still, when Wendt signed his CEO package in June of that year, few were ready yet to conclude that the bust had finally come, that there was no more fuel to boost stock prices yet higher. Some of the most embarrassing business "models" of the era had been jettisoned. Fashion retail Web site Boo.com, after burning through more than $120 million on marketing and parties, vanished with barely a puff of smoke in mid-May. Lightened of such idiocies, many believed, the craft could soar upward for years longer, perhaps forever.

And what a boom it had already been. A bona fide bonanza, a gold rush to stake out chunks of ever-emptier ether. The global markets mania of the early 1990s and the merger mania that began in mid-decade now appeared but simple side-show acts to warm up the crowd for the dot-com extravaganza in the big tent. So grand was the boom that it soon passed beyond the realm of economics into the existential. No longer was the challenge to make money, but to spend it. And why shouldn't the boom challenge all the old rules? Globalization, in and of itself, seemed more than enough to remake all the rules. So, too, the new information technologies. Mixed together, mightn't they just upset all the normal laws of economics? Of physics? By the time of Wendt's windfall, we were already years into the debate over whether America's productivity had been boosted into permanent overdrive. Alan Greenspan, after famously warning investors against "irrational exuberance" in a December 1996 speech, eventually warmed to the idea that the new IT revolution had changed the nature of the game. Even the archskeptics at *The Economist* were tempted to believe. They had declared the boom a bubble in an April 1998 cover story. But by December 1999, they were almost ready to eat their words. "We woz wrong," they wrote, even as they begged that final judgment over their judgment be delayed because they still might be "proved right."[16]

The Internet, Cisco's John Chambers reminded us over and over and over again, had "changed everything." And so it seemed. As the Old Economy became the New Economy, everything in the economy was being dematerialized, pixilated, digitized. We ourselves were becoming weightless, borderless, ageless. Every day, magnificent new wealth-making machines seemed to incorporate out of the digital mists themselves. The challenge was to find ways to reach out to those forms, to lure them closer to us with Web sites that were more sticky, with portals that were more capacious. Money itself was now a commodity to grow simply by scattering a few seeds in the magnificently fertile soils of cyberspace. One online company named iVillage was valued at $1.6 billion, at a time when it was spending nearly $100 million per year to capture annual revenues of less than $25 million. But although iVillage didn't look like much of a company itself, its stock was for a time a very real currency. It could be turned to cash or traded for other assets, some virtual and some very real. We now lived in a world where, as *Fortune* put it, "profligacy pays."[17]

The grand boom remade our perception of ourselves as individuals and as a nation, at least for a time. Politically, the boom seemed to confirm finally and absolutely that the "market" would indeed take care of us and succor us. Now that we had finally left it alone, this remarkable creature seemed to be yielding not only a bounteous prosperity but an ever more perfect harmony among peoples. And this, in turn, reinforced our sense of America's natural and necessary hegemony. America, after all, was the nation that stood most squarely in the light of the market. Hadn't the great newfangled engines of growth—the Internet especially—taken form first in America? Was this not, ipso facto, proof of the wisdom of our faith? Other nations, to grow and prosper, had simply to heed America's gospel. And many did, with ever-greater fervor. We witnessed with not-so-quiet satisfaction the evangelical conversions of Argentina, Thailand, Poland, Peru, the letting in of the market, the ecstatic embrace. Even Europeans got caught in the fever of "cowboy capitalism" and sought to swagger the swagger of the venturous.

Once again America shined as a beacon of liberty to the world. Hadn't our market brought democracy to Taiwan and to South Korea? And now, at least according to Bill Clinton, wasn't the market busy disassembling the authoritarian apparatuses of Beijing? To ship our factories off to China lock, stock, and assembly line was simply to perform the Lord's work. All the salesmen and buyers jockeying for business-class seats of the Shanghai-bound 777s were but the doughboys and GIs of the twenty-first century, expanding a bridgehead of freedom on a dark distant shore. The feudal mercantilisms and monarchical conglomerates and medieval corporate hierarchies of the old worlds were crumbling. In their place we were erecting a new temple, the basic building block the individual human being, set free from the old states, the old corporations, the old communities, not least the old labor unions.

Every so often there was a hint that not all was right in our world. Economically, the Asian financial crisis laid bare some of the dangers of our new interconnectedness. Culturally, there was the sense every so often that "globalization" might just perhaps be creating its own counter-reaction. Harvard professor Samuel Huntington warned of a brewing "Clash of Civilizations" in which the "most important conflicts" will occur along the "cultural fault lines" that separate "civilizations from one another."[18] The December 1999 collapse of the World Trade Organization summit in Seattle into bickering and bottle-throwing revealed that not everyone, at least not yet, had been co-opted into our new system.

But who had time to worry? There was too much money to make, too many new tools to master, the three-way calling and instant messaging and mass-blast e-mails. We had to learn the lingo of Internet cafés and whether to bow, if in Beijing, while exchanging business cards with our Palm Pilots. What we focused on now was our inability to focus. Big books of the era went by names like *Blur* and *Blown to Bits*. One, titled *Faster, the Acceleration of Just About Everything*, didn't even bother to print the vowels.[19] Maybe those problems out in the world would prove to be no more than minor glitches, bumps in the road. And anyway, with a minimal amount of creativity, we should be able to outsource the job of managing it all.

This perhaps was the ultimate lesson: All the necessary work of the world seemed now just to happen, somewhere else, far away, out of sight. Our job had become just to party as heartily as we knew how.

No one disputes that Gary Wendt should be recognized as a pioneer for his work on the ground in India, both at General Electric and with his own ExlService and GW Capital. When Wendt was chosen to deliver the keynote speech at the Outsourcing World Summit in 2003, it was a clear recognition by this industry of his expertise. But it would be wrong to credit Wendt with the discovery of India as the "back-office to the world."[20] The role of Columbus was actually played by Wendt's former boss, Jack Welch. To Wendt would go the role of Cortés or Pizarro, the job of actually extracting the wealth of the land.

Welch's arrival in India took place almost exactly five centuries after the Venetian set sail toward the setting sun to reach the spices of the East. Of course, the challenge of travel had lessened somewhat over the years, and it was in a jet that Welch floated onto the Subcontinent in September 1989. An Italian did act as his guide, though, a lawyer named Paolo Fresco who had long been a senior vice president of GE International. Welch was in the midst of yet another attempt to reorder his company, one that would soon bear fruit as an initiative to make GE "boundary-less," which aimed to erase all sense of physical space in the company and all sense of hierarchical specialization. It was Fresco who convinced Welch to visit India, who set up the meetings with Prime Minister Rajiv Gandhi and other top officials, who organized the soiree at the Maharaja's palace in Jaipur complete with fireworks, who arranged for Welch to visit the Taj Mahal. Welch wrote later that it was all "pinch me stuff" and that he "instantly fell in love" with the Indian people. More to the point, Welch concluded almost instantly that India was a place to make big money.[21]

As it turned out, and as Welch readily admits, he was "dead wrong" about India as a place to sell GE products and services. Big pushes by

GE's lighting and appliance divisions flopped, while the performance of the power-generation and plastics units was at best only blasé. The company's only real success was in medical systems. India had yet to follow China in figuring out how to mine America for hard currency, so the country's companies and people had few dollars to spend for imported goods. Yet India very quickly proved to be of huge value as a source of skills that could be paid for by GE in rupees and used to replace work done on the other side of the world and paid for in dollars.[22]

And GE had no intention of keeping this treasure trove hidden as some sort of competitive secret, not when the company could resell these very same services to third parties for dollars, euros, or yen. Since Welch took over GE in the early 1980s, there has been perhaps no company that has played all sides of the outsourcing business as well as General Electric. Not only has the company been a leader in sloughing off work onto others, it has been a leader in reselling both its own work and that of its suppliers, in the form of a service, to other companies looking to lighten themselves via outsourcing. And during the 1990s, it was Wendt's GE Capital that established itself as the world's most perfect business built on outsourcing, serving up both hype and hope, motive and means, showing companies how to sell assets while conveniently offering to buy them itself.[23]

In the case of India's back-office services industry, GE Capital formalized its fascination in 1997 when it established its own outsourcing operation to consolidate activities that had been outsourced from other GE units. By 2003, this operation would employ some 15,000 people, and would deliver annual savings of some $340 million as some 700 business processes were performed, or partly performed, in the country. But these numbers tell only a small part of the story, as GE's outsourcing operation in India also served as a hub for all sorts of work that was done for GE or in the name of GE by Indian contractors. More than 7,000 software developers, for instance, work for Indian companies on projects for GE or for GE customers. When a company like Kodak hires GE Capital's Vendor Financial Services to manage its customer credit operation, such work gets distributed across many of GE Capital's twenty-eight divisions, many of which actually perform the work in India. In all, about 70 percent of the work done or coordinated by General Electric in India is resold overseas, either to GE units or GE customers.[24]

The second key event that helped lay the foundation for the outsourcing of back-office work took place only a month or so after Welch "discovered" India. On the other side of the world, in Armonk, New York, Eastman Kodak CIO Kathy Hudson signed a $250 million deal in which she hired IBM, Digital Equipment, and Businessland Inc. to run her company's data center operations for the next ten years. This was the "landmark decision" that "gave a blue chip seal of approval" to the concept of outsourcing high-technology services.[25]

The Kodak deal was shocking for a number of reasons. For one, it took place at a company that was still highly vertically integrated in many other respects; Kodak still operated its own steam and electricity plants, still ran its own seventeen-mile railroad, still owned its own firefighting force.[26] For another, Kodak was the first big company to take such a plunge on what seemed to be core corporate information technology. Computer services for hire had been around at least since the early 1960s: Ross Perot's Electronic Data Systems (EDS) was one of the most successful early pioneers. Other back-office services were available even before that.[27] But such services were generally regarded as designed mainly for small, weak companies. At bigger firms, most CFOs and CIOs jealously guarded their turf—and their staffs and budgets—arguing that their particular approach to organizing back-office work was a uniquely brilliant and vital contribution to their firm's competitiveness. Until Kodak, one magazine wrote, "no self-respecting CIO would entrust IT to a *vendor*."[28]

What changed the minds of the CIOs and CFOs and CEOs was that—especially in computer work—huge sums were at stake and these sums were growing fast. At the time Kodak off-loaded its data systems work, the company was spending nearly $250 million per year on the division, including $90 million per year on hardware and software. The outsourcing deal immediately trimmed the annual cost for information system services by between 5 percent and 15 percent, and it cut annual capital expenditures by 95 percent.[29]

The third factor that would finally unleash the outsourcing of business processes appeared only toward the end of the 1990s. This was the realization that many older software systems, and especially databases, would not be able to function correctly in the coming millennium because of a software glitch that prevented them from recognizing the year 2000. The so-called Y2K bug almost overnight created an overwhelming demand for programmers to fix old code and write new, and this demand soon led many toward India or, more likely, to the companies like GE that were reselling Indian-sourced services.

To tell this story, it helps to turn again to Welch's first trip to India in 1989. Amid the parties and meetings with government officials, the GE head met a man named Azim Premji, CEO of a company named WIPRO. Already in a partnership with GE to manufacture lightbulbs, Premji now proposed another deal with GE to help develop low-cost, low-end medical systems products. Premji got the contract, and this work soon led the two companies to a third partnership, one in which WIPRO would handle more and more back-office services for GE. For Premji, this deal would prove to be the second key turning point in a career that began at age twenty-one, in the early 1960s, when his father died and left him a small vegetable oil factory.[30] Premji's first big break had come in 1979 when a nationalist Bharatiya Janata Party government evicted IBM and other multinationals from India, creating a sudden space for domestic companies in India's information technology sector. But the GE deal was the one that would propel Premji into an entirely different orbit. By 2003, the Bangalore-based firm would have 18,000 full-time employees.[31] And for a short while near the end of the great tech boom, Premji, who at the time retained an 84 percent stake in the company, held stock valued at upward of $40 billion,[32] which at the time was equal to about 1.5 percent of India's total GDP.[33]

By 2001, *The Economist* was able to write that India's information technology sector had grown to a point where it was ready to "transform commerce in the developed world."[34] Indian workers were answering phones for American companies, as well as writing software, reading MRIs, filling in tax forms, processing mortgages, managing orders, handling insurance claims, buffing PowerPoint presentations, even coloring in cartoons. Just in the epicenter of the industry, in Bangalore, by November 2003 at least 110,000 Indians were working for Americans, while in all of India, the number was some 350,000. Many expected the total to top 1 million by 2008, if not sooner.[35]

And GE was already on to the next big thing, which was to capture as much of India's top engineering and scientific talent as possible, and to put that talent to work on projects both for the conglomerate and for GE customers. As one reporter put it, GE is "snapping up" India's tech talent "to work on its next-generation refrigerators, jet engines and X-ray machines."[36] And it was reaping huge arbitrage rewards in the process of exporting this work, which it was able to purchase for only about a third of what it cost in America.[37] Not surprisingly, once again many other American companies soon rushed in to emulate GE's strategy, and Microsoft, Cisco, Ford, General Motors, Honeywell, and Cummins Engine have all opened new R&D centers in the country.

Centuries ago, it often took years of hazardous travel for traders to carry the spices of India to Europe, the travails made worthwhile by the ability to charge many times what they had paid. Now GE had found a way to ship the fruits of the human mind around the world, in an instant, and still triple the price.

In 1995, US Robotics purchased a small and nearly bankrupt company with a promising software for running small personal computers. The target firm, named Palm, had a reputation for writing good code, especially handwriting-recognition software. But when it set out to compete with its erstwhile customers in producing a new device known as a personal digital assistant, or PDA, Palm had found itself far short of the cash it needed to launch actual manufacturing. Now, though, the US Robotics deal represented a twofer of sorts for the firm. Not only did the bigger company bring Palm all the capital it needed to roll out its product, it also came stocked with in-house manufacturing experts and high-quality production lines. Yet the Palm team soon opted to continue with their pre-acquisition plan to farm out the work to a small Singapore-based contract manufacturer named Flextronics. Although the decision baffled many, within two years Palm had captured more than 80 percent of the total market for PDAs.[38] And in an almost unheard-of feat for a brand-new product, as fast as demand rose so, too, did production.

There is perhaps no better proof of the potential power of an upstart snap-together corporation than the introduction of the PDA. Only a few years earlier, Japanese firms had seemed unbeatable in any electronics business. The original idea of producing a calculator-size personal computer priced at about $300 had been floated by the American company Apple, and the most commonly used early operating software had been developed by Microsoft. But especially after Apple's Newton MessagePad came to market twice as expensive and twice as heavy as hoped, many figured that one of Japan's powerful electronics firms would soon gobble up the market, as they had so many markets before. The defeatist attitude permeated even many American firms. Tam Chung Ding, president of Motorola's Asia-Pacific semiconductor division, expressed confidence in his own company's plans for what Motorola called a "pocket organizer." But Tam also figured that Motorola's main competition would come not from its American counterparts but rather from Sony, Sharp, and Casio.[39] Yet in the end, the garland would be grabbed by a company no one had heard of, which had rejected production help from a highly respected parent in favor of a contract manufacturer almost unknown at the time.

The success of Palm was therefore much more than a matter of beating the Japanese at manufacturing. What it signified was that the long revolution in the nature of the manufacturer—indeed, of the process of bringing an idea to market—at last appeared complete. Almost all production activities, almost all service activities, had been commodified. And all were available all the time from highly specialized suppliers. Now, at last, absolutely anyone could enter any business as long as they had a plan and some capital. Manufacturing itself, rather than a down-and-dirty deed done on the shop floor, had been transformed into an act of sheer imagination. The conductivity and tensile strength of a particular metal? The vagaries of sourcing materials and managing in-bound logistics? How long to lease a particular parcel of land? How generous a Christmas bonus to give the truck drivers? All such worries had vanished, as all the world's production activities and all the world's business services were transformed into so many Lego blocks, to hunt down in catalogs and online B2B marketplaces. Today's Henry Ford didn't even have to get out of bed, let alone walk an assembly line.

Of course, this power was available not only to particularly precocious engineers, and to start-ups like Palm, and to visionary first-mover innovators like Cisco. It was by nature available to anyone, which meant that it was also very much available to any very powerful firm that felt a need to make a big move, whether against an entrenched competitor or to head off the rare start-up that refuses to be bought.

The story with Microsoft's Xbox is remarkably similar to that of Palm, although unlike Palm this lead firm faced absolutely no early-stage shortage of capital or any lack of name recognition. Only a few years earlier, Microsoft would probably have opted to set up its own production line, hiring manufacturing talent, leasing buildings, buying machinery. But this would have been very expensive, and already Microsoft planned to sell the Xbox at a loss of upward of $100 per unit. Spending tens of millions of dollars learning the secrets of manufacturing would only have swelled that loss, and postponed the day when the new business could turn a profit. Now, thanks to the new system of snap-together production, even giant Microsoft could move fast and cheap.

The story here begins in 1999 when Microsoft awarded a young executive named J Allard the task of opening a beachhead for the company in the digital home entertainment market, in essence to help push the corporation's software into the living room. Allard had already made a reputation for himself when, fresh out of college in 1993, he sold Microsoft honchos on the importance of the Internet. Now Allard concluded that the best first step into home entertainment would be to stake a claim for Microsoft in high-end gaming, and to do so really fast. This meant taking on Sony and Nintendo, which had dominated the business for years. This in turn meant delivering a highly specialized computer in a box, which could be linked to a screen in exactly the same way as Sony's latest PlayStation and Nintendo's new Game Cube.

After working with the game-developer community to set basic specs for the hardware, Allard set out to find someone to build the box. He placed his first calls to Dell, Gateway, and Compaq, but each quickly turned him down. Even though the actual Xbox box would be little different from the basic personal computers these companies assembled, they saw little chance to make a profit on a product branded by another company. Allard then called Flextronics, which already had a small business making joysticks and keyboards for Microsoft, and by February 2001 a deal was done. Almost immediately, Flextronics took over control of the manufacturing side of the project, coordinating the work of the other Xbox suppliers Microsoft was lining up. These included Intel, which was to supply the processor, NVIDIA, which provided the graphics chip, Western Digital, which made the hard drives, and Micron, which supplied the memory. And as it proved, despite the economic disruptions after September 11, by Christmas Day 2001, only ten months after the deal had been signed, Flextronics had shipped more than 1.3 million boxes. Xbox had traveled from first conception to buyers' hands in fourteen months, while avoiding most of the production glitches that have hit Sony and Nintendo over the years.[40]

There are many other recent "virtual manufacturing" successes; TiVo, for instance, falls into the start-up tradition of Palm. Yet in recent years the main beneficiaries have been already large firms, such as Cisco, which recently made an Xbox-like move into branded telephones aimed at consumers and businesses. If anything, it increasingly seems that the computer and electronics industries had already entered into a sort of post-upstart paradigm, in which fewer small companies are willing or able to challenge lead firms. Take, for instance, the path chosen by Pixelworks, a Portland, Oregon–based firm that developed an entire system architecture for plasma-screen televisions, one of the first significant American contributions to television technology since the 1970s. Rather than attempt to snap together its own production system and work to build up its own brand, the company simply licensed its technology to a Chinese company named Xoceco,[41] which assembles it into sets sold in America by branded retailers like Best Buy and Circuit City.

Even the old Japanese manufacturers seemed ever less in control of their destiny. Sony's response to the new industrial system is especially telling. The glittering high-tech leader of Japan's invasion of America in the 1980s, Sony had always tended to contract out more work than most of its home-island competitors, with their so carefully integrated industrial *keiretsus*. And so it was not surprising that Sony was one of the first Japanese firms to experiment with American-style contract manufacturing. Yet in today's ever more commodified world, success is increasingly based on one of four things: retail power, standard-setting power, old-fashioned capital investment power, or monopoly first-mover power, especially in the form of better-designed software or chips. Sony, realizing that it was weak in all of these areas—its own core revenue streams and technology expertise were based on old analog television technologies—by 2003 had taken another tack, protecting its revenue by funneling its own work to its own internal manufacturing units.

Although Sony managers depicted this more as a smart next step in the evolution of manufacturing, the decision can also be viewed as a simple defensive holding action.[42] The aim in many ways seems no more than to enable the firm to keep control over its revenues while it develops some sort of next-generation technologies that will secure its place in the network. Yet even in this effort, Sony increasingly finds itself having to turn to the same American semiconductor designers—IBM and NVIDIA— that partner with Sony's main American competitors.

However fast or brilliant the upstart, however carefully integrated the old-line manufacturer, the initiative seemed to have shifted almost entirely to the retailer and the software firm. Whatever snapping together was to be done, was to be directed by only a few.

Most early avatars of "virtual" manufacturing and "virtual" corporations focused only on how the process of production itself was changing, and on what America as a nation could do to manufacture more effectively and efficiently.[43] Many of these early on became quite extreme in their vision of the future of manufacturing. One 1993 magazine article predicted that the corporation would be replaced by "temporary" networks of "independent" companies that "share skills, costs and access to one another's markets."[44] But like almost all other manufacturing visionaries of that time, the writer of the article simply overlooked the question of how this distribution of work might also redistribute profits.

Which brings us back to Robert Reich's 1992 book *The Work of Nations*. This book, as we saw in Chapter One, is highly useful in understanding the laissez-faire trade policy of the Clinton Administration. Yet its influence on the thinking of the 1990s was actually more profound than that. This is because Reich used the book to make one of the first efforts to address how the disintegration of the old state and the old corporate systems might actually affect the distribution of power in society. What Reich realized was that globalization and outsourcing meant that a fresh new pie had been laid on the table, and so after a long period of relative social peace, once again we would now have to scramble and scrap for our shares. The real question, then, was who among us would end up with bigger slices, and who would have to settle for less.

Reich started off by sketching a downright scary picture. The nation-state and the corporation were two of the only entities over which many citizens felt they had even a modicum of control, and he now detailed how these both were being torn to shreds. But Reich then moved quickly to reassure his readers that they themselves had little to fear from the collapse of these institutions. Other, less gifted Americans—people who worked in "routine production" or who provided "in-person services"—might not fare so well in the new world. But the well-educated, highly creative, politically astute individuals whom Reich actually addressed—whom he called "symbolic analysts" and "problem solvers" and "strategic brokers"—would generally thrive in the emerging world of snap-together business. It would be these individuals who would be most in demand in the new wide-open global market, who would best be able to set their own price for their intellectual assets.[45]

In a sense, Reich resurrected the Jeffersonian image of the American citizen-entrepreneur. The yeoman farmer and yeoman shopkeeper he now morphed into the yeoman information "broker." Now, for the first time since the rise of big corporations in the nineteenth century, it would be these enterprising and hardworking and self-sufficient small holders who would again form the backbone of society. This, Reich made clear in a few of his more exuberant passages, would represent a true revolution in society, as the profits of enterprise shifted away from the "shareholders" toward the "other participants" who add "considerably more value than money." It was a process that would not stop until it had achieved nothing less than the "subordination of capital" to the "brains of the employees."[46]

It was a technocrat's wet dream. And it may help to explain why Reich, in his book and in practice, so eagerly embraced radical laissez-faire economic policy. Where investors saw the unfettering of their corporations as a way to even further expand the power of these enterprises, Reich believed that the absence of state interference would on the contrary speed the dissolution of the corporation itself, which of course for a century had been the main tool for gathering and concentrating capital. As more light filtered through to the plants that for so long had been shadowed by these immensely powerful economic entities, what would flourish would be nothing less than a more perfect market economy and a more perfect democracy.

It is perhaps not surprising that Reich's vision would be adapted into a sort of revolutionary manifesto by the new class of programmers and computer engineers whose personal stock seemed to rise so fast in the New Economy. Of the many takes on *The Work of Nations,* two are worth noting. One appeared first in an article in *Fast Company,* a magazine written for the young, highly paid, proudly overworked, unworldly, sheltered, nerdy symbolic analysts whom Reich identified as among the main beneficiaries of the breakdown of the old economic institutions. Titled "Free Agent Nation," the article trumpeted a revolution in which twenty-five million Americans had declared their "independence" from hierarchy, and had taken control over their own destinies by transforming themselves into truly "independent" contractors and consultants and freelance managers.[47] The other article appeared in the *Harvard Business Review,* written by a professor of management at MIT's Sloan School. America, the professor declared, was at the "dawn of the E-Lance economy,"[48] in which "businesses of one" would no longer be subject to any stable "chains of management." For analogy, he turned to the meltdown of the Hollywood studio system in the 1950s, a time when power "shifted from the studio to the individual." The implication, it seemed, was that all these millions of independent contractors would soon be transmuted into so many Tom Hankses, who could live between projects, presumably, off some sort of residual rights.

When the business press sought to strike a balance between their generally conservative readership and these would-be Robespierres, the result was often a Tocquevillian tone in which the inevitability of democratic revolution was reported even as the writer bemoaned the smashing of the old civilization by the mouse-wielding mob. An article in *Business Week* in late 1999 stands out. In the future, the reporter felt, all commercial relationships will be "low and flat, very adaptable and very cruel," and there would be little room, if any, for "superhero" CEOs. Power had passed at last and forever to a new churning, multiheaded democratic sovereign, in which "success will belong to companies that are leaderless—or, to be more precise, companies whose leadership is so widely shared that they resemble beehives, ant colonies, or schools of fish."[49]

At some point this reverie of revolution—of anarchy—had to pop, just like the stock market bubble that had given it life. And so it would early in the new millennium, as the gentry, shopkeepers, and clergy of the old regime emerged from their cellars to chase the *Red Herring* reading rabble back to their cubicles. No less an eminence than Michael E. Porter, the Harvard Business School professor, finally rose up to declare enough was enough. Porter chose as his target the Internet, or rather those who would believe à la John Chambers that the Internet had "changed everything." The Internet had certainly changed many things, Porter admitted, but any talk of revolution was vastly exaggerated. The Internet doesn't even "represent a break with the past," he wrote. "Rather, it is the latest stage in the ongoing evolution of information technology." Put another way, the vaunted "new economy" appears "less like a new economy than like an old economy that has access to a new technology."

For established companies, Porter's message was very reassuring. Powers and rights won long ago and defended over the course of decades in the fields of competition were a lot less threatened than the upstarts were claiming. Not only would the Internet only "rarely" nullify "the most important sources of competitive advantage in an industry," in many cases it "actually makes those sources even more important." Given a modicum of smarts, Porter said, even the oldest, heaviest, most clay-footed of enterprises could survive, even thrive. It was "established companies," he concluded, that were "often in the best position" to use the Internet "to buttress existing advantages."[50] The means may have changed, as means in business always change, but not the principles. Power was still power, mass was still mass.

And the big corporations, as we have seen, were in fact already hard at work on a myriad of efforts to reassert their power over the would-be geekocracy by turning these "knowledge workers" once again into "plug-and-play pieces." Work was shifted abroad more quickly—to India, for instance, or to China or Russia. Work was transferred onto machines and into software. University assembly lines were cranked up to pump more fresh talent onto the market. And many top managers soon discovered that these efforts not only had enabled them to head off any serious rebellion, but they had actually significantly increased their power vis-à-vis this class of worker.[51] In relatively short order, the militia of self-sufficient yeoman programmers, the New Model Army of educated contractors, had been reduced to a harried, frazzled, self-focused rout of the semi-employed.

Yes, power had been redistributed; yes, the pie had been recut. But it was now clear that it was the lead firm in any production system, or more specifically the investors who were exerting an ever-closer control over the lead firm, who had managed to cut for themselves the biggest slice. Outsourcing shifted work and responsibility outside the company, but it did not shift power. Today's employee may still work ultimately for the same firm as before. But rather than walk every day through a door at a large, vertically integrated corporation, he or she labors at the other end of a contract, or on the other end of a whole series of contracts. And this is the same everywhere in the world. Although outsourcing has spread some significant wealth to India and China, it has not so far spread real power, at least not in the normal everyday world of business (as we will see, today's production networks have created very real *potential political* power in these nations).[52] The story of India's success is not, as *The Economist* put it in 2001, the story of Indians "transforming" world commerce to suit their national interests. It is much more a story of GE, and the global corporations that followed GE's lead, transforming world commerce to better suit their private interests.

Reich would prove very correct about one issue—today's lead corporation is no longer in any sense a community of people engaged in a common pursuit. Where he went astray was in assuming that the disintegration of the physical corporation was synonymous with the destruction of the corporate form itself. What this disintegration actually meant was that capital was left even more able than ever to concentrate itself in order to exert power. The physical dissolution of the corporation into snap-together pieces is what most enabled shareholders to reconceive the corporation as a smart buyer of products and services, preferably in a marketplace over which it was able to exert near-complete control. In the end, it is only the firm's responsibility and liability that have vanished. Its power, by contrast, has grown.

So, yes, the relationship between capital and labor today less and less resembles that between Ford and the assembly-line worker circa 1930. But this does not mean that we have returned to the Arcadian marketplace of the Ohio Valley circa 1830, when small farmers and small dairymen and small tanners all sold their goods on truly free markets. Rather, the relationship today is much more similar to the one that existed between the Union Pacific and the California wheat farmer circa 1885. Like those farmers, who at best were able to group themselves into small towns strung along the rail line, today's employees increasingly find themselves strung out along lines of commerce that stretch around the world. And they are so effectively isolated from one another that all market-making power rests with the lead corporation they must serve.

In 1999, Jose Ignacio Lopez de Arriortua set out to do to automobile manufacturing what Michael Dell had done to the PC industry. It was three years since Lopez had resigned from VW as part of the deal to settle the industrial espionage case GM filed after the German carmaker had lured Lopez away. Now Lopez planned to show them all by launching his own multimodel mass-production automaker.

And why not? If he didn't, it seemed ever more likely someone else would. The chopping up of old-line manufacturers like General Motors and service companies like Conseco into ever-smaller and more commodifiable activities made these corporations lighter and more profitable. But it also seemed to Lopez to have left them more vulnerable, by forcing them to unwind many of their secrets and place them in the hands of suppliers, who could now repackage these secrets and sell them to any comer. This was where, Lopez felt, the real opportunity lay. Had not Michael Dell simply plugged together off-the-shelf components to capture control of the PC industry? Had not John Chambers wired off-the-shelf manufacturing and logistics services into the even more wildly successful Cisco? Had not Lopez himself proved such a model could work in the automotive industry, in VW's new supplier-run assembly plant in Brazil?

Lopez's basic plan seemed brilliant in its simplicity. At its core was his decade-old Plant X dream, reborn as an entirely new automotive firm named Loar (a word Lopez formed by combining the first two letters of his two last names). Final assembly would take place on a 260-acre industrial site near his hometown of Amorebieta, Spain; only 100 of a total of 6,000 employees would work directly for Loar, while the rest would report to fifty-two "supplier partners"; the company would produce 300,000 cars each year in four basic models, each named after a saint important in Lopez's life.[53] The twist was that rather than beg support from the board of a lead firm like GM or VW, Lopez planned to raise all the cash he needed—all $554 million of it—from investors, local governments, and the suppliers themselves.

Nor was Lopez alone in dreaming such dreams. A similar idea struck Robert Lutz, who was Chrysler's president until forced out soon after the Daimler deal. Though long one of the world's most respected developers of new automobiles, Lutz at age sixty-six had been written off as too old for another chance in the big leagues. Then, suddenly, in January 2000, he roared out of semiretirement at the controls of a "virtual carmaker" named Cunningham Motors. Lutz's plan was to design a high-performance luxury car priced at about $250,000, then farm out production entirely to contract manufacturers. And there was the vision of Jeff Hawkins and Donna Dubinsky, developers of the original Palm Computer. At the very height of the success of Palm's Pilot PDA in the summer of 1998, the two quit to launch a new enterprise. Within months they had chosen a name, Handspring,[54] and hired Flextronics and Flextronics's competitor, Solectron, to build bodies for a new PDA, and by the fall of 1999 they were shipping their first products.

In the end, though, few of these ventures would snap together exactly as planned. Hawkins and Dubinsky realized they didn't have the funds to grow Handspring to scale, so they sold out to Palm. Lutz, short of cash and assailed in court by his partner, accepted a new post at General Motors as vice chairman for product development. Lopez, rebuffed by the government of Amorebieta, popped up one last time in Brazil, fishing for a round $1 billion to launch Loar in Bahia, then disappeared again.

No matter how magnificent the man or woman, the inertia of capital remained very great. Early in the decade, Michael Dell had built his company to scale in a highly competitive industry by selling commodified components faster and more efficiently than anyone else. But in the years since, many of the world's big corporations had consolidated their positions, and they had become much more adept at pumping up their own profits via cross-border arbitrage. This meant two things. By the end of the 1990s, the average supplier was less willing and less able to ally with an upstart in order to challenge the big lead firms. And it meant that investors often saw less space to compete directly against existing powers. The increasing rigidity of global production systems had given the average lead corporation more security, and more time to adjust how it exercised its power and earned its profits.

This new approach, in turn, affected how these shareholders viewed the role of top management. Just as the essential activity of the corporation had changed, so too had the essential responsibilities of the CEO. The main goal now was to continue the process of disassembly, of disaggregation. And by the end of the decade, this process was increasingly extending right through to the position of the CEO itself. In other words, although a few brilliant men and women still sought to take advantage of the snap-together model to challenge existing conglomerations of capital, what actually took place was that the shareholders entered the final stage of their long-running effort to disintegrate the power of the manager.

For much of the twentieth century, one of the more intense debates in business was little noticed by the public. This was the question of who was in charge of the corporation and in whose interest this person worked. When capitalism first began to supplant feudalism, the single most important distinction between the two systems was the idea of private property, the idea that rather than absentee landlords a real person should own and care for the land. The great paradox of the corporate form is that, by its very nature, it severs this direct link by allowing many people to pool their property. At first, this did not seem to pose much of a problem. For decades, the big corporation still struck most people as a private property "owned" by men like Andrew Carnegie and Jay Gould and Pierpont Morgan and John D. Rockefeller and Henry Ford. Yet, by the 1920s, it had become impossible to ignore the fact that the great majority of corporations were no longer overseen directly by individual "owners," but had evolved into extremely complex amalgams of small properties woven into vast and intricate systems of power overseen by professional managers. The first great study of the subject, published in 1932, declared that the corporate form itself had shattered the "atom of property" and had thereby undermined "the very foundation on which the economic order" had stood for the previous three centuries.[55]

Especially after the Bolshevik revolution in Russia, many economists and social theorists began to fret that the corporate form, despite its phenomenal powers of creation, might somehow threaten the workings of the capitalist system itself. Though the subject was touched on by economists as diverse as Alfred Marshall and Thorsten Veblen, it would be carried into our postwar era most eloquently by Schumpeter. "By substituting a mere parcel of shares for the walls of and the machines in a factory," he wrote, the capitalist process "takes the life out of the idea of property." For Schumpeter, who had left his home in Austria at a time when the Socialist and National Socialist parties were growing dramatically in strength, this was no mere theory. On the contrary, his was a very real fear that the coupon-clipping dilettantes of Fifth Avenue would prove unwilling to stand at the door of their factories shooting down the Communist mob.[56] The Gilded Age had devolved into a Gelded Age.

Yet in the years after the war no anarcho-syndicalists materialized on the streets of Detroit and Pittsburgh, so this fear began to dissipate. And so, when the issue of who controlled the corporation again surfaced as a major subject of debate in the late 1950s, it would play out more as an intellectual awakening to the fact that there were no institutionalized political checks on the power of the corporate managers. The reaction to this realization would take two forms. Many politicians and academics concluded that if the shareholder no longer effectively controlled the manager, then the government should create some other power—either within the corporate form itself or within the state—to counterbalance what had evolved into nothing less than "an automatic self-perpetuating oligarchy."[57]

Investors, on the other hand, responded with a simpler argument. Rather than better governance, rather than more regulation, what society really needed to do was place the corporation back under the control of the shareholders. The main difference—and it was a big one—was that whereas the academics focused mainly on making the corporate manager more subject somehow to the will of the people of the United States, such as by giving workers and communities more power within the board of directors, the shareholders sought only to make the manager subject to them alone. The "functionless rentier" now claimed to be ready to serve a real function.[58]

The result was that the shareholders launched a three-pronged attack on managerial power that has played out over the past forty years. One prong, as we will see in more detail in the next chapter, was a legal theory—called Nexus of Contracts—that aimed to greatly strengthen the shareholder's legal "right" to direct the firm's managers while simultaneously increasing the protection these shareholders enjoy from being held liable for any of the actions of the corporation. The second prong was more purely political, and this was to *assert* more actively the already existing "right" of the investor to have more of a say over the day-to-day actions of the corporation. This thrust played out most dramatically in the rebellions by "institutional investors" against CEOs who they felt did not act aggressively enough to protect the profits against the depradations of the other constituencies within the corporation. And this campaign had very real effects. By 2004, the average CEO was three times more likely than in 1980 to get the boot.[59]

The most subtle and effective of the three campaigns was simply to erase any real distinction between the interests of top managers and those of the investor. For years investors had fixated on the idea that the corporate manager was in a position to serve his own interest at the direct expense of the interest of the shareholders, such as by choosing to invest in the long-term survival and success of the corporation rather than on immediate returns.[60] So the response now, in corporation after corporation, in industry after industry, was to increase radically the compensation for top managers, and to pay this out ever more in the form of stock in the company. In 1980, the average CEO earned a salary forty-two times as large as the average employee's. By 2002, this differential had exploded to 531 times;[61] fully loaded with bonuses, the total compensation an executive can earn can run to more than a hundred million dollars per year.[62] Take, for instance, Gary Wendt, who a month after pocketing his initial $45 million bonus was awarded a stock grant worth more than $30 million, along with more than $100 million in options.[63]

In this way, a new top manager took shape. No longer was he the company's man in the boardroom, committed and loyal to particular projects and processes and fellow managers and workers and communities and technologies and fellow oligopolists and institutions and traditions, and to the corporation itself as a productive entity. Rather, he was now the investor's man in the company, his interest made absolutely synonymous with theirs, the fantastic payouts and stock options serving ultimately not so much to confirm these men and women as singular human beings but, on the contrary, to dissolve their more human instincts entirely and thereby transform them into extensions of the marketplace itself.

The disintegration of the old corporation was now complete. Greed, Adam Smith believed, was a socially valuable passion. But it is a blind and mindless passion. For more than a century, the corporate form had contained a counterbalance to that blind passion, first in the person of the on-site entrepreneur, then in the person of the on-site manager. But now the shareholder, as a class, had at last completed the subversion of the old CEO. Which meant that for the first time in its more than a century of life, the corporation was left truly unguided by any internal rational authority, even as it found itself ever less controlled by the external rational authority of the state. The modern equivalent of the absentee landlord—the nameless and faceless horde of investors—was now in control. And so was completed the transformation of the corporation from an institution designed primarily to commercialize new and better products and to maintain the machinery necessary to make these products. From now on, it would be a much more simple mechanism designed mainly to carve wealth from others, entirely without regard to the consequences, entirely without any interest in understanding the social ramifications of what it is doing.

CHAPTER EIGHT

WARNINGS UNHEEDED

Risk vs. Reward

A t 1:00 P.M. on September 11, 2001, NBC's Tom Brokaw reported that the borders of the United States had been "closed." A few hours later, on *The NewsHour with Jim Lehrer,* a guest described the attack on the World Trade Center as a blow against the "entire international system." Not that many Americans noticed the huge disruption in international trade and finance that took place that day, nor would many have expected the government to respond in any other way than it did. Given the magnitude of the catastrophe, a break in the flow of goods in and out of the country seemed the least of our worries. More disturbing by far were the other new realities: the fighter jets that circled the capital and Manhattan, the indefinite suspension of trading on the stock markets, the shutdown of all domestic and international airline service, the rescue workers who had only just begun to gather the dead. In such a context, it seemed only natural that stores and movie theaters and restaurants would close, that professional baseball and football would cancel their games, that almost all commerce would cease. A shocked America wanted to huddle at home. By that night a sort of silence had fallen across the nation. America, the AP reported, "was locked down."[1]

Yet for managers of cross-border businesses, the reaction to the September 11 attacks posed a very different challenge entirely—how not to be shut down, how to keep the components moving and the assembly lines in gear, how to keep the information and most especially the cash flowing. And they had to do so in a very unclear landscape, which would remain unclear for a long time.

The immediacy of the challenge was obvious. By noon on September 11, many just-in-time supply chains were already shutting down. In the automotive industry, the intricate network of factories that stretches from Mexico to Canada seemed to have been rent. General Motors closed assembly plants in New Jersey, Delaware, and Maryland, Daimler-Chrysler shut all U.S. operations, Ford closed all plants in both the United States and Canada.[2] Most of the factories would struggle back on line by the next day, but the feat seemed at best temporary, owing to the continued grounding of all commercial aircraft. Though air cargo accounts for only a tiny fraction of the physical volume of trade in and out of the United States, jets carry about 40 percent of all trade by value.[3] Just from South Korea, the United States at the time of the attacks imported more than $30 million per day by air, while from Taiwan, the number was higher yet.[4] Intel, Dell, Hewlett-Packard, Gateway, Cisco, and IBM all faced almost immediate disruptions due to the break in the flow of components from Asia, and soon so would their customers. In the automotive industry, although few components are regularly shipped by air, what does fly tends to be important, and so by the end of the week a new series of closures began to ripple through the industry.

Manufacturers overseas were not in much better shape. Many faced shortages of high-technology components from America. In Japan, NEC and Fujitsu warned of imminent shortages of U.S.-made components.[5] So, too, Taiwanese computer manufacturers.[6] Not that the managers of transport companies weren't scrambling, often with great ingenuity, to find alternatives. FedEx and UPS shifted domestic air shipments onto trucks. Dell adjusted its sales machine to steer buyers to select those components that were actually on hand. At Chrysler, top managers set up a special committee to oversee the 55,000 shipments that flow each day into the company's eighteen assembly plants.[7] But the manufacturers often found themselves blindsided by the smallest of items. General Motors scrambled to hire special couriers to distribute paychecks normally delivered by air. Ford on September 13 sent home workers at its plant in Wixom, Michigan, because of a lack of door hinges.[8] Chrysler faced an imminent cutoff of a key steering component for its Ram pickup trucks.[9] Mobile phone production around the world was threatened by a shortage of a component designed to control the heat in the handsets. For personal computer makers, it was a shortage of one of the most simple parts, which was the power supply box.[10]

By the time international air service was fully restored on Saturday,[11] more than four days after the attack, many industries were on the verge of seizing up. Experienced logistics managers who in normal times brag of stopping trains to pull off a desperately needed container, or of landing a helicopter at a truck stop to loft a case of high-cost electronics straight to the assembly line, had more than met their match. The global assembly line—in a world suddenly and dramatically defined once again by national borders—looked way too global. And this was despite the fact that Tom Brokaw was actually wrong in his news reports on September 11. The U.S. government had never actually shut the nation's borders. The road tunnel from Windsor to Detroit was closed for about three hours as U.S. Customs officials adjusted their security system. But the Ambassador Bridge across the Detroit River had remained open,[12] as did Canadian Pacific's train tunnel under the river. At the Laredo crossing from Mexico into Texas, there were two short closures, but such closures occur most days.[13] America's seaports never closed. Nor were the disruptions due to added security in the days that followed as significant as they sometimes sounded. Yes, increased security inspections often resulted in twelve-hour waits by trucks entering from Canada, but by the Monday following the attack many just-in-time shipments were again being precleared. And shipping managers at many manufacturers also quickly adjusted, loading more components onto each trailer, delaying shipments of well-stocked items, diverting air cargo to truck or even ship. Making this challenge easier yet was that the economic recession that began earlier in the year had left significant slack in a transport system that only a few months earlier had been functioning full out.

Yet so tightly and intricately interconnected was the global production system that this smattering of slowdowns cascaded into disruptions that would take weeks to work through the system. Despite the marvelous flexibility of many of the supply chains run by individual companies, despite great feats of ingenuity by experienced shipping managers, despite the fact that trade during the first ten days in September was normal, despite the fact that air travel was suspended for only four days, America's exports for the whole month of September plunged more than 16 percent compared with September 2000, while imports dropped more than 14 percent. This was well more than double any effect due to the recession that had started the previous winter.[14]

Other events would soon refine the lesson:

- On December 13, 2001, militants killed seven people on the grounds of India's parliamentary building. India blamed the Pakistani government for sponsoring the attack, and within two weeks tensions mounted so high that the two nations began to mobilize hundreds of thousands of troops, and to threaten to launch nuclear weapons at each other. Under extreme pressure from other nations, the two governments eventually stood down. But the close call petrified many of the companies, like GE, that depend on operations in India.[15]

- On September 27, 2002, West Coast port employers locked out stevedores who were members of the longshoremen union. Ports from San Diego to Seattle would stay closed for ten days until President Bush invoked Taft-Hartley to order them reopened. Despite months of warnings before the lockout, during which many companies bulked up their inventories, the closure caused an estimated $2 billion per day in damage to the American economy. Among the factories that would close were automotive plants belonging to Honda, Mitsubishi, Toyota, and General Motors.[16] To keep some semblance of normal production, some companies even took to flying in steel components on 747 freighters.[17]

- On December 5, 2002, Venezuelans striking against the government of Hugo Chavez used commercial fishing vessels to block the navigation channel into Lake Maracaibo, through which some 1.5 million barrels per day of crude oil are shipped abroad, mainly to the United States. Soon, a country that supplied some 13 percent of American gasoline imports, which had long been regarded, along with Saudi Arabia, as one of the United States's two strategic oil partners, found itself importing refined gasoline from Brazil.[18]

- On March 13, 2003, the World Health Organization issued an alert about the outbreak of a deadly flulike respiratory illness that had been observed in Vietnam, Hong Kong, and China. By early April, many businesses began to worry that the disease—nicknamed SARS, for Severe Acute Respiratory Syndrome—might cause severe breaks in their supply of finished goods and components; one consultancy warned that any quarantine of China would create a "nuclear winter" in the semiconductor and electronics industries. And so it nearly proved. SARS forced Matsushita Electrical to shut assembly lines and Motorola to close its Beijing headquarters, before tapering off as mysteriously as it began.[19]

Nor did such supply-chain crises begin on September 11. Rather, the attack simply shed new light on a long catalog of at times nearly catastrophic disruptions over the previous decade. Among the most significant:

- The July 1993 explosion at a Sumitomo Chemical plant in Niihama, Japan, which cut off roughly half the world capacity for a high-grade epoxy resin, called cresol, used in the plastic casing of semiconductor chips; by August, the price of memory chips had doubled and PCs had spiked up by $100 per machine.[20]
- The January 1995 quake that smashed the Japanese city of Kobe, killing more than 5,000 people. Industrial effects ranged from the stranding of Mitsubishi-made engines destined for Chrysler assembly lines in America to a severe slowdown of production at Hosiden Corp., a liquid crystal display manufacturer that supplied Compaq, Apple, and Boeing, among other American firms.[21]
- The February 1997 fire at Toyota supplier Aisin Seiki that destroyed the company's only line for proportioning valves used in brakes; Toyota lost five days of production—70,000 vehicles—even though the component was simple to make and easily replicable by other companies.[22]
- The September 21, 1999, earthquake in Taiwan, which cut off high-tech exports for a full week and led to the shutdown of manufacturing lines around the world.

In the 1990s, the equation seemed simple enough: Just-in-time plus outsourcing plus global network equaled big savings. But it had now been made dramatically evident that such advances also entailed a huge rise in the likelihood of cascading economic breakdowns, from causes that are often all but impossible to conceive until the moment they hit. Many of these threats would clearly result in damage that is mainly local or regional in nature. Others would have effects that are only temporary, much like a blizzard. Some potential threats have clearly been trumped up.[23] But it is not hard to conceive of scenarios that would clearly result in global economic catastrophes of almost inconceivable proportions, by collapsing large swaths of our ever more specialized, rigid, and extended global production system.

In the wake of September 11, corporate managers were treated to a plethora of warnings about the strategic nature of the threat to their now globally exposed companies, and to the new global production system as a whole. "The brave new world," wrote Stephen Roach, the chief economist at Morgan Stanley, suddenly "looks a lot less seamless";[24] *Foreign Policy* magazine wondered if September 11 spelled globalization's "last hurrah."[25] Nor was there any shortage of more practical, tactically oriented studies that aimed to show how executives could make their company's supply chains more robust and flexible. James Womack, one of the main experts in Toyota-style production, urged managers to really think "lean" in the more traditional sense, and to locate "as many of the manufacturing steps as possible in close proximity" to one another.[26]

But in general, the response by executives was not to adjust but to resist. A Booz Allen Hamilton survey of Fortune 1000 CEOs over the last two months of 2001 reported that most still felt "comfortable with their ability to handle threats and discontinuities."[27] Even before the World Trade Center fires had been put out, there was a growing chorus of complaints about the government's plans to capture more information about incoming containerized cargo and airfreight. "Once the spooks take over, there's concern that trade facilitation goes out the window," complained Erik Autor, vice president of the National Retail Federation.[28] Even European Union bureaucrats got in the way; to protect their own prerogatives, they took legal action against the governments of Germany, France, the Netherlands, and Belgium for allowing U.S. Customs officers to work in their ports.[29] By April 2002, many consultants again felt free to push yet faster, tighter supply chains.[30]

At many companies, the only real practical response to the attack was to bulk up inventories slightly. Xerox raised its buffer supply of Japanese semiconductor chips from one day to four. Ford added slightly to overall inventory but remained fully committed to "lean" manufacturing. Toyota leaned on some suppliers to double their inventories. But few companies planned to rebuild the shelves they had eliminated when they first adopted just-in-time lean production. Fewer yet planned to shift any work back home to suppliers in the United States, not least because there were so few factories left to which work could be shifted. As one EDS consultant put it, the American plants "that might have once stepped into the breach have long since closed."[31]

In retrospect, the failure to adjust is not surprising. The response was little different after the Taiwan earthquake in 1999, even though that breakdown of the production system was in some ways more distressing, and it was an event easier to isolate and understand. There were at least a few significant attempts to learn from the lessons of the quake, and in the months and weeks afterward many companies actively tried to lessen their dependency on production based on the island. Some firms—Dell, for instance, as we saw in Chapter Six—set out to study their entire supply chains, to trace their own purchases and the purchases made in their name, component by component through tier after tier. Other big lead firms required their suppliers to split their orders between different factories, even different nations. Such pressure led Taiwan's number-two wafer foundry, UMC, to forge new production partnerships in Japan and in the United States. The semiconductor industry was one of the few to pursue such changes at the level of the whole sector. The Semiconductor Industry Association commissioned a study on how to limit the dangers of overdependence on a single region.[32]

Yet it wasn't long before most of these efforts began to falter. There was no shortage of reasons why: The recession that began in 2000 cut deeply into company budgets; many firms feared too much attention on supply problems would attract unwanted government regulation; the rigors of quarterly reporting remained as confounding of long-term planning as ever; tensions between Taiwan and China distracted government officials and company managers from their attempts to diversify supply; a growing glut of electronics and semiconductor capacity cut the appetite for new investment elsewhere. Most important was the fact that the nature of competition today makes it almost impossible for any company to adjust on its own, or even for any industry to do so. Absent government action to ensure that all companies around the world face the same costs of making their supply chains more secure, the marketplace tends to dictate one fact: Taking more precautions than your competitor is a good way to lose market share big-time. So despite the initial flurry of concern, within a year it was clear that few companies or industries that depended on production in Taiwan would do anything to lessen the danger they faced from any future disruption of production within that country or of trade to and from that country.

Another clear lesson from the Taiwan quake is that existing institutions outside of the corporation also failed to force firms to revamp their operations. This is most evident in two of the social institutions most clearly charged with the task of forcing corporations to analyze and lessen the risks they take: the insurance industry and the stock market. In the first, the main reaction to the new forms of risk posed by global production has been to protect its own assets as much as possible, while in the second the main reaction has been simply to ignore it.

Of the two, the insurance industry at least has shown some awareness of the new dangers that have been built into the world's industrial systems. Aon, for instance, in 2003 published a short paper on "protecting supply chains against political risks." The paper listed four "tip-offs" that a company's operations might be subject to "political risk" such as a war in Korea or a port strike in the United States. The tip-offs were: just-in-time production, highly customized products, reliance on single sources of supply, and dependence on production capacity located in a single geographic region.[33] Yet the insurance industry appears to be only slowly coming to understand that almost all of its large customers face such threats, even firms that mainly source services abroad. As one article put it, "Until recently, insurers have focused on protecting customers that don't get paid for their exports rather than on companies that don't receive their imports."[34] But the difference between these two types of loss can be profound. The first, at worst, amounts to a clearly quantifiable loss. The second, if it disturbs the functioning of an intricate and tightly geared supply chain or business operation, can result in a potentially massive disruption of production, and hence in the flow of all cash through a company.

A growing number of insurers have introduced what they term "business interruption" coverage. Unfortunately, quantifying the potential damage of even a modest break in supply is nearly impossible, and in many cases the goal for the insurer has evolved into figuring out how to limit coverage to such a degree that the carriers themselves are clearly not liable for covering even the most basic of risks. One common limit, for instance, is not to cover any chain of production that traces back to Hsinchu industrial park in Taiwan. As one underwriter at GE Francona puts it, "If Hsinchu goes up, then it's all over."[35]

The stock market's shortcomings in managing such risk seem to be even more obvious. Though in theory the stock market is one of the main places where a corporation's ability to manage risk is evaluated—firms, after all, are required to disclose basic "risks" to investors—the market performs this task in a grossly imperfect way. First, the stock market includes only some players; private firms and foreign firms do not have to report risk at all or in the same manner. Second, there is no clear definition of what constitutes risk, especially process risk, so while some firms go into detail about the potential for disruptions in their supply chains, others ignore the subject entirely. Third, it is not clear how quickly risk must be reported. Fourth, there are no clear penalties when a company makes untrue statements regarding risk.[36]

If anything, the stock market is shaped to punish those firms that actually maintain more redundancy than their competitors. It does so in two ways. First, it rewards upstarts that have nothing to lose—the Dells and Ciscos of the world—for turning the more old-fashioned redundant production systems of onetime market leaders like Compaq and Lucent against those corporations. Second, as we will see in a moment, the stock market punishes companies that suffer misfortune only after the fact. Such timing of punishment serves mainly to encourage managers to keep quiet about real and near disasters, at least up to the point where all hope of fixing the problem has been lost.

The overall effect of such an economic structure is to shift the risk from the individual venture to society as a whole. As the sociologist Charles Perrow has noted, given that true catastrophes are rare, "individual calculators" often rationally decide that the personal "benefits" of "creating and running risky systems" clearly "outweigh the risks" to their individual careers. Unfortunately, for society as a whole the exact opposite is true. When all the risky behavior of individual firms is added together, the risk of catastrophe is often "substantial" and in many cases it is increasing.[37]

The inescapable conclusion is that today's institutional structure serves to encourage companies to tear apart the very attributes we once celebrated in our traditional vertically integrated corporations, such as the ability to plan and protect, to invest and innovate, to provide stability and security. Opportunity lies in turning the more formal and carefully made structures of the past against the owners of these assets. The very goal of many upstarts is to break down these older, safer systems in order to free up and capture the wealth that has been built into what are, in essence, privately managed social infrastructures. And from the point of view of the managers at these more old-fashioned firms, who must strive on a day-to-day, even moment-to-moment basis to keep up with the upstarts, it is safety itself that begins to look most deadly.

In March 2000, a fire damaged a section of a Philips Electronics semiconductor plant in New Mexico. What happened in the weeks and months after that isolated event helps to show how today's corporations are, more and more, simply no longer built to manage production systems safely.

The chain of events—and its significance in the realm of business—was later captured concisely by a *Wall Street Journal* reporter. "Caused by a lightning bolt, the blaze in an Albuquerque semiconductor plant burned for just 10 minutes last March. But far away in Scandinavia, the fire touched off a corporate crisis that shifted the balance of power between two of Europe's biggest electronics companies." The first signs of the real impact of the fire would not emerge for four months, and it was only the following July that Swedish mobile phone manufacturer Ericsson would admit to investors that it faced a shortfall in revenue of $450 million for the year. The company, it turned out, had relied on the New Mexico plant for the entire production of an ASIC semiconductor chip named Edith-P27, a key component in its latest-model handsets. Absent that chip, the company simply could not build its new cell phone, and getting a new line up and running would take six to eight months.

The company's archrival, Nokia of Finland, had also sourced chips out of the same New Mexico plant. But unlike at Ericsson, where one executive later admitted the firm simply "did not have a plan B," Nokia in this instance had lined up a backup source of supply, and the firm was able to keep production largely unaffected. Not only was Nokia able to recover more quickly by ramping up production elsewhere, but the firm also gained significant market share.[38] At Ericsson, meanwhile, the impact was immediate and long-lived. Within hours of the announcement, the company's stock had plummeted 14 percent, and then it just kept falling, dropping by more than 50 percent over the next six months. Early the following year, the company's board decided to off-load manufacturing almost entirely to Flextronics.

The pain of Ericsson can reasonably be viewed as no more than the proper working of the market, a weeding out of a company that made a very poor decision. But it would be more accurate to view this particular change in fortune more as a matter of luck. As we have seen, all large corporations rely increasingly on single sources of supply, so in a normal world of everyday accidents and everyday disasters, whether a company rises or falls is less a matter of the wisdom of its choices than the timing and nature of particular crises. Had the fire occurred at a different time or place, it could easily have been Nokia and not Ericsson that saw its system seize up. If anything, the growing prevalence of single sourcing is proof that today's average production-oriented corporation is, in its physical organization, less and less designed to care for itself over the long or even the medium term, and more and more designed simply to maximize the immediate return on investment. And as the Ericsson case proves, this is true within the normal everyday landscape of risk, not just in cases of true catastrophes like earthquakes or wars.

The outsourcing revolution, it is now clear, has delivered a sort of triple blow to the strength of the global production system. Outsourcing eats away at the ability of the lead firm to understand and manage the system as a whole; the insistence of lead firms on steadily ratcheting down the prices they pay suppliers erodes the ability of these smaller firms to manage their own systems; and the hyperspecialization of activity that often results undermines the health of the entire production system as a whole. Of these three, outsourcing's effects on the ability of the lead firm to manage information is perhaps the most obvious effect. As we saw in Chapter Five, outsourcing is attractive not least because firms view the shifting of work outside as an excuse to do away with many of the managers and systems that once kept track of the internal operations. Although the stated hope is that responsibility for certain activities will get picked up by the suppliers, often the real result is that responsibility is not shifted onto any other set of managers but rather onto no one. A good analysis of the issue was made in 1996 by James J. Conerty, who at the time was IBM's director of risk and insurance management. In a short paper, Conerty bemoaned what the combination of outsourcing and just-in-time production had done to his company. Not least among the challenges Conerty faced was that IBM had outsourced not only much of its production but most of its risk management department itself, trimming the number of in-house staffers from fifty-five to six. "We are being asked to do more with less," Conerty said, "precisely at a time when the demands on us are increasingly heavy and the scope of our job is expanding." Even worse, he wrote, the company was coming to "depend" increasingly "on people who, no matter how highly trained and skilled, don't know our business as well as we do."[39]

The ways in which a system that allows lead firms to arbitrage among suppliers, eating away at both the strength of the individual firm and the strength of the system as a whole, are worth looking at in more detail. In today's industrial networks, the power of the lead firm, as we have seen, is increasingly directed not against other lead firms, and not only against the buyer and employee, but perhaps most consistently against the supplier that actually does the work of production. It is the savings from this that are then directed against other lead firms, not in terms of new products but lower prices. The brute power over suppliers is supplemented, as we saw in the last section, by the taking of more risks. One of the more common risks taken by upstart firms is to single-source. Here again, the savings are then used as a sort of weapon against firms that opt for the more expensive tactic of maintaining multiple sources.

On the surface, these two strategies can seem highly contradictory, given that single sourcing would seem to undermine the ability of the lead firm to pit suppliers against one another. Today's biggest companies aim, as we have seen, to be nimble, flexible, almost protean traders of commodity manufacturing services and commodity business processes, to use their ability to bestride multiple national and regional markets to buttress their power over smaller producers, who by their nature remain trapped within the cost structure of an individual nation or an individual plant. Single sourcing obviously seems to eliminate many of these advantages and to put power right back into the hands of the supplier.

But the power of arbitrage, it must be remembered, derives not from a credible threat to shift business away immediately, but from a credible threat to shift business away at some time in the not-too-distant future. With rare exceptions, time is always on the side of the lead firm, which merely has to maintain the ability to threaten to shift contracts to another supplier six months or even a year hence. Such power is somewhat more fragile than when the lead firm is able to pick and choose from among a robust set of suppliers, but in any capital-intensive activity the overall savings from consolidating the supply base can more than make up for any increase in pricing power enjoyed by the suppliers. Even when supplier industries like semiconductors and steel manage to gain pricing power, such power is usually only temporary. One of the main reasons is that many suppliers have only a few real potential customers for their products.

One result of a system in which the supply base is highly consolidated, yet in which the lead firm retains most of the pricing power, is a rather strange combination of attributes among suppliers. Many of these firms tend to be big enough that they feel little real fear of actually being driven out of business; there is simply too much capital and know-how parked under their roofs. But lacking pricing power, they also lack the ability to collect the sort of profits that would enable them to invest consistently in long-term-oriented research and development work. Take, for instance, the average automotive supplier. As one McKinsey report put it recently, a growing number of these firms now earn "less than their cost of capital," which in turn leads inevitably to cuts in their ability to improve "innovation and quality."[40] It also leads—and this is what is important to us—to an erosion of their ability to manage risk.

Some supply-chain experts argue, reasonably, that today's lean and flexible production systems are in some ways actually safer than the vertically integrated, company-delimited production organizations of two decades back.[41] But this is true only at the level of the individual firm, and only when that company faces a relatively discrete problem, such as a crisis at an individual supplier, and only in cases where the supply base in the particular industry has not been fully consolidated at a global level. The benefits to society from outsourcing, it would seem, tend to be only temporary. As outsourcing progresses though an industry, the almost inevitable result is not more and more suppliers, but a more and more consolidated supply system that is stripped ever more of its redundancy by lead firms that depend on the system yet are alienated from it by contracts. As time goes on, such systems become more and more likely to witness the sort of collapse we saw in flu vaccine in the fall of 2004, when the United States suddenly found itself without half of the supply it had ordered.[42]

The hyperspecialized and hyperrigid production system that is emerging is, if we are honest, the natural outcome of what happens when globalization and outsourcing are combined with an entire lack of regulation by governments. When the borders of the nation and the borders of the firm are both simultaneously ripped open, the result, in industry after industry, is a chain reaction that results very quickly in a single highly networked and highly specialized system of production. Except in the case of a few highly dominant market leaders, like Intel, which still generate enough wealth to maintain largely vertically integrated manufacturing systems, once outsourcing begins to work its way through any industrial sector it often becomes nearly impossible for any one firm to stand alone against the pricing pressures that are unleashed. In general, once a top-tier competitor within an industry begins to disaggregate— either to capture new market share or to protect existing market share against upstarts—the pressure grows on everyone else to do the same. And this means that all firms end up knowing less and less about their own operations, and indeed that they simply come to care less and less.

Tocqueville long ago wrote admiringly of American traders who "show a sort of heroism" in their fixation on accomplishing the task at hand as quickly and cheaply as possible. He illustrated this by looking at American sailing ships, which at the time he wrote were able to offer cheaper rates than their European competitors even though American sailors were better paid. European captains, Tocqueville observed, tended to touch often at different ports, losing time, paying anchorage fees. American captains, by contrast, sought only to perform. To get their tea, they sailed straight to Canton, stayed but a few days, then returned. "In less than two years," the American has traversed "the entire circumference of the globe and has seen land but once." He has drunk brackish water, eaten salt meat, contended with disease and weariness. But "upon his return he can sell a pound of his tea for a halfpenny less than the English merchant, and his purpose is accomplished."

It is tempting to flatter ourselves that little really has changed in the last 175 years except for the scale of our trading entities. Wal-Mart and Dell and today's other dominant trading corporations may seem to be simply large versions of their ancestors. Like the traders of old, the goal of these firms is, after all, to reach across the seas to buy products to sell here. The big difference, however, is that whereas in Tocqueville's day the risk was run by the single ship and its financial backers, today the risk is increasingly run at the level of the system itself, and therefore by all the members of society together.

In the 1960s, Milton Friedman and other economists began to advocate a new concept of the corporation. The immediate spur, as we saw in Chapters Three and Seven, were the many campaigns in those years to expand the rights of the consumer. Friedman and his allies contended that such an expansion of rights would come at the expense of the rights of the shareholder and the overall efficiency of the economy. The interest of society would be best served, Friedman held, by a sort of back-to-basics movement in which the corporation acted ultimately only to serve the interests of its shareholders—not the consumer, nor the employees, nor the "community," nor the state nor the manager nor any other interest group. By concentrating solely on maximizing the return on the shareholder's investment, the corporation would be able to organize business in a more efficient way and thereby "serve" society best by generating bigger overall profits, which would then be available for investment in other activities in order to generate more overall wealth.

So far this book has focused mainly on the effects of the efforts to take apart the physical corporation through outsourcing. But the corporation is at its core not a physical but a legal institution, so to understand the full extent of the changes that have taken place in the production system that existed through most of the twentieth century, it is vital to understand just how radically the corporation's legal nature has been changed over the last two decades. This requires a short look at the efforts in certain segments of the American legal community to translate Milton Friedman's ideas into the realm of law. Their campaign proved remarkably successful within a remarkably short period of time, and that success has greatly complicated the challenge we face today.

Friedman's central argument was based on two closely intertwined assertions: that corporations do not owe any "responsibility" to society, and that they are "owned" by their shareholders.[43] One of his main methods for promoting this idea was to assail the view that the corporation is some sort of person. Economists have traditionally regarded the corporation as a sort of "black box," a single undissectable whole that acts within the economy. Until the 1930s, economists did not look in any depth at how the actions of the marketplace could help explain the dynamics at play within the firm. In law, meanwhile, a somewhat similar concept also held the corporation to be a single whole actor. This meant that even if a firm combined the investment of a million shareholders and directed the work of a million people, within the law it was still regarded as a single "person," and therefore able to enjoy certain "rights" like any other person.[44] Although both the economic and the legal conceptions of the corporation were useful simplifications, until Friedman no one put much effort into linking the two.

What served to spark Friedman's interest in the legal analogy that the corporation is a person was one of the strands in the various campaigns in the 1960s to make corporations act in a more "socially responsible" manner. This strand traced its argument to the work of Harvard law professor E. Merrick Dodd, who in the 1930s wrote that since the corporation had been granted the rights of a person, these firms should also have "responsibilities" like any other citizen. In his writings, Friedman attacked with special vehemence Dodd's idea. "Only people can have responsibilities," he insisted.[45] Later, other economists would develop this line of argument in more detail, and to do so they often turned to the work of Ronald Coase. As we saw in Chapter Five, Coase in the 1930s had sought to break through the walls of the "black box" and develop an economic theory to explain how a firm decided whether to make or buy a particular input.

Coase's goal was to extend the marketplace right through the firm in order to better understand the decisions made by the managers of the firm. Although his work was highly useful in understanding the nature of a firm, it was never of any importance in the realm of law. Beginning in the 1970s, however, economists began to hold up Coase's work as proof of Friedman's contention that the corporation should not be regarded, even in a purely legal sense, as a person. The firm "is not an individual," is how one of the early theorists put it. It is "simply one form of legal fiction which serves as a nexus for contracting relationships."[46]

What a particular subset of economists believes traditionally has been unlikely to sway the thinking of many American politicians. Until quite recently, it was generally accepted that the job of the economist was simply to judge whether a particular politically determined organization of the economy was more or less efficient than some other politically determined organization of the economy, fully understanding that politicians might well choose to ignore the economists' advice entirely if it ran counter to the interests of their constituents. So it was not surprising that in the 1970s and 1980s there proved to be little sympathy in the Democrat-controlled Congress of that era for any major reconception of the corporation based on the somewhat esoteric writings of a group of economists led by a self-proclaimed libertarian. What in retrospect seems much more surprising was the degree of success this group would enjoy in pushing its ideas into the realm of law anyway, which they did mainly by influencing the thinking of certain legal scholars, many of whom were then appointed to influential judgeships by the Reagan Administration.

Within the legal community, the concept came to be known mainly as Nexus of Contracts Theory, and its transit from economics into the realm of law took place largely at the University of Chicago.[47] The primary goal of the theory was to give the shareholder much more clear control over the actions of the manager of the corporation while reinforcing the legal structures that protected the shareholder from liability for the actions of the corporation. At a time when many progressives were attempting to make the corporation into a truly two-way institution by creating mutual responsibilities between society as a whole and the shareholder, this countermovement sought to ensure that the corporation remained essentially a unidirectional entity, answerable more than ever only to the will of the shareholder. Though little noted in the press, the Nexus of Contracts Theory's influence within the ranks of the judiciary grew so quickly that by early in the Clinton Administration it was possible to conclude that it lay at the center of the biggest change in corporate law since the early days of the Depression.

Nexus of Contracts Theory has been attacked by progressives for undermining the corporation as a "community" and for setting the individuals who work in the corporation into a more Hobbesian relationship that is "adversarial, episodic, and economically self-interested."[48] Yet this analysis focuses too much on the effort to increase the protections against liability and not enough on the assertion of shareholder control, and so it misses much of the point of the theory. Nexus of Contracts Theory is not an effort to unleash a Hobbesian war of "all against all," though it has stumbled dangerously close to that point.[49] Nor does it aim at a sort of legal dissolution of the corporation to go along with the physical dissolution of the means of production. On the contrary, Nexus of Contracts Theory has made the corporation into a far more perfect tool by which to centralize power while at the same time placing that power in the hands of only a few.

For our purposes, what is important is that at much the same time when the managers of the corporation were taking advantage of new technologies and new political freedoms to revolutionize the physical organization of the firm, a group of legal scholars working off a script written by libertarian economists forged a radically new legal theory that sought to eliminate all the age-old troublesome ambiguities about the nature of the firm. No longer could the corporation legally be considered an institution designed to organize production and to transform raw material into useful goods. No longer could the firm be considered legally to be primarily a social institution that joined various constituencies into a common effort, the ultimate purpose of which was somehow to serve society. Today's corporations exist, in the legal sense, only to enable the shareholders to exert pure power, unmitigatable by other members of society whether working individually or through government. And such power increasingly is directed against lesser capitalists, and individual employees, and the social infrastructure itself, in order not to build and create but merely to extract wealth and transfer this wealth into the hands of the shareholder.

The sheer scope and power of Wal-Mart is astounding. Though familiar, the numbers are worth repeating. Wal-Mart is the biggest company in the world. Its sales of $256 billion in 2003 far surpassed those of ExxonMobil and General Motors and were three times as much as the world's No. 2 retailer, France's Carrefour. Every week, close to 140 million shoppers visit Wal-Mart's nearly 5,000 stores. The company sells almost a third of all paper towels, toothpaste, and shampoo consumed in the United States each year. The company does more business than Sears, Target, Safeway, K-Mart, Kroger, and JCPenney combined. More than 1.3 million Americans work directly for Wal-Mart, which is nearly one percent of the working population. The company accounts for 2.3 percent of the U.S. GDP. [50]

For most of the last century, our production system was managed mainly by the vertically integrated, production-oriented manufacturer. Until recently, it was the industrial manager who was charged with ensuring the safe, intelligent, efficient, and sustained functioning of the great production machines, which were aligned in largely autonomous compartmentalized independent corporations. But outsourcing means that at the very moment when information has enabled the corporation to expand the scope of its activities far beyond what anyone had imagined possible, and to engage in outsourcing to a degree never before seen, the old managerial systems no longer exist to ensure the safe operation of the system. Instead, the basic responsibility for running the operation of the system has now been placed in the hands of a very different sort of firm, which is focused mainly on trading in the production of other firms. So, besides all the other things that Wal-Mart does for us, we should also understand that this company, and the growing number of firms designed to act like it, are the private-sector entities to which we have outsourced de facto management of our production system (and, as we will see in the next chapter, management of much of our relations with other nations).

It is not unreasonable to expect an entity of the scope and scale of Wal-Mart to be able to manage the section of the global production system that lies under its power. It is also not unreasonable to expect that Wal-Mart and similar firms would have a natural interest in doing so. The problem, however, is that Wal-Mart is built to be a retailer and a trader, so it is built only to demand and to respond to demands, not to produce. It is a company that by its very nature perceives no need even to understand the processes of supply and of production, let alone manage them carefully for the long term. In other words, for all of Wal-Mart's power, which is as immense as that of any firm in American history, the company is not built to use that power to preserve the production system. On the contrary, it is much more likely to use that power to sap the strength of that system.

To understand what it means to replace the production-oriented, management-driven firm with a stripped-down successor vastly less able to analyze, plan for, manage, or control risk, it helps to look at the results of Wal-Mart's efforts to exert power over its producers. The firm is able to deeply influence the workings of almost all of the companies that supply it, and much of this influence can be highly positive, taking the form of demands that these producers "modernize" their operations and become "more efficient."[51] But, as we saw in Chapter Four, Wal-Mart's power is so extreme that—like many lead firms in a production chain—it can all but dictate how much producers earn and, to a growing degree, how much they spend and how they spend it. Take, for instance, Levi's. When that company finally decided it had no option but to distribute its clothes through Wal-Mart, the big retailer required Levi's to both revamp its entire logistics system and to introduce a new lower-quality and lower-cost version of its famous pants. Meeting Wal-Mart's first demand resulted in huge savings for Levi's throughout its entire business; meeting Wal-Mart's second demand led to deep fears among top executives that Levi's was undermining the value of a brand built up over more than a century of business.

The shift in power over the last decade away from the firms that actually do the work of manufacturing can seem shocking. In 1992, when GM was still the biggest firm in America, purchasing czar Jose Ignacio Lopez de Arriortua was almost run out of Detroit by automotive suppliers enraged by his cost-cutting campaign. Even within a truly immense production-oriented corporation, the supplier still had a real say over the operation of the system. Today, however, Wal-Mart is so powerful that even many giant and long-independent producers—firms like Procter & Gamble and Unilever—dare not question its dictates. Every one of these firms is, of

Over the last half century, humans have developed many phenome-nally complex systems, along with the ability to manage them safely—at least most of the time. Among the systems that have proven to be highly reliable, if not perfect, are air traffic control, the generation of electricity using nuclear-powered plants—even, some may argue, the management of nuclear weapons during the Cold War. Further, our soci-ety continues to make some systems more resilient, such as the Federal Reserve's post–September 11 efforts to force financial institutions to back up their records more securely.[54] Other systems, meanwhile, have repeat-edly proven their value. The oil production system, for all of its prob-lems, has proven remarkably resilient over the years.[55]

Hence there would seem to be no reason why we would not be able to develop the strategies and processes by which to manage our global pro-duction system in a more secure way. Yet a closer look shows that for every success in recent years there are at least as many instances in which it seems society is actually losing its ability to manage systems safely. For instance, even as the Federal Reserve insists that financial firms back up data far enough outside of New York to account for any conceivable dis-aster in that city, more and more of these same financial institutions are coming to rely on a day-to-day basis on highly lean services located on the other side of world, in far less stable locales than the United States. In the case of oil, meanwhile, even as we use force to ensure that friendly regimes control the reserves in the Gulf region, we have allowed our private-sector energy firms to consolidate refining and transportation facilities to an extreme degree.[56]

In recent years, the theoretical debate over how best to manage high-risk systems has been dominated by two contending schools of thought. One, following in the steps of Yale sociologist Charles Perrow, holds that accidents are "normal" and therefore to some degree unavoidable, espe-cially when a system combines what he calls "interactive complexity" with "tight coupling." Interactive complexity arises when multiple fail-ures can create unexpected consequences, while Perrow has defined tight coupling as a system in which "processes happen very fast and can't be turned off, the failed parts cannot be isolated from other parts, or there is no other way to keep the production going safely." The only way to really avoid big breakdowns, Perrow wrote, is to radically redesign the complex system, scale it back drastically, or shut it down entirely.[57] The competing approach to managing high-risk systems is known as "high-reliability organization theory." Members of this school hold that almost any system can be made almost perfectly safe, as long as the system is characterized by strong management, is highly redundant, has developed an autarkic culture of safety, and is able to learn from mistakes.[58]

Yet today, in the case of our global production system, we increasingly violate both of these theories. We depend intimately on a system that we are making ever more interactively complex and tightly coupled. At the same time, we are abandoning redundancy, abandoning close management attention, abandoning closed monocultural safety systems. And we have opened the production system to vastly more political risk than ever before. Humans can brag of many instances where they have devised systems that account for all the known vagaries of nature. They have never proven able to consistently account for the vagaries of man.

So clear are some of the dangers we face, and so extreme some of our efforts to ignore them, it is reasonable to wonder whether we have finally reached some limit of the human imagination. As two crisis management experts wrote in the *Harvard Business Review* in April 2003, "Quite simply, the tenets of traditional crisis management are not serving us well anymore. Something critical is missing: the ability to think comprehensively."[59]

Thirty years ago, Langdon Winner, a political scientist who writes on how technology affects society, published an essay on how humans over the centuries have perceived the issue of social and technological complexity. While noting that in the works of most philosophers there is a "crucial gap at exactly the point where complexity appears relevant," Winner believed that in recent decades the complexity of life in our technologically complex world had begun to leave people feeling disoriented, frustrated, even powerless. One result was that more and more people now respond to complexity by throwing their hands up in "despair," in essence surrendering themselves to the belief that, in Winner's words, "the world has fallen to the rule of an artificial self-determining, self-propelling God."[60]

In many senses, our faith that free trade and the free market will somehow manage automatically the global production system for us lies in this tradition. Managing the world economy is a big and tough task, which globalization has made far more complex and confusing than ever. It is highly tempting to regard the truly vast and revolutionary workings of this system teleologically, and to view the global marketplace as some sort of irresistible, ineluctable, mechanistic force that—because it has so far proven relatively beneficent—can be trusted with "managing" ever more of the task for us.

Yet we also know that our production system is not some sort of god. And nor, for that matter, is the market. Both are made up of regular people and are run by regular people, which means that every yielding of power to the "free market" is nothing more than a ceding of management of some sector of the economy to private-sector entities, whose interests may or may not coincide with those of society as a whole, and who in some cases may not even understand what exactly it is we want them to manage. However much we may wish these to be wise yieldings to the workings of a somehow robotically rational system, every such decision may simply mean that no rational mind—human or artificial—is judging the safety of any particular activity.

The political wisdom of these decisions—the ways in which the shift of management from the state to the private sector affects the distribution in society of the proceeds and power of business—should probably be debated far more intensely than they are now. The more pressing question is whether the private-sector institutions to which we are ceding these tasks and these powers are up to the job. Over the last century, it was not the Market that somehow magically brought forth the wonders that distinguish our life from the lives of our great-grandparents. Nor was it the Market that over these many decades has maintained and groomed the production system itself. Both tasks were overseen by rationally managed firms that existed within and sometimes over the marketplace, and that interacted intimately with rational actors in government whose ultimate goal was to ensure that the process in its entirety served the interests of a democratically organized society. The Market did not provide. It was the hand of man that provided, rationally directed by the mind of man. The Market served us only as a tool to help us ensure that these human institutions operated in a somewhat efficient manner.

Unfortunately, the private actors to which we have turned over management of this system are, compared to their predecessors, rather simple-minded creatures; indeed, it is questionable whether we should really regard them as intelligently minded at all. The shifting of the power to direct economic activity from the producer to the retailer and the trader, and from the professional manager to the shareholder, means the production system today is overseen less and less by the rational human mind and more and more by some sort of pure desire, some sort of pure appetite. At a time when the system itself is far more complex than ever before, and at a time when it faces threats unlike any it has ever faced, it would seem that we have placed it all under the control of our stomach.

CHAPTER NINE

RENT AND RENDING

Stretched to the Limit?

In April 2004, Boeing's board of directors approved plans to introduce a new jetliner named the 7E7. Although the craft did not represent a quantum leap in performance—the 7E7 gives passengers more space while using 20 percent less fuel—it was still one of the most important technological advances in jetliner design in decades. Yet by the end of the year Boeing would barely eke out enough orders to keep the project on track. And this was despite the fact that for Boeing, the stakes in producing the 7E7 were much higher than they first appeared. In the seven years before the new aircraft was announced, Boeing's airliner manufacturing division had watched its share of new orders plunge from some 70 percent of the total to 40 percent. A failure to sell the 7E7 may well have spelled the end for Boeing's commercial business.

Blame for Boeing's woes is usually put on the European aircraft maker Airbus; Boeing defenders say Europe's extensive subsidization of Airbus allows that firm to sell under the real cost of production.[1] Although true in part, this argument only begins to touch on what is going on in the industry, and the recent trans-Atlantic talks on cutting subsidies will likely do little to alter the basic trends. Boeing is a true pioneer in both globalization of production and in outsourcing, and the evolution of its commercial unit in recent years offers one of the best windows into the processes at work in many of today's global industries. The picture that comes through is not so much of how a profit-fixated American corporation nearly failed in competition with firms from more mercantile-minded societies, but of how a global industrial system composed of many suppliers and many na-tions tends, ever so slowly at first and then faster and faster, to eat itself up. It is not a story of winners and losers, but of a sort of cannibalism of a global common property that leaves everyone less well off.

As in so many other industries, commercial airline production has been marked by a major shakeout among suppliers. And as in so many other industries the reason for this shakeout has less to do with old-fashioned competition than with the efforts of an American lead firm to refashion itself into a newfangled "systems integrator." Although the avi-ation industry supply base has been shrinking for a long time, the process gained speed once Boeing launched its effort to off-load manufacturing activities, and like Dell and Nike focus mainly on design and marketing.[2] Since then, the effects have proven to be more dramatic than in most other sectors—not least because the process began soon after Boeing's December 1996 purchase of McDonnell Douglas reduced the industry to a duopoly.[3] From more than ten in the late 1970s, the number of major commercial aerospace suppliers in the United States fell to two by 2004.[4] In Europe, the shrinkage was just as striking.[5]

Up to this point, we have focused mainly on how such a process of con-solidation and outsourcing affects the distribution of power within the economy, how companies derive their profits, and the ability of private-sector entities to manage risk within the systems on which they depend. In these respects, the situation with Boeing and in the commercial-aircraft in-dustry is little different. For a variety of reasons—not least the collapse of profitability at airlines after deregulation in the late 1970s—the makers of aircraft long ago settled into a business model more in the tradition of Henry Ford and his Model-T than of Howard Hughes; each firm produces a few basic aircraft architectures into which they every so often blend a few new technologies.[6] Yet as Boeing's difficulties prove, even this model of slow-motion progress now seems at risk. It is increasingly clear that in today's air-liner industry, for many promising technologies there is simply no longer any private-sector production pathway that leads to the marketplace.[7]

What we have not looked at in much depth is the role of the state in today's global industries; if anything, we have focused more on the state's absence. The Boeing case is especially useful in illuminating the role of the state in two ways. First, the firm long ago emerged as one of the true masters of the business of trading manufacturing contracts for airliner orders. Commonly called "offsets," such agreements require Boeing to locate a certain amount of production work in a country in exchange for a certain number of orders from that country, usually from state-owned or state-influenced airlines.[8] Second, Boeing and Airbus are clearly two different types of corporation, their basic aims reflecting the different purposes to which they have been set by their respective states. The prime goal of one, Boeing, is to earn a return on the investment of its shareholders. The prime goal of Airbus, meanwhile, is to provide European citizens with work and to serve as a sort of ark to carry useful technologies and human skills into the future. To meet its goals, Boeing cannot turn to its home government for funds; the company can, depending on the political winds, sometimes summon support in state-to-state negotiations. To meet its goals, Airbus, by contrast, has long been able to tap into super-low-cost "loans" from EU governments, and has long been able to count on unwavering support at the negotiating table. Such an analysis is not all that new. Its main shortcoming is that it does not go far enough in detailing how competition between two such different entities—when played out in today's global system—tends ultimately to harm the system as a whole rather than to build it up.

Boeing's reaction to Airbus's challenge was not that of an old-fashioned vertically integrated managerial-directed American corporation, rooted securely within the American state. The firm did not respond by investing in really significant innovation in its product, nor did it beg Washington to bail it out, nor did it simply abandon the commercial jetliner business, though it threatened to do so.[9] Instead, Boeing found an easier and simpler way to match the subsidies that Airbus receives from Europe even while continuing to pay out profits to its shareholders. This was to apply screws to its global array of suppliers and, through the suppliers, to some of the states that still believe it important to preserve industry, be it for the sake of jobs or technologies. In other words, in today's multistate industrial system, the American shareholders in a giant firm, put on the defensive by subsidies from the European state, in the process of beating their retreat from the sector, are able to extract a matching set of subsidies from whatever state entities feel they have a stake in the survival of the organization these shareholders still control. In an increasingly outsourced yet consolidated global industry, this comes at the expense of the overall health of the system itself.

To understand how today's aviation industry works, it helps to view Boeing's commercial division not as a traditional "modern" twentieth-century corporation but rather a form of cooperative, composed of suppliers. Increasingly, the main job for executives in Boeing's Chicago headquarters is to sit quietly as these lower-tier firms dicker over which will cough up the last few dollars to set the whole process of production into motion. When a top Boeing executive tells an audience in Japan that "Boeing is less concerned about market share than profitability,"[10] the message is clear—Boeing's Japanese suppliers must drop their prices further or take on more responsibility. And so it proved. With the 7E7, Boeing's longtime suppliers in Japan—Mitsubishi, Kawasaki, and Fuji—for the first time accepted a designation as "risk-sharing partners."[11] This means not that they got a bigger share of profits, but that they got to pick up a bigger share of the total cost of development of the aircraft. Boeing also forced suppliers in Australia, Italy, and China to become "risk-sharing partners." Even mighty GE was coerced into reaching into its pocket in exchange for future engine contracts.[12]

More and more, it is not only these private-sector firms that kick in the money Boeing demands. The price point is often beyond their means; so the danger is not only to their profits but to their survival. Often, the result is that the various states where these firms are located make up the difference, essentially matching the subsidies that Europe's governments pay to Airbus, but in a piecemeal fashion. In the case of the 7E7, the most generous offers came, perhaps not surprisingly, from Tokyo. In order to enable Mitsubishi, Kawasaki, and Fuji to play their new roles as "risk-sharing partners," the Japanese government had to grant the 7E7 project "national project" status, which cleared the way for a wide array of state subsidies to the three firms.[13] This was in addition to the money Tokyo had already paid out to support development of the lightweight composite materials that will be used to build the frame of the 7E7. Nor were these indirect subsidies the only concession Boeing extracted from the Japanese. Boeing's board approved 7E7 production only after the Japanese airline ANA placed an order for fifty aircraft. And it was another Japanese airline, JAL, that later became the first member of the airline "establishment" to order the craft.[14]

Boeing also plays this game directly, in its own name. After conducting a sort of auction that pitted U.S. state against U.S. state, Boeing announced that it would keep final assembly of the 7E7 located in its long-time home of Washington, but only after Washington officials agreed to pony up $3.2 billion.[15] Indeed, so many suppliers feel dependent on doing work for Boeing, and so many states around the world feel some obligation to these suppliers, or directly to Boeing, that the offers can soon add up to huge sums. In all, Boeing was able to leverage at least 45 percent of the total development costs for the 7E7 from offshore suppliers and foreign governments,[16] while the total from domestic public and private sources may have been nearly as high. Boeing in a sense has figured out how to harvest the fear that it will simply disappear, and then transfer the fruits of this fear not into some sort of socially useful lasting infrastructure but into the pockets of its shareholders, by guaranteeing them almost no real risk on their investment.[17]

To those with a more mercantile view of the world, it can seem that Boeing has died, and that legions of ants are carving up its carcass and carrying off big chunks to nations where the manufacturing corporation is still viewed as a public good. But what is really happening is that two forms of transfer are taking place—one from the now global system of aircraft production to the European and Japanese worker and producer, and one from that same system to the American shareholder. Neither of these transfers is wrong, in and of itself. The problem is that in the present structure of the industry, both of these transfers serve in the end only to eat away at the strength of the common system. If we look closer, it becomes clear that no one anywhere is really winning anything more than they have now. When work was divvied out for Airbus's swollen 555-passenger A380, as much as 45 percent went to suppliers located in the United States, despite the fact that Europeans have long tried to keep almost all early-stage Airbus work close to home. At least in part, this was because Boeing's sell-off of so many assets in recent years, in order to turn itself into a sleek and svelte "systems integrator," lured many European aviation firms into making big investments in existing capacity in the United States. Naturally, these firms now view as irrational any suggestion that they should replicate such facilities at home.[18] Similarly, the cost of the giant A380 and the cost of the new A350—which was launched almost entirely to lure potential buyers away from the 7E7—are clearly harming Airbus's near-term performance.[19]

In today's outsourced globalized world it seems that competition increasingly serves not to drive innovation, or to drive down prices through improvements in the process, but to drive corporations back ever so slowly at first, then faster and faster toward the harbor of the state. In the case of Boeing, what we have is a de facto nationalization of production not by Washington, but by Tokyo and Washington State. Yet it is a nationalization that does not transfer effective control to any state, and so only perpetuates the shareholders' ability to profit at the direct expense of these social assets. Even in instances of duopoly, the result today is not two separate corporations competing only at the margins and only to keep their skills sharp—they are not, in the words of Schumpeter, "corespective" firms. Rather, today's mature industries look and act ever more like Soviet-style utilities, bereft even of the clumsy care of the Soviet bureaucrat. On the contrary, they increasingly are being torn to pieces by a sort of hybrid competition-to-the-death between the European and Japanese governments and the American investor.

The launch of the 7E7 may well prove to be the last big leap for this particular industrial system. In order to introduce the plane, Boeing hunted down almost all the potential suppliers, and stripped these lesser capitalists of most of their easy-to-grab wealth as well as that of their state protectors. From now on the system itself will likely become only that much more sclerotic, and technological advances that much slower.[20] Indeed, the 7E7 announcement itself set off a further round of collapses in the system, the most important of which is Pratt & Whitney's expected retreat from making jet engines for the commercial market.[21]

In a sense, Boeing's commercial unit truly has become an absentee landlord, able simply to collect rent from those who still actually wish to do the work, who are willing to do the sales, who still have access to capital, who still have states that they can milk. Yet even this status is only temporary. In the same way that the absentee landlords of the past often destroyed their own land—by demanding ever more return while making ever less investment—Boeing's directors, however unintentionally, will simply run down the so marvelous machine that our society built up so carefully over the years and that we entrusted to them to run. In the end, when they have extracted all there is to extract, they will return the scrap to the state. But by then it is not clear which state will sign for delivery. In a global system in which all nations are tied together in mutual dependence, no one will likely feel any need to take sole responsibility for building it all back up again.

When terrorists crashed jetliners into the towers of the World Trade Center and into the west wall of the Pentagon in September 2001, the shock was instantaneous. In three moments that Tuesday morning, America's sense of invulnerability was destroyed and an enemy within revealed. Yet the news of the attack itself was only the first of many blows to the American psyche that day. Over the next few hours, as citizens struggled to make sense of the event, they had to absorb a series of sickening revelations. America's vast military power had done nothing to prevent the attack, our extravagantly funded intelligence system had failed to process the most basic of information, and the federal government had no real plan to maintain control in a crisis.

Yet the most crushing blow that day came when the twin towers fell. Over the years we had seen other tall buildings catch fire or suffer bombings or be shaken by earthquakes. But none had simply collapsed. Before the South Tower began to implode at 9:59 that morning, most Americans watching the event in person or on television naturally expected the fires simply to burn up toward the roof, gutting much of the buildings but leaving the nation with a task of restoration, not of reconstruction from the bedrock up. Had the buildings stood, the attack would have testified to many things: the randomness of death, the invisibility of threat, the inevitability of conflict among cultures. But the fact that the towers fell, that one of our most basic of systems failed so catastrophically, made the day far more disturbing. The attack now testified also to the tenuousness of our social structure itself, the fragility of our civilization.

And so we should understand that although today's global industrial system poses many grave dangers, the ultimate peril is that it will crash. In today's ever more intricate, ever more tightly geared system, the risk increasingly is that a single relatively isolated event will set in motion a cascading series of industrial shutdowns that cannot be stopped, and that this will wipe out the system's ever more thinly spread reserves of components and cash. Such a catastrophe would ultimately be mainly financial in nature, and not all that different from a stock market crash or a bank run, though in this case it would be industrial firms that would knock one another over. But unlike such purely financial crashes, a physically precipitated crash would likely prove far more destructive. Unlike cash, industrial components are not fungible, which means this system could prove very hard to restart.

In the 1960s, many Americans feared that a production-oriented alliance of interests was "bending" the consumer, and society as a whole, to the needs of the machines.[22] Since then a revolution has been achieved, one in which the globe-straddling trader has replaced the vertically integrated manufacturer as the world's primary organizer of economic activity. The main question today then is how the shareholders bend the machine to their needs and desires. The answer is that they do not so much bend as bust. Today's dominant corporations, as we have seen, do not have any built-in interest or ability to plan or to invest. Their power is mainly extractive and increasingly destructive. Rather than working to ensure their own long-term well-being and that of the system on which they depend, they are designed in such a way that their actions tend overall to make the problems only worse.

Coming to terms with this new reality will not be easy. One reason is that in so many other respects, our American-made global economy can appear to be truly a vision of beauty. More than two centuries ago, Adam Smith celebrated the power of common human effort. "Without the assistance and co-operation of many thousands," he wrote, "the very meanest person in a civilized country could not be provided, even according to, what we very falsely imagine, the easy and simple manner in which he is commonly accommodated."[23] Each of us today now counts in the course of our lives on the labor of many millions to clothe and shelter and feed us, and to transport us and educate us and entertain us, and keep us healthy and safe, and clean up after us. One result of this magnificent symphony is a material well-being that would make Faust blush. And so it is not unreasonable to believe that we have arrived at a state of near perfection, but only if we ignore entirely such factors as politics, power, and time.

Another hurdle to coming to terms with the fragility of the production system is that the idea contrasts so sharply with so many of our basic expectations of what "trade" among nations is supposed to deliver. Deep in many of our minds is engraved the conviction that "free trade" results not merely in a more efficient world, nor merely a politically safer world, but a world that is also safer economically. When the British parliament first began to debate the merits of free trade, the poet and politician Thomas Babington Macaulay assailed Great Britain's protectionist Corn Laws. The average citizen paid more for bread, he said, but in return the nation was made no more secure. On the contrary, Macaulay declared, it was free trade, not protectionism, that was the source of true "independence," because the global market for grain was by nature free from the control by any one government or any one company. "Next to independence, and indeed, amounting to practically the same thing, is a very wide dependence, a dependence on the whole world, on every state and climate."[24]

But there is a big difference between a global market for grain and a global production system. Free trade among corn-growing nations can indeed create a single great sea of grain able to wash providentially into any corner of scarcity (assuming the absence of strong global cartels of nations or of global-scale grain-trading corporations). Manufacturing, by contrast, when blended into a single global system, will naturally tend—absent government regulation to the contrary—to evolve straight and fast toward a single global structure, defined by a degree of rationalization and specialization that amounts to the exact opposite of the independence Macaulay envisioned, yet which is, if we are honest, exactly what Adam Smith envisioned as he walked the floor of the pin factory.[25]

Not everyone has failed to understand what happens when a process of rationalization continues for too long. Indeed, although many economists are still under the spell of the dreams of their ancestors, experts in other fields have taken into account that the balances of human systems do change over time, and that under certain circumstances a society can become too efficient and too specialized.

Take, for instance, the insight of the military planner. In 1943, the U.S. Army Air Force sought to paralyze Nazi industry by bombing Germany's capacity to manufacture ball bearings, which were viewed as sort of the microchip of the era, a "keystone" industrial product.[26] During the Cold

War, the Eisenhower Administration promoted the interstate highway system not least as a way to decentralize America's industrial base, in order to better protect it from nuclear attack.

Take also the insight of the anthropologist, not least some studies on the demise of "complex societies." In one, a scholar using the lens of "efficiency" concluded there may come a point where a crisis that a less efficient state can easily master becomes "insurmountable" because otherwise rational-seeming efforts have left a society "lack[ing] reserves" and flexibility.[27] In another, two professors concluded that in highly "specialized" societies "disruptions occurring anywhere will be spread everywhere, whereas in less complex settings a society would be cushioned" by, among other things, "less interlinkage among parts" and "greater time delays between cause and ultimate outcome."[28]

And take, for instance, the insight of the natural scientist. Charles Darwin is best known for his theory of natural selection, which describes a process that tends ultimately toward divergence and specialization. What is especially useful to note is that Darwin's work did not descend only from that of Linnaeus and Lamarck. Darwin was also a close student of Adam Smith, and he drew much of his inspiration directly from the industrial revolution he saw in action all around him in nineteenth-century Britain. The species of the world, Darwin felt, evolved much in the way manufacturers evolved their products and firms, toward ever-greater degrees of what we now call "biodiversity." Unfortunately, as modern naturalists have proven, such highly specialized and highly interlinked systems, if disturbed, often result in massive ecological collapse.

When deciding how to manage our global economy, these days we rarely if ever consider such non-economic insights. Instead, we insist on believing that the "market" will handle it all, which really is to insist that the private-sector entities that dominate most markets have a built-in interest in planning for the safety of our society. But as we have seen, these private-sector entities are no longer designed to maintain the machines on which we depend, which means our so beautiful system, as now balanced, seems doomed sooner or later to some sort of collapse. Every day by its nature, its built-in urge to use every iota of material within the system in the absolute most efficient way possible and hence the most unique way possible, its blind desire to strip all redundancy from the system and shift that wealth into the pockets of the shareholder, today's global production system undermines its own foundations, excavating the bricks it uses to build our ever-finer spires from the deepest columns on which we all stand.

Today no leader in the world talks, like Bismarck, of a "marriage of rye and iron," by which the German chancellor meant self-sufficiency in food and industry for the sake of making war. Almost all nations today are, on the contrary, joined in a sort of marriage of East and West, in which human industry itself is the tie that binds. The era of national industrialisms honed to win power and glory is over. America's arms and mass producers cleared the way, and America's system-building vision and system-maintaining acumen completed the job. Rarely anymore must Americans march down the halls of Montezuma, if only they march often enough down the halls of the Mall of America.

This is a very good thing, at least as long as it makes the world a safer place. At the point where risk begins to increase—be it of an economic breakdown or of a political conflict or a debilitating political compromise—intimate interdependence can become a very bad thing. Up through 1989, in the hands of every American president from Franklin Roosevelt through Ronald Reagan, all of whom were "realistic liberals" when it came to managing global economic integration, the strategy worked very well indeed. The overall result was to expand the power and reach of the American state, not least by enmeshing Western Europe and Japan almost inextricably in the American economy, in such a way as to impinge only minimally on the liberty of any of the nations and individuals within the system. In the fifteen years since the Cold War ended and management of the system was turned over to the private sector, the results have been nothing short of disastrous, not only economically but politically. In exchange for truly marginal increases in the overall "efficiency" of the global economy, the welfare of America has been tied intimately to that of societies we do not control and do not really understand.

Thanks to the volatile mix of globalization and outsourcing, Americans now find themselves locked into many deeply interdependent economic relationships with many new states, and we live now in a world in which a conflict on the Korean peninsula or between India and Pakistan would create great havoc right in the heart of the American economy. To illustrate how little we understand the dynamics of such relationships, it is sufficient to discuss only the example of China. No longer is there any doubt just how closely the economies of our two nations are intertwined.[29] What is doubtful, indeed downright laughable, is the confidence that we have any idea whatsoever of how this economic interdependence will play out in the coming years in the realm of politics. This is made starkly clear if we look at the analogies we use to try to understand what it means to be shackled to a very powerful and yet socially fragile nation, with a very different sense of how the world works.

Some argue, for instance, that a valid model for predicting how the U.S.-China relationship will evolve is America's long-standing symbiotic relationships with Japan and Europe, which have proven to be so beneficial to all parties. This is a reasonable starting point, but only if we also recognize the ways in which our relationship with China differs from these others. Most obvious is that China is far more populous, far poorer, and far less democratic than any nation with which America has made itself intimately interdependent in the past. China also differs from many of these traditional allies in that it was not defeated in war, is not occupied by American troops, and is not bound to America by treaty or by fear of any common enemy.

Others believe a more accurate model for predicting the evolution of the U.S.-China relationship is the U.S.-Soviet relationship. The nuclear face-off between the United States and the Soviet Union was the only time in history when America found itself intimately interdependent with another nation that was not an ally. Given that Americans and Russians did not blow each other up, it is not unreasonable to look to that experience for lessons that might apply to our relationship with China. This analogy was made often in the tense days after China forced down an American spy plane in April 2001. Intel chairman Andrew Grove, for instance, dismissed the likelihood of any hot conflict between the United States, China, and Taiwan, precisely because it would be "the computing equivalent of mutually assured destruction."[30] Indeed, this belief has become so commonplace that it is worth looking at in some detail.

First off, it is not at all clear this analogy applies either. The most obvious difference is that the stakes in an economically interdependent relationship are far less immediately absolute than in a nuclear face-off. An extended cutoff in trade may cause grievous economic harm, but this is still qualitatively different from the near-immediate national suicide guaranteed by firing nuclear warheads at each other. A cutoff in trade can be viewed as no more than one in a series of actions that fall well short of war. For days, and indeed weeks, the nations involved would retain great room for maneuver, for testing each other's endurance and resolve, for exploiting internal divisions, for rattling sabers and moving aircraft carriers into position. In this sense at least, a more useful analogy for understanding our relationship with China is the labor strike. The pain is immediate; but actual bankruptcy and destitution may lie weeks away. Which is one reason why labor strikes happen every day.

Second, this sort of threat-defined interdependence means we also depend on stability within each state. Even if the leaders of the two nations are truly devoted to the same goals—which in and of itself is a highly debatable assumption—this does not mean that all the people within both nations are similarly inclined. What may seem to the ruling clique to be an unacceptable degree of economic destruction may seem a perfectly reasonable cost to a faction eager to seize power from that clique. Further complicating our relationship with China are the interests of third-party states and factions within these states. Foremost among these is Taiwan, where one of the main political groups appears to view the deep economic interdependence in the region as a sort of lever that might help them pry their nation more completely away politically from the Mainland.

Even more disturbing is the fact that today's interdependence may serve actually to trigger conflict. Even under the best of circumstances, interdependence can create resentments in one or even all nations in a relationship in which compromise is enforced outside of any respected political structure.[31] For another, deep interdependence can create temptations that would not otherwise exist. Before the First World War, Germans were able to view their nation's extensive economic interlinkages with France and Britain simultaneously as proof of the weakness of their opponents, and as a source of strength and opportunity for their own nation.[32] In the case of China, that nation's leaders—and factions opposed to that leadership—fully understand that China's hold over America's supply base may be temporary; if the Chinese economy sours or if social upheaval grows or if automated production becomes much cheaper, the next round of investment may shift elsewhere, even without government intervention.[33] The rational temptation for a Chinese government then may become to try to get what they want politically sooner rather than later. This, we should understand, China can do in relatively passive ways. To cause great harm to the U.S. economy, the Chinese need only close their own ports and airports, or even individual production plants.[34] To do so would be a very high-stakes game, and hopefully they will not play it. Whether they do play that game is, for the moment, not really up to us.

At best, the fact that the United States and China depend on the same industrial system does serve as some sort of a restraint on the two nations, a force that dissuades adventurism, at least most of the time. At a minimum, however, this comes at the cost of political compromise to a degree that may already be undermining the basic interests of the American people. The degree to which we have been *politically integrated* with China can be understood if we imagine how we might now react if Chinese citizens rose up to throw off their authoritarian government, which of course was the fundamental reason cited by Bill Clinton and the libertarians in favor of greater trade between the two nations. If anything, the depth of our economic integration with China today means that any social upheaval there would hit our economy almost as immediately as it hits the economy of China. No longer would we be mere onlookers, as we were during the Tiananmen massacre in 1989. If anything, to protect our supply lines, we may find ourselves cooperating with Beijing hard-liners to suppress the will of the Chinese people.[35]

Nowhere is *our* society's *irrationality* in managing this mutual reliance of politically independent nations on the same global industrial commons more evident than it is in the level of confusion in the Pentagon over how to deal with China. As noted in the introduction, the retirement of the State Department from the field has left the Pentagon as perhaps the prime forum in the United States for making sense of our relationship with China today. On one side the old military-power-oriented "realists" have gathered—sometimes arm in arm with adventurous conservatives—with their fifty-year strategies for "containing" China's rise through displays of force, and through the control of energy resources and other basic commodities.[36] On the other side stands a new generation of idealists who declare that China has now been so "integrated" into the global production system that the potential for conflict has all but disappeared.[37]

The point here is not that this debate reflects in any way poorly on the Pentagon—at least in this one corner of our government there is an awareness that our ideologically shaped economic policies have thrust us deep into political realms we have never before visited. What the debate does reflect is the fact that since the end of the Cold War, the political leadership of the United States has failed utterly at the single prime task the voters hire them to manage, which is to ensure the safety and sovereignty of our nation. Instead, they have simply handed the keys to a blind and inherently amoral mob of investors.

In the early years of our nation, Americans learned how to grow and husband our commercial strength, and to use this strength to promote our own security. In the last decades of the nineteenth century, Americans began the process of learning how to regulate our new big businesses, to ensure prosperity and sustainable growth while protecting the basic freedoms of the individual citizen. In the years after the Second World War, the American state began to combine these two traditions, using liberal international commerce to reinforce our nation's military power and secure our peace in a globalizing world. The system was never perfect, but this grand semi-imperial experiment has worked far better overall than the original architects could have hoped. For nearly six decades this economic system has helped us to avoid major war while spreading prosperity and freedom around the world.

Then one day not long ago we decided it would be much better for our government simply to get out of the way. Despite the phenomenal success of our efforts, many Americans suddenly became convinced that in shaping this world we no longer needed to rely on the wisdom of the human mind expressed through our democratic institutions. From now on we would instead allow the "marketplace" itself to "manage" the domestic and international economies for us. What this really meant of course was that we were turning the work of management over to private-sector enterprise. Yet as it proved, this transition never had any real chance of success, because even as we were busting open the borders of the nation, we were also busting open the borders of the traditional firm. The two great economic planning entities of the twentieth century were chased from the stage at almost the exact same moment. So far no one has taken their place.

Perhaps our biggest challenge now is to accept the urgent need for the state to act to restore what the economist F. A. Hayek once called the "carefully thought out legal frame work . . . required" to ensure the safe operation of an economy, especially one as complex as our global system. This will not be easy. The "dogmatic laissez faire attitude" Hayek himself so often condemned now deeply infuses the thinking of most of the people who make our economic and foreign policies.[38] Yet there is no going back; we have truly reached the end of an era. It is only a matter of time till some big government awakes to the urgent need to protect its citizens by reinforcing our new global industrial commons or by beginning the process of withdrawing from it entirely. It is only a matter of time until a reasonable, responsible state rejects the radically dangerous dogma that the "market" will somehow "take care of us." A market is not even able to take care of itself, any more than any human tool is able to take care of itself.[39] On the contrary, it is up to us to take care of the market; only we can ensure that this marvelous tool continues to serve our needs. To say otherwise is to deny the need for the rule of law within the society of man.

In a global world, everyone gets to hold the reins. Right now many states have the power to steer us into the trees; only a few—Europe, Japan, China, the United States—have any real ability to keep us on the road. Each of these, naturally, acts ultimately for the benefit of its own people, and according to its own cultural prejudices and instincts. And so our choice now is this—to trust one or a few of these other nations to manage the global system that America built, and that we designed to orbit around an American center. Or to work with them to do the job together, most immediately by acting in our own national interest.

Once we throw off our ideological blinders, the task can look surprisingly easy. Indeed, there are two very big reasons for hope, at least for those nations or parties within nations able to grasp the vital need to act. The first is that our challenge today on the global level is very similar to the challenge America faced a century ago in our domestic economy. In our now truly global system, the prime task no longer is to promote trade among nations. Rather, it is to manage a single world system made up of world-straddling oligopolies and monopolies, and to do so in the name not of the shareholder, or of the worker, or of a particular class of producers, or of a particular set of communities, but of all American citizens.

This means doing what is necessary to guarantee that Americans always have access to the industrial capacity on which we depend, in much the same way that our government acts to ensure that we always have access to the financial resources on which we depend. We have many tools—proven in use in the past—that can help us to this end.

The second reason for hope is that many of the actions we can take toward this goal not only eliminate much of the risk we face but also help to promote a more just and intelligent distribution of wealth and opportunity in America and around the world. Although the first impulse will often be toward greater protectionism, this is by no means necessary. With the right vision, and with some imagination, we can achieve our ends not through retreat but by pushing forward to build a much more perfect global system, one that is more sustainable and flexible and fair. Perhaps the most effective and efficient—and safe—way to ensure the long-term well-being of Americans is to aim for more discrete industrial units, distributed across more nations, split among more owners, counterbalanced by stronger competitors and stronger suppliers and stronger workers. Fundamental to this vision is to understand once again that it is private-sector capital that must compete for the benefit of the citizen, and not the citizen who must compete for the benefit of the private sector.

In his final speech as president, George Washington warned Americans not to "entangle our peace and prosperity in the toils of [the] ambition, rivalship, interest, humor or caprice" of other nations. Today the opposite could not be more true. We find ourselves deeply enmeshed in the lives of many powerful and politically independent nations, not merely the prosperous and peaceful lands of Europe and Japan, but also nations far less stable and often far less rich.

But herein lies our opportunity. By acting now to ensure that the global industrial commons, which the American state created in the first place, continues to serve the needs of American citizens, we will in the process also clear a space in which all of these other peoples can work more safely to attain their own prosperity, and to limit their own risks, which in turn will help us all work together toward peace. The peoples of the world, it seems, are depending on us to depend on them with a lot more prudence and a lot more wisdom.

OUR GLOBAL COMMONS
Whose Rules?

We must choose. We can act to make our global economy continue to work for peace and prosperity. Or we can develop alternative methods of governing our world and our lives. We must understand, however, that opting to change nothing is itself a choice. Sticking with the same laissez-faire economic "strategy" adopted at the end of the Cold War will ensure the demise of today's America-centric global system and may well erode much of the world's faith in free-market capitalism.

The global economy was created by the American state. Absent a clear-minded effort by the United States to manage this system—in ways amenable to the large majority of the peoples around the world who now depend on it—it will slowly fall to pieces. The end may not be far off. Even before the attacks of September 11, the great political economist Robert Gilpin warned that "all the political elements that have supported an open global economy have considerably weakened" during the 1990s. In the four years since the attacks, the Bush Administration has abandoned even the distracted and ideologically tainted management methods of the Clinton era, turning instead to a shortsighted and counterproductive effort to militarize relations among nations. Not coincidentally, one result has been to cede even greater freedom to the private-sector entities that now manage our global economy. These have used this freedom to pit, ever more effectively, individual against individual and nation against nation, for the sake of private gain.

As such unmitigated economic power increasingly undermines the security and well-being of our societies, a growing number of states will inevitably react against the status quo. Those that do so will have to choose from among a great variety of potential pathways. There are many actions that will reduce or even eliminate the most grave of the dangers I illustrate in this book, at least in the near term. Unfortunately, the policies most likely to emerge may create yet greater dangers over time. Given that the American state and American corporations are increasingly perceived, in capitals around the world, as predatory entities addicted to the use of force means that other governments are ever more likely to retreat into reactionary protectionism.

We must never forget that the germ of our global economy was the desire of America's postwar governments to foster peace by forging cooperation. In recent years, the preachers of dogmatic laissez-faire economics have reduced globalization to a starkly materialistic equation. Over and over we are told the only measure that matters is the number of items in our shopping carts. But this is to confuse a felicitous by-product of America's Cold War–era policy—which is the greater efficiency that derives from the creation of multination marketplaces—with the ultimate end itself. In so doing, we substitute a marginal gain—one recent study says economic globalization has increased American living standards by 10 percent—with an absolute gain, which is the avoidance of war and the spread of true liberty.

As the debate over how to regulate the global economy takes shape, we can expect to hear all sorts of highly arcane proposals. In the United States, the most likely immediate response will be to declare there is nothing wrong that can't be fixed by a few swift kicks to the mechanism, or a few technological patches. But the problem is structural in nature. There is only so much that can be done through advances in supply-chain-management software, revisions in the tax structure, reorientation of overseas investment subsidies, the tightening of export-control regimes, the revamping of insurance regulations, or bilateral and multilateral trade treaties. If our real goal is a system that helps to perpetuate peace and freedom, then much bolder action is required.

The era of trade among nations is over, at least for manufactured goods, at least for now. American corporations—operating within a marketplace shaped by the American state—have created a single global industrial system marked by an extreme degree of specialization. Free trade, we must remember, is a process of becoming—bigger, more efficient, more interlinked. In many industrial sectors today, however, the scale is as big as it will ever get. This means it is vital to move beyond our old conception of a world economy in which nations exchange complete products across borders. They still do so, of course, but less and less. Much more useful is to understand that industry has become a global common property, and that all peoples must work together to maintain it.

More than any other global commons, however, our industrial commons must be regulated to ensure that it operates safely, and that it never provides any one nation with a tool of political coercion or a temptation to power. The following list of proposals is my own take on what is necessary. By no means is it the only approach. I strongly believe, however, that the following program would eliminate most of the risks I describe, while also promoting growth, fairness, and the *long-term* efficiency of our global system. Given the nature of the threat—too tight an industrial interdependence among nations and too fragile a production system—I concentrate on policies that will help to compartmentalize production. Given the pressing need for action, I list only policies that have been proven effective and safe in the past. Given the obvious and huge obstacles to forging any multination agreement in the near term, I list policies that can be enacted unilaterally but that also would do no harm to other peoples, and that indeed would benefit most nations. The list is ordered roughly in terms of urgency:

- Use antitrust power to ensure that no global lead firm controls more than a quarter of any American market.
- Limit how much of any key input any industry, as a whole, can source from capacity located in a single foreign nation, to no more than a quarter of the amount consumed in the United States.
- Require firms to double- or even triple-source all components and all business-process services, in real time, from suppliers in two or more different nations.
- Strengthen the ability of true manufacturers to counterbalance the price-setting power of global lead firms, by strengthening and enforcing anti-monopsony laws. This would enable true manufacturers to capture a greater share of the profit in a production chain, and thereby be able to invest more in the maintenance of their productive assets.

- Require managers to make public their sourcing and supply-chain relationships, to enable investors to shy from firms that take unnecessary risk.
- Enable workers to more effectively counterbalance the power of shareholders by giving them an absolutely equal right to act collectively within the U.S. economy. Practically, this would reduce the ability of large corporations to seek profits by mining the social infrastructure.
- Professionalize management of the U.S. corporation by compensating top management only in salary and not in stock or stock options. One result would be a very different assessment by top managers of risk within the production system and of the attractiveness of owning, developing, and maintaining productive assets.
- Reconsider the nationality of the global-scale lead firm, even if it maintains its headquarters in the United States. Practically, this would give Americans a much clearer sense of how to shape national and state-level tax policies, where and how to subsidize research, and how to employ the private sector to develop defense technologies.

In combination, this set of policies would orient the global industrial machine to work in an economically safe manner, to sustain growth through innovation, and to perpetuate our long peace. Vital industrial capacity would be geographically distributed, competition would be made more fluid and vibrant, peoples in more nations integrated as both producers and consumers. None of the policies would require any government to manage the marketplace. On the contrary, the program would make most marketplaces far more free and open than they are now, by restricting the ability of today's ever more powerful lead firms to manage competition for their own private interests. Ultimately, the program should be viewed as highly analogous to that which American governments enacted at home early in the twentieth century, when our nation learned how to subjugate the new and immensely powerful economic actors of that era to the interest of society in such a way that the yoke did not strangle the ox.

It is obviously vastly easier to sketch out such a program than to enact it in the real world. We will need to overcome profound intellectual inertia, and we will be opposed by global-scale economic behemoths able to spend vast sums to protect their privileged positions. Opposition may also come from many foreign governments and peoples sure to blanch at the merest specter of American economic unilateralism, let alone a program that would fundamentally reshape the global economy. Yet I think both of these obstacles will prove far less daunting than they now appear.

First, the power of these corporations, as vast as they seem now in the virtual absence of any government effort to regulate them, is no match for that of a state with a coordinated program and the will to act. As Americans come to understand the degree to which many of today's biggest lead corporations are truly global and hence inherently foreign actors, it will become ever easier to take the actions necessary to shape these entities in such a way that they serve the interests of our communities and of our nation. Politically, meanwhile, no other single state in the world has the power to upset such a program, at least not through peaceful means. Indeed, most opposition may prove fleeting once other nations come to understand that such a program is not "protectionist" in any traditional sense whatsoever, and that on the contrary this set of policies would increase the economic opportunities available to all peoples around the world. This is especially true of middle-income semi-industrialized nations like Brazil, India, Russia, Malaysia, Mexico, and South Africa. It is also true for many rich nations, especially in Europe.

In all the world, the only states that might reasonably consider themselves losers in a global industrial system designed to distribute capacity and ownership more widely are Japan and China. Here too, however, I believe there is reason for hope. In the case of Japan, the nation's deepening demographic crisis and profound distrust of overly intimate industrial interdependence with China will probably lead Tokyo to welcome a more truly global system, in which Japanese remain free to control what they regard as national technologies, as long as industrial capacity and ownership is dispersed. In the case of China, there are four reasons why I believe Beijing would not seriously oppose the main elements of this program. First, such a set of policies would enable Chinese authorities to manage their own nation's phenomenal economic and political transition more carefully, such as by developing financial and legal systems truly independent of state, military, and corporate power. Second, today's Chinese leaders would likely welcome a less intimate interdependence with other nations precisely because this would reduce the ability of opposition groups within China to play for power by threatening to disrupt overly tight production processes. Third, as an ever more mature member of the community of industrial nations, China should welcome any change that makes the global production system more secure for all peoples who depend on it. Last, China can mount no reasonable claim that one nation, which accounts for a fifth of the world's total population, has any "right" to control more than, say, a quarter of any human productive activity.

Some will object to the idea that the program is national rather than multinational in nature. This is not because I see no room for multilateral actions. On the contrary, there is an urgent need for new multilateral actions in many areas closely related to our industrial commons, most especially the international financial and monetary systems, which obviously can be managed only by nations acting in concert. Rather, it is because I believe that when it comes to industry, it is far faster to act at the national level, not least because it is far easier for policy makers and citizens to understand the benefits. Similarly, acting at the national level will make it far easier for other nations to follow our lead.

Which leads to a seeming contradiction—that America's national security lies in using national power to engineer a more truly global system that ultimately cedes more freedom and independence to other peoples. Going forward, it is absolutely necessary to show far more respect for the right of other peoples to experiment economically, as long as such experiments do not increase the likelihood of armed conflict in the world. Indeed, given the spread of democracy in recent decades, and of the transparency demanded by international capital, there is simply far less need than in the past for the U.S. government to insist on extreme economic orthodoxy, and so we should stop insisting. If the French people want to devote much of their own wealth to protecting their agricultural heritage, or if the Brazilian people want to subsidize and protect a few infant industries, is it a legitimate or intelligent goal of American policy to try to stand in their way? Milton Friedman famously declared that protectionism hurts the importer as much as or more than the exporter. This is certainly so in many instances. But is it not up to the people of each individual nation, acting through democratic institutions, to decide for themselves what policies pain them? Is not one of the strengths of democracy that it enables a people to identify, debate, and eliminate economic policies that benefit only a small minority, without any instruction or interference from abroad? More to the point, should not all people be entirely free, in the words of the economist F. A. Hayek, "to be rational and efficient only when and where we think it worth while"?

From the first, the American nation has been unique in the world in that we have so rarely allowed the power of our state to be used to increase the glory of some one person or class, or of some one specific way of organizing life, or even of the nation itself. America has always worked best when we have instructed our representatives to act not toward some specific end, but rather toward the perfection of the means. Our democratic political system is one such means, our free-market economic system another. Both serve to enable individual members of society, and individual communities (and since the Second World War, individual nations), to work with great liberty toward their personal and communal (and national) ends, rather than toward some end set for them by bureaucrats, or by the managers of private-sector monopolies.

Yet our effort to perfect the processes through which we are enabled to fulfill our role as citizens and as entrepreneurs and as workers is always under siege. There is always some group willing to pursue its own private advantage by seeking to restrict the freedoms of the great majority of Americans, either by stifling or corrupting the political process, or by using state or private power to manage markets for private benefit. Right now is such a time. Great economic powers have been assembled, ever more able to extract the wealth they seek from lesser firms, and from small and desperate states, and from individual citizens. These powers are not always self-conscious. Few of their directors are more than vaguely aware of the destructiveness of the enterprises they oversee, of how these powers are undermining the economic and political balances that have ensured America's well-being and security for more than half a century. These powers will insist that their way is the only way, the right way, the natural way. But their way increasingly is unable to generate enough truly *new* wealth to trickle down to the rest of us. Their way increasingly relies on the use of consolidated brute economic force to extract wealth from the individual and from the social infrastructure, and hence from the security of us all. Fortunately, their strength, and the ideology on which it rests, is ever more brittle. After all, these powers depend ultimately on our approval. As Friedrich Hayek put it so well, "In social evolution nothing is inevitable but thinking makes it so."

ACKNOWLEDGMENTS

This book is the culmination of two decades of work and study and travel, going back to when I first stepped off a plane in Bombay, fresh out of college, intent on seeing a world of which I had only read. A year or so later, I returned home and took my first job as a reporter, covering the consumer electronics industry. Ever since, I have lived largely within the boundaries I set out then, seeking to understand the nature and needs of different peoples and the ways in which business and government could make those lives better and safer. For much of the late 1980s and early 1990s, I lived in Latin America, working mainly as a wire-service reporter. For most of the 1990s, I edited *Global Business* magazine, which covered what business executives really do when they engage in cross-border enterprise. My many experiences, friends, and colleagues from those times continue to deeply inform my work today.

I began to work on *End of the Line* four years ago, and since then I have conducted more than 250 interviews, while reading or rereading more than 200 books. By the time I finished writing, the work had evolved tremendously from what I had first imagined. Although I would like to claim this was due entirely to my own diligence and open-mindedness, the truth is the credit really belongs to the dozens of people who pushed me to dig deeper, to read more, to rewrite another time.

There is no fair way to list these many people except chronologically. So I begin with Lewis Lapham at *Harper's* magazine, who offered to buy the article on which this book is based the day he received my pitch letter. At *Harper's,* I also owe a special thanks to my friend Ann Gollin, and to my editor Ben Metcalf. I next carried my idea to my agent, Rafe Sagalyn, who with great patience and vision helped me shape my idea into the form of a book proposal. Rafe, in turn, soon carried my project to Adam Bellow at Doubleday, and his assurances that Adam was the right editor for me have proven true many times since. Adam's intellect ranges wide and delves deep, and my debt to him is immense. So, too, my appreciation of his methods. Adam can do more with a sigh than most editors can in a week of work with a red pen.

The early stages of my research work were supported generously by the Rockefeller Foundation, and I am deeply grateful. I am especially indebted to Katherine McFate at the Foundation, both for her insights and for her early confidence that I was working toward something of value. There are many people in many foundations who have spent many dollars to support many studies on various facets of globalization. Katherine is almost entirely alone in backing work that gets into the mechanics of how the systems really work.

For most of the eighteen months during which I sat at a keyboard writing, I did so at the New America Foundation in Washington, and the book benefited greatly as a result. There are many reasons why New America is an inspiring place for a writer, but all of them lead in one way or another back to Ted Halstead, who keeps the place in balance with his energy and wit and charm. I also am very grateful to Michael Lind for his careful readings, his insightful comments, and his ceaseless but always constructive provocations. I want to thank Steve Clemons for his brilliant and often usefully blunt comments, and James Fallows for hearing me out in the first place and for his encouragement at various points since. Of all the people at New America, I especially wish to thank Sherle Schwenninger, who combines patience and wisdom with the ability to remember every article published on any policy subject for the last twenty years. Sherle's careful readings and commentaries on early drafts were invaluable. Many others at New America also helped in one way or another. These include Marcellus Andrews, Philip Longman, John Gravois, Max Vilimpoc, Mark Goldberg, and especially Hannah Fischer and Simone Frank.

I could never have written this book without a great deal of cooperation from many in the business community. Among those who aided me in understanding the issues were Xilinx CEO Willem Roelandts and George Scalese, president of the Semiconductor Industry Association. Michael Marks and Jim Sacherman of Flextronics were very helpful. Christopher Gopal, formerly of Ernst & Young, Greg Stein, formerly of Cisco Systems, and Walter Zinn at the University of Ohio helped me make sense of supply-chain and logistics issues. Kenichii Ohmae was very generous with his time. Dell Computer was very cooperative, especially in the early stages of my work. So, too, were UPS, FedEx, and TNT. There were many many others, meanwhile, whom I would like to mention but who prefer to remain anonymous.

I am also deeply indebted to many in the Washington policy arena and in academia who took the time to discuss some of my ideas at some point in the development of this book. There are too many to list, but I must especially thank Arthur Hartman, Jeffrey Garten, James Schlesinger, Lester Thurow, Charlene Barshefsky, Thomas Donnelly, Larry Wortzel, James Lilly, and John Deutch. Rupert Hammond Chambers of the U.S.-Taiwan Business Council helped me in many ways at many times. Michael Borrus, Gary Gereffi, Timothy Sturgeon, Dieter Ernst, and John Zysman all contributed, not least with their own groundbreaking work. I am also very thankful for a series of very useful conversations during the early stages of this project with John Cavanagh, Ivar Andersen, Thea Lee, Douglas Brinkley, Atsuko Horiguchi, Jeff Faux, and Jock Nash. I also wish to thank the ARCA Foundation, Janet Schenk, Tracy Staton, and officials in the governments of Japan, Taiwan, India, Singapore, and China.

If there is a single one influence on my work, it is Edward Taylor, my professor of Shakespeare at Columbia College. Professor Taylor taught me how to read, write, and think.

Of all this list, there is only one person without whom I could not have written this book, and that is my wife, Anya Schoolman. A book is a terrible thing to bring into a family, but Anya from the first was incredibly supportive, remarkably forbearing, and brilliant in her insights. For four years, Anya had to put up with mad ramblings about supply chains and networks of production and interdependencies among nations. This book has kept me away from our home for too many hours, and it has kept me away from too much fun with our two glorious sons, Walter and Ezra. I can never express enough of my gratitude and my love.

NOTES

CHAPTER ONE The Old West: *Running from Japan*

1 James B. Treece, "The Lessons GM Could Learn for Its Supplier Shakeup," *Business-Week,* August 31, 1992, p. 29; Alan Adler, "Key GM Supply Executive Says Customer Happiness Is All That Counts," Associated Press, August 25, 1992; "Roger Cohen, GM Cost Cutter Sharpens His Ax," *New York Times,* June 9, 1992, Section D, p. 1; Micheline Maynard, "GM Wages War for Survival," *USA Today,* August 26, 1992, p. 2B; Alan Adler, "Dr. Lopez Brings Tough Medicine to Ailing Automaker," Associated Press, October 2, 1992.

2 Phil Frame, "Tough Guy Lopez Takes Charge of GM's Purchasing," *Automotive News,* May 25, 1992, p. 1; John McElroy, "His Turn to Speak," *Automotive Industries,* November 1992, p. 53; Micheline Maynard, "GM Wages War for Survival," *USA Today,* August 26, 1992, 2B.

3 Alan Adler, "GM Takes More Profound Steps to Revamp American Carmaking," Associated Press, April 24, 1992.

4 James B. Treece, *Business Week,* August 31, 1992; Raymond Serafin, "Shops Pray to Escape Knife of GM 'Inquisitor,' " *Advertising Age,* August 24 1992, p. 3; Alan Adler, "Purchasing Guru Lopez Staying Put—For Now," Associated Press, March 1, 1993; Micheline Maynard, "GM's Lopez Is Driven by Cost-Cutting Mission," *USA Today,* November 24, 1992, p. 5B.

5 Maynard, *USA Today,* November 24, 1992, p. 5B; Phil Frame, "Lopez: Japanese Must Play Fair," *Automotive News,* May 25, 1992, p. 10.

6 Gary Witzenburg, "How to Turn Around a Car Company," *Automotive Industries,* November 1, 2003, p. 22; Steve Coll, "A Rivalry with a World of Difference," *Washington Post,* April 18, 1993, p. H1.

7 Roger Cohen, *New York Times,* June 9, 1992, Section D, p. 1.

8 Alan Adler, "Key GM Supply Executive Says Customer Happiness Is All That Counts," Associated Press, August 25, 1992.

9 Lance Morrow, "Yankee Doodle Magic," *Time,* July 7, 1986, p. 12.

10 Michael Barrone, "Mondale's Choice," *Washington Post,* July 1, 1984, p. C8.

11 James Barron, "Huge Japanese Realty Deals Breeding Jokes and Anger," *New York Times,* December 18, 1989, Section B, p. 1; Rick Hampson, "Rockefeller Center: No Godzilla at Radio City," Associated Press, November 1, 1989; Judy Temes, "Rocky

Repercussions," *Crane's New York Business,* November 6, 1989, p. 1; John Hillkirk, "Japanese Buying Spree: They Pocket High Profile Properties," *USA Today,* November 1, 1989, 1B.

12 Theodore H. White, "Danger from Japan," *New York Times Magazine,* July 28, 1985, Section 6, p. 19. Karel G. van Wolferen, "The Japan Problem," *Foreign Affairs,* 1986/1987 Winter, p. 288.

13 Clyde Farnsworth, "U.S Japan Trade Showdown," *New York Times,* March 27, 1982.

14 James Barron, "Congressman Says Iacocca Sent Conciliatory Note," *New York Times,* March 5, 1985, Section A, p. 13.

15 "America and Japan: Bad Sports," *Economist,* February 25, 1989, p. 22; Malcolm Forbes, "Fact and Comment," *Forbes,* November 27, 1989, p. 19.

16 Henry Adams, *The Education of Henry Adams,* Boston, Houghton Mifflin, 1973 (copyright 1918), Chapter 25.

17 Much of this information is from David Hounshell, *From the American System to Mass Production, 1800–1932,* Baltimore, Johns Hopkins University Press, 1984.

18 Alexis de Tocqueville, *Democracy in America,* New York, Knopf, 1994, Vol. 1, p. 252.

19 Robert Kanigel, *The One Best Way: Frederick Winslow Taylor and the Enigma of Efficiency,* New York, Penguin, 1997, pp. 130 and 272.

20 "Government, Industry Haunted by Specter of U.S. Protectionism," Kyodo News Service, Japan Economic Newswire, November 4, 1992.

21 Nancy Dunne, "Clinton Tiptoes Around Trade Issue," *Financial Times,* October 23, 1992.

22 Martin Fletcher, "Clinton Aides Advised the EC Against Reaching Export Pact," *London Times,* October 23, 1992.

23 Chalmers Johnson, *MITI and the Japanese Miracle,* Stanford, Calif., Stanford University Press, 1982.

24 Paul Krugman, "Introduction: New Thinking About Trade Policy," in *Strategic Trade Policy and the New International Economics,* ed. Paul Krugman, Cambridge, MIT Press, 1986, p. 15.

25 Robert Reich, *The Work of Nations,* New York, Vintage, 1992, p. 140.

26 E.J. Dionne, "Changing of the Gurus?" *Washington Post,* April 14, 1991.

27 One reporter called it the single best "primer" for "Clintonomics." E.J. Dionne, "Inventing Clintonomics," *Washington Post,* October 15, 1992, p. A1.

28 By the summer of 1990, one of George Bush's top economic aides, Roger B. Porter, was warning that "the old notion of nations, companies and markets rigidly defined by national borders . . . is outdated and dangerous." Nancy Dunne, "Friends Rally to Ailing Trade Talks," *Financial Times,* July 3, 1990, p. 3.

29 Paul H. Weaver, "Robert Reich's Fascinating Flip-Flop," *Fortune,* March 25, 1991, p. 135.

30 Paul Magnusson, "Whatever You Call It, Industrial Policy Is On the Way," *BusinessWeek,* December 28, 1992, p. 34.

31 Editorial, "Nature Boy vs. Texas Chihuahua," *Atlanta Constitution,* November 9, 1993, Section A, p. 8.

32 Maureen Dowd, "A Made-For-TV Debate," *New York Times,* November 10, 1993, Section B, p. 14.

33 The state of South Carolina unilaterally stopped paying federal tariffs on imports in 1832, precipitating one of the greatest constitutional crises in America before the Civil War.

34 NAFTA's most practical goal was to make it much easier for corporations from America and Canada (and other industrial nations as well) to operate in Mexico.

Most of the agreement's nearly 2,000 pages are devoted to such issues as regulating the privatization of Mexico's utilities, the entry into Mexico of foreign-owned banks, and the protections offered by Mexico to foreign capital. In other words, the goal of NAFTA was not so much to increase the sale of American-made automobiles to Mexico, but to transform North America into a single market for automobiles and a single integrated manufacturing economy.

35 Paul Krugman, "The Uncomfortable Truth About NAFTA," *Foreign Affairs,* November 1993.

36 Excerpts from "Presidential Debate," Associated Press, October 15, 1992.

37 The trading bloc model even came with a highly important stamp of approval, at least among progressives. The British economist Maynard Keynes in the 1930s had spoken approvingly of a world system based on semimercantilist economic blocs, after the economic catastrophe occasioned by the Versailles Peace agreement forced him to abandon his hopes for a worldwide liberal free trade system (Robert Gilpin, *U.S. Power and the Multinational Corporation,* New York, Basic Books, 1975, p. 235).

38 In the event that one of the blocs should turn militaristic, Reich contended that the fact that the global corporations had replicated their capacity in all three regions would help deter rash action. In any crisis, the American military would still have access to whatever industrial capacity it might need. "During World War II, Ford's German subsidiary dutifully produced trucks for the Nazis," he wrote. "What is in the United States is indubitably under America's political control" (Reich 144).

39 Terrence Petty, "Kohl to Try to Allay Soviet Fears," Associated Press, February 8, 1990.

40 The competition, Thurow said, was now between different forms of capitalism, and the American form looked conspicuously unfit for the tough new world. "The individualistic Anglo-Saxon British-American form of capitalism," he wrote, is "going to face off against the communitarian German and Japanese variants of capitalism" (Lester Thurow, *Head to Head,* New York, HarperCollins, 1992, p. 32). None of these more alarmist thinkers ever made clear exactly why France and Italy and England would willingly enlist in some new German-conceived plan for global domination. Nor did anyone make it clear exactly how Japan's growing technological prowess would be made to threaten America.

41 John Eisenhammer, "Crusader at the Wheel," *The Independent,* July 14, 1993, p. 14.

CHAPTER TWO China and the Global Moment: *Clinton's Counterstroke*

1 Pete Engardio, "A Great Leap Forward," *BusinessWeek,* May 17, 1993, p. 58.

2 Chris Galvin, quoted in internal Motorola interview, October 7, 1994, provided by Motorola.

3 "Motorola Milestones in China," published by Motorola (China) Electronics Ltd., 1997.

4 David Oliver Relin, "Why Lost U.S. Jobs Are Heading Abroad," *Scholastic Update,* January 26, 1987, p. 8.

5 "Motorola Receives Approval to Build China Factory," Associated Press, March 27, 1992. "Motorola Commits $720 Million to China," Associated Press, September 25, 1995.

6 Some estimates put the total as high as 2,700. "Death Toll from Military Crackdown May Never Be Known," Associated Press, May 21, 1990.

7 Frederick Merk, *Albert Gallatin and the Oregon Problem,* Cambridge, Mass., 1950,

p. 13. Cited in Richard W. Van Alstyne, *The Rising American Empire*, New York, Norton, 1974, p. 94. Among Benton's more practical acts was to dispatch his son-in-law, the explorer and later presidential candidate John C. Fremont, to find easy land routes to San Francisco.

8 The lineage went back even farther, to Jefferson's father Peter, who in 1749 had co-founded a company dedicated to finding a water route across America to the Pacific and hence to China.

9 Thomas J. McCormick, *China Market*, Chicago, Quadrangle Books, 1967, p. 31.

10 *China Market*, 107.

11 The administration of President James K. Polk first offered Mexico $25 million for northern California.

12 Admiral Dewey quickly made clear the value of America's new possession. Almost as soon as Manila had been taken, he sailed back to the coast of China, his ships replete with troops from the U.S. expeditionary force.

13 Harold Isaacs, *Images of Asia*, New York, Capricorn Books, 1962, p. 195.

14 U.S. Secretary of State Richard Olney in 1896 instructed the American ambassador to Beijing to oppose plans to build manufacturing plants in China, even when owned, operated, or funded by Americans. "Our interest," he wrote, is "to keep foreign markets open for our manufactures" (*China Market*, 74).

15 His thinking could be traced back to Henry Clay's "American System," as systematized by Friedrich List, and as refined by nineteenth-century Germany, Meiji Japan, and late Czarist Russia. By the 1920s, the Chinese version of national industrialism had even taken on a Soviet flavor, especially in Sun Yat-sen's belief that the state should own all the most important means of production.

16 First came the Great Depression, which dried up flows of foreign capital. Then came Japan's invasion of Manchuria in 1931 and of China proper in 1937. Then came civil war between the Nationalist and Red armies, and starting in 1950 the war in Korea against the United States.

17 The most extravagant project during this period was the Baoshan Iron & Steel Works, a $5 billion behemoth to be overseen by the Japanese Nippon Steel Corporation. The project became a huge public relations fiasco for China in which dozens of foreign companies lost hundreds of millions of dollars of investment.

18 Jim Mann, *Beijing Jeep*, New York, Simon & Schuster, 1989.

19 Thomas Lippman, "Turmoil in Running Shoes," *Washington Post*, January 31, 1982, p. F1.

20 Julienne Bostic, "It's the Real Thing: America Makes Mark," *Financial Times*, November 23, 1982, p. VII.

21 Louis Kraar, "Your Next PC Could Be Made in Taiwan," *Fortune*, August 8, 1994, p. 91.

22 Commodore Mathew Perry was the first American to envision such a role for the island, recommending in the 1850s that the United States seize Taiwan for use as a base to police the China trade.

23 Taiwan was more developed industrially than most of its neighbors, thanks to extensive Japanese public- and private-sector investments between 1895 and 1945, when the island was a Japanese colony. Robert Wade, *Governing the Market*, Princeton, Princeton University Press, 1990, pp. 74 and 117.

24 Ibid., 84.

25 Ibid., 83.

26 Ralph N. Clough, *Island China*, Cambridge, Mass., Harvard University Press, 1978, p. 24.

27 Taiwan was also favored because its economy was not dominated by large conglomerates, as in Japan and Korea. Taiwanese companies tend to be small, specialized, and highly independent, making them much more amenable to the sorts of partnerships that American companies favor (Wade, 66).

28 This semilegal and illegal trade grew so fast and was so accepted that by the mid-1980s Taiwan's government was advertising the island publicly as the world's best offshore base for doing business in China.

29 James Mann, *About Face: A History of America's Curious Relationship with China, from Nixon to Clinton,* Alred A. Knopf, New York, 1998, p. 262.

30 Which was then, and still remains today, the rates established by Smoot-Hawley.

31 U.S. Newswire, Transcript of Clinton Remarks in Address on China, October 24, 1997.

32 Yoichi Funabashi, Michel Oksenberg, Heinrich Weiss, "An Emerging China in a World of Interdependence," The Trilateral Commission, New York, Paris, Tokyo, May 1994, pp. 2 and 65.

33 Paul Wolfowitz, then assistant secretary for East Asian and Pacific affairs, in September 1984 said in a speech that "we believe that an increasingly prosperous China will be more stable, more secure, and more able to resist outside pressure and intimidation." "The U.S.-China Trade Relationship," Department of State Bulletin, September 1984, p. 25.

34 President Ronald Reagan, in a September 1984 address to the U.N. General Assembly, declared that America's "desire to cut down trade barriers" was part of an overall strategy to bring about "a world where prosperity is commonplace, conflict an aberration, and human dignity and freedom a way of life." Text of Reagan's United Nations Speech, Associated Press, September 24, 1984.

35 Milton Friedman, "Economic Freedom and Political Freedom," in *Capitalism and Freedom,* University of Chicago Press, 1962, p. 10.

36 Mann, *About Face,* p. 241.

37 The United States has often chosen to sanction individual firms rather than their parent nations for actions of which it did not approve.

38 Francis Fukuyama, *The End of History,* The National Interest, Summer 1989.

39 Georg Wilhelm Friedrich Hegel, *Philosophy of Right,* translated by T.M. Knox, Oxford University Press, New York, 1967, Section 244.

CHAPTER THREE Our World: *America's System in Transition*

1 The deal was brokered by Acting Secretary of the Navy Franklin Roosevelt, who was concerned about British dominance of the radio business. Roosevelt also turned over the Navy's own radio patents to the new subsidiary and helped to convince Britain's Marconi to sell control of its American radio unit to GE. Over the next few years, the government raised no objection as GE convinced AT&T, Westinghouse, and the United Fruit Company to also turn over their radio technologies to the new subsidiary in exchange for stock.

2 James F. Peltz, "GE, RCA Announce Merger Agreement," Associated Press, December 11, 1985.

3 Paul Richter, "GE and RCA Say They Expect No Regulatory Obstacles to Merger," *Los Angeles Times,* December 13, 1985, Part 4, p. 1.

4 Marilyn A. Harris, "Not Just Another Takeover—Or Is It?" *BusinessWeek,* December 30, 1985, p. 48.

5 Eric N. Berg, "GE Says Merger May Take a Year," *New York Times,* December 13, 1985, Section D, p. 10.

6 Michael Schrage, "Merger Seen Boosting U.S. Competitiveness," *Washington Post,* December 13, 1985, p. D7.

7 In the 1970s, RCA squandered a big technological lead in video recording technology, failing to commercialize its highly advanced videodisc player and all but ceding the market to Japanese firms with their tape-based videocassette recorders.

8 These weapons were first used in combat in 1944, when a technician in a TBF Avenger airplane used a remote control to steer a camera-equipped missile into a Japanese radar station near the port of Rabaul. Kenneth Bilby, *The General: David Sarnoff,* New York, Harper & Row, 1986, p. 157.

9 Peter Petre, "GE's Gamble on American-Made TVs," *Fortune,* July 6, 1987, p. 50.

10 Paul Richter, "GE and RCA Say They Expect No Regulatory Obstacles to Merger," *Los Angeles Times,* December 13, 1985, Part 4, p. 1. Welch did not have to worry about the Reagan Administration. On the contrary, the Justice Department a few months earlier had quietly cleared the way for the RCA deal by abandoning the antitrust "consent decree" that since 1932 had prevented GE from owning any part of RCA.

11 David Sanger, "GE, A Pioneer in Radio and TV, Is Abandoning Production of Sets," *New York Times,* July 23, 1987, p. 1.

12 Mark Potts, "GE Sells Consumer Electronics Unit," *Washington Post,* July 23, 1987, p. E1.

13 Philip Elmer-DeWitt, "Jumping Jack Strikes Again," *Time,* August 3, 1987, p. 44.

14 RCA Records had gone to Bertelsmann, RCA's satellite operations had gone to private investors, the NBC Radio Network had gone to a California radio syndicator, and RCA's Sarnoff Research Center at Princeton was given to the Stanford Research Institute in exchange for a tax write-off. Thomas F. O'Boyle, *At Any Cost,* New York, Alfred A. Knopf, 1998, p. 97.

15 Christine Winter, "GE Bids Adieu to Electronics," *Chicago Tribune,* July 23, 1987, p. 1.

16 Thane Peterson, "Overnight, Thomson Has the Stuff to Take on the Titans," *BusinessWeek,* August 10, 1987, p. 36.

17 Anatole Kaletsky, "A Hollow Feeling in the Great American Manufacturing Revolution," *Financial Times,* July 24, 1987, p. 16.

18 Sanger, *New York Times,* July 23, 1987, p. 1.

19 Thomas Jefferson, *Notes on the State of Virginia,* 1785, Chapter 19.

20 David Ricardo, *On the Principles of Political Economy and Taxation,* 1817, Chapter 7. In order for this theory to work, however, Ricardo assumed a system of "perfectly free commerce," and he had to assume away any transfer whatsoever across borders of labor, or capital, or tools, or even of certain other commodities. Despite these limitations, his theory of comparative advantage undergirds the trade theories of most economists working in America to this day.

21 Douglas A. Irwin, *Against the Tide,* Princeton, Princeton University Press, 1996, p. 16. In English politics, meanwhile, the idea is present by early in the seventeenth century. When a ship of the British East India Company landed in Aceh in Sumatra in 1602, the captain carried a letter of introduction from Queen Elizabeth. God, she wrote, in His "infinite and unsearchable wisdom" had ordained that no nation should be self-sufficient in all things, but rather that "out of the abundance" some regions enjoy, "the necessity or want of others should be supplied." John Keay, *The Honourable Company,* New York, Macmillan, 1991, p. 10.

22 Immanuel Kant, *Perpetual Peace,* First Supplement, 1795.

23 Richard Cobden, Speech delivered in Manchester, January 15, 1846. In *Speeches on Questions of Public Policy,* London, T. Fisher Unwin, 1908.

24 Within the English political context of the mid-nineteenth century, Cobden's pioneering work in political organizing had the most immediate impact. Not only did he turn the Anti-Corn Law League into the world's first self-funding political agitation machine—the great-grandfather of the National Rifle Associations and Sierra Clubs of today—he also designed what was probably the world's first direct-mail operation and the first true voter registration campaign. It was only late in his life that Cobden began to promote his causes more as an end in themselves rather than as a means to power. Nicholas C. Edsall, *Richard Cobden, Independent Radical,* Cambridge, Mass., Harvard University Press, 1986, pp. 333 and 353.

25 Cobden also bemoaned the militarization of Prussia and especially the brewing naval arms race between Britain and France.

26 The *Communist Manifesto* is filled with odes to globalization that could easily have been published in any of a number of magazines or newspapers in the late 1990s. "In place of the old local and national seclusion and self-sufficiency," reads one early passage, "we have intercourse in every direction, universal inter-dependence of nations. And as in material, so also in intellectual production. The intellectual creations of individual nations become common property. National one-sidedness and narrowmindedness become more and more impossible, and from the numerous national and local literatures, there arises a world literature." Indeed, of all the theories conjured up by the capitalists of their day, Marx and Engels clearly held free trade to be one of the most usefully subversive. Not only did free trade undermine the "national ground" on which the old feudal powers had stood, they believed it was clearing the way for the workers' revolution to take place on a truly global scale.

27 As early as the 1830s, industrialists in the north began to defend the protective tariff not as something good for the American producer but as something good for the American worker. In the words of Massachusetts senator Daniel Webster, protection against the "cheaper, ill-paid, half-fed, and pauper labor of Europe" was a "duty" the American government owed to its citizens. Robert Remini, *Daniel Webster,* New York, Norton, 1997, p. 464.

28 John Maynard Keynes in *The Economic Consequences of the Peace* wrote that the new political frontiers drawn by the victors often sliced across the natural regional economies that had been built up over many decades and thereby ensured the eventual collapse of the new Europe. "Even if there is no moral solidarity between the nearly race-related races of Europe," Keynes wrote after surveying the shambles of France in 1919, "there is an economic solidarity which we cannot disregard" (p. 295).

29 Al Gore used the myth that Smoot-Hawley killed jobs to great effect in his NAFTA debate against Ross Perot, calling it the "principal cause" of the Great Depression. Larry King Transcript, CNN, November 9, 1993.

30 The one important exception came when the government founded the Springfield Armory in 1794.

31 The principal prophet was a German-born economist named Friedrich List, who came to America as an exile at age thirty-six. During seven years in the country, List failed as a farmer, helped develop a horse-drawn railroad, and met many of America's more prominent thinkers, including Henry Clay. List then sailed home to write a four-volume work, *The National System of Political Economy,* which spread the gospel of Hamiltonianism around the world.

32 Mahan is often called the "father" of the modern navy, owing to the worldwide influence of his 1890 book *The Influence of Sea Power Upon History*.

33 A.T. Mahan, *Armaments and Arbitration*, Harper & Brothers, 1911, reissued by Kennikat Press, Port Washington, N.Y., 1973, pp. 9 and 13.

34 Norman Angell, *The Great Illusion*, 1909, reissued by Garland Publishing, New York, 1972.

35 At the time, negotiations to shape the ITO were seen as a big victory for the United States. Not only did the Roosevelt Administration quash a British proposal for a monetary system that would have limited American power and centrality in the global economy, but in forging the ITO the Americans rejected British plans to revive the Commonwealth trading system after the war. Daniel Drache, "The Short but Significant Life of the International Trade Organization: Lessons for Our Time," Working Paper No. 62/00, Centre for the Study of Globalisation and Regionalisation, University of Warwick, Coventry, November 2000. See also Charter of the International Trade Organization (Excerpts), posted online by The Avalon Project at Yale Law School.

36 The ITO was left to flounder for a few years before expiring quietly in the U.S. Senate early in the Korean War.

37 Robert Gilpin, *U.S. Power and the Multinational Corporation*, New York, Basic Books, 1975, p. 102.

38 Ibid., 103.

39 Albert O. Hirschman, *National Power and the Structure of Foreign Trade*, Berkeley, University of California Press, 1945, p. xvi.

40 Key instances include President Eisenhower's 1957 demand that European nations treat American investors the same way they treat domestic corporations, and Lyndon Johnson's stillborn proposal for a North Atlantic Free Trade Agreement to complement the radical Asia-focused "Kennedy Round" of trade negotiations.

41 Gilpin, 110.

42 Michael Schaller, *Altered States: The United States and Japan Since the Occupation*, New York, Oxford University Press, 1997, pp. 58 and 59.

43 Gilpin, 110, 111.

44 Schaller, 235, 244.

45 In 1954, the Eisenhower Administration imposed tariffs on Swiss watches; in 1973, President Nixon acted to protect America's ball bearing industry; in 1983, the Reagan Administration took steps to protect U.S. makers of machine tools.

46 U.S. Congress, Office of Technology Assessment, *Arming Our Allies: Cooperation and Competition in Defense Technology OTA-ISC-449* (Washington, DC: U.S. Government Printing Office, May 1990), Chapter 1, p. 15.

47 Many factors seem to have played some role in distracting Americans from the nature of industrial interdependence of nations. First, the American companies and workers most eager for protection from Japanese competition had little interest in acknowledging any common interest with the Japanese people. A second factor was the resurgence in the early 1980s of the "realist" school of international relations; since the days of Mahan there is nothing that military-oriented realists have enjoyed more than accusing theorists who focus on interdependence of being softheaded. A third factor was the reputation of the main critics of American strategies to promote interdependence and their peculiar choice of targets. Columnist and sometime nativist presidential candidate Pat Buchanan and political cult leader Lyndon LaRouche both assailed the idea by attacking the Trilateral Commission for undermining the sovereignty of the United States.

48 Robert O. Keohane and Joseph S. Nye, *Power and Interdependence,* 3rd Edition, New York, Longman, 2001, p. xvii.

49 One of the first instances anywhere of overseas direct investment for the sake of manufacturing came on January 1, 1853, when Samuel Colt opened an armory on the banks of the Thames. Colt's venture was unprofitable, but only a decade later Isaac Singer's sewing machine factory in Glasgow would prove a huge success.

50 The British also exported capital, but they tended to rely on a "portfolio" approach, which meant that investment bankers directed the capital to locally organized ventures rather than via cross-border firms managed from London (Gilpin, 64).

51 They also learned how to escape from the control of individual American states. This was thanks mainly to a highly creative interpretation of the Fourteenth Amendment to the Constitution, which was designed to protect the rights of former slaves but was also now used to protect the "rights" of corporations. The rise of giant corporations was also made possible by the introduction of extremely friendly corporate laws in New Jersey and Delaware.

52 Raymond Vernon, *Sovereignty at Bay,* New York, Basic Books, 1971, p. 61.

53 Mira Wilkins, *The Emergence of Multinational Enterprise,* Cambridge, Mass., Harvard University Press, 1970, p. 64.

54 As early as the 1830s, Tocqueville was able to put it simply, in observing the political power of European manufacturers. "Manufacturers govern us," he wrote, and the state "govern[s] manufacturers" (Alexis De Tocqueville, *Democracy in America,* Volume II, New York, Knopf, 1994, p. 312).

55 The United States is the only industrialized nation in the world that depends on the private sector rather than the state to manage these services.

56 Jacob Viner, "Political Aspects of International Finance," *The Journal of Business of the University of Chicago* 1 (April 1928), 170.

57 Gilpin, 139.

58 Vernon, 137.

59 Alfred E. Eckes Jr., *Opening America's Market,* Chapel Hill, University of North Carolina Press, 1995, p. 206.

60 Gilpin, 139.

61 Governments and peoples abroad were not always thrilled by the arrival of American multinationals. Both industrialized and less developed nations have generally tended to welcome the infusion of technology and skills that American ventures bring with them. But the appearance of "aggressive and indefatigable rivals" from America (Vernon, 81) has often led not to an embrace of the newcomers but to efforts to counterbalance them with homegrown alternatives. One of the more dramatic such responses took place in Japan after the Meiji Restoration in 1868. Not only did the nation adopt a Hamiltonian industrial policy (as filtered through List), but it copied the corporate form from America (Vernon, 223). Sometimes, foreign citizens grew to resent the American multinationals they had at first welcomed. One notable instance was the France of Charles de Gaulle in the 1960s, after the Johnson Administration ordered IBM's subsidiary in France not to sell an advanced computer to the French nuclear program. Yet such cases of gross interference were rare. Washington was much more intent on winning and keeping allies than on using multinationals to micromanage the affairs of foreign governments.

62 Vernon, 156.

63 Gilpin, 147.

64 John Kenneth Galbraith, *The New Industrial State,* Boston, Houghton Mifflin, 1967, p. 398.

65 Low points include China's firing of missiles into the sea off Taiwan in July 1995 and again in January 1996, which led the U.S. government twice to dispatch aircraft carriers to near China's coast. Another bad moment came when an American cruise missile struck the Chinese Embassy in Belgrade during NATO's war against Serbia. Chinese authorities responded by permitting rioters to attack the U.S. Embassy in Beijing. At one point, a Chinese general even threatened to destroy Los Angeles with a nuclear-armed missile.

CHAPTER FOUR Thinking in Links: *The Logistics Revolution*

1 Charles Boisseau, "The Company That Dell Built Isn't Finished Yet," *Houston Chronicle,* February 25, 1996, Magazine, p. 6.

2 Jan Hopkins, "Entrepreneur Michael Dell Discusses Computer Industry," CNN Moneyline, June 29, 1994.

3 Kevin Kelly, "Michael Dell: The Enfant Terrible of Personal Computers," *BusinessWeek,* June 13, 1988, p. 61.

4 David Henry, "Dell Stock: Beyond the Wildest Dreams," *USA Today,* February 18, 1999, p. 3B.

5 Peter Burrows, "The Computer Is in the Mail," *BusinessWeek,* January 23, 1995, p. 76; Kirk Ladendorf, "Lean Inventory Helps Dell Post Record Quarter," *Austin American-Statesman,* May 15, 1996, p. D5; "Dell's Direct Model Fuels Record Quarterly Performance," PR Newswire, August 19, 1997; Henry, *USA Today,* February 18, 1999, p. 3B.

6 Julie Pitta, "Why Dell Is a Survivor," *Forbes,* October 12, 1992, p. 82.

7 Sam Walton with John Huey, *Made in America,* New York, Doubleday, 1992.

8 Pitta, *Forbes,* October 12, 1992.

9 Aliza Pilar Sherman, "The Idol Life," *Entrepreneur,* January 1, 2002, p. 55.

10 Alfred D. Chandler, *The Visible Hand,* Cambridge, Mass., Harvard University Press, 1977, pp. 229 and 232.

11 "Corporate Culture Provides Wal-Mart Competitive Advantage," *Refrigerated Transporter,* July 1, 2002, p. 14.

12 Walton, 110.

13 Walton, 237.

14 Fred Smith, "How I Delivered the Goods," *Fortune Small Business,* October 2002; Blane Harden, "Overnight Success," *Washington Post,* February 22, 1981, p. 10.

15 "Good Ideas and Big Money Aren't All You Need," *Forbes,* November 15, 1975, p. 30; "Why Airlines Fear the 'Federal Express Bill,'" *BusinessWeek,* September 13, 1976, p. 116; Robert Flaherty, "Breathing Under Water," *Forbes,* March 1, 1977, p. 36; "Flying High at Federal," *Forbes,* February 6, 1978, p. 12; "Federal Express Says Profit Rose by 4.7 Percent in Latest Quarter," Associated Press, July 17, 1984.

16 Paul Page, "Federal Express and National Semiconductor Plan Global Parts Bank in SE Asia," *Traffic World,* November 23, 1992, p. 27.

17 Ronald Henkoff, "Delivering the Goods," *Fortune,* November 28, 1994, p. 64.

18 Henkoff, November 28, 1994.

19 Henkoff, November 28, 1994.

20 Thomas Friedman, "Autos: Studying the Japanese," *New York Times,* February 27, 1982, Section 2, p. 29.

21 Peter Drucker, *Concept of the Corporation,* New York, John Day Company, 1946, pp. 154 and 155.

22 Douglas Brinkley, *Wheels for the World*, New York, Penguin, 2003, pp. 270 and 285.

23 James P. Womack, Daniel T. Jones, and Daniel Roos, *The Machine That Changed the World*, New York, Rawson Associates, 1990, pp. 12 and 13.

24 Alfred P. Sloan, *My Years with General Motors*, Garden City, NY, Doubleday, 1964, p. 124.

25 Taiichi Ohno, *Toyota Production System*, Cambridge, Mass., Productivity Press, 1988, p. 45.

26 Staff Report, "Can Kanban Ban Inventory Blues?," *Industry Week*, July 26, 1982, p. 21.

27 Al Wrigley, "Chrysler Aiming to Double Inventory Turnover," *American Metal Market*, January 31, 1983, p. 12; *The Machine That Changed the World*, p. 266.

28 John Kenneth Galbraith, *The Affluent Society*, Boston, Houghton Mifflin, 1958, p. 105.

29 Eckes, 206.

30 Michael Borrus, *Left for Dead: Asian Production Networks and the Revival of U.S. Electronics*, The China Circle, Washington, Brookings Institution Press, 1997, pp. 150 and 151.

31 Borrus wrote that the trans-Pacific production system was characterized by a deep and growing "division of labor, in which U.S. firms specialize in 'soft' competencies (definition, architecture, design-standards areas) and Asian firms specialize in hard competencies (components, manufacturing stages, and design and development thereof)."

32 Borrus, 147.

33 Borrus, 145.

34 Borrus, 149.

35 Michael Dell, *Direct from Dell*, New York, HarperCollins, 1999.

CHAPTER FIVE Assets Backwards: *Outsourcing and the Arbitrage Firm*

1 Robert Slater, *The Eye of the Storm: How John Chambers Steered Cisco Through the Technology Collapse*, New York, HarperCollins, 2003, p. 18; Glenn Collins, "For This Couple, the Royal Tour Starts Here," *New York Times*, September 7, 2000, Section B, p. 1; Maitland Zane, "Belgian Premier in S.F. Today," *San Francisco Chronicle*, September 8, 2000, p. 2; Betsy Pisik, "Leaders of the World Arrive in New York for U.N. Summit," *Washington Times*, September 5, 2000, p. A11; "Belgian Government Tries to End Road Blockade Crisis," *Xinhua*, September 12, 2000.

2 Andy Reinhardt, "Mr. Internet," *BusinessWeek*, September 13, 1999, p. 128.

3 Jeffrey S. Young, *Cisco Unauthorized*, Roseville, Calif., Prima Publishing, 2001, p. 11.

4 John Chambers, Keynote Address, Government Technology Conference West, May 1999, published in "Visions," *Government Technology* magazine, August 1999.

5 Young, 4.

6 Chris Ayres, "American Evangelist Brings Britain the Word on the Web," *Times of London*, March 19, 1999.

7 Andrew Chetham, "Man on a Mission Preaches Conversion to the Internet," *South China Morning Post*, September 28, 1998.

8 Cisco was not the only company to adopt radical outsourcing in the early 1990s. SUN Microsystems and Hewlett-Packard pursued similar strategies at roughly the same time. But generally, these companies acted on a smaller scale, or in a more limited part of their operations, or kept more control over the integration of the final product.

9 Interview with Greg Stein, Cisco's former Senior Manager for Global Supply Chain Logistics.

10 Ismini Scouras, "Contract Manufacturing Is Changing Industry Map," *Electronic Buyers News,* November 11, 1996; *Case Study: Cisco Systems,* Published by InfoEdge, Stamford, Conn., 2001.

11 Ahmad Diba, "Blessed Are the Piece Makers," *Fortune,* May 1, 2000, p. 293.

12 Slater, 147; Young, 49–50.

13 Andy Serwer, "There's Something About Cisco," *Fortune,* May 15, 2000, p. 114.

14 Slater, 144.

15 Adam Smith, *The Wealth of Nations,* New York, Random House, 1994, p. 3.

16 Chandler, 337–339.

17 In the case of GM, the company under early CEO William C. Durant rolled up a variety of existing automobile makers—from Cadillac to Chevrolet—to sell to a wide range of buyers. In the case of GE, the company began with the merger of two integrated companies that made a variety of electric products, ranging from lightbulbs to dynamos, then grew by spinning internally developed products into separate industrial units. General Foods took form when the Postum breakfast cereal company went on an acquisition spree, buying Jell-O in 1925, Baker's Chocolate in 1927, Maxwell House Coffee in 1928, and the Birdseye frozen food company in 1929 (Brinkley, 255, and company history).

18 Brinkley, 34 and 47.

19 Ford, after watching the cost of materials soar during the First World War, "determined that his company would never again suffer at the mercy of commodity market pricing" (Brinkley, 255).

20 Richard Langlois and Paul Robertson, "Explaining Vertical Integration: Lessons from the American Automobile Industry," *Journal of Economic History,* Vol. 49, Issue 2, June 1989, p. 367.

21 Brinkley, 109.

22 Chandler, 231 and 232.

23 Langlois, 368.

24 Timothy J. Sturgeon, "Modular Production Networks: A New American Model of Industrial Organization," *Industrial and Corporate Change,* Vol. 11, No. 3, June 2002, p. 466.

25 One article in the magazine of the Institute of Industrial Engineers listed eight reasons to outsource. These were (1) to free resources for other purposes, (2) to share risks, (3) to accelerate reengineering benefits, (4) to assist with a function that is difficult to manage or out of control, (5) to use resouces that are not available internally, (6) to reduce and control operating costs, (7) to infuse cash into the enterprise, (8) to make capital funds available. Dean Elmuti, Yunus Kathawala, Mathew Monippallil, "Outsourcing to Gain a Competitive Advantage," *Industrial Management,* Vol. 40, No. 3, May 15, 1998, p. 20.

26 Richard Langlois and Paul Robertson, *Firms, Markets, and Economic Change: A Dynamic Theory of Business Institutions,* London: Routledge, 1995.

27 Ibid.

28 Langlois, "Explaining Vertical Integration," 370 and 371.

29 Ray Windecker, "DaimlerChrysler's Rocky Road," *Automotive Industries,* December 2001.

30 Langlois, "Explaining Vertical Integration," 368 and 369.

31 Womack, 139.

32 James Womack and Daniel Jones, *Lean Thinking,* New York, Simon & Schuster, 1996, p. 235.

33 Ronald Coase, "The Nature of the Firm," *The Firm, the Market, and the Law,* Chicago, University of Chicago Press (reprint edition), 1990.

34 Michael Porter, "Strategy and the Internet," *Harvard Business Review,* March 2001.

35 Sturgeon, "Modular Production Networks," 488; Timothy Sturgeon, "Exploring the Risks of Value Chain Modularity," MIT Industrial Performance Center, Working Paper Series, MIT-03-003, p. 33.

36 Greg Stein interview.

37 Other well-honed tools that allow better control over suppliers include industry-specific interfirm standards such as those published by the International Electrotechnical Commission, and "procurement standards" such as those published by the International Organization for Standardization, including the popular ISO 9000 series.

38 Andrew Rappaport and Schmuel Halevi, "The Computerless Computer Company," *Harvard Business Review,* July/August 1991, p. 301.

39 Among the more important technologies were software systems designed for "enterprise resource planning" or "supply chain management," and which provide a frame in which to manage much or most of the key information that flows through a company. Similarly, the advent of "computer-aided design" and "computer-aided engineering" software tied engineers much more closely to the factory floor, no matter where that floor was located. Finally, the rise of electronic business standards, like RosettaNet, simplified the transfer of financial and pricing information among companies within a network, and thereby gave big companies a yet wider window into the processes and cash flow of their suppliers.

40 Michael Borrus and John Zysman, "Globalization with Borders: The Rise of Wintelism as the Future of Industrial Competition," *Industry and Innovation,* Vol. 4, No. 2, December 1997, p. 141.

41 David Bunnel, *Making the Cisco Connection,* New York, John Wiley & Sons, 2000, 34 and 119.

42 Borrus and Zysman, 39.

43 Timothy Sturgeon and Richard Florida, "Globalization and Jobs in the Automotive Industry," MIT Industrial Performance Center, Globalization Working Paper 01-003, March 2000, Figure 9-2, p. 76.

44 In China, the situation remains highly complex, as the nation slowly abandons the Maoist-era model in which the employer provided not only pensions and unemployment insurance (mainly by keeping unnecessary employees on the payroll), but also housing, clinics, and kindergartens.

45 Jacob Hacker, *The Divided Welfare State,* New York, Cambridge University Press, 2002.

46 O'Boyle, 71.

47 Sturgeon and Florida, 76.

48 John McMillan, "Reorganizing Vertical Supply Relationships," in *Trends in Business Organization,* ed. Horst Siebert, Tubingen, J.C.B. Mohr, 1995, p. 203.

49 William J. Baumol, Alan Blinder, and Edward Wolff, *Downsizing in America: Reality, Causes, and Consequences,* New York, Russell Sage Foundation, 2003.

50 Alfred Chandler traces the origins of middle management in the American corporation to the rise of complex railroad networks in the 1860s and 1870s, not least because of the obvious need to coordinate information to ensure safe operation (Chandler, 107). Over the next century, as corporations grew ever larger, middle management

became the primary means of coordinating diverse activities, which they did through an increasing mastery of both the "science" and "art" of statistics (Chandler, 109). The middle manager, ensconced behind banks of IBM accounting machines, reached a sort of apotheosis in the 1950s and 1960s under executives like Robert Mc-Namara at Ford. This was an era when "large staffs of corporate controllers, planners, and auditors acted as the executives' eyes and ears, ferreting out data about divisional performance, and intervening to adjust the plans and activities of operational managers" (Michael Hammer and James Champy, *Reengineering the Corporation,* New York, HarperBusiness, 1993, p. 15).

51 The process was well expressed by Peter Drucker. "Restructuring the organization around information . . . invariably results in a drastic cut in the number of management levels and, with it, the number of 'general' management jobs." Peter Drucker, "Tomorrow's Restless Managers," *Industry Week,* April 18, 1988, p. 25.

52 Kanigel, pp. 462 and 473.

53 Take, for instance, the ability of Enterprise Resource Planning (ERP) systems to automate much of the money flow and accounting that had been handled manually. As *CIO* magazine put it, "The things accountants used to monitor manually—such as making sure that two signatures from the right people went on every check, or reconciling purchase orders against invoices—all became automated inside ERP systems" (Christopher Koch, "The Sarbox Conspiracy," *CIO,* July 1, 2004, p. 58). In the 1990s, it became popular to talk about "flat" organizations. Up to that point, management structures in American corporations had traditionally followed a certain formula, with many firms adopting a ratio similar to that of the military. This meant one manager for every six or seven employees, and so on up through layer upon layer of managers till the whole pyramidal structure peaked with the CEO. Now, though, consultants and executives began to speculate about much greater "spans" of management. Business guru Tom Peters thought such spans could reach to one per fifty or even one per seventy. One Dartmouth professor wrote that corporations could even reduce middle management down to one person per 200 workers (William Davidow and Michael Malone, *The Virtual Corporation,* New York, HarperBusiness, 1992, p. 169).

54 Slater, 171.

55 InfoEdge Case Study, 2001.

56 Davidow, 4.

57 Richard Chase and David Garvin, "The Service Factory," *Harvard Business Review,* July/August 1989, p. 61.

58 Davidow cited with special approval Toyota's plan to develop a vehicle that would be delivered within three days of a customer's order. "The closer a corporation gets to cost-effective instantaneous production of mass-customized goods and services," he wrote, "the more competitive and successful it will be." Davidow traced his concept back to the futurist Alvin Toffler, who in his book *Third Wave* had written of "prosumers," which he defined as consumers who produced what they consumed (Davidow, 5 and 137).

59 Chandler, 413.

60 Sloan, 47. Human resources, or personnel, would soon be added to the list (Peter Drucker, *The New Realities,* New York, Harper & Row, 1989, p. 224).

61 Porter, *Harvard Business Review,* March 2001.

62 Young, 57.

63 Slater, 127–134.

64 Robert Hof, "A New Era of Bright Hopes and Terrible Fears," *Business Week,* October 4, 1999, p. 84.

65 Other American-managed firms include Celestica and Sanmina-SCI. Another top player is the Taiwanese-managed, China-based company Foxxcon.

66 Michael Marks, CEO, Flextronics, interview.

67 Sturgeon, "Modular Production Networks," 456.

68 Timothy Sturgeon and Richard Lester, "The New Global Supply Base, MIT Industrial Performance Center," Working Paper Series, MIT-IPC-03-001, Table 4, p. 26.

69 Sturgeon and Lester, 20.

70 The power of the lead firm was made clear in 2004, when the Big Three automakers took steps to blend more Chinese components into the vehicles they assemble in the United States. Restrained from doing so directly by labor contracts, they instead ordered their top suppliers to source more from China, whether these firms wanted to do so or not (Norihiko Shirouzu, "Big Three's Outsourcing Plan: Make Parts Suppliers Do It," *Wall Street Journal,* June 10, 2004).

71 Sturgeon, "Modular Production Networks," 1.

72 Sturgeon, "Exploring the Risks of Value Chain Modularity," p. 13.

73 Letter to Stakeholders, by Jeffrey Immelt, Annual Report 2002. An excellent description of how corporate managers view globalization as an opportunity to pit suppliers and workers against one another can be found in the 1999 book *Race for the World.* In a chapter titled "Cross-Geographic Arbitrage," the authors, who were all consultants with McKinsey & Co., write that "the transition economy offers opportunities to transfer labor and productivity advantages developed in one geography to another. A company can lower its production costs while living under the price umbrellas of producers with lower productivity or higher factor costs." And thanks to the spread of outsourcing, such benefits have become available to much smaller players. "Now," they write, "it is possible to capture these opportunities by means of external agreements with other players. Counterparty agreements give companies the flexibility necessary to take advantage of these opportunities without making large capital investments" (Jane Fraser, Jeremy Oppenheim, and Wilhelm Rall, *Race for the World,* Boston, Harvard Business School Press, 1999, p. 235).

74 Geri Smith and Cristina Lindblad, "Mexico: Was NAFTA Worth It?" December 2, 2003, p. 66. Minxin Pei, "Beijing's Social Contract Is Starting to Fray," *Financial Times,* June 4, 2004, p. 17.

CHAPTER SIX   The Great Consolidation: *Of Scope & Scale*

1 Alex Taylor III, "Is the World Big Enough for Jurgen Schrempp?" *Fortune,* March 6, 2000, p. 140.

2 Timothy Ryback, "The Man Who Swallowed Chrysler," *The New Yorker,* November 16, 1998; Alex Taylor III, "The Germans Take Charge," *Fortune,* January 11, 1999, p. 92; Karen Lowry Miller, "The Auto Baron," *Business Week,* November 16, 1998, p. 82; Bill Vlasic and Bradley Stertz, *Taken for a Ride,* New York, HarperCollins, 2000, pp. 130–132.

3 Vlasic and Stertz, 242.

4 Tim Larimer, "Nissan Calls for a Tow," *Time,* March 1, 1999, p. 48.

5 Chalmers Johnson, *MITI and the Japanese Miracle,* Stanford, Calif., Stanford University Press, 1982, p. 9.

6 Japan was most successful, building on an industrial base already highly advanced before the war, and leveraging the profits of a protected home market to subsidize ex-

ports. South Korea has proven highly adept at emulating the Japanese, albeit on a much smaller scale. Elsewhere, though, results have been mixed at best. Malaysia managed to fill its roads with a heavily subsidized "national car" named the Proton, based on a kit purchased from Mitsubishi. Less successful was Yugoslavia's Yugo, which grew out of a seed planted by Fiat. Less successful yet was Indonesia's car project, based on a kit supplied by Korea's Kia. Most Latin American nations, meanwhile, took a different path. Rather than seek to develop their own branded vehicles, even large nations like Brazil and Mexico opted instead to force American and European companies to build plants locally in exchange for access to their markets. China in recent years has generally followed the Latin American model, though with a twist. In contrast to most other sectors in the country, China still refuses to allow foreign car companies to own a majority of their business (David Sedgwick, "Automaker Stays in Hot Market Despite Possible Patent Loss," *Automotive News,* June 16, 2003, p. 43).

7 "Mercedes Goes to Motown," *The Economist,* May 5, 1998, p. 2. Indeed, the purchase of Chrysler was the crowning event in what was actually a fourth round of cross-border ventures in the sector. The first acquisitions took place after the First World War, when GM opted to match Ford's organic expansion into Europe with the same roll-up strategy it had used at home, purchasing the British company Vauxhall in 1925 and Germany's Adam Opel in 1929. The second wave of consolidation did not hit until the early 1970s, when all three big American automakers bought what were essentially controlling stakes in the second tier of Japanese companies. The results here were long-term relationships between General Motors and Isuzu, Chrysler and Mitsubishi, and Ford and Mazda. In the late 1980s, Ford and BMW rolled up the remnants of the British auto industry, acquiring Jaguar and Rover respectively, and GM took a controlling stake in Sweden's Saab. Now, in the late 1990s, it seemed that the final rush for "global scale" was on, as managers scrambled to do away with the post-Asian-contagion "glut" of capacity before it did away with them (Merrill Goozner, "Excess Capacity Demands a Sleeker Auto Industry," *Chicago Tribune,* May 8, 1998, p. 1).

8 Vlasic and Stertz, 180.

9 Keith Naughton, "The Global Six," *BusinessWeek,* January 25, 1999, p. 68.

10 Sang-Hun Choe, "GM Acquires Daewoo Units," Associated Press, April 30, 2002.

11 Hyundai's ability to pay was helped out by a roughly $400 million infusion of cash from DaimlerChrysler in June 2000, in exchange for 10.5 percent of the company (Don Kirk and John Schmid, "Eyes on Asia, Daimler Links Up with Hyundai," *International Herald Tribune,* June 24, 2000, p. 1).

12 Carol J. Williams, "Deal Would Give DaimlerChrysler Foothold in Asia," *Los Angeles Times,* March 28, 2000, p. C1.

13 Geoffrey Colvin, "Year of the Mega Merger," *Fortune,* January 11, 1999, p. 62.

14 Editorial, "The Best Managers: What It Takes," *BusinessWeek,* January 10, 2000, p. 158.

15 Jack Welch, *Straight from the Gut,* New York, Warner Books, 2001, Appendix A.

16 O'Boyle, 87.

17 Welch, 186 and 304. Another early mover was Whirlpool, which in the mid-1980s set off on a world-spanning acquisition spree, buying out KitchenAid's business in the United States, Philips's appliance business in Europe, and expanding into India. In the 1990s, Whirlpool just kept going, pushing into eastern Europe, into South America, into China, and emerging as the world's biggest appliance maker, a neck ahead of Sweden's similarly expansive-minded Electrolux.

18 "After the Deal," *The Economist,* January 9, 1999, p. 21; Sandra Sugawara, "Merger Wave Accelerated in '99," *Washington Post,* December 31, 1999, p. E1; "The World's First Three-Way Cross-Border Merger Rolls Out," *Corporate Finance,* January 2000.

19 John R. Wilke, "How Driving Prices Lower Can Violate Antitrust Statutes," *Wall Street Journal,* January 27, 2004.

20 "Sony, Samsung in Talks on Making Liquid Crystal Display Panels Together," Associated Press, October 17, 2003; Larry Wilson, "Corning Inc. 150th: Wherever It Leads Us," *Elmira NY Star-Gazette,* June 17, 2001, p. 20H; Peter Marsh, "General Electric Plans for Growth," *Financial Times,* June 21, 2002, p. 26; "Airbus Soars Higher Than Boeing," *Le Figaro,* January 3, 2003; "Polatechno to Acquire U.S. Optical Components Venture Moxtec," *Asia Pulse,* January 8, 2004; "Chipmakers in Tie-Up to Reclaim Top Spot," *Asahi News,* September 5, 2003; Peter Smith, "Owens-Illinois Leads Global Market with E1.6 Billion Deal," *Financial Times,* February 19, 2004, p. 22.

21 International Harvester figure comes from Ron Chernow, *The House of Morgan,* New York, Grove Press, 1990, p. 109.

22 Chandler, 442.

23 Robert Litan and Carl Shapiro, "Antitrust Policy During the Clinton Administration," UC Berkeley, Center for Competition Policy Working Paper, No. CPC01-22, July 2001, p. 1.

24 Ken Auletta, "Final Offer: What Kept Microsoft From Settling Its Case," *The New Yorker,* January 15, 2001, p. 40.

25 One historian has termed the 120-year career of American antitrust policy a "rhetorical omelet" of "scrambled categories of large and small, powerful and weak." Rudolph Peritz, *Competition Policy in America,* New York, Oxford University Press, 1996, p. 225.

26 Chandler, 331. In the decade after the Sherman Act became law, the number of consolidations soared. The first wave came immediately after the Act—and a radical revision of New Jersey's corporate law—with a total of fifty-one deals taking place between 1890 and 1893. A second and much bigger wave began in 1898, after a series of Supreme Court interpretations of the Sherman Act clarified that although cartels were prohibited, corporations were perfectly free to merge into single enterprises. The wave peaked in 1899, almost exactly a century before the DaimlerChrysler deal, when 108 deals were struck in a single year (Chandler, 332). The process would continue, at a slower pace, through industry after industry until around the First World War, when most American industries had acquired "their modern structure" (Chandler, 364).

27 Peritz, 72–75. Many early progressives strongly supported the idea of consolidation. Compared to the small, old-fashioned firms that dominated production before the Sherman Act, many progressives welcomed the ability of the new mass manufacturers to drive down prices, improve quality, even provide better jobs. When J. P. Morgan partner George Perkins described trusts as "socialism of the highest, best, and most ideal sort," socialist and socialist-influenced progressives nodded in eager agreement (Chernow, 110). Jacksonian populism, meanwhile, was increasingly condemned as tending inherently to anarchy. The view was famously expressed by Supreme Court Justice Oliver Wendell Holmes, a progressive, who in 1904 warned that those who advocated competition for competition's sake were dangerously naive. The problem, as Holmes saw it, was that to limit combination at any point was, if pursued to the logical endpoint, to limit combination at all points. To act to protect small businesses from big would simply doom those same small businesses to later attack by yet smaller entities.

The prospect gave Holmes a case of Hobbesian shivers, as he foresaw a "universal disintegration of society into single men, each at war with all the rest" (Peritz, 42).

28 New Deal thinkers were strongly influenced by Edward Chamberlin's theory that big industrial entities tended naturally, and often harmlessly, toward oligopoly and monopoly (Edward Hastings Chamberlin, *The Theory of Monopolistic Competition*, Cambridge, Mass., Harvard University Press, 1933). Later, they proved amenable to Schumpeter's theory that such corporations were often more innovative than smaller corporations that had to make their way in more competitive markets (Joseph Schumpeter, *Capitalism, Socialism, and Democracy*, New York, Harpers & Brothers, 1942).

29 As Supreme Court Justice William J. Brennan put it, the general goal was to prohibit mergers that resulted in "undue percentage share" in any market, of "at least 30%," or that resulted in a significant increase in concentration, beyond 33 percent. The Antitrust Division went further in its 1968 "Merger Guidelines," announcing a policy to challenge any merger in a sector where the four largest firms were responsible for 75 percent or more of production (Peritz, 217 and 232).

30 Commerce Secretary Malcolm Baldrige captured this sentiment when he defended the Reagan Administration's proposal to relax antitrust law. "The world economy has changed, trade patterns have changed, but the antitrust laws have not" (Peritz, 278).

31 Mark Roe, "From Antitrust to Corporate Governance," in *The American Corporation Today*, ed. Carl Kaysen, New York, Oxford University Press, 1996, p. 106.

32 Litan and Shapiro, 2; Assistant Attorney General Anne Bingaman, Justice Department Press Release, March 3, 1994.

33 Chandler, 374.

34 Alfred Chandler, *Inventing the Electronic Century*, New York, Free Press, 2001, p. 249. So profound was the effect of this policy that Chandler has compared the "middle-level bureaucrats" in the Cold War-era Antitrust Division to "gods."

35 As Peter Drucker has written, "Schumpeter's economy is not a closed system like Newton's universe—or Keynes's macroeconomy. It is forever growing and changing and is biological rather than mechanistic in nature." Peter Drucker, "Schumpeter and Keynes," *Forbes*, May 23, 1983, p. 124.

36 Schumpeter, 90 note.

37 Schumpeter believed "perfectly competitive" markets were able to exist only in agriculture, and then only sometimes (78–81).

38 Schumpeter, 82–83.

39 Schumpeter, 132.

40 Schumpeter, 101.

41 These included Antitrust Division chief Thurmond Arnold and the growing number of jurists open to arguments of Supreme Court Justice Louis Brandeis and others who favored competition for competition's sake (Wyatt Wells, *Antitrust & the Formation of the Postwar World*, New York, Columbia University Press, 2002, p. 41). As Learned Hand, chief justice of the 2nd Circuit Court of Appeals, wrote in 1945 in ordering the breakup of Alcoa, the purpose of antitrust is "to perpetuate and preserve, for its own sake and in spite of possible cost, an organization of industry in small units which can effectively compete against each other" (Steve Lohr, "Is Wal-Mart Good for America," *New York Times*, December 7, 2003, Section 4, p. 1).

42 Schumpeter, 91 and 102.

43 This competition theory was influenced by an investigation into the corporate use of intellectual property, completed only months before America entered the war in 1941. The investigation, by the Temporary National Economic Committee

(TNEC), composed of congressmen and members of the Roosevelt Administration, found that many corporations simply hoarded their patents. In its final report, the committee recommended "legislation which will require that any future patent is to be available for use by anyone who may desire its use and who is willing to pay a fair price" (Wells, 39–40). Although Congress did not act on this recommendation, the Antitrust Division put it into practice almost immediately after the end of the war.

44 David M. Hart, "Antitrust and Technological Innovation in the U.S.," *Research Policy,* Vol. 30, No. 6 (June 2001), p. 928.

45 Carlos Correa, "Intellectual Property Rights and the Use of Compulsory Licenses: Options for Developing Countries," South Centre Working Paper, October 1999, Section V, p. 22.

46 F.M. Scherer, Testimony before Federal Trade Commission, Hearings on Global and Innovation-Based Competition, DKT/CASE NO: P951201, November 29, 1995.

47 In April 1952, AT&T's manufacturing arm, Western Electric, had invited representatives of twenty-five American and ten foreign firms to learn about the transistor that Bell Labs had invented in 1948.

48 IBM agreed to "license existing and future patents to any person making a written application" (Chandler, "Inventing the Electronic Century," 250).

49 The last big compulsory licensing decree would be signed in 1975 by Xerox, though it can be reasonably argued that the last de facto licensing decree was IBM's decision in the early 1980s, at the end of another drawn-out antitrust investigation of the company, to outsource its semiconductor technology to Intel and its operating system to Microsoft.

50 One of the more important technological programs of the Clinton-Gore team was the Partnership for a New Generation of Vehicles (PNGV), which aimed to help American automobile makers to design a highly fuel-efficient and commercially viable automobile. In a direct reversal of pre-Reagan policy on intellectual property, PNGV arranged for the transfer of publicly developed technologies into the vaults of private-sector corporations, without any sort of quid pro quo guarantee these technologies would ever be put to use.

51 Information from StarTrek.com, Paramount Pictures, 2004.

52 Ed Paulson, *Inside Cisco,* New York, John Wiley & Sons, 2001, Appendix D.

53 Chernow, 67–68.

54 Not that Microsoft is always averse to buying its way into a new market. In mid-2004, the firm made the "eye-popping" disclosure that it had tried to acquire Germany's giant business software company SAP. Jay Greene, "The Message in Microsoft's SAP Quest," *BusinessWeek Online,* June 9, 2004.

55 Laurie Flynn, "Oracle Says Fear of Microsoft Led to PeopleSoft Bid," *New York Times,* July 1, 2004, Section C, p. 1.

56 David Hounshell, *Science and Corporate Strategy: Du Pont R&D 1902–1980,* New York, Cambridge University Press, 1988, pp. 595, 597, and 600.

57 Paulson, 52.

58 Young, 63.

59 Paulson, 20.

60 At GE's Corporate Research and Development Center in Schenectady, New York, Welch cut the staff by 30 percent in the seven years up to 1993 (O'Boyle, 136).

61 By 2000, GE would be purchasing more than one hundred small to mid-size companies each year. Amy Barrett, "Jack's Risky Last Act," *BusinessWeek,* November 6, 2000, p. 40.

62 Michael Arndt, "3M's Rising Star," *Business Week,* April 12, 2004, p. 62.

63 Barnaby Feder, "Johnson and Johnson Decides It Needs Devices," *New York Times,* December 8, 2004.

64 Spencer Reiss, "Size Matters," *Wired,* February 2004.

65 "Foundry Father," *The Economist,* May 19, 2001. Cameron Cooper, "Risk Taker Became King of Microchips," *The Australian,* October 10, 2001, p. 25.

66 Samuel Weber, "A New Endangered Species: Mulling a Fabless Future," *Electronics,* July 1991, p. 36.

67 Other design firms that have carved out lucrative though highly circumscribed niches include Qualcomm, which designs chips for mobile phones, NVIDIA, which specializes in graphics chips for video games, and Broadcom, which focuses on broadband and networking applications.

68 "AMD Delays Some Chips, Plans Factory," *AFX,* November 6, 2003.

69 As Michael Porter put it, "Purchasing everything from one supplier may yield that supplier too much of an opportunity to exercise power" (Michael Porter, *Competitive Strategy,* New York, Free Press, 1980, pp. 27 and 44. Quoted in Paul D. Larson, "Single Sourcing and Supplier Certification," *Industrial Marketing Management,* January 1998).

70 "The fear of supply disruption has long been regarded as the Achilles' heel of single-source alliances" (John Sheridan, "Betting on a Single Source," *Industry Week,* February 1, 1988, p. 31). Production managers have always known that the key question was not whether their suppliers produced products that looked exactly alike, but whether they could rely on one supplier to ramp up quickly to replace production handled by another supplier.

71 Business consultant W. Edwards Deming wrote that American manufacturers should move fast to "end the practice of awarding business on the basis of the price tag" alone. Instead, the goal should be to "minimize total cost" by moving "toward a single supplier for any one item, on a long-term relationship of loyalty and trust" (W. Edwards Deming, *Out of the Crisis,* Boston, MIT Press, 1986, p. 23. Quoted in Paul D. Larson, *Industrial Marketing Management,* January 1998).

72 Womack, *The Machine That Changed the World,* 159.

73 *Industry Week,* February 1, 1988.

74 Many firms now aimed to form "partnerships" with their suppliers. These were presented as "win-win" relationships marked by a "collaborative approach" in which the lead firm and its suppliers "work closely together, sharing the risks and rewards of a cooperative relationship that focuses on continuous improvement" (Ronan McIvor, "Partnership Sourcing," *Journal of Supply Chain Management,* June 22, 2000). Practically, the aim of such "partnerships" was to cut costs by reducing the number of transactions and relationships a lead firm needed to manage by shifting management responsibility to the suppliers. As we saw with the relationship between Cisco and Flextronics, fewer, bigger, more capable suppliers meant fewer plants to visit, fewer contracts to negotiate, a greater ability to shift responsibility—and management costs—down the supply chain. By early 1997, Dell had whittled its Tier 1 supply base down to 47 companies, from 204 in 1992 (Gary McWilliams, "Whirlwind in the Web," *Business Week,* April 7, 1997, p. 132). Cisco in 2003 announced plans to reduce its supplier base from more than 1,300 to about 350, of whom only 50 to 70 were to get most of the work (Mike Angell, "Cisco System Drastically Paring Its Suppliers," *Investors Business Daily,* March 6, 2003, p. A6).

75 John Kenneth Galbraith, *The New Industrial State,* Boston, Houghton Mifflin, 1967, p. 391.

76 "If I had gone and said Chrysler would be a division, everybody on their side would have said: 'There is no way we'll do a deal'" (Tim Burt, "The Schrempp Gambit," *Financial Times,* October 30, 2000, p. 26).

77 James Surowiecki, "Chrysler's New Best Friend," *The New Yorker,* December 25, 2000, p. 64.

78 Jeffrey Ball and Joseph White, "Grinding Gears," *Wall Street Journal,* October 27, 2000.

79 Steven Pearlstein, "Schrempp Wrecking DaimlerChrysler," *Washington Post,* May 19, 2004, p. E1.

80 Talk now was of selling off Chrysler's still highly profitable Jeep division, or perhaps merging Chrysler and Mitsubishi, or even of dumping Chrysler's car division onto the market for whatever price it would fetch (Gail Edmondson, "Stalled," *Business-Week,* September 29, 2003, p. 55). In May 2004, DaimlerChrysler announced plans to forgo any further infusions of cash into Mitsubishi, even if this meant bankruptcy for its Japanese partner.

81 Edmondson, *BusinessWeek,* September 29, 2003.

82 "The Worst Managers: Jurgen Schrempp," *BusinessWeek,* January 12, 2004, p. 72.

CHAPTER SEVEN The Virtual Moment: *The Snap-Together World*

1 Cheryl Strauss Einhorn, "There's No Magic," *Barron's,* August 28, 2000.

2 Otis Port, "Customers Move Into the Driver's Seat," *BusinessWeek,* October 4, 1999, p. 103.

3 Dave Beal, "Signing Bonus of $45 Million Stirs Comment," *St. Paul Pioneer Press,* July 23, 2000, p. 1D.

4 "GE to Buy 7 Satellites," *New York Times,* July 1, 1994, p. 2; "GE Unit to Buy Polish Bank from Chase Enterprises," *AFX,* August 18, 1995.

5 Robert Garsson, "Houston Astros Take GE Credit to Full Count in Lending Game," *American Banker,* July 8, 1985, p. 8.

6 Welch, 240.

7 Tim Smart, "A Mover and Shaker, GE Style," *BusinessWeek,* March 8, 1993.

8 "The House That Jack Built," *The Economist,* September 18, 1999.

9 Welch, 244.

10 John Curran, "Jack Welch's Secret Weapon," *Fortune,* November 10, 1997, p. 116.

11 Betsy Morris, "It's Her Job Too," *Fortune,* February 2, 1998, p. 64; Denise Lavoie, "GE at Center of Top Executive's Divorce Case," Associated Press, January 26, 1997; Nathan Cobb, "The Ex-Wife's Club," *Boston Globe,* December 23, 1997, p. C1.

12 Tim Smart, "GE Capital's Grand Tour of Europe," *BusinessWeek,* October 16, 1995, p. 71; Nathan Cobb, *Boston Globe,* December 23, 1997; "List of Accepted Invitations to Forbes Birthday Bash," Associated Press, August 18, 1989.

13 *Indianapolis Star,* April 20, 2001.

14 *St. Paul Pioneer Press,* April 21, 2001.

15 Chris O'Malley, "Conseco to Buy India Firm," *Indianapolis Star,* April 23, 2001, p. 1A

16 "We Woz Wrong," *The Economist,* December 18, 1999.

17 Justin Fox, "Net Stock Rules, Masters of a Parallel Universe," *Fortune,* June 7, 1999, p. 66.

18 Samuel Huntington, "Clash of Civilizations?," *Foreign Affairs,* Summer 1993.

19 Stan Davis and Christopher Meyer, *Blur: The Speed of Change in the Connected Economy,* New York, Warner Books, 1999; Philip Evans and Thomas Wurster, *Blown to Bits: How the New Economics of Information Transforms Strategy,* Boston, Harvard Business School Press, 1999; James Gleick, *Faster: The Acceleration of Just About Everything,* New York, Pantheon, 1999.

20 "Back Office to the World," *The Economist,* May 5, 2001.

21 Welch, 304, 308, and 309.

22 As Welch put it, the "real benefit of India turned out to be its vast intellectual capability and the enthusiasm of its people" (Welch, 310).

23 Beginning in the late 1980s and accelerating in the 1990s, GE Capital bulked up on capital assets, which it would buy from the user and then lease back in a long-term deal. By 2003, GE Capital owned more airliners, 1,161, than any airline in the world (GE Capital Aviation Services Report). The company also owned thousands of railroad cars in the United States and Europe, fleets of trucks and rental automobiles, British taxis, even oil rigs. The numbers were so huge that in 1996 alone, the company was able to claim some $2 billion in annual depreciation. As other firms went light, often in emulation of GE's strategies elsewhere, GE Capital was there to take on their burdens.

24 GE Capital India Fact Sheet, downloaded May 12, 04; Justin Fox, "Where Your Job Is Going," *Fortune,* November 24, 2003, p. 84; Manjeet Kripalani and Pete Engardio, "The Rise of India," *BusinessWeek,* December 8, 2003, p. 66; Joanna Slater, "GE Reinvents Itself in India," *Far Eastern Economic Review,* March 27, 2003; "Kodak Will Sell 3 Units," Reuters, November 24, 1992.

25 Tom Field, "10 Years that Shook IT," *CIO,* October 1 1999; Mary Lacity, "IT Outsourcing: Maximize Flexibility and Control," *Harvard Business Review,* May/June 1995, p. 84; Jonathan Weber, "Computer Services for Hire," *Los Angeles Times,* August 2, 1992, p. D1.

26 David Kirkpatrick, "Why Not Farm Out Your Computing?" *Fortune,* September 23, 1991, p. 103.

27 Automatic Data Processing began to offer its payroll services in 1949. Warren McFarlan and Richard Nolan, "How to Manage an IT Outsourcing Alliance," *Sloan Management Review,* December 22, 1995, p. 9. See also, John Byrne, "Has Outsourcing Gone Too Far?" *BusinessWeek,* April 1, 1996, p. 216.

28 Field, *CIO,* October 1, 1999.

29 At almost the same time, Enron closed a $750 million outsourcing deal with EDS. A decade later, company leaders credited the outsourcing agreement with enabling Enron to focus on developing a "freewheeling, deal-making, spin-off kind of culture" (*CIO,* August 15, 1999).

30 WIPRO was originally an acronym for Western India Vegetable Products. Premji expanded his company's product line first into soaps and then into hydraulic machinery and finally into data processing services.

31 *Le Figaro,* January 6, 2003 (from WIPRO Web site).

32 "The Stars of Asia: Azim Premji," *BusinessWeek,* July 2, 2001.

33 Premji, in Jack Welch's words, was the "poster child of India's high-tech industry" (Welch, 308). Other early beneficiaries of GE deals include Infosys, which employs some 21,000 people, and Tata Consulting Services (TCS), which employs some 22,000 people. As of 2003, GE continued to cultivate new entrants, spreading new BPO contracts to companies including Satyam Computer, Birlasoft, Mascot Sys-

tems, and Patni. For many of the first-generation companies, the "big break" came in the desperate run-up to fix computer programs before January 1, 2000 (Kripalani and Engardio, *Business Week,* December 8, 2003).

34 *The Economist,* May 5, 2001.

35 Justin Fox, *Fortune,* November 24, 2003. GE, meanwhile has already moved on to its next stage of development in India. Continuing its countercyclical tradition, GE Capital announced that it was looking to split its wholly owned back-office subsidiary in India in half, or sell it off entirely. This was at the same time that IBM and Citigroup were exercising options to gain more direct control of their back-office partners in India, IBM paying upward of $170 million for control of Daksh and Citigroup paying $126 million for control of e-Serve International (Indrajit Basu, "Indian BPOs in Sell Mode," UPI, April 22, 2004).

36 Slater, *Far Eastern Economic Review,* March 27, 2003.

37 Kripalani and Engardio, *Business Week,* December 8, 2003.

38 Mary Eisenhart, "How Palm Beat Microsoft," *Salon,* September 17, 1998.

39 Pete Engardio, "How Motorola Took Asia by the Tail," *Business Week,* November 11, 1991, p. 68.

40 Jeffrey O'Brien, "The Making of Xbox," *Wired,* November 2001; Raoul Mowatt, "They're Playing for Keeps," *Chicago Tribune,* December 31, 2001, p. 3.

41 Evan Ramstad and Phred Dvorak, "Off-the-Shelf Parts Create New Order in TVs, Electronics," *Wall Street Journal,* December 16, 2003.

42 Michiyo Nakamoto, "Sony Struggles to Get Back in the Race," *Financial Times,* October 28, 2004.

43 William Davidow, in *The Virtual Corporation,* wrote that the firm was becoming "edgeless" and "permeable" with "constantly changing interfaces between company, supplier, and customer." But he still operated in an essentially twentieth-century context in which both the corporation and the nation retained their traditional nature within the system. Davidow's book is full of exhortations toward "teamwork" and "learning together," in which the goal is for all stakeholders in a corporation to join together to beat the foreign competitor rather than to battle among themselves over the fruits of work. For Davidow, the goal is for American managers and workers to cooperate, to ensure that the American nation not be reduced to a "colony of economic serfs" (Davidow, 2).

44 John Byrne, "The Virtual Corporation," *Business Week,* February 8, 1993.

45 Reich, 99 and 102.

46 Reich, 101 and 105.

47 The article was written by Daniel Pink, who had recently served as one of Al Gore's speechwriters. *Fast Company* was eager to stake out a role for itself as the *Cosmopolitan* of programmer lifestyle, with cover-to-cover coverage of the glorious lives of the rising geekocracy, the climbing walls in the office gym and BMWs in the parking lot, the games of team-building laser tag and the concierges in the corporate lobby (Daniel Pink, "Free Agent Nation," *Fast Company,* December 1997).

48 Thomas Malone and Robert Laubacher, "Dawn of the E-Lance Economy," *Harvard Business Review,* September/October 1998.

49 John Byrne, "The Global Corporation Becomes the Leaderless Corporation," *Business Week,* August 30, 1999, p. 88.

50 Michael Porter, *Harvard Business Review,* March 2001.

51 One survey showed that more than 28 percent of the American workforce in 2002 was made up of "temporary and contract employees, freelancers, independent pro-

fessionals, and consultants," up from 22 percent in 1998 (Steven Berchem, "The Flexible Workforce," *OfficeSolutions,* March 1, 2004, p. 18).

52 Although there is little doubt that the rise of the business process services industry has been beneficial for India, the boom has not resulted in the transfer of much real power over the process. The relatively small size and high number of Indian firms providing business process services makes the whole industry vulnerable to manipulation by customers that tend to be much larger and more powerful. GE, for instance, uses its huge market power to pay well below the going rate for most computer and back-office services, so much so that WIPRO and fellow early mover Infosys have both stopped doing business process work for GE (Pankaj Mishra, "GE Changes Outsourcing Paradigm for India," *Express Computer Online,* April 15, 2002). A recent article summed up GE's strategy well, urging buyers of India-based business process services to strive always to "have multiple vendors continually bidding against each other" (Stephanie Overby, "Inside Outsourcing in India," *CIO,* June 1, 2003).

53 Which Lopez had named after four saints important in his life —Virgen del Carmen, Virgen del Pilar, Virgen de Begonia, and Virgen de Lourdes (Al Goodman, "A Lopez in Every Garage," *New York Times,* October 26, 1999, Section C, p. 1; "Lopez Stands Alone on Amorebieta Car Project," *Financial Times Expansion,* September 30, 1999, p. 10).

54 Melanie Warner, "A Much Anticipated Sequel," *Fortune,* January 11, 1999, p. 152.

55 Adolf Berle and Gardiner Means, *The Modern Corporation & Private Property,* New Brunswick, N.J., Transaction Publishers (Reprint Edition), 1991, p. 8. Originally published by Harcourt, Brace & World, 1932. The concern traces back to the American economist Thorsten Veblen and beyond him to the nineteenth-century British economist Alfred Marshall.

56 "Dematerialized, defunctionalized and absentee ownership does not impress and call forth moral allegiance as the vital form of property did," he concluded (Schumpeter, 142).

57 Adolf Berle, *Economic Power and the Free Society,* New York, Fund for the Republic, 1957, n. 4, p. 9, quoted in Abram Chayes, "The Modern Corporation and the Rule of Law," in *The Corporation in Modern Society,* ed. Edward Mason, Cambridge, Mass., Harvard University Press, 1959, p. 40.

58 Edward Mason, Introduction, *The Corporation in Modern Society,* p. 2.

59 Barbara Rose, "CEO Chair Becomes Hotter Seat," *Chicago Tribune,* February 2, 2004. Among the CEOs booted in the 1990s for "underperformance"—which often meant too much loyalty to workers or communities—were Robert Stempel at General Motors, Kay Whitmore at Kodak, John Akers at IBM, and James Robinson III at American Express.

60 Though certainly well paid, the CEOs of the past were by no means rich. This meant they often perceived their own long-term interest more in promoting harmony within the corporation and in investing in innovation, rather than in absolutely maximizing the price of their firm's stock.

61 Christopher Farrell, "Stock Options for All," *BusinessWeek Online,* September 20, 2002.

62 The reasoning is simple, transparent, and has been noted often elsewhere. As *Barron's* wrote, in an article inspired by Wendt's payday at Conseco, compensation for CEOs increasingly "consists largely of shares or options," which serves mainly to make the CEO's "primary goal the same as shareholders'—to get the stock price up" (Cheryl Strauss Einhorn, *Barron's,* August 28, 2000).

63 Christopher Carey, "Conseco CEO's Perk-Laden Deal Surpasses Exclusive $100 Million Mark," *Indianapolis Star,* July 11, 2000, p. A1.

CHAPTER EIGHT Warnings Unheeded: *Risk vs. Reward*

1 Tom Brokaw, "Attack on America," NBC News Transcripts, September 11, 2001, 1:00 P.M. ET; Arlene Levinson, "U.S. Under Lockdown After Attacks," Associated Press, September 11, 2001; *The NewsHour with Jim Lehrer,* "Day of Terror," Transcript #7152, September 11, 2001; David Levee, "Our Sense of Normalcy May Never Return," *Chicago Tribune,* September 12, 2001.

2 James Prichard, "Attacks Have Almost Immediate Impact on Michigan," Associated Press, September 11, 2001.

3 Humphrey Hudson, "Air Traffic Ban to Hit Hi-Tech Sector," World Trade, Reuters, September 12, 2001.

4 "Korea Losing $30 Million Daily in Airfreight Exports," Reuters, September 13, 2001; "U.S. Airport Shutdown Halts Taiwan Tech Exports," Reuters, September 14, 2001.

5 Yuri Kageyama, "US Terror Attacks Worry Asia Companies," Associated Press, September 13, 2001.

6 Mark Landler and Richard Oppel Jr., "Ban on Airliners' Freight Has Businesses Scrambling," *New York Times,* September 15, 2001.

7 Jeffrey Ball, "How Chrysler Averted a Parts Crisis," *Wall Street Journal,* September 24, 2001.

8 "Border Slowdown Affects Automakers," *Detroit Free Press,* September 14, 2001.

9 Ball, *Wall Street Journal,* September 24, 2001.

10 Eric Auchard, "Cargo Disruptions the Least of Asian High Tech's Worries," Reuters, September 13, 2001.

11 "International Air Travel to U.S. Resumes," Agence France-Presse, September 15, 2001.

12 "Closures and Evacuations Nationwide," Associated Press, September 11, 2001.

13 Dan Schiller and Allison Gregor, "INS Straps on Extra Muscle Along Borders," *San Antonio Express-News,* September 11, 2001.

14 "U.S. Total Import Trade in Goods and Services," "U.S. Total Export Trade in Goods and Services," U.S. Census Bureau, Foreign Trade Division.

15 At GE, for instance, the showdown "prompted an internal debate" over "how much work to concentrate" in India. Joanna Slater, "GE Reinvents Itself in India," *Far Eastern Economic Review,* March 29, 2003.

16 Toyota's Fremont, California, plant, for instance, which produces 1,500 cars per day, suddenly found itself cut off from forty container loads per day of imports from Asia. Ford, which imports 360 different parts through the port of Tacoma, faced imminent shutdowns at ten assembly plants and four power train plants (John Porretto, "West Cost Port Shutdown Threatens Auto Industry," Associated Press, October 3, 2002).

17 Vanessa Hua, "Looking for Alternatives," *San Francisco Chronicle,* October 4, 2002.

18 "Stratfor, Alert—Oil Blockade Under Way," Economist Intelligence Unit Riskwire, December 5, 2002; T. Christian Miller, "Strike in Venezuela Widens," *Los Angeles Times,* December 5, 2002; Christopher Toothaker, "Venezuela Gets 1st Foreign Gas Shipment," December 28, 2002; Nick Ashwell, "Fitch Upgrades Venezuelan Debt as Oil Production Rebounds," World Markets Research Centre, June 24, 2003.

19 Russ Craig and Peter Kastner, "SARS Virus Attacks the Electronics Industry," AberdeenGroup Consulting, March 31, 2003; "Japanese Firms Adapt to a Market In-

fected with Fear," *Asahi News,* April 24, 2003; Rebecca Buckman, "Worries About
SARs Crimp Toy Industry's Buying Season," *Wall Street Journal,* April 30, 2003;
Gabriel Kahn and Ann Zimmerman, "In Age of SARS Wal-Mart Adjusts Global
Buying Machine," *Wall Street Journal,* May 28, 2003; Toshiya Ono, "SARS Puts
Component Makers at Risk," *Nikkei Weekly,* April 28, 2003; Darrell Dunn, "Mo-
torola Monitors SARS in China," *Financial Times Global News Wire,* May 9, 2003.

20 Evan Ramstad, "Computer Memory Chip Prices Double," Associated Press, July 20,
1993; James Coates, "Crunch Is Likely to Boost PC Prices," *Chicago Tribune,* August
6, 1993.

21 Larry Holyoke, "Day of the Troubleshooter," *Business Week,* February 6, 1995, p. 19.

22 "Toyota Output Returns to Normal After Parts Company Fire," Associated Press,
February 27, 1997; Toshihiro Nishiguchi and Alexandre Beaudet, "Case Study: The
Toyota Group and the Aisin Fire," *Sloan Management Review,* Vol. 40, No. 1, 1998.

23 One instance is the fretting in Southeast Asia over dangers posed to Malacca Straits
shipping by pirates and terrorists ("Going for the Jugular," *The Economist,* June 12,
2004).

24 Stephen Roach, "Back to Borders," *Financial Times,* September 28, 2001.

25 "Globalization's Last Hurrah?" *Foreign Policy,* January 1, 2002.

26 James Womack, "Manufacturers Can't Panic and Discard JIT," *Advanced Manufac-
turing,* November 2001. Other responses can be found in: Lisa Hauser, "Risk-
Adjusted Supply Chain Management," *Supply Chain Management Review,* November
2003; *Creating Resilient Supply Chains: A Practical Guide,* Cranfield University
School of Management, Bedford, U.K., 2003; David Katz, "The O-Ring in Your
Supply Chain," *CFO,* March 11, 2004; Gary Lynch and Karen Avery, "A Five-Step
Business Continuity Plan for CEOs," *Strategy + Business,* September 24, 2002.

27 Mark Gerencser and DeAnne Aguirre, "Security Concerns Prominent on CEO
Agenda," *Strategy + Business,* February 12, 2002.

28 "Shipper Groups Worry About Impact of Homeland Security Department," *Logistics Management,* January 2003.

29 Gregory Crouch, "Europe Acts Against U.S. Effort on Ports," *New York Times,* January 28, 2003.

30 One article even urged companies to create "a real-time economy" (Mark Roberti,
"From Just-in-Time to Real Time," *CIO Insight,* April 2002). "What is remarkable,"
lamented two Booz Allen Hamilton consultants a year after the attack, is how little
CEOs worry about "their company's business continuity—short-term or long-
term—in the face of disruption, let alone disaster" (Lynch and Avery, *Strategy +
Business,* September 24, 2002).

31 Said Frank Vargo, the vice president for international affairs at the National Associa-
tion of Manufacturers, a month after the attacks: "None of our members are build-
ing warehouses to cope with the aftermath of September 11." Claudia Deutsch, "A
Nation Challenged: The Suppliers," *New York Times,* October 9, 2001; Jim Ericson,
"Supply Chain Interrupted," *Line56.com Magazine,* December 2001, p. 41; Greg Ip,
"Companies Are Seeing Efficiencies Erode," *Wall Street Journal,* October 24, 2001.

32 In part this was due to the concerns of SIA members such as Xilinx CEO Wim Roelandts. In part it was because SIA president George Scalise had experienced such a
near industrial collapse once before. In 1993, as a top manager at Motorola, Scalise
had been put in de facto charge of rationing out resin to the semiconductor industry
after an explosion at a Sumitomo plant in Japan (interviews with Roelandts and
Scalese).

33 Aon, "Protecting Supply Chains Against Political Risks," August 2003.

34 Katz, *CFO,* March 11, 2004.

35 Brian Byrnes, director of property facultative reinsurance, GE ERC (Employers Re Corporation), interview, 2003.

36 In early 2003, Cisco managers told *Circuitree* magazine that "every part at Cisco must be dual sourced, to assure a continuous supply and avoid line stops" (Walt Custer, "They Might Be Giants: An Interview with Cisco's PCB Group," *Circuitree,* April 1, 2003). But in Cisco's annual report for 2003, the company admits that it "receives certain of its components from sole suppliers" (Cisco Annual Report 2003, p. 39, note 2).

37 When risk is "socialized" in this manner the result, Perrow says, is to "minimize" the "consequences" faced by "those who take the risks" in order to "increase profits" (Charles Perrow, *Normal Accidents,* New York, Basic Books, 1984, pp. 360, 361, 370, and 371).

38 Almar Latour, "Trial by Fire," *Wall Street Journal,* January 29, 2001; "Flextronics Sees Opportunity in Ericsson's Cell-Phone Business," Bloomberg, January 27, 2001; Jeff May, "Wireless Circuit Maker Warns of Revenue Drop," *The Star-Ledger,* September 16, 2000; "Ericsson's Financial News Not the Hot Variety It Prefers," *CT Wireless,* July 24, 2000; Robert Lineback, "Anadigics Expects Sales Drop," *Silicon Strategies,* September 15, 2000; Ursula Kraus, "Philips/Ericsson Suppliers Extension Claim," *Exposure,* published by GE Francona Re, No. 5, February 2001.

39 James Conerty, "Business Interruptions: Is This What Corporate Reengineering Left in Its Wake?" FM Global Library, Collection of Speeches, 1996.

40 Stephen Doig, et al., "Has Outsourcing Gone Too Far?," *McKinsey Quarterly,* September 22, 2001, p. 25. And rather than letting up, the automotive lead firms continue only to demand further price cuts by the suppliers (Norihiko Shirouzu, "Ford and GM Put Squeeze on Parts Suppliers for Price Cuts," *Wall Street Journal,* November 18, 2003). This is despite the fact that a solid majority of lead firms already feel that engineering work done by these suppliers is inferior to engineering work done in house (Tom Murphy, "Has Engineering Outsourcing Gone Too Far?" *Wards Auto World,* March 2001).

41 Kenichii Ohmae, interview, September 2003.

42 In the 1970s, some thirty firms made vaccines for the U.S. market. That number is down to five, only three of which make flu vaccine. Britain, by contrast, splits flu vaccine orders among five suppliers, precisely to avoid breakdowns in the system (Denise Grady, "Before Shortage of Flu Vaccine, Many Warnings," *New York Times,* October 17, 2004).

43 This was well captured in a 1970 article in the *New York Times* (Milton Friedman, "The Social Responsibility of Business Is to Increase Its Profits," *New York Times Magazine,* September 13, 1970).

44 The image of the corporation as a sort of person traces back centuries in Anglo-Saxon common law, but the concept per se had little legal importance until after the adoption of the Fourteenth Amendment to the Constitution in 1868. Drawn up to protect the newly freed slaves from having their rights denied by southern state legislatures, the Fourteenth Amendment declared that all citizens were entitled to the same basic protections under federal law. Enterprising lawyers soon began to claim that corporations deserved the same level of protection from the "arbitrary" powers of the states as any other "person."

45 Friedman, *New York Times Magazine,* September 13, 1970.

46 Michael Jensen and William Meckling, "Theory of the Firm: Management Behavior, Agency Costs and Ownership Structure," *Journal of Financial Economics,* Vol. 3, No. 4, October 1976, p. 305.

47 Most important was a series of law review articles by two professors at the University of Chicago Law School, Daniel R. Fischel and Frank H. Easterbrook. These were later collected into a book, *The Economic Structure of Corporate Law,* Cambridge, Mass., Harvard University Press, 1991. Though Fischel and Easterbrook were at first dismissed as "enfants terribles," interested mainly in shocking their readers, by the turn of the century their work would evolve into what was widely regarded as the "dominant perspective among legal scholars" (Gaurang Mitu Gulati, William Klein, and Eric Zolt, "Connected Contracts," *UCLA Law Review,* Vol. 47, p. 887, 2000). And they were enfants no more. Fischel had been named dean of the University of Chicago Law School while Easterbrook was appointed to a judgeship on the 7th Circuit Court of Appeals in Chicago.

48 Peritz, 290.

49 By far the most effective attack on Nexus of Contracts theory has come from within its ranks. Take, for instance, "Connected Contracts" theory, inspired by the emergence of the "virtual" companies of the 1990s (see earlier, note 47). The authors contended that the Nexus of Contract insistence on a clear channel of control by shareholders over management ignored the growing complexity of ownership in the postmodern virtual firm. For these authors, the answer was to go yet further and do away entirely with any "implicit notion of a core or centralizing entity" within the corporation. In place of the corporation, there will remain only "interrelated agreements or relationships among all participants in an economic activity." It was a system in which there would be "no primacy, no core, no hierarchy, no prominent participant, no firm, no fiduciary duty" (Gulati, "Connected Contracts," 907). One of the main responses came from UCLA law professor Stephen M. Bainbridge. Long a committed proponent of nexus of contracts theory (see "Community and Statism: A Conservative Contractarian Critique of Progressive Corporate Law Scholarship," 82 Cornell L. Rev. 856, 877, 1997), Bainbridge now concluded there must be at least some reification of the firm. "Perhaps some deference should be shown the corporation's status as a legal person," he wrote, if only to ensure that liability continue to be limited. It is vital, Bainbridge wrote, to ensure that "corporate constituents contract not with each other, but with the corporation" (Stephen M. Bainbridge, "The Board of Directors as Nexus of Contracts," January 2002, UCLA School of Law Research Paper, No. 02-05). To limit the significance of his admission, Bainbridge immediately went on to condemn the "mindless formalism" of the "traditional insistence" that the firm is some sort of "real entity." Bainbridge's goal, in essence, was to keep the physical body of the corporation healthy enough to absorb all liabilities, but then to lobotomize it to ensure that it would be unable to assume any social responsibilities.

50 Anthony Bianco and Wendy Zellner, "Is Wal-Mart Too Powerful?" *BusinessWeek,* October 6, 2003, p. 100; Charles Fishman, "The Wal-Mart You Don't Know," *Fast Company,* December 2003; Jim Hopkins, "Wal-Mart's Influence Grows," *USA Today,* January 23, 2003; Jeff Madrick, "Wal-Mart May Be the New Model of Productivity, But It Isn't Wowing Workers," *New York Times,* September 2, 2004, p. C1.

51 When Levi's reorganized its entire supply chain to win Wal-Mart's approval, the company was able to boost its on-time delivery performance to all customers from 65 percent to 95 percent (Kim Girard, "How Levi's Got Its Jeans Into Wal-Mart," *CIO,* July 15, 2003).

52 Norihiko Shirouzu, "Big Three's Outsourcing Plan: Make Parts Suppliers Do It," *Wall Street Journal,* June 10, 2004.

53 Keynes wrote famously of the everyday task of the investor to predict the future course of the economy, even if only a year or two out. "The outstanding fact is the extreme precariousness of the basis of knowledge on which our estimates" are made (Maynard Keynes, *The General Theory of Employment, Interest, and Money,* New York, Harcourt, Brace, 1936, Chapter 12, Section III).

54 One excellent example is the post–September 11 effort by the Federal Reserve Board and the Securities and Exchange Commission to force banks and other financial institutions to make their systems more redundant. Another successful program was the Critical Infrastructure Assurance Office, created in May 1998 by the Clinton Administration. Although the main goal was to harden government agencies against cyberattacks, CIAO also established innovative public-private committees to help corporations share information within and across industries.

55 Here the model has long been relatively simple—maintain a multiplicity of sources and a multiplicity of middlemen. Winston Churchill, in a 1913 speech urging Parliament to buy a private oil company to ensure the British Navy a steady supply of inexpensive oil, put it best: "On no one quality, on no one process, on no one country, on no one route and on no one field must we be dependent. Safety and certainty in oil lie in variety and variety alone" (Daniel Yergin, *The Prize,* New York, Touchstone, 1993, p. 160). The U.S. government in the 1970s added an important layer to this system when it began to set aside vast reserves of oil in underground reservoirs to afford the nation a chance to respond to any major disruptions in supply.

56 The total number of oil refineries in the United States has been consolidated from 321 in 1976 to 149 now (Jeffrey Ball, "Lack of New Capacity Is Spotlighted by High Oil Prices," *Wall Street Journal,* June 7, 2004). Electricity utilities have slashed expenditures on new plants and on the maintenance of existing systems. Pharmaceutical companies have been allowed to dramatically cut their capacity to manufacture vaccines. Defense contractors have concentrated production of cruise missiles on a single assembly line and even to single-source critical chips from offshore plants. Railroads have cut staff to the point where a slight glitch can create a "rolling bottleneck" that severely affects U.S. economic performance (Daniel Machalaba, "Woes at Union Pacific Create a Bottleneck in the Economy," *Wall Street Journal,* July 22, 2004).

57 Perrow, 4 and 369.

58 Scott Sagan, *The Limits of Safety,* Princeton, N.J., Princeton University Press, 1993, p. 17.

59 Ian Mitroff and Murat Alpasian, "Preparing for Evil," *Harvard Business Review,* April 2003, p. 209.

60 Langdon Winner, "Complexity and the Limits of Human Understanding," in *Organized Social Complexity: Challenge to Politics and Policy,* ed. Todd R. La Porte, Princeton, N.J., Princeton University Press, 1975, pp. 49 and 74.

CHAPTER NINE Rent and Rending: *Stretched to the Limit?*

1 Stanley Holmes, "A Plane, a Plan, a Problem," *BusinessWeek,* December 1, 2003.

2 Don Tapscott, "Rethinking Strategy in a Networked World," *Strategy + Business,* Issue 24, 2001. In recent years, Boeing has dumped many of its plants onto the market, not only in its home state of Washington but in McDonnell Douglas's old home of Mis-

souri, as well as big operations in Texas and Kansas (John Gillie, "British Company Eyes Boeing Plants," *The News Tribune [Tacoma]*, April 20, 2004). Increasingly, the expectation is that any major capital investments will be made by suppliers. Indeed, Boeing has long neglected its own capital assets, and one recent study showed that most of Boeing's machine tools dated back to the 1960s and 1970s and were therefore nearing the end of their useful lives (Alan MacPherson and David Pritchard, "International Decentralization of US Commercial Aircraft Production," Canada–United States Trade Center, Occasional Paper No. 26, p. 7).

3 Boeing paid $13.3 billion, yet compared to Daimler's takeover of Chrysler eighteen months later, the deal was hardly noticed in the press. In large part, this was because McDonnell Douglas's share of the world market had fallen to some 5 percent, so few questioned Boeing CEO Phil Condit when he reassured reporters that "you're not going to see any less competition" (Anne Willette and Keith Alexander, "Boeing Pays $13.3 Billion for McDonnell Douglas," *USA Today*, December 16, 1996, p. 1B). The only real objections to the deal were by the governments of Taiwan and South Korea, which had invested substantially in subsidizing businesses that were developing technology for McDonnell Douglas's planned MD-95. (In 1991, Taiwan Aerospace had even tried to buy control of McDonnell Douglas's commercial division.) For Americans, a more important objection was raised by officials in Europe, who feared the purchase would only boost Boeing's dominance of the industry, where it already controlled nearly 70 percent of the business. But given that neither firm had substantial operations in Europe, the authorities in Brussels opted not to challenge the deal.

4 MacPherson and Pritchard, 4.

5 In Britain, a "perfect storm" of weak defense orders, a strong currency, and the maturation of Tier 3 and Tier 4 suppliers in Asia means that as much as half the nation's aircraft component manufacturers will close by mid-2006 (Nick Cook, "Aerospace Suppliers Brace for a Nosedive," *Financial Times*, April 12, 2004).

6 The commercial airline industry has not been a driver of technological progress for decades. The half century of technological advances between the Wright Flyer of 1903 and the Boeing 707 prototype of 1953 was one of the most phenomenal chains of innovation in the history of the world. Well into the 1960s, more than a dozen big companies still competed in the building of jet-powered airliners. In the United States there was Boeing, Lockheed, Douglas, and Convair. In Britain there was De-Havilland, Hawker-Siddeley, Vickers, and the British Aircraft Corporation. In France there was Aerospatiale and Dassault-Breguet. In the Soviet Union, Ilyushin and Tupolev. In Holland, Fokker. But the amount of capital required, the complexities of aeronautical regulation, the competition unleashed among the airlines by deregulation of competition, the nature of state intervention in Europe and Japan, the ability of many airplane makers to profit more easily off defense contracts, all combined to push the industry to rationalize dramatically.

7 As one magazine recently made clear, the huge improvements in aerodynamics in recent years mean that it is now much more affordable to build a plane like the Concorde than was the case when that supersonic aircraft was introduced thirty-five years ago. Yet given the present structure of the market for commercial aircraft, the writer figured that any recommercialization of these technologies lies at least twenty years in the future, or more than half a century after civilian passengers first flew faster than the speed of sound (Will Knight, "Supersonic Successor to Concorde Will Take 20 Years," NewScientist.Com Newsservice, April 10, 2003).

8 Offsets in the aviation industry date back at least to the 1960s, when Douglas

awarded wing and fuselage assembly work to Alenia in Italy and to DeHavilland in Canada, in exchange for big contracts to sell its DC-9 and DC-10 aircraft to those nation's airlines (MacPherson and Pritchard, 3). Over the years Boeing, often in close cooperation with the U.S. government, has agreed to shift production work to countries as far afield as the Philippines, South Africa, Taiwan, and India, among many others. The foreign-made content in the average Boeing aircraft has progressed steadily since then. When the 767 came on line in the early 1980s, the share made abroad had risen to 15 percent, and with the 777 in the early 1990s, the total would rise to 30 percent.

9 Stanley Holmes, "Is Boeing Bailing Out of Passenger Jets?" *BusinessWeek Online,* April 11, 2003.

10 "Boeing to Boost Ties with Japan Suppliers," *The Daily Yomiuri,* April 3, 2004.

11 "Airbus Beats Boeing for Second Year in Row on Jetliner Deliveries," *Seattle Post Intelligencer,* January 6, 2004.

12 "The House That Jack Built," *The Economist,* September 18, 1999.

13 Brendan Sobie, "Japan's Big Hope," *Flight International,* February 17, 2004, p. 76.

14 Michael Mecham, "Year-End Dividends," *Aviation Week & Space Technology,* January 3, 2005, p. 38.

15 Boeing demanded that Kansas promise $500 million, which it did, despite the fact that the state was already facing a $230 million budget gap. Boeing up to that time employed 12,000 people in Wichita and directly and indirectly contributed 7 percent of the state's total tax revenue ("Boeing Asks Kansas for $500 Million Incentive Package," Knight Ridder Tribune Business News, March 28, 2003). In the end Boeing simply passed, and located the work elsewhere (Phyllis Jacobs Griekspoor, "Officials Wait for Boeing Decision," *Wichita Eagle,* April 12, 2004).

16 J. Lynn Lunsford, Daniel Michaels, Neil King and Scott Miller, "New Friction Puts Airbus, Boeing on Course for New Trade Battle," *Wall Street Journal,* June 1, 2004.

17 Many Americans continue to fret about how corporations don't pay taxes anymore—and indeed the majority do not (John McKinnon, "Many Companies Avoided Taxes Even As Profits Soared in Boom," *Wall Street Journal,* April 6, 2004). More disturbing yet, however, is the degree to which they demand that public revenues be paid to them.

18 J. Lynn Lunsford, *Wall Street Journal,* June 1, 2004.

19 Carol Matlack, "Is Airbus Caught in a Downdraft" *BusinessWeek,* December 27, 2004.

20 A recent book by industrial research expert Ralph Gomory and economist William Baumol noted that capital-intensive industries are increasingly becoming fixed in space. Governments, with the general exception of United States, tend to protect whatever industrial activities they have captured, making it more expensive for new companies (and nations) to enter such markets. "Whatever may have been true two centuries ago, we know that in today's world a good part of international trade consists of products that are definitely not characterized by ease of entry on a small scale." This means that in a world in which "each product is produced by just one nation, any specialized assignment of products among countries will tend to persist" (Ralph Gomory and William Baumol, *Global Trade and Conflicting National Interests,* Cambridge, Mass., MIT Press, 2000, pp. 16 and 19).

21 One of the best examples in any industry of how a weakness in the supply base can cripple a lead firm took place in the commercial aircraft sector three decades ago. In the early 1970s, the bankruptcy and reorganization of Rolls Royce resulted in a nearly

one-year delay in delivery of the first of a new generation of jet engines the company planned, and this resulted in a one-year delay in delivery by Lockheed of its new L-1011 TriStar. Even though the L-1011 was regarded as perhaps the most advanced jetliner in the world, Lockheed lost so many sales to Douglas's new DC-10 that the company almost followed Rolls Royce into insolvency.

22   Galbraith, *New Industrial State,* 6.

23   Smith, *Wealth of Nations,* 13.

24   Hirschman, 7.

25   As recently as 2004, psychology professor Barry Schwartz decried what he called a "tyranny of choice" in the modern marketplace (Barry Schwartz, "The Tyranny of Choice," *The Chronicle of Higher Education,* January 23, 2004). *BusinessWeek* not long afterward celebrated the "vanishing" of the mass market under a "proliferation" of highly targeted products (Anthony Bianco and Michael Arndt, "The Vanishing Mass Market," *BusinessWeek,* July 12, 2004). On the surface, such statements certainly appear true enough. Even in a "heavy" industry like automobiles, buyers today choose from more than 600 models around the world ("Cadillac Comeback," *The Economist,* January 24, 2004). But as with the sixty-four manifestations of Shiva, most of these varied faces lead back to but a few gods, and if anything the pantheon of true powers is slowly shrinking.

26   The Germans had left themselves vulnerable by locating well more than 50 percent of their ball bearing machinery in three plants in the small town of Schweinfurt. In the event, the bombs caused less damage than hoped, and Germans responded by breaking up ball bearing production into small, highly disguisable units (Report of the Commanding General of the Army Air Force to the Secretary of War, from the U.S. Air Force Museum Web site. See also Gian Gentile, *How Effective Is Strategic Bombing?* New York, New York University Press, 2001; and Robert Pape, *Bombing to Win,* Ithaca, N.Y., Cornell University Press, 1996).

27   Joseph A. Tainter, *The Collapse of Complex Societies,* New York, Cambridge University Press, 1988, p. 55. Tainter based this on work done by David A. Phillips, curator of archaeology at the Maxwell Museum at the University of New Mexico.

28   Tainter, p. 55. Tainter based this idea on work done by Roy Rappaport and Kent Flannery of the University of Michigan Department of Anthropology.

29   After management of the U.S.-China commercial relationship was turned over to the private sector in the early 1990s, the economic integration of the two nations progressed far faster than most at that time would have imagined possible. The purchasing decisions of firms like Wal-Mart and GE and Dell often vastly outweigh in political importance the economic tweakings of the State Department during the Cold War era. Indeed, to such sweeping reorganizations of global trade as those unleashed by the Kennedy and Tokyo rounds of the GATT we should probably add the Wal-Mart Round of the 1990s. No longer is this integration simply a matter of hand towels, T-shirts, and cheap trade beads, but increasingly some of the world's most advanced production lines are located in China. The country is the world's top producer of both basic commodities like shoes and brassieres as well as laptops and microwaves, cell phones and washing machines, televisions and digital cameras, even key hardware destined for the U.S. military (Nancy Cleeland, Evelyn Iritani and Tyler Marshall, "The Wal-Mart Effect: Scouring the Globe to Give Shoppers an $8.63 Polo Shirt," *Los Angeles Times,* November 24, 2003).

30   Mark Landler, "These Days 'Made in Taiwan' Often Means 'Made in China,'" *New York Times,* May 29, 2001.

31 "The paradox of an interdependent world economy is that it creates sources of insecurity and competition . . . which exacerbate international relations," Robert Gilpin wrote in 1975 (Gilpin, 256). Take, for instance, the attitude of economist Jagdish Bhagwati, long one of the most eloquent of writers in favor of free trade as a way to alleviate poverty in his native India and in other poor nations. "When I read about interdependence, a red light flashes in my head that reads *dependence*" (Jagdish Bhagwati, *In Defense of Globalization*, New York, Oxford University Press, 2004).

32 German nationalists tended to view talk of economic interdependence as a sign of weakness. General Friedrich von Bernhardi in 1911 wrote, "This desire for peace has rendered most civilized nations anemic, and marks a decay of spirit and political courage." Von Bernhardi went on to quote the German nationalist historian von Treitschke, to the effect that it is only "the weary, spiritless, and exhausted ages which have played with the dream of perpetual peace" (Friedrich Adam Julius von Bernhardi, *Germany and the Next War*, London, E. Arnold, 1912). The Germans at the very same time also saw interdependence as an opportunity. In 1914, German military planners launched the war knowing full well that their nation had developed a more advanced and much larger steelmaking capacity than England, because before the war England was highly dependent on purchases of German steel. As it proved, the cutoff in steel shipments in the summer of 1914 left England immediately in deep trouble, without the capacity to build sufficient numbers of explosive shells or the merchant ships on which its supply lines depended. Winston Churchill would later describe the war as a "steel war," yet it was America's steel capacity, not Britain's, that enabled the survival of the British military effort. Nor were the English able quickly to build back their capacity even when pressed. This was because the country had outsourced much of machine tool industry to the Germans. As a postwar report made clear, it was "only the importation of machine tools from America, Switzerland, and Sweden that prevented a total breakdown of the British effort to create new industries between 1914 and 1916" (Thomas Howell, "Dumping: Still a Problem in International Trade," in National Research Council, *International Friction and Cooperation in High Technology Development and Trade*, Washington, National Academies Press, 1997).

33 MIT economist Lester Thurow wrote, after a Chinese fighter had forced an American spy plane to land in China, that the power in the U.S.-China relationship lies with Americans in the "long run," because U.S. companies and the U.S. government can steer buying away from a China that acts in an overly aggressive way. But in the near term, Thurow wrote, real power probably lies with the Chinese, who can deprive Americans of what they want and need (Lester Thurow, "Behind Plane Crisis: Who's In Control Economically?" *USA Today*, April 11, 2001).

34 TSMC Chairman Morris Chang warned after the spy plane crisis that "if in the future China were to stop shipping I.T. products, that could shut down a large part of the I.T. industry in the U.S." (Mark Landler, *New York Times*, May 29, 2001).

35 Many experts on China believe something in that nation will give soon. The economic revolution there is in fact unleashing many of the sorts of demands for political liberalization that Bill Clinton and the libertarians predicted. Yet the huge imbalance in the distribution of wealth in China is also creating deep resentments among the poor, which may play out in political actions and reactions we do not expect.

36 Douglas Streusand, "Geopolitics Versus Globalization," in *Globalization and Maritime Power*, Sam Tangredi, ed., Washington, National Defense University, 2002.

37 Greg Jaffe, "At the Pentagon Quirky Powerpoint Carries Big Punch," *Wall Street Journal,* May 11, 2004; Thomas Barnett, "The Pentagon's New Map," *Esquire,* March 2003.

38 F. A. Hayek, *The Road to Serfdom,* Chicago, University of Chicago Press, 1944 (reprinted 1994), p. 41.

39 The idea that the market "manages" the economy is a crude myth. When not managed by the state, the economy will still be managed, only now by private sector actors. By no means is this necessarily a bad thing if the private-sector entity acts in such a way that it serves the overall interest of society. Right now, however, in most global industries this is not the case.

BIBLIOGRAPHY

Acheson, Dean, *Power and Diplomacy,* Cambridge, Mass., Harvard University Press, 1958.

Adams, Henry, *The Education of Henry Adams,* Boston, Houghton Mifflin, 1973 (copyright 1918).

Almeida, Beth, "Are Good Jobs Flying Away?: U.S. Aircraft Engine Manufacturing and Sustainable Prosperity," Center for Industrial Competitiveness, University of Massachusetts Lowell, Working Paper No. 206, August 1997.

Angell, Norman, *The Great Illusion,* 1909. Reissued by Garland Publishing, New York, 1972.

———, *The Fruits of Victory,* 1921. Reissued by Garland Publishing, New York, 1972.

Bainbridge, Stephen M., "The Board of Directors as Nexus of Contracts," January 2002, UCLA, School of Law Research Paper, No. 02-05.

Barnett, Thomas P.M., *The Pentagon's New Map,* New York, Putnam, 2004.

Bauer, Michael, et al., *e-Business: The Strategic Impact on Supply Chain and Logistics,* Oak Brook, Ill., Council of Logistics Management, 2001.

Baumol, William J., Alan Blinder, and Edward Wolff, *Downsizing in America: Reality, Causes, and Consequences,* New York, Russell Sage Foundation, 2003.

Baxter, Maurice, *Henry Clay and the American System,* Lexington, Ky., University Press of Kentucky, 1995.

Beeching, Jack, *The Chinese Opium Wars,* San Diego, Harcourt Brace Jovanovich, 1975.

Bergere, Marie-Claire, *Sun Yat-Sen,* Janet Lloyd, trans., Stanford, Calif., Stanford University Press, 1998.

Berle, Adolf, *The 20th Century Capitalist Revolution,* New York, Harcourt, Brace and Company, 1954.

———, and Gardiner Means, *The Modern Corporation & Private Property,* New Brunswick, N.J., Transaction Publishers (Reprint Edition), 1991. Originally published by Harcourt, Brace & World, 1932.

Bernhardi, Friedrich Adam Julius von, *Germany and the Next War,* London, E. Arnold, 1912.

Bhagwati, Jagdish, *In Defense of Globalization,* New York, Oxford University Press, 2004.

Bilby, Kenneth, *The General: David Sarnoff,* New York, Harper & Row, 1986.

Borrus, Michael, "Left for Dead: Asian Production Networks and the Revival of U.S. Electronics," in *The China Circle,* Washington, Brookings Institution Press, 1997.

———, and John Zysman, "Globalization with Borders: The Rise of Wintelism as the Future of Industrial Competition," *Industry and Innovation,* Vol. 4, No. 2, December 1997.

Brinkley, Douglas, *Wheels for the World,* New York, Penguin, 2003.

Bunnel, David, *Making the Cisco Connection,* New York, John Wiley & Sons, 2000.

Butler, Michael, *Cautious Visionary: Cordell Hull and Trade Reform 1933–1937,* Kent, Ohio, Kent State University Press, 1998.

Carr, Edward Hellett, *The Twenty Years' Crisis,* New York, St. Martin's, 1939 (reprinted by HarperCollins, New York, 2001).

Chamberlin, Edward Hastings, *The Theory of Monopolistic Competition,* Cambridge, Mass., Harvard University Press, 1933.

Chambers, William Nisbit, *Old Bullion Benton: Senator from the New West,* Boston, Little, Brown & Company, 1956.

Chandler, Alfred, *The Visible Hand: The Managerial Revolution in American Business,* Cambridge, Mass., Harvard University Press, 1977.

———, *Scale and Scope: The Dynamics of Industrial Capitalism,* Cambridge, Mass., Harvard University Press, 1990.

———, *Inventing the Electronic Century,* New York, The Free Press, 2001.

Chang, Ha-Joon, *Kicking Away the Ladder: Development Strategy in Historical Perspective,* London, Atheneum Press, 2002.

Chernow, Ron, *The House of Morgan,* New York, Grove Press, 1990.

Clough, Ralph N., *Island China,* Cambridge, Mass., Harvard University Press, 1978.

Coase, Ronald, "The Nature of the Firm," in *The Firm, the Market, and the Law,* Chicago, University of Chicago Press (reprint edition), 1990.

Cobden, Richard, *Speeches on Questions of Public Policy,* London, T. Fisher Unwin, 1908.

Collis, Maurice, *Foreign Mud,* London, Faber & Faber, 1946 (reprinted by New Directions, New York, 2002).

Correa, Carlos, "Intellectual Property Rights and the Use of Compulsory Licenses: Options for Developing Countries," South Centre Working Paper, October 1999.

Cousins, Paul, "Supply Base Rationalisation: Myth or Reality?" *European Journal of Purchasing & Supply Management* 5 (1999).

Cumings, Bruce, "Webs with No Spiders, Spiders with No Webs," in *The Development State,* Meredith Woo-Cumings, ed., Ithaca, Cornell University Press, 1999.

Davidow, William, and Michael Malone, *The Virtual Corporation,* New York, HarperBusiness, 1992.

Dell, Michael, *Direct from Dell,* New York, HarperCollins, 1999.

Deming, W. Edwards, *Out of the Crisis,* Boston, MIT Press, 1986.

Dertouzos, Michael, Richard Lester, and Robert Solow, *Made in America: Regaining the Productive Edge,* Cambridge, Mass., MIT Press, 1989.

Drache, Daniel, "The Short but Significant Life of the International Trade Organization: Lessons for Our Time," Working Paper No. 62/00, Centre for the Study of Globalisation and Regionalisation, University of Warwick, Coventry, November 2000.

Drucker, Peter, *Concept of the Corporation,* New York, John Day Company, 1946.

———, *The Age of Discontinuity,* New York, Harper & Row, 1968.

———, *The New Realities,* New York, Harper & Row, 1989.

Eckes Jr., Alfred E., *Opening America's Market,* Chapel Hill, The University of North Carolina Press, 1995.

Edsall, Nicholas C., and Richard Cobden, *Independent Radical,* Cambridge, Mass., Harvard University Press, 1986.

Ellsberg, Daniel, "The Theory and Practice of Blackmail," Santa Monica, Calif., The Rand Corporation, 1968, paper P-3883.

Ernst, Dieter, "From Partial to Systemic Globalization: International Production Networks in the Electronics Industry," Berkeley Roundtable on the International Economy, Working Paper 98, April 1997.

Evans, Philip, and Thomas Wurster, *Blown to Bits,* Boston, Harvard Business School Press, 2000.

Fallows, James, *Looking at the Sun: The Rise of the New East Asian Economic and Political System,* New York, Vintage, 1994.

Fischel, Daniel R., and Frank H. Easterbrook, *The Economic Structure of Corporate Law,* Cambridge, Mass., Harvard University Press, 1991.

Flamm, Kenneth, *Mismanaged Trade?: Strategic Policy and the Semiconductor Industry,* Washington, Brookings Institution Press, 1996.

Fraser, Jane, Jeremy Oppenheim, and Wilhelm Rall, *Race for the World,* Boston, Harvard Business School Press, 1999.

Freeland, Robert, "Creating Holdup Through Vertical Integration: Fisher Body Revisited," *Journal of Law and Economics,* 2000, Vol. 43, Issue 1.

Friedman, Milton, *Capitalism and Freedom,* Chicago, University of Chicago Press, 1962.

Friedman, Thomas, *The Lexus and the Olive Tree,* New York, Anchor Books, 1999.

Fukuyama, Francis, *The End of History and the Last Man,* New York, Avon Books, 1992.

Funabashi, Yoichi, Michel Oksenberg, and Heinrich Weiss, "An Emerging China in a World of Interdependence," The Trilateral Commission, New York, Paris, Tokyo, May 1994.

Galbraith, John Kenneth, *The Great Crash 1929,* Houghton Mifflin, 1954.

———, *The Affluent Society,* Boston, Houghton Mifflin, 1958.

———, *The New Industrial State,* Boston, Houghton Mifflin, 1967.

Gattorna, John, ed., *Strategic Supply Chain Alignment,* Brookfield, Vermont, Gower, 1998.

General Accounting Office of the United States, "Export Controls: Rapid Advances in China's Semiconductor Industry Underscore Need for Fundamental U.S. Policy Review," April 2002, GAO-02-620.

Gentile, Gian, *How Effective Is Strategic Bombing?* New York, New York University Press, 2001.

Gereffi, Gary, "Shifting Governance Structures in Global Commodity Chains, with Special Reference to the Internet," in *American Behavioral Scientist,* Vol. 44, No. 10, June 2001.

Gereffi, Gary, "The Global Economy: Organization, Governance, and Development," in *Handbook of Economic Sociology,* Neil Smelser and Richard Swedberg, eds., Princeton, N.J., Princeton University Press, 2003.

———, and Miguel Korzeniewicz, eds., *Commodity Chains and Global Capitalism,* Westport, Conn., Greenwood Press, 1994.

Gill, Stephen, *American Hegemony and the Trilateral Commission,* Cambridge, England, Cambridge University Press, 1990.

Gillingham, John, *Coal, Steel, and the Rebirth of Europe,* New York, Cambridge University Press, 1991.

Gilpin, Robert, *U.S. Power and the Multinational Corporation,* New York, Basic Books, 1975.

———, *The Challenge of Global Capitalism,* Princeton, N.J., Princeton University Press, 2000.

Gomory, Ralph, and William Baumol, *Global Trade and Conflicting National Interests,* Cambridge, Mass., MIT Press, 2000.

Goodwin, Craufurd, *Economics and National Security,* Durham, N.C., Duke University Press, 1991.

Greider, William, *One World, Ready or Not,* New York, Touchstone, 1997.

Grove, Andrew, *Only the Paranoid Survive,* New York, Doubleday, 1996.

Grunwald, Joseph, and Kenneth Flamm, *The Global Factory: Foreign Assembly in International Trade,* Washington, Brookings Institution Press, 1985.

Gulati, Gaurang Mitu, William Klein, and Eric Zolt, "Connected Contracts," *UCLA Law Review,* Vol. 47, 2000, p. 887.

Hacker, Jacob, *The Divided Welfare State,* New York, Cambridge University Press, 2002.

Hammer, Michael, and James Champy, *Reengineering the Corporation,* New York, Harper-Business, 1993.

Harrison, Bennett, *Lean and Mean: The Changing Landscape of Corporate Power in the Age of Flexibility,* New York, Basic Books, 1994.

Hart, David M., "Antitrust and Technological Innovation in the U.S.," *Research Policy,* Vol. 30, No. 6, June 2001.

Hawley, Ellis, *The New Deal and the Problem of Monopoly,* New York, Fordham University Press, 1995.

Hayek, F.A., *The Road to Serfdom,* Chicago, University of Chicago Press, 1944 (reprinted 1994).

Hegel, Georg Wilhelm Friedrich, *Philosophy of Right,* translated by T.M. Knox, Oxford University Press, New York, 1967.

Heller, Francis, and John Gillingham, *The United States and the Integration of Europe,* New York, St. Martin's Press, 1996.

Helper, Susan, John Paul MacDuffie, and Charles Sabel, "Pragmatic Collaborations: Advancing Knowledge While Controlling Opportunism," in *Industrial and Corporate Change,* Oxford University Press, Vol. 9(3), September 2000.

Hirschman, Albert O., *National Power and the Structure of Foreign Trade,* Berkeley, University of California Press, 1945.

Hobbes, Thomas, *Leviathan,* New York, Norton, 1997.

Hobsbawm, Eric, *Industry and Empire, The Birth of the Industrial Revolution,* New York, New Press, 1999 (originally published 1968).

Horwitz, Morton, *The Transformation of American Law 1780–1860,* Cambridge, Mass., Harvard University Press, 1972.

Hounshell, David, *From the American System to Mass Production, 1800–1932,* Baltimore, Johns Hopkins University Press, 1984.

———, *Science and Corporate Strategy: Du Pont R&D 1902–1980,* New York, Cambridge University Press, 1988.

Howell, Thomas, "Dumping: Still a Problem in International Trade," in *International Friction and Cooperation in High Technology Development and Trade,* Washington, National Academies Press, 1997.

Hunt, Michael, *The Making of a Special Relationship: The United States and China to 1914,* New York, Columbia University Press, 1983.

Irwin, Douglas A., *Against the Tide: An Intellectual History of Free Trade,* Princeton, Princeton University Press, 1996.

Isaacs, Harold, *Images of Asia,* New York, Capricorn Books, 1962.

Jefferson, Thomas, *Notes on the State of Virginia,* New York, Norton, 1972.

Jensen, Michael, and William Meckling, "Theory of the Firm: Management Behavior, Agency Costs and Ownership Structure," *Journal of Financial Economics,* Vol. 3, No. 4, October 1976.

Jespersen, T. Christopher, *American Images of China: 1931–1949,* Stanford, Calif., Stanford University Press, 1996.

Johnson, Chalmers, *MITI and the Japanese Miracle,* Stanford, Calif., Stanford University Press, 1982.

Jorde, Thomas, and David Teece, eds., *Antitrust, Innovation, and Competitiveness,* New York, Oxford University Press, 1992.

Kanigel, Robert, *The One Best Way: Frederick Winslow Taylor and the Enigma of Efficiency,* New York, Penguin, 1997.

Kant, Immanuel, *Perpetual Peace,* First Supplement, trans. Lewis White Beck, Indianapolis, Hackett, 1983.

Kantorowicz, Ernst, *The King's Two Bodies,* Princeton, N.J., Princeton University Press, 1956 (reprinted 1997).

Kaysen, Carl, ed., *The American Corporation Today,* New York, Oxford University Press, 1996.

Keay, John, *The Honourable Company: A History of the English East India Company,* New York, Macmillan, 1991.

Kennedy, Paul, *The Rise and Fall of Great Powers,* New York, Vintage, 1989.

Keohane, Robert O., *Power and Governance in a Partially Globalized World,* New York, Routledge, 2002.

————, and Joseph S. Nye, *Power and Interdependence,* 3rd Edition, New York, Longman, 2001.

Keynes, John Maynard, *The Economic Consequences of the Peace,* New York, Harcourt Brace Jovanovich, 1920 (reissued by Penguin Books, New York, 1995).

————, *The General Theory of Employment, Interest, and Money,* New York, Harcourt, Brace, 1936.

Krugman, Paul, ed., *Strategic Trade Policy and the New International Economics,* Cambridge, MIT Press, 1986.

Lamoreaux, Naomi, Daniel Raff, and Peter Termin, "Beyond Markets and Hierarchies: Toward a New Synthesis of American Business History" (June 2002). NBER Working Paper No. W9029.

Lampton, David, *Same Bed Different Dreams,* Berkeley, University of California Press, 2001.

Langlois, Richard, "The Vanishing Hand: The Changing Dynamics of Industrial Capitalism" (September 12, 2001). UConn Center for Institutions, Organizations, & Markets, Working Paper No. 01-1.

Langlois, Richard, and Paul Robertson, "Explaining Vertical Integration: Lessons from the American Automobile Industry," *Journal of Economic History,* Vol. 49, Issue 2, June 1989.

————, *Firms, Markets, and Economic Change: A Dynamic Theory of Business Institutions,* London: Routledge, 1995.

Larson, Paul D., "Single Sourcing and Supplier Certification," *Industrial Marketing Management,* January 1998.

Lazonick, William, *Competitive Advantage on the Shop Floor,* Cambridge, Mass., Harvard University Press, 1990.

LeFeber, Walter, *The Clash: U.S.–Japanese Relations Throughout History,* New York, Norton, 1998.

Lind, Michael, *Hamilton's Republic: Readings in the American Democratic Nationalist Tradition,* New York, Free Press, 1997.

Litan, Robert, and Carl Shapiro, "Antitrust Policy During the Clinton Administration," UC Berkeley, Center for Competition Policy Working Paper, No. CPC01-22, July 2001.

Lundestad, Geir, *The American "Empire,"* London, Oxford University Press, 1990.

————, *"Empire" by Integration: The United States and European Integration, 1945–1997,* New York, Oxford University Press, 1998.

Luttwak, Edward, *Turbo Capitalism: Winners and Losers in the Global Economy,* New York, HarperCollins, 1999.

MacArthur, John, *The Selling of "Free Trade,"* New York, Hill & Wang, 2000.

MacPherson, Alan, and David Pritchard, "International Decentralization of U.S. Commercial Aircraft Production," Canada–United States Trade Center, Occasional Paper No. 26.

Mahan, A.T., *Armaments and Arbitration,* Harper & Brothers, 1911. Reissued by Kennikat Press, Port Washington, N.Y., 1973.

Mann, James, *Beijing Jeep: A Case Study of Western Business in China,* New York, Simon and Schuster, 1989.

———, *About Face: A History of America's Curious Relationship with China,* New York, Vintage Books, 1998.

Marx, Karl, "On the Question of Free Trade," Speech to the Democratic Association of Brussels at its Public Meeting of January 8, 1848, in *Marx/Engels Collected Works,* Moscow, Progress Publishers, Vol. 6, p. 450 (available online at Marxists.org).

———, *The Communist Manifesto,* in *The Marx-Engels Reader,* 2nd Edition, ed., Robert Tucker, New York, Norton, 1978.

Mason, Edward, ed., *The Corporation in Modern Society,* Cambridge, Mass., Harvard University Press, 1959.

McCormick, Thomas J., *The China Market: America's Quest for Informal Empire,* Chicago, Quadrangle Books, 1967.

McDonald, Forrest, *Alexander Hamilton: A Biography,* New York, Norton, 1979.

McIvor, Ronan, "Partnership Sourcing," *Journal of Supply Chain Management,* June 22, 2000.

McMillan, John, "Reorganizing Vertical Supply Relationships," in *Trends in Business Organization,* ed. Horst Siebert, Tubingen, J.C.B. Mohr, 1995.

Millon, David, "The Ambiguous Significance of Corporate Personhood," Stanford, *Agora: An Online Journal of Legal Perspectives,* January 2001.

Nishiguchi, Toshihiro, and Alexandre Beaudet, "Case Study: The Toyota Group and the Aisin Fire," *Sloan Management Review,* Vol. 40, No. 1, 1998.

Nye, Joseph, *Understanding International Conflicts,* New York, Longman, 1993.

Nye, Joseph, *The Paradox of American Power: Why the World's Only Superpower Can't Go It Alone,* New York, Oxford University Press, 2002.

———, Kurt Biedenkopf, and Motoo Shiina, "Global Cooperation After the Cold War: A Reassessment of Trilateralism," New York, Paris, Tokyo, The Trilateral Commission, 1991.

O'Boyle, Thomas F., *At Any Cost: Jack Welch, General Electric, and the Pursuit of Profit,* New York, Alfred A. Knopf, 1998.

Ohmae, Kenichi, *The Borderless World,* New York, HarperCollins, 1990.

———, *The End of the Nation State,* New York, Free Press, 1995.

Ohno, Taiichi, *Toyota Production System,* Cambridge, Mass., Productivity Press, 1988.

Pape, Robert, *Bombing to Win,* Ithaca, N.Y., Cornell University Press, 1996.

Paulson, Ed, *Inside Cisco,* New York, John Wiley & Sons, 2001.

Pempel, T.J., "The Development Regime in a Changing World Economy," in *The Development State,* ed., Meredith Woo-Cumings, Ithaca, Cornell University Press, 1999.

Peret, Geoffrey, *A Country Made by War,* New York, Random House, 1989.

Peritz, Rudolph, *Competition Policy in America,* New York, Oxford University Press, 1996.

Perrow, Charles, *Normal Accidents,* New York, Basic Books, 1984.

Plehwe, Dieter, "Why and How Do National Monopolies Go Global?: International Competition, Supranational Regionalism and the Transnational Reorganization of

Postal and Logistics Companies in Europe," Discussion Paper FS 99-102, Wissenschaftszentrum Berlin fur Sozialforschung.

Porter, Michael, *Competitive Strategy*, New York, Free Press, 1980.

Posner, Richard, *Antitrust Law*, Chicago, University of Chicago Press, 1976.

Pratt, Julius, *Cordell Hull*, New York, Cooper Square Publishers, 1964.

Reich, Robert, *The Work of Nations*, New York, Vintage, 1992.

Remini, Robert, *Henry Clay: Statesman for the Union*, New York, Norton, 1991.

———, *Daniel Webster: The Man and His Time*, New York, Norton, 1997.

Ricardo, David, *On the Principles of Political Economy and Taxation*, London, J.M. Dent & Sons, 1992.

Roosevelt, Theodore, *Life of Thomas Hart Benton*, Boston, Houghton Mifflin, 1894 (reprinted by Scholarly Press, St. Clair Shores, Mich., 1970).

Russett, Bruce, and John Oneal, *Triangulating Peace: Democracy, Interdependence, and International Organizations*, New York, Norton, 2001.

Sagan, Scott, *The Limits of Safety*, Princeton, N.J., Princeton University Press, 1993.

Schaller, Michael, *Altered States: The United States and Japan Since the Occupation*, New York, Oxford University Press, 1997.

Scherer, F.M., *Competition Policies for an Integrated World Economy*, Washington, Brookings Institution Press, 1994.

Schumpeter, Joseph, *Capitalism, Socialism, and Democracy*, New York, Harper & Brothers, 1942.

Skidelsky, Robert, *John Maynard Keynes: The Economist as Savior 1920–1936*, London, Papermac, 1994.

———, *John Maynard Keynes: Fighting for Freedom 1937–1946*, New York, Penguin, 2000.

Sklar, Martin, *The Corporate Reconstruction of American Capitalism: The Market, the Law, and Politics*, New York, Cambridge University Press, 1988.

Slater, Robert, *The Eye of the Storm: How John Chambers Steered Cisco Through the Technology Collapse*, New York, HarperCollins, 2003.

Sloan, Alfred P., *My Years with General Motors*, Garden City, N.Y., Doubleday, 1964.

Smith, Adam, *The Wealth of Nations*, New York, Random House, 1994.

Smith, Henry Nash, *Virgin Land: The American West as Symbol and Myth*, Cambridge, Mass., Harvard University Press, 1971.

Strange, Susan, *The Retreat of the State: The Diffusion of Power in the World Economy*, New York, Cambridge University Press, 1996.

Streusand, Douglas, "Geopolitics Versus Globalization," in *Globalization and Maritime Power*, ed. Sam Tangredi, Washington, National Defense University, 2002.

Strum, Philippa, *Louis D. Brandeis: Justice for the People*, Cambridge, Mass., Harvard University Press, 1984.

Sturgeon, Timothy, "Modular Production Networks: A New American Model of Industrial Organization," *Industrial and Corporate Change*, Vol. 11, No. 3, June 2002.

———, "Exploring the Risks of Value Chain Modularity," MIT Industrial Performance Center, Working Paper Series, MIT-03-003.

———, and Richard Florida, "Globalization and Jobs in the Automotive Industry," MIT Industrial Performance Center, Globalization Working Paper 01-003, March 2000.

———, and Richard Lester, "The New Global Supply Base," MIT Industrial Performance Center, Working Paper Series, MIT-IPC-03-001.

Tainter, Joseph A., *The Collapse of Complex Societies*, New York, Cambridge University Press, 1988.

Taussig, Frank, *Tariff History of the United States*, New York, G.P. Putnam's Sons, 1910.

Thorelli, Hans Birger, *Federal Antitrust Policy: Origination of an American Tradition,* Baltimore, The Johns Hopkins Press, 1954.

Thurow, Lester, *Head to Head,* New York, HarperCollins, 1992.

Tocqueville, Alexis de, *Democracy in America,* New York, Knopf, 1994.

Tyndall, Gene, Christopher Gopal, and Wolfgang Partsch, *Supercharging the Supply Chain,* New York, John Wiley & Sons, 1998.

Tyson, Laura D'Andrea, *Who's Bashing Whom? Trade Conflict in High-Technology Industries,* Washington, Institute for International Economics, 1992.

Van Alstyne, Richard W., *The Rising American Empire,* New York, Norton, 1974.

Vernon, Raymond, *Sovereignty at Bay,* New York, Basic Books, 1971.

———, *In the Hurricane's Eye,* Cambridge, Mass., Harvard University Press, 1998.

Viner, Jacob, "Political Aspects of International Finance," *The Journal of Business of the University of Chicago* 1 (April 1928).

———, *Studies in the Theory of International Trade,* Cambridge, Mass., Harvard University Press, 1965 (reprint).

Vlasic, Bill, and Bradley Stertz, *Taken for a Ride,* New York, HarperCollins, 2000.

Vogel, Steven, ed., *U.S.–Japan Relations in a Changing World,* Washington, Brookings Institution Press, 2002.

Wade, Robert, *Governing the Market,* Princeton, Princeton University Press, 1990.

Walton, Sam, with John Huey, *Made in America,* New York, Doubleday, 1992.

Weick, Karl, and Kathleen Sutcliff, *Managing the Unexpected: Assuring High Performance in an Age of Complexity,* San Francisco, Jossey-Bass, 2001.

Welch, Jack, *Straight from the Gut,* New York, Warner Books, 2001.

Wells, Wyatt, *Antitrust & The Formation of the Postwar World,* New York, Columbia University Press, 2002.

Whitman, Marina v.N., *New World, New Rules: The Changing Role of the American Corporation,* Boston, Harvard Business School Press, 1999.

Wilkins, Mira, *The Emergence of Multinational Enterprise,* Cambridge, Mass., Harvard University Press, 1970.

———, *The Maturing of the Multinational Enterprise,* Cambridge, Mass., Harvard University Press, 1974.

Winner, Langdon, "Complexity and the Limits of Human Understanding," in *Organized Social Complexity: Challenge to Politics and Policy,* ed. Todd R. La Porte, Princeton, N.J., Princeton University Press, 1975.

Womack, James P., Daniel T. Jones, and Daniel Roos, *The Machine That Changed the World,* New York, Rawson Associates, 1990.

Womack, James P., and Daniel T. Jones, *Lean Thinking,* New York, Simon & Schuster, 1996.

Woo-Cumings, Meredith, ed., *The Developmental State,* Ithaca, Cornell University Press, 1999.

Yergin, Daniel, *The Prize: The Epic Quest for Oil, Money, and Power,* New York, Touchstone, 1993.

Young, Jeffrey S., *Cisco Unauthorized,* Roseville, Calif., Prima Publishing, 2001.

Zsidisin, George, and Lisa Ellram, "An Agency Theory Investigation of Supply Risk Management," *Journal of Supply Chain Management,* No. 3, Vol. 39, June 22, 2003.

INDEX